Objects and Attention

COGNITION Special Issues

The titles in this series are paperback, readily accessible special issues of *COGNITION: An International Journal of Cognitive Science*, edited by Jacques Mehler and produced by special agreement with Elsevier Science Publishers B.V.

Published by The MIT Press:

Visual Cognition
Steven Pinker, guest editor

The Onset of Literacy: Cognitive Processes in Reading Acquisition
Paul Bertelson, guest editor

Spoken Word Recognition
Uli H. Frauenfelder and Lorraine Komisarjevsky Tyler, guest editors

Connections and Symbols
Steven Pinker and Jacques Mehler, guest editors

Neurobiology of Cognition
Peter D. Eimas and Albert M. Galaburda, guest editors

Animal Cognition
C. R. Gallistel, guest editor

COGNITION *on Cognition*
Jacques Mehler and Susana Franck, guest editors

Computational Approaches to Language Acquisition
Michael R. Brent, guest editor

Similarity and Symbols in Human Thinking
Steven A. Sloman and Lance J. Rips, guest editors

Object Recognition in Man, Monkey, and Machine
Michael J. Tarr and Heinrich H. Bülthoff, guest editors

The Cognitive Neuroscience of Consciousness
Stanislas Dehaene, guest editor

Objects and Attention
Brian J. Scholl, guest editor

Published by Blackwell:

Numerical Cognition
S. Dehaene, guest editor

Lexical and Conceptual Semantics
Beth Levin and Steven Pinker, guest editors

Reasoning and Decision Making
P. N. Johnson-Laird and Eldar Shafir, guest editors

Objects and Attention

edited by Brian J. Scholl

A Bradford Book

The MIT Press
Cambridge, Massachusetts
London, England

© 2002 Elsevier Science Publishers, B.V., Amsterdam, the Netherlands

All rights reserved. No part of this book may be reproduced in any form by any electronic or mechanical means (including photocopying, recording, or information storage and retrieval) without permission in writing from the publisher.

Reprinted from COGNITION: *International Journal of Cognitive Science,* Volume 80, Numbers 1–2, June 2001. The MIT Press has exclusive license to sell this English-language book edition throughout the world.

Library of Congress Cataloging-in-Publication Data

Objects and attention / edited by Brian J. Scholl.
   p.   ; cm. — (Cognition special issues)
 Includes bibliographical references and index.
 ISBN 0-262-69280-5 (pbk. : alk. paper)
 1. Attention I. Scholl, Brian J. II. Series.

BF321 .025 2002
15.7'33—dc21

2002022920

Contents

1	Objects and attention: the state of the art *Brian J. Scholl*	1
2	Attention-based visual routines: sprites *Patrick Cavanagh, Angela T. Labianca, and Ian M. Thornton*	47
3	Segmentation, attention, and phenomenal visual objects *Jon Driver, Greg Davis, Charlotte Russell, Massimo Turatto, and Elliott Freeman*	61
4	Auditory and visual objects *Michael Kubovy and David Van Valkenburg*	97
5	Visual indexes, preconceptual objects, and situated vision *Zenon W. Pylyshyn*	127
6	What is a visual object? Evidence from target merging in multiple object tracking *Brian J. Scholl, Zenon W. Pylyshyn, and Jacob Feldman*	159
7	Infants' knowledge of objects: beyond object files and object tracking *Susan Carey and Fei Xu*	179
Index		215

1

Objects and attention: the state of the art

Brian J. Scholl*

Department of Psychology, Yale University, P.O. Box 208205, New Haven, CT 06520-8205, USA

Abstract

What are the *units* of attention? In addition to standard models holding that attention can select spatial regions and visual features, recent work suggests that in some cases attention can directly select discrete objects. This paper reviews the state of the art with regard to such 'object-based' attention, and explores how objects of attention relate to locations, reference frames, perceptual groups, surfaces, parts, and features. Also discussed are the dynamic aspects of objecthood, including the question of how attended objects are individuated in time, and the possibility of attending to simple dynamic motions and events. The final sections of this review generalize these issues beyond vision science, to other modalities and fields such as auditory objects of attention and the infant's 'object concept'. © 2001 Elsevier Science B.V. All rights reserved.

Keywords: Objects; Attention; State of the art

1. Introduction

In the vast literature concerning visual attention, perhaps no topic has engendered more recent work and controversy than the nature of the underlying *units* of attentional selection. Traditional models characterized attention in spatial terms, as a spotlight (or perhaps a 'zoom lens') which could move about the visual field, focusing processing resources on whatever fell within that spatial region – be it an object, a group of objects, part of one object and part of another, or even nothing at all. Recent models of attention, in contrast, suggest that in some cases the underlying units of selection are discrete visual objects, and that the limits imposed by

---

* Fax: +1-617-495-3764.
  E-mail address: brian.scholl@yale.edu (B.J. Scholl).

attention may then concern the number of objects which can be simultaneously attended.

This special issue of *Cognition* is concerned with the idea that attention and objecthood are intimately and importantly related. The papers in this collection review the evidence for object-based attention, discuss what attentional objects are, and discuss links both to other modalities (e.g. auditory objects of attention) and to other fields of study (e.g. developmental work on the nature of the infant's 'object concept').

1.1. Why study objects and attention?

These issues are important and timely for at least three reasons. First, the nature of the units of attention is clearly a central question for vision science: among the most crucial tasks in the study of any cognitive or perceptual process is to determine the nature of the fundamental units over which that process operates. A second reason for exploring objects and attention involves the breadth of interest in these topics: research on objects and attention has involved a convergence between many different fields of study, including experimental cognitive psychology, neuropsychology and cognitive neuroscience, philosophy of mind, developmental psychology, computer modeling, and the psychology of audition. Indeed, in a larger context, this concern for 'objecthood' can be seen as a type of 'case study' in cognitive science – an issue which is being addressed in surprisingly similar ways across traditional academic boundaries – and one of the primary goals of this special issue is to explore such connections.

A third reason for exploring these questions is that the nature of the units of attention may also prove crucial for other fields, wherein assumptions about attention frequently play a role in guiding theories of higher-order cognitive processing. As an example taken from cognitive developmental psychology, consider the following claim:

> Perceptual systems do not package the world into units. The organization of the perceived world into units may be a central task of human systems of thought... The parsing of the world into things may point to the essence of thought and to its essential distinction from perception. Perceptual systems bring knowledge of an unbroken surface layout... (Spelke, 1988b, p. 229)

The context of this historical claim is a discussion of the nature of the processes underlying various looking-time results concerning the infant's 'object concept'. The inference is that the architectural locus of these results must be 'conception', since 'perception' doesn't parse the world into units (see Scholl & Leslie, 1999 for discussion and other examples of this inference).[1] Yet, just because processing is not based on a continuous retinal layout does not necessarily mean that it has left the

---

[1] This type of inference continues to be influential (see Scholl & Leslie, 1999), despite the fact that many researchers in cognitive development (notably the quote's author) now take a much more nuanced view which does allow for explanations involving attention (e.g. see Spelke, Gutheil, & Van de Walle, 1995).

domain of perception. Indeed, many object-based attention results suggest that this 'packaging of the world into units' (and fairly sophisticated units at that!) may occur quite early, and even preattentively. The relation between objects and attention is thus of interest beyond vision science, and may play a role in theorizing about other cognitive processes.

1.2. A roadmap for this paper and this special issue

The goal of this paper is to review the state of the art with regard to objects and attention, and to provide a context from which the other papers in this special issue can be related to each other. This review is divided into six additional primary sections. Section 2 provides a brief review of the evidence for object-based attention, drawing on work from both experimental psychology and neuropsychology. In Section 3, these objects of attention are related to other fundamental concepts, including locations, reference frames, perceptual groups, surfaces, and parts. This section also introduces the paper by Driver and colleagues (Driver, Davis, Russell, Turatto, & Freeman, 2001), which discusses in more detail the relationship between attention and segmentation. Section 4 discusses another fundamental contrast, between objects and the individual visual features which characterize them. Section 5 discusses the dynamic aspects of objecthood, including the question of how object tokens are individuated and maintained over time. Pylyshyn's paper (Pylyshyn, 2001) focuses on this topic, and on how the earliest stages of this process serve to link up the mind and the world. This section also discusses how attention might interact directly with information which is inherently dynamic, for example simple stereotypical motions of objects. Such representations are the focus of the experiments on 'attentional sprites' reported by Cavanagh, Labianca, and Thornton (2001). Section 6 emphasizes the importance, for future work, of determining the precise properties which mediate the degree to which visual feature clusters are treated as objects. Some early work along these lines is reviewed, including the experiment reported by Scholl, Pylyshyn, and Feldman (2001a). Finally, Section 7 generalizes these issues beyond vision science, focusing on the nature of auditory objects of attention (the topic of the paper by Kubovy & Van Valkenburg, 2001), and relations to the infant's object concept (the topic of the paper by Carey & Xu, 2001).

1.3. What is attention?

Before getting to object-based attention, however, we can briefly consider a more fundamental question: what is attention, that it might be object-based? The notion of attention has been variously characterized as both obvious and intuitive, and as somehow vague and suspect. Compare:

> Everyone knows what attention is. It is the taking possession by the mind, in clear and vivid form, of one out of what seem several simultaneously possible objects or trains of thought. (James, 1890, pp. 403–404)

> [P]eople talk about attention with great familiarity and confidence. They speak of it as something whose existence is a brute fact of their daily experience and therefore something about which they know a great deal, with no debt to attention researchers. (Pashler, 1998, p. 1)

> But [attention's] towering growth would appear to have been achieved at the price of calling down upon its builders the curse of Babel, 'to confound their language that they may not understand one another's speech'. For the word 'attention' quickly came to be associated ... with a diversity of meanings that have the appearance of being more chaotic even than those of the term 'intelligence'. (Spearman, 1937, p. 133, quoted in Wright & Ward, 1998)

Some of the central aspects of our everyday notion of attention are reviewed by Pashler (1998): the fact that we can process some incoming stimuli more than others (*selectivity*), an apparent limit on the ability to carry out simultaneous processing (*capacity limitation*), and the fact that sustained processing of even visual stimuli seems to involve a sometimes aversive – though sometimes enjoyable – sense of exertion (*effort*). Intuitively, attention seems to be an extra processing capacity which can both intentionally and automatically select – and be effortfully sustained on – particular stimuli or activities.

The *explananda* of theories of attention are difficult to characterize precisely, and seem to comprise a family of questions related to the selectivity, effort, and capacity limitation embodied in our pretheoretical notions: why do certain events seem to automatically distract us from whatever we are doing, 'capturing' our attention? How is it that you can sometimes focus so intently on some task that you fail to perceive otherwise salient events occurring around you? Why is it that you sometimes fail to perceive clearly visible objects or events occurring right in front of you, even when you are searching for them? How is it that some activities which initially seem to require substantial effort eventually seem to become automatic and effortless? Why is it that other practiced activities do not? Why is Waldo hard to find, and how do we actually go about finding him?[2] Each of these questions has been operationalized in various experimental paradigms, many of which are reviewed below.

Because the *explananda* of attention comprise a family of 'intuitive' questions rather than a detailed operationalized problem, many people dismiss talk of 'attention' as vague or unscientific. This attitude seems misguided, however: rigor and concreteness are to be desired in scientific explanations, but cannot always be imposed on *explananda*. The questions asked above are indeed vague and hard to specify precisely, but acknowledging this does not make them go away. In this article it will be assumed that such questions are real and important, and that

---

[2] *Where's Waldo?* is a popular series of children's activity books which embody difficult visual search tasks. Note that this is one case in which the effort involved in the allocation of attention seems to be enjoyable.

there are (possibly several different) types of selective processing – which will collectively be called 'attention' – that play a ubiquitous and important role in visual processing. Our topic will be the nature of the basic *units* of such selection.[3]

2. Evidence for object-based attention

In this section, some of the evidence for object-based attention is introduced. (For earlier reviews of some of this evidence, see Driver and Baylis (1998) and Kanwisher and Driver (1992).) After briefly discussing the most influential evidence for spatial selection, evidence from four experimental paradigms is reviewed (selective looking, divided attention, attentional cueing, and multi-element tracking), along with object-based phenomena in two neuropsychological syndromes (neglect and Balint syndrome).

2.1. Evidence for spatial selection

The contrast which most directly motivated the study of object-based attention was between objects and locations. Does attention always select spatial areas of the visual field, or may attention sometimes directly select discrete objects? (See Section 3.1 for a more detailed discussion of how objects and locations might be related.) The canonical evidence for spatial selection, which gave rise to the dominant 'spotlight' and 'zoom lens' models of spatial attention, comes from spatial cueing studies. Posner, Snyder, and Davidson (1980), for instance, showed that a partially valid cue to the location where a target would appear speeded the response to that target, and slowed responses when the cue was invalid and the target appeared elsewhere. A similar experiment was conducted by Downing and Pinker (1985), this time cueing one of a row of ten boxes with a partially valid cue. Detection of the targets was fastest in the cued box, and slowed monotonically as the distance between the cued box and the actual target location increased on invalid cue trials. These types of results suggested that attention was being deployed as a spatial gradient, centered on a particular location and becoming less effective as the distance from that location increased. For other spatial studies, focusing on the 'spotlight' and 'zoom lens' characterizations of attention, see the influential papers of Eriksen, Hoffman, and colleagues (Eriksen & Eriksen, 1974; Eriksen & Hoffman, 1972, 1973; Eriksen & St. James, 1986; Eriksen & Yeh, 1985; Hoffman & Nelson, 1981) and the recent review by Cave and Bichot (1999).

2.2. Early suggestions from 'selective looking'

Some of the earliest evidence for object-based selection came from the work of

---

[3] For general reviews of attention research, see Pashler (1998) and Styles (1997). For experimental phenomena which pose these broader questions of attention in a salient manner, and which highlight the difference between attention and vision more generally, see recent work on change blindness (e.g. Rensink, O'Regan, & Clark, 1997; Simons & Levin, 1997) and attentional resolution (e.g. He, Cavanagh, & Intriligator, 1997).

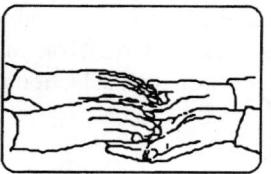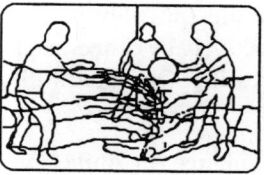

Fig. 1. Sample displays from Neisser and Becklen (1975). The two scenes – the 'hand game' and the 'ballgame' – are superimposed, and subjects are then induced to attend to only one of them, for example to count the number of times the hands clap each other. In this case, subjects fail to perceive incredible sustained events which occur in the other scene, despite the superimposition. See text for details.

Ulric Neisser on what he called 'selective looking' (Neisser, 1967, 1979; Neisser & Becklen, 1975). Subjects in these experiments simultaneously viewed two spatially superimposed movies, as in Fig. 1, and were given a 'selective looking' task which required them to attend to one of the scenes (e.g. a 'hand game', in which they had to count the number of times one set of hands hit another) and ignore the other (e.g. a ballgame, with several men passing a basketball in the background). While engaged in such tasks, these subjects failed to notice unexpected events which happened in the unattended scene (e.g. several women walking on and replacing the men in the 'ballgame' scene). By today's standards these early studies had several methodological flaws, but the essential finding – that subjects were unaware of events occurring in the unattended scene – has been replicated in more recent work (Simons & Chabris, 1999), including studies which adapted this 'selective looking' idea to computerized displays with simple shapes, wherein the details of the displays could be rigorously controlled (Most et al., in press).

This type of attentional selection seems unlikely to be spatially mediated, since the two scenes were globally superimposed: if a spatial spotlight was focused on one scene, it would also be focused on at least part of the other, and would encompass the unexpected event. As such, this early work provides evidence that attention does not simply consist of a single unitary region of spatial selection. One ironic aspect of this work, though, is that it used more naturalistic and dynamic displays than most recent studies. As discussed below, it is unclear that a movie in these experiments constitutes a single object (rather than a perceptual group, or an extended event). A ripe strategy for further research might thus involve combining the richness of Neisser's 'selective looking' stimuli with the more recent and rigorous divided attention and cueing paradigms described below.

2.3. 'Same-object advantages' in divided attention

The type of 'overlapping' strategy used by Neisser and Becklen (1975) and others to avoid purely spatial explanations was also employed in a seminal study of divided attention by Duncan (1984) (see also Treisman, Kahneman, & Burkell, 1983). Subjects viewed brief masked displays, each containing a box with a single line drawn through it. Both the box and the line varied on two dimensions: the box could

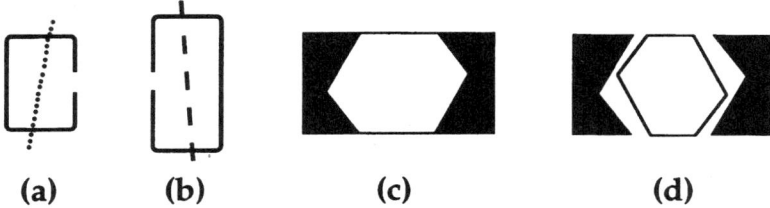

Fig. 2. Sample displays from Duncan (1984) and from Baylis and Driver (1993). (a,b) Stimuli from Duncan (1984). Each stimulus has four degrees of freedom: the line can be either dashed or dotted and can be tilted to the right or left, and the box can be either tall or short and have a right gap or left gap. Subjects are better at reporting two features from a single object compared to two features from two different objects. (c) A stimulus from Baylis and Driver (1993): subjects report the relative height of the two inner vertices while grouping the stimulus as either a single white object or two black objects (the actual colors were red and green), and are better in the single-object case. (d) An 'incongruent' control condition used to insure that subjects were grouping as they were instructed. (Adapted from Baylis and Driver (1993) and Duncan (1984).)

be tall or short, and had a small gap on either its left or the right side, and the line could be either dotted or dashed, and was oriented slightly off vertical, to either the left or the right. Fig. 2a,b present two examples of this type of stimulus. On each trial, subjects saw a brief masked box/line pair, and simply had to judge two of these properties. Some subjects were asked to make both judgments about the same object (e.g. the size of the box and the side of its gap), whereas others made a judgment about two different objects (e.g. the size of the box and the orientation of the line). As in earlier studies showing deficits for reporting two targets in a single display (Duncan, 1980), subjects were less accurate at reporting two properties from separate objects, but were able to judge two properties of a single object without any cost; this has been termed a 'same-object advantage'. Again, space-based theories cannot easily account for this result: because of the overlapped objects, the spatial extents involved in the two-object judgments were never greater than those involved in the single-object judgments.

Later studies have carried this demonstration through several iterations of proposed confounds followed by replications with the appropriate controls. Watt (1988), for instance, proposed a computational algorithm which accounted for Duncan's results in a completely data-driven manner (involving fine-grained versus course-grained spatial filters), without individuating the line and the box as different objects. A later study (Baylis & Driver, 1993) countered by using stimuli for which Watt's alternative explanation (and any such explanation based on image statistics) was inadequate: they used the same physical display for the one-object versus two-object cases, with the difference being defined by perceptual set (see Fig. 2c,d for details). Space-based theories cannot easily account for such results, since spatial location does not vary with the number of perceived objects. Note, however, that the interpretation of these divided attention tasks is still controversial because of other spatial concerns (see also Baylis, 1994; Chen, 1998; Gibson, 1994; Lavie & Driver, 1996). It has recently been argued, for instance, that the results of these divided

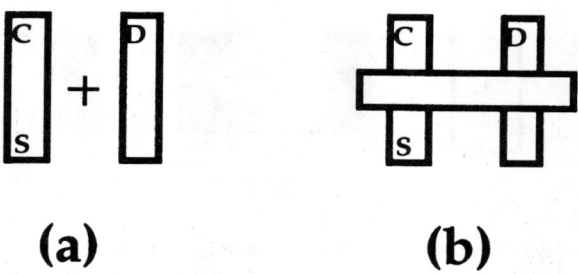

Fig. 3. Stimuli from various experiments used to demonstrate 'same-object advantages' in the automatic spread of attention: (a) Egly, Driver, and Rafal (1994); (b) Moore, Yantis, and Vaughan (1998). In each case 'C' indicates the cued location, 'S' indicates a same-object target location, and 'D' indicates a different-object target location. See text for details. Note that the Moore et al. study actually used a slightly different task. (Adapted from Egly, Driver, and Rafal (1994) and Moore et al. (1998).)

attention studies are due to the fact that automatic attentional spread has a greater area to fill with two objects than with one object, and that no same-object advantages are observed when this confound is removed (Davis, Driver, Pavani, & Shepard, 2000). The details of this interpretation still implicate object-based attention, but the mechanism responsible is seen to be automatic spread of attention, as discussed in Section 2.4. For other studies which have explored same-object advantages in divided attention tasks (some of which are discussed in later sections), see Duncan (1993a,b), Duncan and Nimmo-Smith (1996), Kramer and Watson (1996), Kramer, Weber, and Watson (1997), Valdes-Sosa, Cobo, and Pinilla (1998), Vecera and Farah (1994), and Watson and Kramer (1999).

2.4. 'Same-object advantages' in the automatic spread of attention

The studies reviewed in Section 2.3 were divided attention tasks, in which subjects attended to parts of multiple objects. Other similar studies have looked at the automatic spread of attention in response to the same type of cueing used by Posner et al. (1980) and many others to demonstrate spatial effects. Using displays such as those in Fig. 3a, Egly, Driver, and Rafal (1994) cued subjects to one end (labeled 'C') of one of two bars on each trial, using cues which were 75% valid. The subjects' task was to detect a luminance decrement at one end of a bar immediately after the cue. For the invalid cues, subjects were faster to detect targets that appeared on the uncued end of the cued bar ('S' for 'same object' in Fig. 3a), compared to the equidistant end of the uncued object ('D' for 'different object'). This is another 'same-object advantage', since the spatial distance between the cued location and the two critical locations is identical (see also He & Nakayama, 1995, described in Section 3.5).

This paradigm has also been used to demonstrate that the units of selection are at least complex enough to take occlusion into account, since the 'same-object effect' replicates with displays such as that in Fig. 3b, where the two bars are amodally

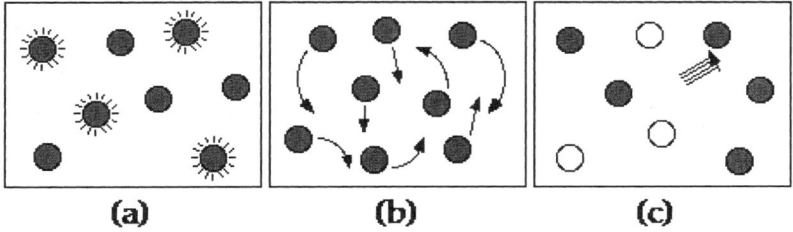

Fig. 4. A schematic depiction of a multiple-object tracking task. (a) Four items are initially flashed to indicate their status as targets. (b) All items then begin moving independently and unpredictably around the screen. (c) At the end of the motion phase, the subject must move the cursor about the screen to highlight the four targets – here the subject has just highlighted three of the targets, and is moving the mouse to the fourth. Animations of this task can be viewed or downloaded over the Internet at http://pantheon.yale.edu/~bs265/bjs-demos.html.

completed behind an occluder and so are physically separated in the display (Behrmann, Zemel, & Mozer, 1998; Moore et al., 1998). Similar results have been found for objects defined by illusory contours (Moore et al., 1998). The fact that the objects of attention in this paradigm can be defined in such ways comports with evidence from visual search paradigms that amodal completion and illusory contour formation occur preattentively (e.g. Davis & Driver, 1994; Enns & Rensink, 1998). For other studies which have explored same-object effects in the automatic spread of attention (some of which are discussed in later sections), see Atchley and Kramer (in press), Avrahami (1999), He and Nakayama (1995), Lamy and Tsal (2000), Lavie and Driver (1996), Neely, Dagenbach, Thompson, and Carr (1998), Stuart, Maruff, and Currie (1997), and Vecera (1994).

2.5. Multiple object tracking

The object-based nature of attentional selection is also apparent in dynamic situations, in which object tokens must be maintained over time. (Such dynamic objects are the focus on Section 5 of this paper.) One dynamic paradigm which has been used for this purpose is multiple object tracking (MOT), wherein subjects must attentionally track a number of independently and unpredictably moving identical items in a field of identical distractors. In the canonical MOT experiment (Pylyshyn & Storm, 1988), subjects viewed a display consisting of a field of identical white items. A certain subset of the items was then flashed several times to mark their status as targets. All of the items then began moving independently and unpredictably about the screen, constrained only so that they could not pass too near each other, and could not move off the display. At various times during this motion, one of the items was flashed, and observers pressed a key to indicate whether the flash had been at the location of a target, a non-target, or neither (see Fig. 4 for a schematic representation of this basic MOT task). Since all items are identical during the motion phase, subjects can only succeed by picking out the targets when they were initially flashed, and then using attention to track them through the motion interval.

Subjects can successfully perform this task (with over 85% accuracy) when tracking up to five targets in a field of ten identical items.[4]

Several additional results suggest that it is the items themselves which are attentionally pursued in this task as distinct objects. First, simulation results confirm that the observed performance cannot be accounted for by a single spotlight of attention which cyclically visits each item in turn, even with liberal assumptions about the speed of attentional shifts and sophisticated guessing heuristics (Pylyshyn & Storm, 1988). Second, attention has been found to speed response times to attended objects, and this advantage appears to be target-specific in MOT: in particular, it doesn't hold for non-targets, even those which are located within the convex polygon bounded by the moving targets (Intriligator, 1997; Sears & Pylyshyn, 2000). Third, as discussed below in Section 6, only certain types of visual clusters – namely those which intuitively constitute discrete objects – can be tracked in this manner (Scholl et al., 2001a). In Intriligator's terms, these results all indicate that attention is *split* between the target objects rather than being *spread* among them.[5] For other studies which have explored object-based attention with MOT, see Culham et al. (1998), Culham, Cavanagh, and Kanwisher (2001), He et al. (1997), Scholl, Pylyshyn, and Franconeri (2001b), Viswanathan and Mingolla (in press), and Yantis (1992).

2.6. Object-based neglect

'Unilateral neglect' is the name given to a collection of disorders in which patients, typically with lateralized parietal lesions, fail to perceive or respond to certain stimuli in their contralateral visual fields (for overviews, see Rafal, 1998; Robertson & Marshall, 1993). The basic phenomenon of neglect has striking practical consequences: in severe cases, neglect patients will fail to orient to people located in their neglected hemifield, will not dress the neglected side of their body, will ignore food on the neglected side of their dinner plate, etc. Historically, this class of stimuli was characterized spatially, and from an egocentric reference frame: patients were thought to neglect entire halves of their visual fields. Recent evidence,

---

[4] Pylyshyn himself has written of MOT as not involving attention per se, but rather an earlier preattentive tracking system (Pylyshyn, 1989, 1994, 2001). Attention, in this view, is seen as perhaps contributing to an 'error recovery' stage when a target item is 'lost', but as not being centrally involved in the tracking itself. This view is discussed at length in Pylyshyn's contribution to this special issue, but in this paper I will follow most other researchers in considering MOT as a paradigmatic case of attentional selection and attentional 'pursuit'.

[5] Yantis (1992) suggested that MOT can be enhanced by imagining the targets as being grouped into a single virtual polygon (VP), and then tracking deformations of this polygon. He demonstrated that such grouping does indeed play a role in MOT by showing that performance was facilitated simply by informing subjects of this strategy, or by constraining the items' trajectories such that the VP could never collapse upon itself. While this strategy (or, indeed, any grouping strategy, for example pairing items into virtual tumbling line segments) can indeed enhance performance, it is not necessary for successful tracking, and the enhancement seems likely to be due to an improved error recovery process when one item is lost: when items are being perceptually tracked as virtual groups, one can make an educated guess as to where a lost item 'should' be, given the overall contour of the virtual shape (Sears & Pylyshyn, 2000). In addition, Scholl and Pylyshyn (1999) have shown that dynamic information which is local to each item (or 'vertex' in the VP strategy) does greatly impact on tracking performance.

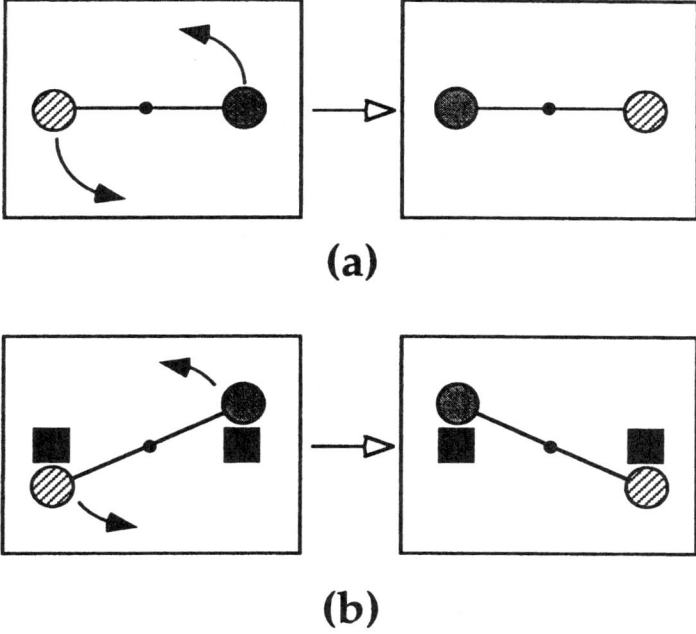

Fig. 5. Sample displays shown to neglect patients by Behrmann and Tipper (1994, 1999). (a) Subjects are shown a dumbbell which then rotates 180° in place. Left-neglect patients initially neglect the disc on the left side. After the rotation, neglect of the disk which is now on the left is attenuated, while neglect is now evident for the disk which ended up on the right. (b) The same event occurs, but two stationary boxes are added. After the rotation, left-neglect patients show some neglect for the left box but the right disc. (Adapted from Behrmann and Tipper (1994, 1999).)

however, has suggested that in some situations neglect may also be object-based, such that patients neglect entire halves of objects with salient axes regardless of the visual field in which they are presented (e.g. Caramazza & Hillis, 1990; Driver, Baylis, Goodrich, & Rafal, 1994; Driver & Halligan, 1991; Humphreys & Riddoch, 1994; Subbiah & Caramazza, 2000; Ward, Goodrich, & Driver, 1994; for many other studies, see Rafal, 1998). Here I will discuss just a single set of 'object-based' studies.

Behrmann and Tipper (1994) used a task in which left-neglect patients were required to detect targets in various 'dumbbells' consisting of two discs connected by a line. As expected, these patients were slower to detect targets presented on the left side of the dumbbell. When the whole dumbbell visibly rotated through 180°, however, these same patients then showed less neglect for the disc which ended up on the left, and were slower to detect targets presented on the disc which ended up on the right after the rotation (see Fig. 5a). Crucially, Tipper and Behrmann (1996) showed that this only held for the connected dumbbells, which were apparently treated as single objects: when the line connecting the two discs was removed, subjects were always slower to respond to targets on the left side of the display,

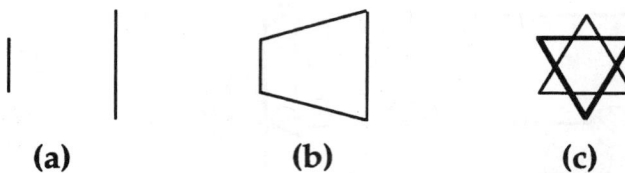

Fig. 6. Stimuli used to demonstrate object-based effects in simultanagnosic patients. Patients viewing (a) cannot determine whether the lines are of equal lengths, but they can tell that the shape in (b) is a trapezoid rather than a rectangle (Holmes & Horax, 1919). Patients of Luria (1959) could see only a single triangle from (c) at once, when the two triangles were colored differently.

regardless of their motion to or from any other location. This suggests that in some contexts these patients neglect not halves of egocentric space per se, but rather halves of specific objects with salient axes, and that the object-based reference frame which defines 'left' and 'right' persists through such rotation, such that the 'left' (i.e. the neglected) side of a just-rotated object can be located on the right side of the display after the rotation.

Furthermore, this type of object-based neglect can occur simultaneously with scene-based neglect (Behrmann & Tipper, 1999). When stationary squares were added to the dumbbell display, as in Fig. 5b, patients simultaneously showed some neglect for the stationary square on the left side of the display, but the dumbbell disc on the right side (to which it had rotated after being initially located on the left). This fascinating finding suggests that neglect can not only operate in multiple reference frames (including object-based ones), but can also do so simultaneously. More generally, egocentric neglect and object-based neglect may interact in other ways: for instance, the primary axis of an off-vertical object may serve to *define* egocentric left and right for an observer, such that neglect might still be considered as a primarily egocentric disorder, but with object-based contributions to the egocentric axis (e.g. Driver, 1998; Driver & Halligan, 1991).

2.7. Balint syndrome

Additional evidence for the object-based nature of visual attention comes from the study of Balint syndrome, in which (typically bilateral) parietal patients exhibit surprising object-based deficits (see Rafal, 1997, for a review). Balint syndrome, even more than neglect, is best characterized as a true syndrome, incorporating many different types of deficits which may not all share a common cause; these include near-complete spatial disorientation (including the inability to indicate an object by pointing or even by verbal description), abnormal eye movements, optic ataxia (a disorder of visually-guided reaching), and impaired depth perception. The most relevant – and startling – component of Balint syndrome, however, is termed *simultanagnosia*: the inability to perceive more than one object at a time, despite otherwise preserved visual processing, including normal acuity, stereopsis, motion detection, and even object recognition. (Such pure cases of simultanagnosia are very rare, however, and many simultanagnosic patients also have various forms of agnosia, alexia, prosopagnosia, and related deficits.) Such patients fail even the simplest of tasks which require them to compute a relation between two separate objects (Coslett & Saffran, 1991; Holmes & Horax, 1919; Humphreys & Riddoch, 1993; Luria, 1959; Rafal, 1997).

The object-based nature of this disorder emerged very early (and, indeed, seems intrinsic to the definition of simultanagnosia). Holmes and Horax (1919), for instance, noted that although Balint patients were unable to determine if two parallel lines were of equal lengths (as in Fig. 6a), they could tell whether a simple shape was a rectangle or a trapezoid (as in Fig. 6b) when the two lines were simply connected by other lines at each end to form a single shape. Similarly, although simultanagnosic patients are typically unable to see two separate discs simultaneously, they are perfectly able to see a single dumbbell (Humphreys & Riddoch, 1993; Luria, 1959). It was even noted in early work by Luria (1959) that this object-based percept seemed untied to particular locations: if the two overlapping triangles composing a 'Star of David' were colored separately, as in Fig. 6c, patients often perceived only one of them! Further aspects of Balint syndrome, involving the perception of locations and visual features, will be discussed in later sections.

2.8. Other evidence for object-based attention

Some additional evidence for object-based attention is discussed later in this article, in the context of other topics (e.g. the perception of groups, surfaces, features, and events). The goal of this review is to highlight major themes in the study of objects and attention, though, and not to exhaustively discuss the empirical evidence. As such, the rest of this article focuses on various theoretical issues and connections to other fields, and many additional studies supporting the existence of object-based selection are not discussed. These include studies of negative priming (Tipper, Brehaut, & Driver, 1990), inhibition of return (Tipper, Driver, & Weaver, 1991; Tipper, Jordan, & Weaver, 1999), symmetry judgments (Baylis & Driver, 1995; Driver & Baylis, 1996), repetition blindness (Chun, 1997; Kanwisher, 1987, 1991), attentional capture (Yantis and Hillstrom, 1994), visual illusions (Cooper & Humphreys, 1999), response competition (Kramer & Jacobson, 1991), intra-object attentional effects (Hochberg & Peterson, 1987; Peterson & Gibson, 1991), visual search (Maljkovic & Nakayama, 1996; Mounts & Melara, 1999), and visual marking (Watson & Humphreys, 1998). Other neuropsychological studies which are not discussed here include studies of early object recognition effects on scene segmentation (Peterson, Gerhardstein, Mennemeier, & Rapcsak, 1998) and suggestions of hemispheric specialization for object-based processing (Egly, Rafal, Driver, & Starrveld, 1994; Reuter-Lorenz, Drain, & Hardy-Morais, 1996).

3. Objects in context: locations, reference frames, groups, surfaces, and parts

Having now presented some of the evidence that discrete objects can in some cases serve as units of attention, it is worth stepping back from this evidence, and considering more carefully how such attended objects relate to other units and processes, including spatial locations, reference frames, perceptual groups, scene segmentation, and visual surfaces.

3.1. Objects and locations

As discussed above, the contrast which has done most to fuel research on object-based attention is between objects and locations. One general way to characterize this issue is in terms of the degree of preattentive processing in the visual system (Driver & Baylis, 1998): is an initial 'packaging of the world into units' computed before – or as a result of – attention? Viewing the question this way is much in the spirit of the classic distinction which has motivated attention research, between 'early selection' and 'late selection' theories (see Johnston & Dark, 1986; Pashler, 1998). That question typically focused on whether stimuli were processed to the level of meaning before or after the limits imposed by attention. In this context we are asking a similar question, about whether various feature clusters are parsed as independent *individuals* before an attentional bottleneck, or if the foci of attention are simply spatial in nature.[6]

It seems clear, though, that these two notions – objects and locations – should not be treated as mutually exclusive. Attention may well be object-based in some contexts, location-based in others, or even both at the same time. The 'units' of attention could vary depending on the experimental paradigm, the nature of the stimuli, or even the intentions of the observer. Perhaps attention will prove location-based *within* complex extended perceptual objects (Neely et al., 1998), or will prove object-based only under relatively distributed global spatial attention (Lavie & Driver, 1996; though see Lamy, 2000). The distinction between objects and locations may also blur in other ways, for example if the shape of a spatial spotlight is allowed to deform around an object (cf. LaBerge & Brown, 1989). It may even be, as suggested by Rafal (1997) (see also Driver, 1998; Laeng, Kosslyn, Caviness, & Bates, 1999), that object-based disorders such as simultanagnosia have their origin in disruptions of perceived space:

> A real object is perceptually distinguished from others based on its unique location; it must be in a different place from any other object. Even if it is superimposed in the retinal image, occlusion cues normally assign each of the two objects to different distances from the observer and will engender an experience of depth. Because patients lack conscious access to a visual representation of topographic space, there is only one 'there' out there – and hence there can be only one object. (Rafal, 1997, p. 350)

---

[6] Note that such references to preattentive processing might be a matter of degree, such that a 'preattentive' process is really best characterized as one which requires relatively little attention. It remains unclear whether there are any truly preattentive processes in the strongest sense of the term (see Nakayama & Joseph, 1998).

3.2. Object-based processing and object-based reference frames

The discussion so far has focused on the units of attentional selection. A related foundational question concerns the nature of the underlying *reference frame* into which visual features are encoded. (A reference frame here just refers to the specification of a set of axes with an origin; relational terms such as 'to the left', and 'towards the front' are then defined relative to these axes.) In an *environment-based* reference frame, visual features are encoded into some absolute coordinate system. In *viewer-based* reference frames, features are encoded relative to egocentric properties such as gaze direction or body orientation. In *object-based* reference frames, features are coded relative to axes defined by individual objects. Though it is often assumed that object-based attentional effects also implicate object-based reference frames (e.g. Behrmann & Tipper, 1999), this is not necessary (Mozer, 1999): there are many ways in which attention could spread throughout an object and not the surrounding context, even though all of the features on that object were still represented in environment- or viewer-based coordinates. One obvious way would be for the processes implementing the spread of attention to be constrained by principles of grouping, such as connectedness.[7]

The distinction between object-based processing and object-based reference frames has also been stressed (in different terms) in the context of visual attention (Vecera & Farah, 1994). Here it was noted that there are two fundamentally different ways that attention could fail to be entirely location-based. First, attention could select *groups of locations*, bound together by object formation principles (such as connectedness) but still represented in terms of their spatial coordinates; this was called a '*grouped array*' theory. On the other hand, objects could be attended without any regard for spatial position; this *spatially invariant* account is related to the idea of an object-based reference frame. (Note that while Vecera and Farah (1994) refer to only this latter type of model as 'object-based', I am considering both to be object-based accounts, since in neither case is selection based entirely on spatial location.) Which of these object-based accounts is correct appears to depend on the specific paradigm. The 'same-object advantages' in divided attention (discussed in Section 2.3) appear to reflect spatially invariant processing, since when the spatial distance between the two previously superimposed stimuli is varied, the magnitude of the object-based effect is unchanged (Vecera & Farah, 1994). In contrast, the 'same-object advantages' in spatial cueing (Section 2.4) appear to reflect the processing of grouped arrays, since manipulations of the spatial distance between the probe

---

[7] Mozer (1999) demonstrates this point by modeling object-based effects from the study of neglect (Behrmann & Tipper, 1999; Tipper & Behrmann, 1996, which are described in Section 2.6) in a connectionist framework which does not employ object-based reference frames. He suggests that this result supports the importance of such network models for the understanding of object-based processing, but on inspection it seems clear that all of the relevant work is done by the fact that the network operates according to the rule that, "Locations adjacent to activated locations should also be activated" (p. 458). This simply implements the connectedness constraint mentioned above, which of course could also be implemented in many other ways which did not share the details of these connectionist models.

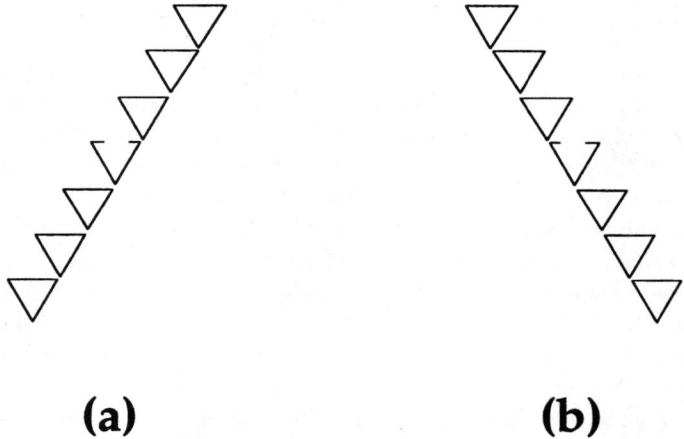

(a) **(b)**

Fig. 7. Stimuli shown to neglect patients by Driver et al. (1994) to demonstrate the role of perceptual grouping in determining the axis on which the neglect is based. See text for details.

locations do attenuate the object-based effect (Vecera, 1994; though see Kramer et al., 1997; Lavie & Driver, 1996, for critiques of these conclusions).

3.3. Attention and perceptual groups

Several older research traditions have emphasized that scenes are organized into perceptual groups defined by the traditional Gestalt principles of continuity, proximity, common fate, etc. (for an excellent summary see Chapter 6 of Palmer, 1999). How does the notion of object-based attention differ from these earlier ideas? Though work on perceptual grouping has typically been conducted without reference to 'attention', many of these demonstrations could easily be reinterpreted as involving attention. For example, Driver and Baylis (1998) note that "the subjective feeling that a column or row of dots belongs together ... may arise because when trying to attend to a single dot, our attention tends to spread instead across the entire group in which it falls" (pp. 301–302). Perhaps, in other words, the Gestalt psychologists were studying attention all along (see also Driver et al., 2001)!

This intriguing possibility deserves to be pursued in future work. In particular, it would be of interest to determine if the evidence for object-based selection described in Section 2 would replicate when Gestalt groups are used as stimuli instead of single objects. Some evidence suggests that it will. The 'same-object advantages' using the cueing paradigm of Egly, Driver, and Rafal (1994) (see Section 2.4), for instance, have been replicated when using two groups of circles arranged into parallel rows (Rafal, in press, cited in Egly, Driver, & Rafal, 1994; see also Driver & Baylis, 1998, pp. 303–304) – a 'same-group' advantage. In addition, some neuropsychological studies suggest a more direct role for grouping (e.g. Boutsen & Humphreys, 2000; Driver et al., 1994; Ward et al., 1994). In one study, neglect

Fig. 8. A stimulus whose natural grouping is of two crossing lines, but which can also be perceived in other ways, for example as two birds' beaks touching each other.

patients reported whether a small triangle in a briefly flashed display had a gap in its contour, where this triangle was surrounded by other triangles such that it was perceptually grouped into a right-leaning or a left-leaning global figure, as in Fig. 7 (Driver et al., 1994). When the critical triangle was grouped into the left-leaning global figure, as in Fig. 7b, the gap was on the right side of this overall group; when it was perceptually grouped into the right-leaning figure, as in Fig. 7a, the gap was on the left of the overall group. This manipulation greatly affected whether the patients perceived the gap, even though the critical triangle was always drawn identically.[8]

Such evidence suggests that 'object-based' attention and 'group-based' attention may reflect the operation of the same underlying attentional circuits – a conclusion which echoes William James' comment that "however numerous the things [to which one attends], they can only be known in a single pulse of consciousness for which they form one complex 'object'" (James, 1890, p. 405). This is not a foregone conclusion, however. It may be, for example, that attention is more easily moved effortfully within *any* perceptual group that can be intentionally perceived, compared to movement between groups, but that attention will *automatically* spread only within a subset of such groups, comprising those that reflect the most 'intuitive' percepts. The line segments in Fig. 8, for example, are most naturally grouped into two crossing lines, though it is possible to perceive them in other ways, for example as two birds' beaks facing each other. Here attention might automatically spread only along the two crossing lines, despite the fact that the line segments can be grouped in several additional ways. Another way to put this is that attention may automatically spread (e.g. by 'exogenous' cues) only within groups defined primarily by 'bottom-up' factors, but that 'top-down' factors may additionally form groups which can be independently attended by intentional, endogenously-cued processes. For a more complete discussion of the relation between perceptual grouping and objecthood, see Feldman (1999).

---

[8] Related evidence – and, indeed, some of the earliest evidence for stimulus-based neglect – comes from studies which used words (i.e. groups of letters) as units (e.g. Caramazza & Hillis, 1990; Subbiah & Caramazza, 2000). In these cases, words seem to be treated as special cases of objects or groups (see also Kahneman & Henik, 1981).

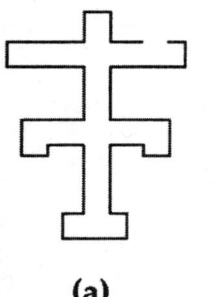 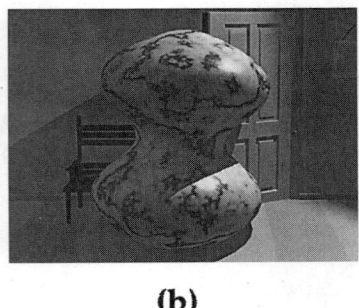

(a) **(b)**

Fig. 9. Stimuli used to explore part-based attention. (a) A stimulus with intuitive 'crossbar' parts, used by Vecera et al. (2000). (b) A stimulus used by Singh and Scholl (2000) with parts defined by negative minima of curvature, the magnitude of which can be varied continuously. See text for details.

3.4. Attending to parts

Just as multiple objects can be perceptually grouped together, so can individual visual objects be composed of multiple parts (e.g. Hoffman & Richards, 1984; Palmer, 1977). The part structure of complex objects has played a major role in theorizing about the recognition of specific objects, where several researchers have proposed that specialized processes for the recognition of specific volumetric parts help to 'jumpstart' the recognition process (e.g. Biederman, 1987; Marr, 1982). In the study of attention, recent research has demonstrated 'same-part advantages' (cf. Sections 2.3 and 2.4) for complex objects composed of hierarchical part arrangements, as in Fig. 9. In one study, for example, Duncan's divided attention paradigm (Section 2.3) was tested with stimuli consisting of 'poles' with 'crossbars' (see Fig. 9a), and same-part effects on accuracy were observed concurrently with same-object effects in displays with multiple figures (Vecera, Behrmann, & McGoldrick, 2000; see also Vecera, Behrmann, & Filapek, in press).[9]

Similarly, a 'same-part advantage' was observed in a spatial cueing study (Section 2.4) with stimuli such as the one depicted in Fig. 9b (Singh & Scholl, 2000). The parts in this study were defined by minima of curvature on a 3D surface, which has been found to accurately predict where observers judge part boundaries to exist (Hoffman & Richards, 1984). This study has two advantages over the divided attention study. First, due to the nature of the experimental paradigm (based on Egly,

---

[9] The cueing method used in this study appears to introduce a confound, however. When subjects reported two features from a single part (e.g. whether the upper crossbar in Fig. 9a was short or long, and the side of its gap; or, alternately, whether the bottom crossbar was short or long, and the direction of its 'prongs'), they always reported all of that part's features, with the relevant part indicated by the location of a cue. In contrast, on different-part trials, subjects had to use the color of the cue to determine which feature of a part to report. This raises the possibility that the observed 'same-part advantage' simply reflects the difficulty of remembering or working through the mapping between cue color and feature-to-report in the different-part trials. In single-part trials, no such memory is required, since all features of the part are reported.

Driver, & Rafal, 1994; Moore et al., 1998), it is not subject to the confound discussed in Footnote 9. Second, defining the parts in this way allows for continuous variation in the magnitude of the curvature defining the parts, which has been found to correlate with part salience (Hoffman & Singh, 1997). Since the naturalism of the objects used here provides larger than normal cueing effects (see Atchley & Kramer, in press), it is thus possible to demonstrate that the magnitude of the 'same-object effect' varies with the magnitude of the curvature and the length of the part cuts. Both of these studies suggest that it may be worthwhile in future work to bring the literatures on attention and perceptual part structure into closer contact (Singh & Scholl, 2000; Vecera et al., 2000).

3.5. Attending to surfaces

The previous sections considered both multi-object units such as groups, and intra-object units such as parts. Visual *surfaces* constitute another level of representation which can encompass both of these categories: complex objects can consist of multiple surfaces, while multiple objects can be arrayed along a single surface. One research tradition which has been developed largely independently of the work discussed above has focused on the role of visual surfaces in 'mid-level vision' (Nakayama, He, & Shimojo, 1995). Nakayama and his colleagues argue that a surface-based level of representation is a critical link between low-level vision and high-level perception, and they have shown that several visual phenomena are based not on the retinal makeup of the visual field, but rather on the perceived interpretation of the visual field in terms of surfaces.

For example, He and Nakayama (1995) explored how attention can spread along surfaces in non-fronto-parallel depth planes. In one experiment, observers had to search for an odd-colored target in the middle depth plane of a stereoscopically presented display, ignoring the items in two other arrays at depths above and below the critical plane (see Fig. 10). When the items to be searched for were tilted so that

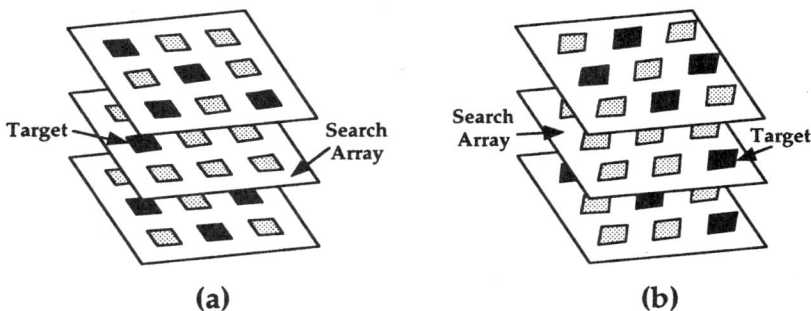

Fig. 10. Stimuli used by He and Nakayama (1995) to demonstrate that attention can efficiently select surfaces even when they span a range of depths. Subjects must detect an odd-colored item in the middle depth plane in each case. When the items are arrayed along a perceptual surface corresponding to this depth plane (a), the search is efficient. When the items do not lie along such a surface (b), attention can no longer select that depth plane, and the search is impaired. (Adapted from He and Nakayama (1995).)

they appeared to lie along a surface at this middle depth plane (Fig. 10a), subjects were able to efficiently confine their search to those items, speeding search. However, when the items were tilted so that they were not seen to lie along such a surface (Fig. 10b), subjects could no longer confine their search to the middle depth plane, and response times increased. This indicates that attention can efficiently select individual surfaces, even when they span an extreme range of depths. In another experiment, He and Nakayama used a cueing study (very similar to that of Egly, Driver, & Rafal, 1994) to demonstrate that in some cases attention *must* spread along surfaces. Subjects had to detect a target in one of two rows of items, and a cue indicated the row which was 80% likely to contain the target. When the disparity of the two rows was increased, observers were able to more efficiently select the cued row, but only if the items did not lie along a common perceptual surface; when the items did lie along a common surface, increased disparity between the rows was unable to facilitate selection of the cued row. He and Nakayama conclude that "The visual system ... can direct selective attention efficiently to any well-formed perceptually distinguishable surface" (p. 11155), and while they do not explain 'well-formedness', they hint that local co-planarity and collinearity of surface edges may play important roles. These roles are considered again in Section 6 below.

As with perceptual groups, it is possible that attending to objects, surfaces, and parts all reflect the operation of the same underlying attentional circuits. Future work along these lines must investigate the extent to which phenomena of object-based attention will replicate with such units, and must also take care to pursue rigorous ways of distinguishing surfaces, objects, and parts, rather than relying on intuitive conceptions of such units (see Feldman, 1999).

3.6. Attention, segmentation, and proto-objects

As the previous three sections have emphasized, there may be a hierarchy of units of attention, ranging from intra-object surfaces and parts to multi-object surfaces and perceptual groups. It remains an open question whether attention to each of these levels reflects the operation of the same or distinct attentional circuits. Another complication is that each of these units may be computed multiple times within the course of visual processing. In general, segmentation processes – that is, processes that bundle parts of the visual field together as units – probably exist at all levels of visual processing. Some of these processes are early, using 'quick and dirty' heuristics to identify likely units for further processing. This results in a visual field which has been segmented into 'proto-objects', which are thought to be volatile in the sense that they are constantly regenerated rather than being stored in visual working memory (VWM) (Rensink, 2000a,b).

In this scheme, it is these 'proto-objects' which serve as the potential units of attention. Then, once a proto-object is actually attended, additional object-based processes come into play. In Rensink's 'coherence' theory (Rensink, 2000a,b), attention to a proto-object gives rise to a more detailed representation of that unit, and one that persists in VWM. It seems likely, however, that this attentional processing could in some cases override the earlier parsing characterized by the proto-objects. For instance, the additional processing which results from attention to a proto-object may result in a higher-level representation of that portion of the visual field as a pair of intertwined objects, or as only a part of a more global object or group of objects. In general, since such processes can occur at multiple levels, 'segmentation' cannot be considered as synonymous with object-based attention. The units of some segmentation processes may serve as the focus of attention, while the units of other segmentation processes may be in part the *result* of (proto-)object-based attention.

The relation between attention and segmentation is treated at length in the paper by Driver and colleagues in this special issue (Driver et al., 2001). They address the issues discussed above, and focus on the question of whether – and how much – image segmentation occurs with attention, without attention, and with attention otherwise occupied in a competing task. In experiments studying a wide array of phenomena – transparency, change blindness and inattentional blindness, modal and amodal completion, and low-level flanker tasks – Driver and colleagues stress how unattended (and even un*seen*) portions of the visual field can still enter into segmentation processes, while at the same time attention can influence even very early types of segmentation. Throughout this work, Driver and colleagues discuss the conscious phenomenology of scene segmentation, and the limited degree to which it represents the complexity of visual processing.

4. Objects and features

In the previous sections we considered hierarchical objects, and the possibility of attending to individual parts and surfaces. Objects are also seen as comprising individual features, however, such as color, luminance, shape, and orientation. In this section object-based selection is contrasted with feature-based models, in which attention can select individual visual features, and in which the limits imposed by attention may concern the number of such features which can be simultaneously encoded into VWM.

One recent experiment which highlights this contrast used a change detection paradigm to demonstrate that the units of VWM are in some cases discrete objects, apparently regardless of the number of visual features which make up those objects (Luck & Vogel, 1997; see also Irwin & Andrews, 1996). On each trial, subjects saw a display such as that in Fig. 11a for 100 ms, followed by a brief blank delay and then Fig. 11b for 2000 ms, and simply had to determine whether there had been a change. Using simple features such as colored boxes and oriented lines, VWM was found to have a capacity of four features, as evidenced by change detection accuracy. Surprisingly, this same limit of four discrete objects held whether the items were colored boxes (Fig. 11a,b) or oriented lines of different colors (with two features per object), or even colored oriented bars which came in two possible sizes and which either did or did not have a gap (see Fig. 11c,d), in which case all 16 features from the four objects could be retained as accurately as only four features from four objects. It thus

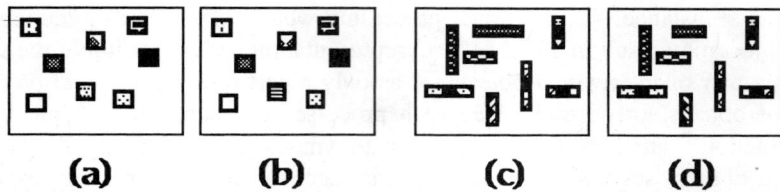

Fig. 11. Sample change detection displays from Luck and Vogel (1997), with texture standing in for color. Displays (a) and (b) contain colored boxes. Displays (c) and (d) contain bars of two different sizes and orientations and several colors, and can either have a gap or no gap. Subjects are shown display (a) for 100 ms, followed by display (b) after a 900 ms delay, and must indicate whether a change occurred (here it did: one item changed 'color'). A similar method is used for displays (c) and (d), where one of the items has changed size. In each case, subjects are accurate with displays containing up to four items in total, regardless of the number of features comprising those items. See text for details. (Adapted from Luck and Vogel (1997).)

appears that object-based processing can trump feature-based processing as well as purely spatial processing, at least in some circumstances and for some 'objects'.[10]

4.1. The link between object-based attention and feature encoding

The studies of VWM described above support a view which is often taken as a hallmark of object-based selection: that attending to an object automatically entails encoding all of its features into VWM. This thesis was proposed in early theorizing about object-based attention (e.g. Kahneman & Henik, 1981), and remains pervasive today (Duncan, 1993a,b; Duncan & Nimmo-Smith, 1996; O'Craven, Downing, & Kanwisher, 1999). Kahneman and Henik (1981), for instance, suggested that, "Attention can be focused narrowly on a single unit, or else it can be shared among several objects. To the degree that an object is attended, however, all its aspects and distinctive elements receive attention. An irrelevant element of an attended object will therefore attract – and waste – its share of attention." (p. 183). More recently, O'Craven et al. (1999) have suggested that "the central claim of object-based theories" is that "task-irrelevant attributes of an attended object will be selected along with the task-relevant attribute, even when these attributes are independent" (p. 585).

Converging evidence for this view comes from a recent neuroimaging study (O'Craven et al., 1999). Previous neuroimaging studies have identified a part of the fusiform gyrus which responds selectively to faces (the 'fusiform face area' or

---

[10] More recent work with this paradigm supports the existence of an object-based component to VWM, but with two important limitations. First, whereas Luck and Vogel (1997) obtained an object-based result even for objects defined by a conjunction of two identical dimensions (e.g. a colored border around a colored box), later studies have failed to replicate this effect when the second display could not contain any entirely new colors (Wheeler & Treisman, 1999; Xu, 2001b). Second, the types of 'objects' that enjoy this effect may be highly constrained. An attenuated object-based effect with color and orientation is found for colored oriented bars, for example, but not for colored 'beach balls' with colored oriented stripes running through them (Xu, 2001a).

FFA; Kanwisher, McDermott, & Chun, 1997) and also a part of parahippocampal cortex which responds selectively to the shape of the local environment (the 'parahippocampal place area' or PPA; Epstein & Kanwisher, 1998). fMRI was used to identify these brain areas in subjects, and their activations were then measured when the subjects viewed superimposed photographs of houses and faces, as in Fig. 12. Despite this spatial superimposition, the activations of the FFA and PPA were highly dependent on which stimulus subjects attended to, indicating an object-based attentional modulation of these areas' activations. Furthermore, even task-irrelevant features of the attended stimulus resulted in activation of the corresponding neural areas. When subjects had to attend only to a small motion in the face, for instance, *both* the motion area (MT/MST) and the FFA were activated, though again in this case the PPA was not activated. Again, it seemed that entire objects were being selected, rather than individual features.

4.2. The priority of spatiotemporal features

This strong view of feature processing, wherein *all* the features of an object are necessarily encoded when an object is attended, breaks down at high attentional loads. In the MOT paradigm (see Section 2.5), for example, successfully attending to the targets throughout the tracking phase appears to result in the encoding of spatiotemporal properties such as location and direction of motion, but *not* featural properties such as color and shape (Scholl et al., 2001b). To investigate whether items' locations were encoded as a result of being tracked, an item disappeared suddenly at the end of the motion phase, and subjects had to report the missing object's location using the mouse, and also indicate whether that item was a target or a distractor. As expected, performance was much better for successfully tracked target items compared to the unattended distractors. Similar results held when subjects had to use the mouse after the MOT motion phase to indicate the direction in which an item

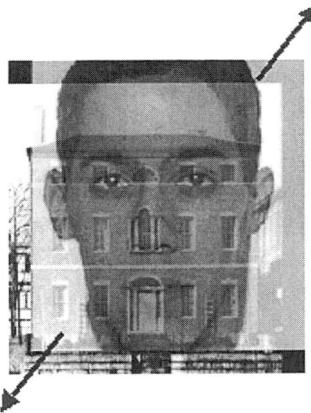

Fig. 12. Example of a superimposed face/place stimulus used by O'Craven et al. (1999) in an fMRI study of object-based attention. See text for details. A dynamic version of the figure is also available on the Internet at http://web.mit.edu/bcs/nklab/objects_att.html.

had been moving. A striking dissociation emerged, however, when certain other properties were examined. To investigate whether items' colors and shapes are encoded as a result of being tracked in MOT, the colors and shapes of items were occasionally permuted when the items were occluded or 'flashed', and subjects reported these properties when a single probe item disoccluded or 'unflashed' as a simple placeholder. (After the disocclusion of the placeholder, for instance, the subject would have to report what color it had been a moment before, and whether or not it was a target.) Here, surprisingly, property encoding was very poor, and was no better for attended targets than for unattended distractors: in the context of the attentional load induced by MOT, items' spatiotemporal properties but not their featural properties seem to be reliably encoded as a result of attention.

This pattern of results is in line with other earlier results obtained using briefly presented static stimuli (e.g. Sagi & Julesz, 1985), and suggests that attended object representations may in some circumstances be represented more robustly in terms of their spatiotemporal properties (especially location) than their featural properties (see also Jiang, Olson, & Chun, 2000; Johnston & Pashler, 1990; Nissen, 1985; Quinlan, 1998; Simons, 1996). This view is also supported by anecdotal evidence from Balint syndrome, where the objects seen by simultanagnosic patients do not seem to be tied to any particular set of visual features enjoyed by that object. Such patients, for instance, will often see many of the colors from each of the objects in the display 'float' through the single object which they are perceiving (Robertson, Treisman, Friedman-Hill, & Grabowecky, 1997; see also Humphreys, Cinel, Wolfe, Olson, & Klempen, 2000). As a whole, the evidence relating objects and features suggests that object-based processing may often trump feature-based processing, but that not all features are created equal: in some circumstances, spatiotemporal features may be more tightly coupled with object representations than are surface-based features such as color and shape.

5. Dynamic objects in space and time

The majority of the studies discussed in previous sections were concerned with demonstrating that attention can select discrete objects. Having established that objects can be units of attention, we can also ask about the dynamic nature of object representations. Two such issues are explored in this section: the maintenance of attended object tokens over time, and the possibility of attending to simple motions and events.

5.1. Maintaining object representations through time and motion

When attended objects move about the visual field, what factors constrain sustained attentional allocation to those items? An example of research addressing this question is discussed below, as are two general theories of how object tokens are maintained and updated.

5.1.1. Tracking items through occlusion

The MOT paradigm (Section 2.5) is well-suited to studying questions about the maintenance of object tokens, since only such sustained attention over time can distinguish the otherwise identical targets and distractors after the motion begins. This task has been used, for instance, to determine whether attended object representations survive interruptions in visibility during their motion (Scholl & Pylyshyn, 1999). Subjects tracked four small squares in a field of eight squares in total in a display which contained occluders (which were either drawn on the screen, or else were invisible but still functionally present). Subjects were able to successfully track even when the items were briefly (but completely) occluded at various times during their motion, suggesting that occlusion is taken into account when computing enduring perceptual objecthood (see also Tipper et al., 1990; Yantis, 1995). Unimpaired performance in the context of these occluders, however, required the presence of accretion and deletion cues along fixed contours at the occluding boundaries. Performance was significantly impaired when items were present on the visual field at the same times and to the same degrees as in the occlusion conditions, but disappeared and reappeared in ways which did not implicate the presence of occluding surfaces, for example by imploding and exploding into and out of existence instead of accreting and deleting along a fixed contour (see Fig. 13 for a schematic depiction of these conditions).

This pattern of results confirms that the circuits responsible for the 'attentional pursuit' of the items in this task are not simply robust in the face of any interruption in spatiotemporal continuity, but rather have a specific tolerance for interruptions consistent with occlusion. In other words, the local dynamics of items during brief disappearances help define what 'counts' as a dynamic visual object: items which disappear and reappear via accretion and deletion along a fixed contour are represented as persisting objects, and can be tracked in MOT, whereas those which disappear in other ways cannot be so tracked, as the disappearances seem to disrupt their continuing representation as the same object.

5.1.2. Object files

One general account of how object representations are maintained over time is the 'object file' theory (Kahneman & Treisman, 1984; Kahneman, Treisman, & Gibbs, 1992; Treisman, 1988, 1993; see also Kahneman & Henik, 1981). One traditional model of visual experience contends that visual stimuli are identified as objects when their visual projections activate semantic representations in long-term memory, and that visual experience consists of shifting patterns of this type of long-term memory activation. Kahneman et al. (1992) note the shortcomings of this view. It appears to be the case, for instance, that objects can be perceived and tracked even when they remain unidentified. Furthermore, when objects are initially mis-identified, and later correctly recognized, there is still never any doubt that the object involved was the same object. "Two identical red squares in successive fields may be perceived as distinct objects if the spatial/temporal gap between them cannot be bridged, but the transformation of frog into prince is seen as a change in a single visual object." (Kahneman et al., 1992, p. 179). Kahneman and Treisman argue that an intermediate level of representation is needed to mediate this latter task, which they call 'object files'.

On this theory, attending to an object in the visual field causes a temporary 'object file' representation to be created. Object files store information about the properties of visual objects (e.g. their colors, shapes, and current locations), but are allocated

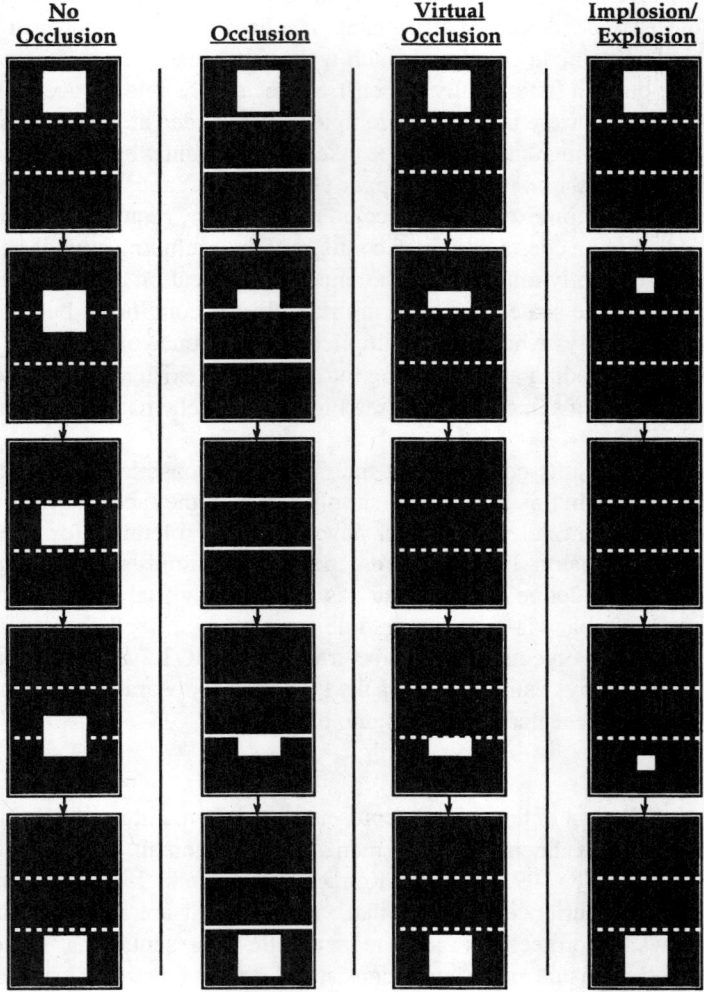

Fig. 13. Some of the different 'occlusion' conditions from Scholl and Pylyshyn (1999). The inherently dynamic nature of the occlusion conditions makes them difficult to represent in a static medium, but here they are presented as sequences of static 'snapshot' diagrams. In each condition, an item travels downward throughout five sequential frames of motion, interacting with a hypothetical occluder position (not to scale). Solid occluder boundaries represent visible occluders, while dashed occluder boundaries represent invisible occluders (presented to aid comprehension). See text for details. Animations of these conditions are available for viewing over the Internet at http://pantheon.yale.edu/~bs265/bjs-demos.html (Adapted from Scholl and Pylyshyn (1999).)

and maintained primarily on the basis of spatiotemporal factors. Three operations are involved in managing object files: (a) a *correspondence* operation, which determines for each object whether it is novel, or whether it moved from a previous location; (b) a *reviewing* operation, which retrieves an object's previous characteristics, some of which may no longer be visible; and finally (c) an *impletion* operation, which uses both current and reviewed information to construct a phenomenal percept, perhaps of object motion. When the features of two objects at different times match (via the reviewing process), the correspondence operation is thought to be facilitated, and the two objects are seen as temporal stages of a single enduring object in the world. When the features do not match, however, the correspondence between those items is inhibited.

This idea was tested with the 'object reviewing' paradigm (Kahneman et al., 1992). A single trial in this paradigm consists of two successive displays, as in Fig. 14. Each display contains small boxes, each of which may contain a single letter, and various manipulations are employed so that particular boxes in the first display are seen as continuous with particular boxes in the second display. The first ('preview') display contains two or more letters-in-boxes, while the second ('target') display contains a single letter-in-a-box, which can either match the letter from 'that' box in the initial display, can contain the letter from a 'different' box from the original display, or can contain an entirely novel letter. Subjects must simply name the single letter in the second display, and the typical result is that such response times are faster when that target is the same letter that filled the corresponding box in the first display (see Fig. 14). Kahneman et al. (1992) call this type of priming the 'object-specific preview effect': a preview facilitates or inhibits the processing of a target only if the preview and target are seen as states of the same object.

5.1.3. Visual indexing

A related theory called 'visual indexing' (Pylyshyn, 1989, 1994, 2001) complements the object file framework by postulating a mechanism whereby object-based individuation, tracking, and access are realized. In order to detect even simple geometrical properties among the elements of a visual scene (e.g. being collinear, or being 'inside'), Pylyshyn argues that the visual system must be able to simultaneously reference – or 'index' – multiple objects. This need is met in Pylyshyn's model by 'visual indexes', which are independently assigned to various items in the visual field on the basis of bottom-up salience cues, and which serve as a means of access to those items for the higher-level processes that allocate focal attention. In this regard, they function rather like pointers in a computer data structure: they reference certain items in the visual field (identifying them as distinct objects), without themselves encoding any properties of those objects. These indexes were referred to in early work as 'FINSTs', for FINgers of INSTantiation, due to the fact that physical fingers work in an analogous way: they can individuate and track items, and provide a means to determine relations such as 'to the left of', but they cannot by themselves encode an object's color or global shape. Visual indexes are thought to be assigned to objects in the visual field regardless of their spatial contiguity (in contrast with spotlight models), but with the restriction that the architecture of the

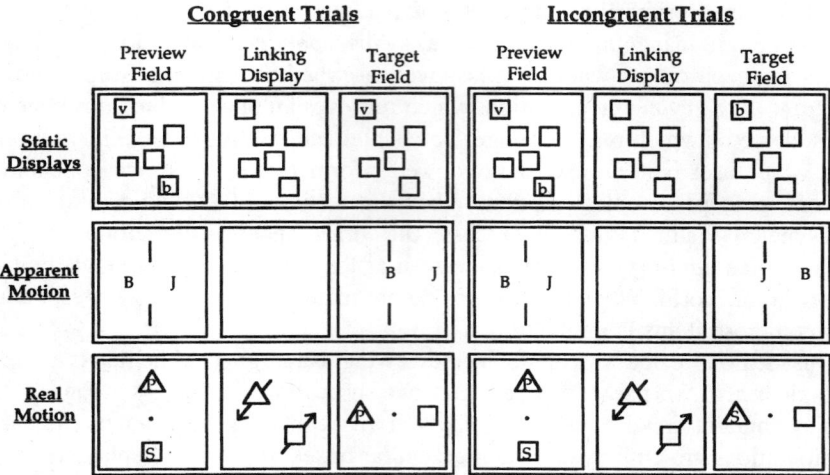

Fig. 14. Displays used by Kahneman et al. (1992). In the static displays, the target is seen as the same object as one of the previews, because it appears in the same location. In the apparent motion displays, the target (i.e. the stimulus between the two lines) is seen as the same object as one of the previews, because it is seen to arrive at its location via apparent motion from one of the preview locations. The same holds for the real-motion displays, mutatis mutandis. In each case, congruent information facilitates target naming, while incongruent information hampers performance. In control conditions (not pictured) in which the target is not seen as the same object as one of the previews, no such effects are observed. (Adapted from various figures in Kahneman et al. (1992).)

visual system provides only about *four* indexes. Furthermore, the indexes are sticky: if an indexed item in the visual field moves, the index moves with it.

Pylyshyn (2001) describes several types of experiments illustrating the need for and the operation of such visual indexes. This paper also stresses the data-driven (or, in Pylyshyn's terms, 'preconceptual') nature of the operation of these visual indexes. This aspect of the proposal serves to link visual processing up with the world, providing an exit to the regress in which various representational systems are explained in terms of other representational systems. If a significant portion of the indexing process is truly data-driven, then this might be a mechanism which 'gets vision off the ground'. In this sense, the visual indexing theory is intended to be a sort of interface between the world and the mind, and could underlie higher-level types of object-based processing.[11]

---

[11] In particular, Pylyshyn argues that the MOT paradigm (see Section 2.5) is a multi-stage process, and that the actual tracking itself illustrates the operation of the visual indexing system. Indeed, Pylyshyn created this paradigm in order to test the indexing theory (Pylyshyn & Storm, 1988). In this paper, in contrast, I have treated MOT as simply involving a standard type of attention. This is because MOT enjoys the salient properties of our pretheoretic notion of attention (it is selective, capacity-limited, and effortful), while it is unclear what aspects of MOT suggest or support a lower-level interpretation. At present, there seems to be no evidence ruling out the hypothesis that paradigms like MOT involve a standard type of attentional selection and 'pursuit', which is simply allocated in a rather complex way, 'split' between multiple items.

Both the object file and visual indexing frameworks embody theoretical assumptions which have been useful for guiding research on object-based attention. Perhaps the most basic assumption of these theories is simply that a level of visual processing exists in which the visual field is parsed and tracked as distinct objects, which are nevertheless not analyzed or recognized as *particular* objects. This is reminiscent of the evidence presented in Section 4 that spatiotemporal properties are more tightly bound to object representations than are surface-based properties.

5.2. Attention, sprites, and event perception

Whereas nearly all of the work on attention reviewed above has concerned either static objects or objects which happened to be in motion, attention may also interact directly with information which is *inherently* dynamic, such as simple stereotypical motions. Cavanagh and colleagues raise this possibility in their contribution to this special issue (Cavanagh et al., 2001). They suggest that the stereotypical motions of familiar objects – such as a person walking or a hand waving – may be stored as such, and that these 'units' of motion may facilitate recognition of the events and the objects participating in them. These stored representations of simple motions, termed *sprites*, are accessed or modeled by attention when viewing dynamic scenes. Such 'animation' of stored stereotypical motions is hypothesized to be among the visual system's standard repertoire of visual routines (in the sense of Ullman, 1984). As with other 'chunking' data structures (e.g. schemas, scripts), attentional sprites let familiar objects and events be recognized even from very sparse dynamic information in the scene. A complex set of sprites, for instance, would be responsible for the robust perception of biological motion (e.g. a person walking) which can arise when viewing even a very simple 'point light walker' composed of around 11 points of light in motion (Johansson, 1973).

The experiments reported by Cavanagh et al. (2001) focus on the attentional demands of using sprites. In particular, they explore whether simple patterns of points in motion can be discriminated without attention. Two such discriminations are tested: pairs of points 'tumbling' or 'orbiting' around a center point (Fig. 15a), and simple biological motion in one of two directions. When such dynamic stimuli are used in visual search tasks, so that the subjects must quickly determine whether a target motion is present in a field of distractor motions, the time taken to make this decision varies with the set size, a result which is taken to indicate that attention is required to 'animate' the sprites used to discriminate even simple motion patterns.

Beyond simple motion patterns, it is also possible that certain inherently dynamic *events* may serve as 'objects' of attention. Consider, for example, the perception of causality in simple 'launch displays', wherein one item is seen to hit another (Fig. 15b). It has been argued that the perception of such events is mediated by automatic low-level processes (Michotte, 1946/1963; see Scholl & Tremoulet, 2000, for a review). Such stimuli – and others, such as pushes, pulls, and even chases – are perceived in *causal* terms which go beyond the objective kinematics of the items in the display. It is possible that attentional sprites of the sort introduced here by Cavanagh et al. (2001) play a role in mediating such percepts by 'animating' the

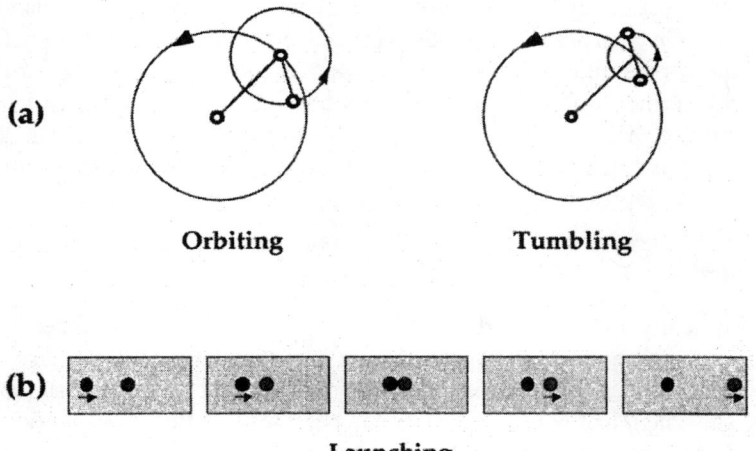

Fig. 15. Examples of simple events and motion patterns. (a) The 'tumbling' versus 'orbiting' pairs which had to be discriminated in visual search tasks in the experiments reported by Cavanagh et al. (2001). (Only the dots are actually drawn.) (b) A simple 'launch' event that has been thought to be perceived 'automatically' (Michotte, 1946/1963; Scholl & Tremoulet, 2000). Can such inherently dynamic animations and events serve as units of attention?

event schemas, and that in this way events might serve as units of attention. Such possibilities remain an intriguing focus for future research.

6. What is a visual object?

In previous sections of this paper, we have identified several different constraints on what can count as 'objects' of attention. For example, we have seen several instances of objects surviving both static and dynamic occlusion (Behrmann et al., 1998; Moore et al., 1998; Scholl & Pylyshyn, 1999; see also Tipper et al., 1990; Yantis, 1995), and we have seen that standard object-based effects are replicated with stimuli which we would intuitively characterize as groups, parts, and surfaces (see Section 3). Beyond these general categories, however, an important task for future work will be to determine the precise properties which mediate the degree to which visual feature clusters are treated as objects of attention. Some researchers, such as David Marr, have been pessimistic about the possibility of providing a useful answer to this question:

> Is a nose an object? Is a head one? Is it still one if it is attached to a body? What about a man on horseback? These questions show that the difficulties in trying to formulate what should be recovered as a region from an image are so great as to amount almost to philosophical problems. There is really no answer to them – all these things can be an object if you want to think of them that way, or they can be part of a larger object. (Marr, 1982, p. 270)

Marr's pessimism is certainly appropriate when considering the mind as a whole; certainly, for instance, we can *conceive* of almost anything as an object (for philosophical treatments, see Hirsch, 1982; Wiggins, 1980). With regard to what mental processes such as visual attention *treat* as objects, however, there may be well-defined answers to such questions.

The majority of work on object-based attention to date has been focused on demonstrating *that* object-based attention exists in various situations, independently of location-based and feature-based attention. In addition, some recent studies have begun to use the tools described in Section 2 to explore more directly what can count as an object of attention. Three such studies are briefly described here.

The first two studies employed the divided attention and spatial cueing paradigms which have previously revealed 'same-object advantages' (see Sections 2.3 and 2.4). In the original object-based cueing study, Egly, Driver, and Rafal (1994) observed a same-object advantage using pairs of rectangles as objects (see Fig. 3a). Avrahami (1999) set out to determine which features of these rectangles were crucial for the effect. She found that their closure was neither necessary nor sufficient: a same-object advantage was observed with simple sets of parallel lines, but not with certain distorted versions of the enclosed rectangles. Other researchers have similarly explored same-object advantages in the divided attention paradigm (Watson & Kramer, 1999). Subjects in these experiments viewed pairs of 'wrenches' as stimuli, and had to decide from extremely brief (50 ms) presentations whether the pair of wrenches contained both an open-ended wrench and a bent-end wrench. When these two features were on the same visual object, they reasoned, this response should be speeded. Using stimuli such as those in Fig. 16 (which shows 'same-object' trials for each condition), Watson and Kramer demonstrated that objecthood can be defined by uniformly connected regions such as those in Fig. 16a, but not by non-uniformly connected regions such as those in Fig. 16b (see also Kramer & Watson, 1996; Van Lier & Wagemans, 1998). They also showed that the magnitude of the same-object effect was attenuated when the ends of the wrenches were easily differentiable from the shafts by concave cusps as in Fig. 16c, compared to when such cusps were either non-existent (Fig. 16d) or not as pronounced (Fig. 16a) (see also Driver & Baylis, 1995; Hoffman & Singh, 1997). A final conclusion from this research was that the nature of visual objecthood varied by task (see also Brawn & Snowden, 2000; Lamy & Tsal, 2000): in other tasks, the existence of these cusps did not make a difference, and even regions which were not uniformly connected were treated as objects.

The issue of what can count as an object of attention is also addressed by Scholl et al. (2001a) in a MOT experiment involving a technique they call 'target merging'. Though subjects still attempted to track multiple independently and unpredictably moving items, the nature of these items was altered so that target/distractor pairs were perceived as single objects – with a target at one end and a distractor at the other end. For example, the pair might be drawn as a simple line segment connecting the two points, or as the convex hull of the two items. Each of the diagrams in Fig. 17, for instance, represents two targets and two distractors paired in various ways. (All of the actual experiments involved eight items in total paired into four target/distractor pairs.) Crucially, each 'end' of a pair still moved completely indepen-

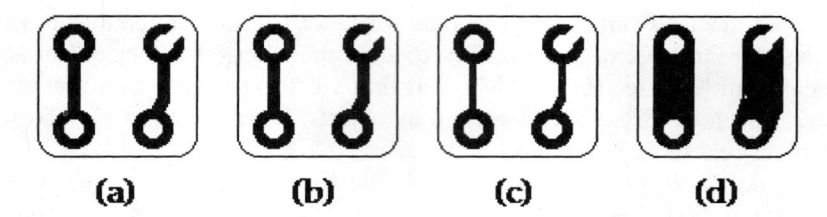

Fig. 16. Depictions of some of the 'wrench' stimuli used by Watson and Kramer (1999). In all displays, subjects must determine from brief (50 ms) presentations whether the display contains both a bent-end wrench and an open-ended wrench. All displays shown here represent 'same-object' target trials, since the two crucial features are always depicted on the same wrench. (a) A uniformly-connected display; (b) a non-uniformly connected display; (c) a display with salient cusps at each end of each wrench; (d) a display with no cusps at the end of the wrenches. See text for details. (Adapted from Watson and Kramer (1999).)

dently. Using a between-subjects design and identical sets of trajectories and target selections for each condition, Scholl et al. (2001a) find that tracking performance is radically impaired when the to-be-tracked items are undifferentiated parts or ends of larger objects such as lines (Fig. 17b) or 'rubber bands' (Fig. 17c). (In these cases, object-based attention is palpable: observers can feel attention being pulled in to the entire line or rubber band as the tracking phase unfolds.) This method is then used to explore the roles of part structure, connectedness, and other forms of perceptual grouping on visual objecthood. For instance, when subjects had to track ends of 'dumbbells' as in Fig. 17d, performance was worse than with boxes alone (Fig. 17a), but better than with lines alone (Fig. 17b) – presumably because of the salient parts at each end. In more complex cases, the precise nature of the connections seemed crucial: for instance, tracking was greatly impaired with 'Necker Cubes' (Fig. 17e), but not in the similar control condition depicted in Fig. 17f.

In most cases, given enough time and leisure, we are free to consider almost anything as an object. As these experiments demonstrate, however, objecthood is more well-defined at earlier levels of visual analysis. To get at such earlier levels, most investigators (e.g. Watson & Kramer, 1999) have used briefly presented and often masked stimuli along with speeded responses. This manipulation confines processing to early mechanisms because of a temporal limitation: the displays are gone before higher levels of analysis have a chance to come into play. The advantages of this method come with a cost, however: they result in small and imperceptible effects. In MOT, in contrast, the higher-level processes are constrained not by temporal limits but by overall sustained attentional load. It is trivially easy to track a *single* end of a line using focal attention, but the higher-level processes which make this possible are not available when attentional capacity is strained by the high load induced by MOT: in this latter case only a limited class of 'visual objects' can be tracked. The experiments described in this section report very preliminary results concerning the nature of visual objecthood, but hopefully these methods can continue to be used in the future to comprehensively explore the properties which give rise to objects of attention.

7. Beyond vision science

To this point, the discussion of objects and attention has been confined largely to aspects of visual processing in adults. In fact, however, the relation between objects and attention is also a central concern in the study of other modalities and even other sub-fields of cognitive science. Since a major goal of this special issue as a whole is to explore such connections, this penultimate section will address two such areas: *auditory* objects of attention (the topic of the paper by Kubovy & Van Valkenburg, 2001) and the infant's object concept (the topic of the paper by Carey & Xu, 2001).

7.1. Auditory objects of attention

There are many analogies between phenomena of object-based visual attention and phenomena of grouping and 'streaming' in audition. Albert Bregman (1990), in his influential book *Auditory scene analysis: the perceptual organization of sound*, pioneered a theory in which auditory scenes are grouped into and perceived as distinct auditory streams or objects of audition: "The stream plays the same role in auditory mental experience as the object does in visual." (p. 11). Each stream is perceived as containing those parts of the incoming auditory scene which 'go together'. In most cases, such analysis is tremendously useful since these different streams will emanate from different sources in the environment.

Kubovy and Van Valkenburg (2001) provide an overview of how to best conceptualize auditory objects, and relate them to visual objects. Early theories, they note,

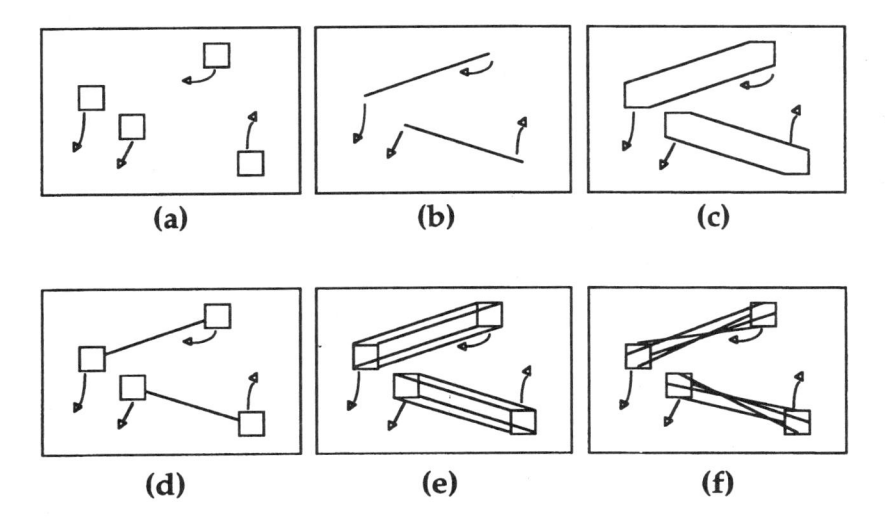

Fig. 17. Sample *target merging* displays from the MOT tasks of Scholl et al. (2001a). Each display shows four items, each of which always moves independently from all other items. (Actual displays had eight items in total.) In displays (b) through (f), the items are merged into pairs in various ways, with each pair always consisting of a target and a distractor, and subjects must track one *end* of each pair. Such manipulations greatly affect tracking performance. See text for details. Animations of these conditions are available for viewing over the Internet at http://pantheon.yale.edu/~bs265/bjs-demos.html.

tended to map auditory spatial processing (i.e. the computation of a sound source's location) onto visual spatial processing, and to map auditory frequency onto a visual property such as color. In contrast to this 'spatial' mapping, Kubovy and Van Valkenburg suggest that a more useful mapping is between auditory frequency and visual space. Just as visual objects exist in space-time, so auditory objects exist in pitch-time. This mapping is motivated by Kubovy's theory of 'indispensable attributes' (Kubovy, 1981), which notes that spatial separation is a necessary precondition for numerosity judgments in vision, while separation in frequency space is a necessary precondition for numerosity judgments in audition. (Two tones of different pitches coming from the same location will be judged as distinct, while two tones of the same pitch coming from different locations will be heard as a single sound.) Auditory spatial processing, in contrast, is seen as supporting visual spatial processing in the service of action, rather than being involved in object formation. Kubovy and Van Valkenburg summarize the existing evidence for this view, as well as the evidence that auditory processing contains separate 'what' and 'where' streams, as does vision. In addition, they discuss how attention interacts with each stream, proposing that attention is typically drawn only to indispensable attributes in each modality (i.e. primarily to objects and locations but not colors in vision, and primarily to pitches but not spatial locations in audition).

The view of objecthood which emerges from this theory is intended to be cross-modal. Early perception – both auditory and visual – aggregates 'elements', which then undergo grouping to form various perceptual organizations. Each of these perceptual organizations is then a potential 'object', and actual objects are formed via attentional selection, which results in figure-ground segregation. An advantage of this particular conception of objecthood is that it can be stated in this modality-independent way. Note, though, that the choice of which of these levels count as the 'objects' is somewhat arbitrary. Most of the 'objects' (and sometimes 'proto-objects'; see Section 3.6) that have figured in the object-based attention work might be termed 'elements' on this model. Of course, it remains an important topic for future research to determine the properties which mediate unit formation at each of these levels in Kubovy and Van Valkenburg's theory: the early 'elements', the mid-level 'groups', and the final 'objects' which emerge as a result of attention (see also Section 3.6).

In addition to these general lessons on how to think about auditory objects and relate them to visual objects, it is also possible to draw more specific analogies between auditory phenomena and experiments on object-based visual attention. Two such examples are discussed in the remainder of this section. First, recall the evidence (presented in Section 2) that attention in some contexts is not a simple unitary spotlight. In the MOT task, for instance, attention can be split between multiple items in space, rather than being spread between them. Keeping to the analogy between visual space and auditory frequency, similar results are obtained: just as some of the results described in Section 2 seem inconsistent with attention to a single region of visual space, so do the results of some audition experiments seem inconsistent with attention to a single region of frequency space. For example, listeners are able to simultaneously monitor for both a low- and a high-frequency

Objects and attention: the state of the art

tone just as easily as they can monitor for the two tones in sequential intervals (Johnson & Hafter, 1980). A more direct source of evidence comes from a monitoring situation where subjects have to determine which of two sequential temporal intervals contains a target tone. In this situation, when the target tones are usually at two separated frequencies, subjects perform well at both frequencies, but perform poorly for those targets which unexpectedly have tones between these typical frequencies (Macmillan & Schwartz, 1975). This demonstrates that attention can be split between multiple auditory tones rather than simply spread between them in frequency space.

A second example of convergences between the general principles of visual and auditory processing involves the processing of occlusion. Many researchers of auditory attention (e.g. Dannenbring, 1976; Warren, 1982) have studied how sounds moving in frequency space can seem to continue 'behind' auditory occluders, such as sudden bursts of noise (see Fig. 18a). This type of situation is in some ways analogous to the experiments of Scholl and Pylyshyn (1999) discussed in Section 5.1.1, where spatial movement is analogous to movement in frequency space. In those experiments the nature of the local disappearance at the occluding boundary made a crucial difference to whether the item could be tracked through that boundary: when the items 'imploded' and 'exploded' at the occluding boundaries, for example, performance was severely impaired (see Fig. 13). Auditory researchers have observed similar effects. For instance, if the initial frequency ends (Fig. 18b) – or begins to gradually diminish in amplitude (Fig. 18b) – a moment before the burst of noise, then the auditory percept of continuation is severely reduced or eliminated (Bregman, 1990; Bregman & Dannenbring, 1977; Warren et al., 1972). In both cases, continuity through occlusion occurs only when all of the 'disappearing' of the tracked visual or auditory object occurs along the contour of the occluding boundary. Bregman (1990) identifies the general principle involved here: "The perceptual systems, both visual and auditory, must use a very accurate analysis of the structure of the sensory evidence to determine whether the parts separated by the occluding material show sufficient agreement with one another to be considered parts of the same thing or event." (p. 347). Such analogies are provocative, if

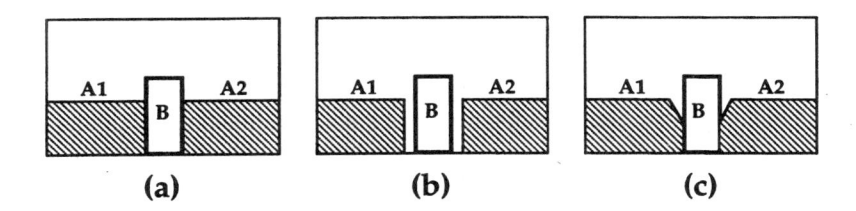

Fig. 18. Depictions of auditory events used by Bregman (1990), Bregman and Dannenbring (1977), and Warren, Obusek, and Ackroff (1972). In each diagram, the horizontal axis represents time, while the vertical axis represents intensity. (a) Sound A1 ceases just as sound B begins, and sound A2 begins just as sound B ceases. Subjects perceive A1 continuing behind the 'auditory occluder' of B. This continuity percept is attenuated or destroyed, however, when A1 stops (b) or diminishes in intensity (c) just before the onset of B. See text for details. (Adapted from Bregman (1990).)

7.2. Object-based attention and the infant's object concept

Cognitive developmental psychology is another area of study which has often focused on issues of objects and attention. Using looking-time measures to study the infant's 'object concept', developmental psychologists have demonstrated that infants even a few months old have a substantial amount of 'initial knowledge' about objects in domains such as physics and arithmetic (for recent reviews and overviews, see Baillargeon, 1995; Carey, 1995; Spelke, 1994; Spelke et al., 1995; Wynn, 1998). Traditional discussions of the nature of such 'initial knowledge' have assumed an implicit dichotomy between 'perception' and 'cognition' (e.g. Bogartz, Shinskey, & Speaker, 1997; Kellman, 1988; Leslie, 1988; Spelke, 1988a,b), and from within this dichotomy 'perception' was often found wanting, largely because it was thought not to be object-based (see the quote from Spelke, 1988b, in Section 1.1). Since 'perception' was thought not to traffic in discrete objects, but 'thought' was, the correct explanations for the infancy experiments were assumed to be 'conceptual' in nature (see Scholl & Leslie, 1999, for discussion). Of course, all of the evidence discussed in this article belies this characterization of perception, and if parts of perception can indeed be object-based, then it is possible that mechanisms of object-based attention play an important role in explaining these infancy results.

Scholl and Leslie (1999) drew just this conclusion, and identified several convergences between these two fields (see also Leslie, Xu, Tremoulet, & Scholl, 1998). To take one example, recall the priority for spatiotemporal over featural properties that was found by Scholl et al. (2001b) (see Section 4.2), and which is inherent in theories of object files and visual indexing (Section 5.1). This pattern mirrors the maturational differences in property encoding obtained with 10–12-month-old infants by Xu and Carey (1996). Ten-month-old infants, for instance, will use spatiotemporal information (seeing two unconnected items emerge from behind a screen at the same time) but not featural information (seeing a red item and a green item emerge sequentially) to infer the existence of two distinct objects behind the screen, as in Figs. 19 and 20 (Xu & Carey, 1996). Twelve-month-olds, in contrast, will use both sorts of information, like adults. In a similar vein, 4-month-old infants have been shown to use spatiotemporal information to infer that two parts are in fact a single unitary object (e.g. the fact that two parts separated by an occluder undergo common motion) but not featural information (e.g. the fact that two stationary parts separated by an occluder have similar colors and/or shapes; Kellman & Spelke, 1983; Kestenbaum, Termine, & Spelke, 1987; see also Van de Walle & Spelke, 1996). (Again, adults and older children will use both sorts of information.) Furthermore, infants at these ages appear to use *only* spatiotemporal information to assess an object's unity: in the situation described above, for example, infants are perfectly happy to conceive of the two parts in common motion as a single object, despite the

Objects and attention: the state of the art   37

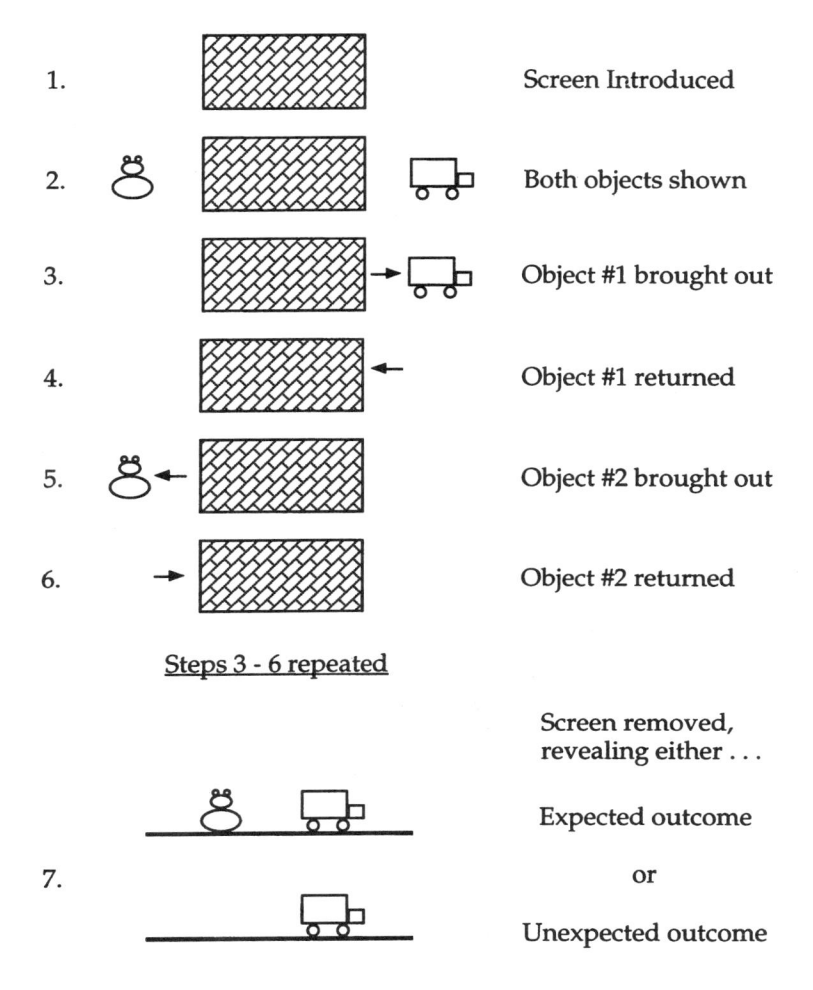

1.   ▨▨▨   Screen Introduced

2.   &   ▨▨▨   🚚   Both objects shown

3.   ▨▨▨ → 🚚   Object #1 brought out

4.   ▨▨▨ ←   Object #1 returned

5.   & ← ▨▨▨   Object #2 brought out

6.   → ▨▨▨   Object #2 returned

            Steps 3 - 6 repeated

                                            Screen removed,
                                            revealing either . . .

            &   🚚   Expected outcome

7.   or

                 🚚
                                            Unexpected outcome

Fig. 19. The 'spatial' condition from Xu and Carey (1996). See text for details. (Adapted from Xu and Carey (1996).)

fact that their colors and shapes suggest strongly (to older children and adults) that they are distinct objects (but cf. Needham, 1997).

Carey and Xu (2001) address the relationship between object-based visual attention in adults and this type of infancy work at length, identifying several other convergences, as well as their limitations. They suggest that the adult mind has two primary representational systems for individuating objects. One, which they call the 'mid-level object file system', involves the types of attentional processes discussed throughout this article. The second is a 'kind-based' system, which is fully conceptual, and can often override the attention-based tracking system (e.g. when you decide that the computer on your desk is the same one that was there yesterday, despite the fact that you did not directly observe the spatiotemporal continuity

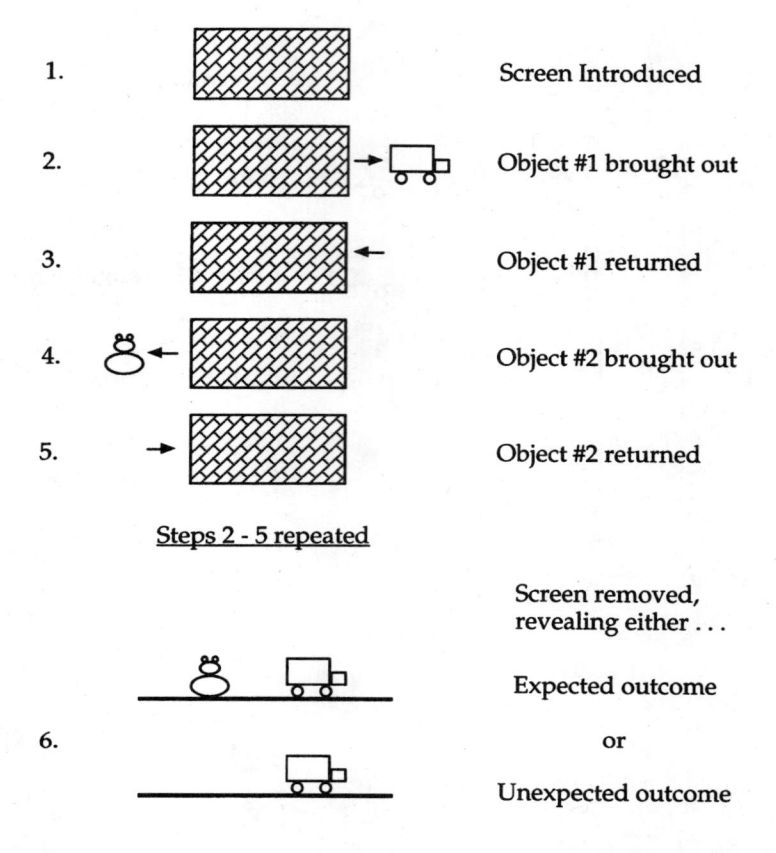

1. Screen Introduced
2. Object #1 brought out
3. Object #1 returned
4. Object #2 brought out
5. Object #2 returned

Steps 2 - 5 repeated

6. Screen removed, revealing either...

Expected outcome

or

Unexpected outcome

Fig. 20. The 'property' condition from Xu and Carey (1996). See text for details. (Adapted from Xu and Carey (1996).)

between the two). Whereas properties such as color and shape may play only a peripheral role in mid-level object tracking, they may play a more central role in kind-based individuation. Because young infants do not yet employ kind-based individuation, Carey and Xu stress that they are ideal 'tools' with which to study mid-level object-tracking: adults, in contrast, are 'contaminated' by both systems, which are often hard to distinguish. In addition to stressing the role of attention-based systems in infant cognition, Carey and Xu also identify several ways in which results from the infant cognition literature might usefully inform work on object-based attention. In particular, they describe a nuanced view of the relation between object-based attention and higher-level processes. They note that the representations formed by processes of object-based attention may still be conceptual in nature, despite their perceptual origin: for example, these representations may end up playing a prominent role in guiding further inferences and actions.

These connections between developmental work and work from vision science on adults should be an exciting topic for future research. Research in these two fields has until this point proceeded largely independently, and it seems certain that each field will have many heuristic insights to offer the other, and that in some cases researchers from the two fields may be studying the same mechanisms of object-based attention.

8. Conclusions: a case study in cognitive science?

The study of objects and attention is important, in the first instance, for intrinsic reasons: a fundamental task in the study of visual attention is to determine the nature of the basic units over which attention operates. As has been reviewed in this paper, the units of attention are often various kinds of visual *objects*. That this is true seems undeniable in the face of converging evidence from so many psychophysical and neuropsychological experiments. Still, there are many important questions which remain to be answered about object-based attention. These include the question of precisely which stimulus features define 'objecthood' from the perspective of the visual system (Section 6), and how (or if) object-based attention differs from notions of group-, surface-, part-, or event-based attention (Sections 3 and 5).

As the additional analogies with other fields (Section 7) begin to suggest, however, the study of objects and attention may also be of interest more generally. The evidence reviewed above consisted largely of experimental psychology and neuropsychology, but there has also been valuable recent input from computational modeling (e.g. Behrmann et al., 1998; Mozer, 1999) which was not reviewed here. Furthermore, in addition to the work on audition and cognitive development discussed in Section 7, the relation of objects and attention has also been of much interest to philosophers (e.g. Hirsch, 1997; Wiggins, 1997; cf. Xu, 1997) and even language researchers (e.g. Landau & Jackendoff, 1993). In few other areas of this young field have so many areas of study converged on so many similar ideas, and as such the research on this topic might be viewed as an emerging 'case study' in cognitive science.

Acknowledgements

B.J.S. was supported by NIH #F32-MH12483-01. For helpful conversation and/or comments on earlier drafts, I thank Jacob Feldman, Jerry Fodor, Steve Franconeri, Alex Holcombe, Alan Leslie, Ken Nakayama, Mary Peterson, Dan Simons, Anne Treisman, and Steve Yantis. Special thanks to Jon Driver and Zenon Pylyshyn for especially careful and critical readings of an earlier draft. Special thanks are also due to the members of my 1999 undergraduate seminar at Rutgers, 'Objects: A Case Study in Cognitive Science', for extremely helpful extended conversation.

References

Atchley, P., & Kramer, A. (in press). Object-based attentional selection in three-dimensional space. *Visual Cognition, 8*(1).

Avrahami, J. (1999). Objects of attention, objects of perception. *Perception & Psychophysics, 61*, 1604–1612.

Baillargeon, R. (1995). Physical reasoning in infancy. In M. S. Gazzaniga (Ed.), *The cognitive neurosciences* (pp. 181–204). Cambridge, MA: MIT Press.

Baylis, G. (1994). Visual attention and objects: two-object cost with equal convexity. *Journal of Experimental Psychology: Human Perception and Performance, 20*, 208–212.

Baylis, G., & Driver, J. (1993). Visual attention and objects: evidence for hierarchical coding of location. *Journal of Experimental Psychology: Human Perception and Performance, 19*, 451–470.

Baylis, G., & Driver, J. (1995). Obligatory edge assignment in vision: the role of figure and part segmentation in symmetry selection. *Journal of Experimental Psychology: Human Perception and Performance, 21*, 1323–1342.

Behrmann, M., & Tipper, S. (1994). Object-based visual attention: evidence from unilateral neglect. In C. Umilta, & M. Moscovitch (Eds.), *Attention and performance. Conscious and nonconscious processing and cognitive functioning* (Vol. 15, pp. 351–375). Cambridge, MA: MIT Press.

Behrmann, M., & Tipper, S. (1999). Attention accesses multiple reference frames: evidence from unilateral neglect. *Journal of Experimental Psychology: Human Perception and Performance, 25*, 83–101.

Behrmann, M., Zemel, R., & Mozer, M. (1998). Object-based attention and occlusion: evidence from normal participants and a computational model. *Journal of Experimental Psychology: Human Perception and Performance, 24*, 1011–1036.

Biederman, I. (1987). Recognition-by-components: a theory of human image understanding. *Psychological Review, 94*, 115–147.

Bogartz, R., Shinskey, J., & Speaker, C. (1997). Interpreting infant looking: the event set × event set design. *Developmental Psychology, 33*, 408–422.

Boutsen, L., & Humphreys, G. (2000). Axis-based grouping reduces visual extinction. *Neuropsychologia, 38*, 896–905.

Brawn, P., & Snowden, R. (2000). Attention to overlapping objects: detection and discrimination of luminance changes. *Journal of Experimental Psychology: Human Perception and Performance, 26*, 342–358.

Bregman, A. S. (1990). *Auditory scene analysis: the perceptual organization of sound*. Cambridge, MA: MIT Press.

Bregman, A. S., & Dannenbring, G. L. (1977). Auditory continuity and amplitude edges. *Canadian Journal of Psychology, 31*, 151–159.

Caramazza, A., & Hillis, A. (1990). Levels of representations, co-ordinate frames, and unilateral neglect. *Cognitive Neuropsychology, 7*, 391–445.

Carey, S. (1995). Continuity and discontinuity in cognitive development. In E. Smith, & D. Osherson (Eds.), *Thinking: Vol. 3. An invitation to cognitive science* (2nd ed., pp. 101–130). Cambridge, MA: MIT Press.

Carey, S., & Xu, F. (2001). Infant knowledge of objects: beyond object files and object tracking. *Cognition*, this issue, *80*, 179–213.

Cavanagh, P., Labianca, A., & Thornton, I. (2001). Attention-based visual routines: sprites. *Cognition*, this issue, *80*, 47–60.

Cave, K., & Bichot, N. (1999). Visuospatial attention: beyond a spotlight model. *Psychonomic Bulletin & Review, 6*, 204–223.

Chen, Z. (1998). Switching attention within and between objects: the role of subjective organization. *Canadian Journal of Experimental Psychology, 52*, 7–16.

Chun, M. (1997). Types and tokens in visual processing: a double dissociation between the attentional blink and repetition blindness. *Journal of Experimental Psychology: Human Perception and Performance, 23*, 738–755.

Cooper, A., & Humphreys, G. (1999). *A new, object-based visual illusion*. Poster presented at the annual meeting of the Psychonomic Society, Los Angeles, CA.

Coslett, H. B., & Saffran, E. (1991). Simultanagnosia: to see but not two see. *Brain, 113*, 1523–1545.

Culham, J. C., Brandt, S., Cavanagh, P., Kanwisher, N. G., Dale, A. M., & Tootell, R. B. H. (1998). Cortical fMRI activation produced by attentive tracking of moving targets. *Journal of Neurophysiology, 80*, 2657–2670.

Culham, J. C., Cavanagh, P., & Kanwisher, N. (2001). Attention response functions of the human brain measured with fMRI. Manuscript submitted for publication.

Dannenbring, G. (1976). Perceived auditory continuity with alternately rising and falling frequency transitions. *Canadian Journal of Psychology, 30*, 99–114.

Davis, G., & Driver, J. (1994). Parallel detection of Kanizsa subjective figures in the human visual system. *Nature, 371*, 791–793.

Davis, G., Driver, J., Pavani, F., & Shepherd, A. (2000). Reappraising the apparent costs of attending to two separate visual objects. *Vision Research, 40*, 1323–1332.

Downing, C., & Pinker, S. (1985). The spatial structure of visual attention. In M. Posner, & O. S. M. Marin (Eds.), *Attention and performance* (Vol. XI, pp. 171–187). London: Erlbaum.

Driver, J. (1998). The neuropsychology of spatial attention. In H. Pashler (Ed.), *Attention* (pp. 297–340). Hove: Psychology Press.

Driver, J., & Baylis, G. (1995). One-sided edge assignment in vision: II. Part decomposition, shape description, and attention to objects. *Current Directions in Psychological Science, 4*, 201–206.

Driver, J., & Baylis, G. (1996). Figure-ground segmentation and edge assignment in short-term visual matching. *Cognitive Psychology, 31*, 248–306.

Driver, J., & Baylis, G. (1998). Attention and visual object segmentation. In R. Parasuraman (Ed.), *The attentive brain* (pp. 299–325). Cambridge, MA: MIT Press.

Driver, J., Baylis, G., Goodrich, S., & Rafal, R. (1994). Axis-based neglect of visual shapes. *Neuropsychologia, 32*, 1353–1365.

Driver, J., Davis, G., Russell, C., Turatto, M., & Freeman, E. (2001). Segmentation, attention, and phenomenal visual objects. *Cognition*, this issue, *80*, 61–95.

Driver, J., & Halligan, P. (1991). Can visual neglect operate in object-centered coordinates? An affirmative single case study. *Cognitive Neuropsychology, 8*, 475–494.

Duncan, J. (1980). The locus of interference in the perception of simultaneous stimuli. *Psychological Review, 87*, 272–300.

Duncan, J. (1984). Selective attention and the organization of visual information. *Journal of Experimental Psychology: General, 113*, 501–517.

Duncan, J. (1993a). Coordination of what and where in visual attention. *Perception, 22*, 1261–1270.

Duncan, J. (1993b). Similarity between concurrent visual discriminations: dimensions and objects. *Perception & Psychophysics, 54*, 425–430.

Duncan, J., & Nimmo-Smith, I. (1996). Objects and attributes in divided attention: surface and boundary systems. *Perception & Psychophysics, 58*, 1076–1084.

Egly, R., Driver, J., & Rafal, R. (1994). Shifting visual attention between objects and locations: evidence for normal and parietal lesion subjects. *Journal of Experimental Psychology: General, 123*, 161–177.

Egly, R., Rafal, R., Driver, J., & Starrveveld, Y. (1994). Covert orienting in the split brain reveals hemispheric specialization for object-based attention. *Psychological Science, 5*, 380–383.

Enns, J., & Rensink, R. (1998). Early completion of occluded objects. *Vision Research, 38*, 2489–2505.

Epstein, R., & Kanwisher, N. (1998). A cortical representation of the local visual environment. *Nature, 392*, 598–601.

Eriksen, B. A., & Eriksen, C. W. (1974). Effects of noise letters upon the visual identification of a target letter in a nonsearch task. *Perception & Psychophysics, 16*, 143–149.

Eriksen, C. W., & Hoffman, J. E. (1972). Temporal and spatial characteristics of selective encoding from visual displays. *Perception & Psychophysics, 12*, 201–204.

Eriksen, C. W., & Hoffman, J. E. (1973). The extent of processing of noise elements during selective encoding from visual displays. *Perception & Psychophysics, 14*, 155–160.

Eriksen, C. W., & St. James, J. D. (1986). Visual attention within and around the field of focal attention: a zoom lens model. *Perception & Psychophysics, 40*, 225–240.

Eriksen, C. W., & Yeh, Y. Y. (1985). Allocation of attention in the visual field. *Journal of Experimental Psychology: Human Perception and Performance, 11*, 583–597.

Feldman, J. (1999). The role of objects in perceptual grouping. *Acta Psychologica, 102* (1), 137–163.

Gibson, B. (1994). Visual attention and objects: one versus two, or convex versus concave? *Journal of Experimental Psychology: Human Perception and Performance, 20*, 203–207.

He, S., Cavanagh, P., & Intriligator, J. (1997). Attentional resolution. *Trends in Cognitive Sciences, 1*, 115–121.

He, Z. J., & Nakayama, K. (1995). Visual attention to surfaces in 3-D space. *Proceedings of the National Academy of Sciences USA, 92*, 11155–11159.

Hirsch, E. (1982). *The concept of identity*. New York: Oxford University Press.

Hirsch, E. (1997). Basic objects: a reply to Xu. *Mind & Language, 12*, 406–412.

Hochberg, J., & Peterson, M. A. (1987). Piecemeal perception and cognitive components in object perception: perceptually coupled responses to moving objects. *Journal of Experimental Psychology: General, 116*, 370–380.

Hoffman, D., & Richards, W. (1984). Parts of recognition. *Cognition, 18*, 65–96.

Hoffman, D., & Singh, M. (1997). Salience of visual parts. *Cognition, 69*, 29–78.

Hoffman, J. E., & Nelson, B. (1981). Spatial selectivity in visual search. *Perception & Psychophysics, 30*, 283–290.

Holmes, G., & Horax, G. (1919). Disturbances of spatial orientation and visual attention, with loss of stereoscopic vision. *Archives of Neurology and Psychiatry, 1*, 385–407.

Humphreys, G. W., Cinel, C., Wolfe, J., Olson, A., & Klempen, N. (2000). Fractionating the binding process: neuropsychological evidence distinguishing binding of form from binding of surface features. *Vision Research, 40*, 1569–1696.

Humphreys, G. W., & Riddoch, M. J. (1993). Interactions between object and space systems revealed through neuropsychology. In D. Meyer, & S. Kornblum (Eds.), *Attention and performance* (Vol. XIV, pp. 183–218). Cambridge, MA: MIT Press.

Humphreys, G. W., & Riddoch, M. J. (1994). Attention to within-object and between-object spatial representations: multiple sites for visual selection. *Cognitive Neuropsychology, 11*, 207–241.

Intriligator, J. M. (1997). *The spatial resolution of visual attention*. Unpublished doctoral dissertation, Harvard University, Cambridge, MA.

Irwin, D., & Andrews, R. (1996). Integration and accumulation of information across saccadic eye movements. In T. Inui, & J. McClelland (Eds.), *Attention and performance*, Vol. XVI. Cambridge, MA: MIT Press.

James, W. (1890). *The principles of psychology*. New York: Holt.

Jiang, Y., Olson, I., & Chun, M. (2000). Organization of visual short-term memory. *Journal of Experimental Psychology: Learning, Memory, and Cognition, 26*, 683–702.

Johansson, G. (1973). Visual perception of biological motion and a model for its analysis. *Perception & Psychophysics, 14*, 201–211.

Johnson, D., & Hafter, E. (1980). Uncertain-frequency detection: cueing and condition of observation. *Perception & Psychophysics, 28*, 143–149.

Johnston, J., & Pashler, H. (1990). Close binding of identity and location in visual feature perception. *Journal of Experimental Psychology: Human Perception and Performance, 16*, 843–856.

Johnston, W., & Dark, V. (1986). Selective attention. *Annual Review of Psychology, 37*, 43–75.

Kahneman, D., & Henik, A. (1981). Perceptual organization and attention. In M. Kubovy, & J. Pomerantz (Eds.), *Perceptual organization* (pp. 181–211). Hillsdale, NJ: Erlbaum.

Kahneman, D., & Treisman, A. (1984). Changing views of attention and automaticity. In R. Parasuraman, & D. R. Davies (Eds.), *Varieties of attention* (pp. 29–61). New York: Academic Press.

Kahneman, D., Treisman, A., & Gibbs, B. J. (1992). The reviewing of object files: object-specific integration of information. *Cognitive Psychology, 24*, 174–219.

Kanwisher, N. (1987). Repetition blindness: type recognition without token individuation. *Cognition, 27*, 117–143.

Kanwisher, N. (1991). Repetition blindness and illusory conjunctions: errors in binding visual types with visual tokens. *Journal of Experimental Psychology: Human Perception and Performance, 17*, 404–421.

Kanwisher, N., & Driver, J. (1992). Objects, attributes, and visual attention: which, what, and where. *Current Directions in Psychological Science*, *1*, 26–31.

Kanwisher, N., McDermott, J., & Chun, M. (1997). The fusiform face area: a module in human extrastriate cortex specialized for the perception of faces. *Journal of Neuroscience*, *17*, 4302–4311.

Kellman, P. (1988). Theories of perception and research in perceptual development. In A. Yonas (Ed.), *Perceptual development in infancy*: Vol. 20. *The Minnesota Symposium on Child Psychology* (pp. 267–281). Hillsdale, NJ: Erlbaum.

Kellman, P., & Spelke, E. (1983). Perception of partly occluded objects in infancy. *Cognitive Psychology*, *15*, 483–524.

Kestenbaum, R., Termine, N., & Spelke, E. S. (1987). Perception of objects and object boundaries by 3-month-old infants. *British Journal of Developmental Psychology*, *5*, 367–383.

Kramer, A., & Jacobson, A. (1991). Perceptual organization and focused attention: the role of objects and proximity in visual processing. *Perception & Psychophysics*, *50*, 267–284.

Kramer, A., & Watson, S. (1996). Object-based visual selection and the principle of uniform connectedness. In A. Kramer, M. Coles, & G. Logan (Eds.), *Converging operations in the study of visual selective attention* (pp. 395–414). Washington, DC: APA Press.

Kramer, A., Weber, T., & Watson, S. (1997). Object-based attentional selection – grouped arrays or spatially invariant representations?: comment on Vecera and Farah (1994). *Journal of Experimental Psychology: General*, *126*, 3–13.

Kubovy, M. (1981). Concurrent-pitch segregation and the theory of indispensable attributes. In M. Kubovy, & J. Pomerantz (Eds.), *Perceptual organization* (pp. 55–99). Hillsdale, NJ: Erlbaum.

Kubovy, M., & Van Valkenburg, D. (2001). Auditory and visual objects. *Cognition*, this issue, *80*, 97–126.

LaBerge, D., & Brown, V. (1989). Theory of attentional operation in shape identification. *Psychological Review*, *96*, 101–124.

Laeng, B., Kosslyn, S., Caviness, V., & Bates, J. (1999). Can deficits in spatial indexing contribute to simultanagnosia? *Cognitive Neuropsychology*, *16*, 81–114.

Lamy, D. (2000). Object-based selection under focused attention: a failure to replicate. *Perception & Psychophysics*, *62*, 1272–1279.

Lamy, D., & Tsal, Y. (2000). Object features, object locations, and object files: which does selective attention activate and when? *Journal of Experimental Psychology: Human Perception and Performance*, *26*, 1387–1400.

Landau, B., & Jackendoff, R. (1993). 'What' and 'where' in spatial language and spatial cognition. *Behavioral and Brain Sciences*, *16*, 217–265.

Lavie, N., & Driver, J. (1996). On the spatial extent of attention in object-based selection. *Perception & Psychophysics*, *58*, 1238–1251.

Leslie, A. M. (1988). The necessity of illusion: perception and thought in infancy. In L. Weiskrantz (Ed.), *Thought without language* (pp. 185–210). Oxford: Oxford Science.

Leslie, A. M., Xu, F., Tremoulet, P., & Scholl, B. J. (1998). Indexing and the object concept: developing 'what' and 'where' systems. *Trends in Cognitive Sciences*, *2* (1), 10–18.

Luck, S., & Vogel, E. (1997). The capacity of visual working memory for features and conjunctions. *Nature*, *390*, 279–281.

Luria, A. R. (1959). Disorders of 'simultaneous perception' in a case of bilateral occipito-parietal brain injury. *Brain*, *83*, 437–449.

Macmillan, N., & Schwartz, M. (1975). A probe-signal investigation of uncertain-frequency detection. *Journal of the Optical Society of America*, *58*, 1051–1058.

Maljkovic, V., & Nakayama, K. (1996). Priming of pop-out: II. The role of position. *Perception & Psychophysics*, *58*, 977–991.

Marr, D. (1982). *Vision*. New York: W.H. Freeman.

Michotte, A. (1963). *The perception of causality* (T. Miles, & E. Miles, Trans.). New York: Basic Books. (Original work published 1946)

Moore, C., Yantis, S., & Vaughan, B. (1998). Object-based visual selection: evidence from perceptual completion. *Psychological Science*, *9*, 104–110.

Most, S. B., Simons, D. J., Scholl, B. J., Jiminez, R., Clifford, E., & Chabris, C. F. (in press). How not to be seen: the contribution of similarity and selective ignoring to sustained inattentional blindness. *Psychological Science*.

Mounts, J., & Melara, R. (1999). Attentional selection of objects or features: evidence from a modified search task. *Perception & Psychophysics, 61*, 322–341.

Mozer, M. (1999). Do visual attention and perception require multiple reference frames? Evidence from a computational model of unilateral neglect. *Proceedings of the 21st annual conference of the Cognitive Science Society* (pp. 456–461). Mahwah, NJ: Erlbaum.

Nakayama, K., He, Z., & Shimojo, S. (1995). Visual surface representation: a critical link between lower-level and higher-level vision. In S. M. Kosslyn, & D. Osherson (Eds.), *Visual cognition*: Vol. 2. *An invitation to cognitive science* (2nd ed., pp. 1–70). Cambridge, MA: MIT Press.

Nakayama, K., & Joseph, J. (1998). Attention, pattern recognition, and popout in visual search. In R. Parasuraman (Ed.), *The attentive brain* (pp. 279–298). Cambridge, MA: MIT Press.

Needham, A. (1997). Factors affecting infants' use of featural information in object segregation. *Current Directions in Psychological Science, 6*, 26–33.

Neely, C., Dagenbach, D., Thompson, R., & Carr, T. (1998). *Object-based visual attention: the spread of attention within objects and the movement of attention between objects*. Paper presented at the 39th annual meeting of the Psychonomic Society, Dallas, TX.

Neisser, U. (1967). *Cognitive psychology*. New York: Appleton-Century-Crofts.

Neisser, U. (1979). The control of information pickup in selective looking. In A. Pick (Ed.), *Perception and its development* (pp. 201–219). Hillsdale, NJ: Erlbaum.

Neisser, U., & Becklen, R. (1975). Selective looking: attending to visually specified events. *Cognitive Psychology, 7*, 480–494.

Nissen, M. J. (1985). Accessing features and objects: is location special? In M. Posner, & O. Marin (Eds.), *Attention and performance* (Vol. XI, pp. 205–220). Hillsdale, NJ: Erlbaum.

O'Craven, K., Downing, P., & Kanwisher, N. (1999). fMRI evidence for objects as the units of attentional selection. *Nature, 401*, 584–587.

Palmer, S. (1977). Hierarchical structure in perceptual representation. *Cognitive Psychology, 9*, 441–474.

Palmer, S. (1999). *Vision science: photons to phenomenology*. Cambridge, MA: MIT Press.

Pashler, H. (1998). *The psychology of attention*. Cambridge, MA: MIT Press.

Peterson, M. A., Gerhardstein, P., Mennemeier, M., & Rapcsak, S. (1998). Object-centered attentional biases and object recognition contributions to scene segmentation in left- and right-hemispheric-damaged patients. *Psychobiology, 26*, 357–370.

Peterson, M. A., & Gibson, B. S. (1991). Directing spatial attention within an object: altering the functional equivalence of shape descriptions. *Journal of Experimental Psychology: Human Perception and Performance, 17*, 170–182.

Posner, M. I., Snyder, C. R. R., & Davidson, B. J. (1980). Attention and the detection of signals. *Journal of Experimental Psychology: General, 109*, 160–174.

Pylyshyn, Z. W. (1989). The role of location indexes in spatial perception: a sketch of the FINST spatial index model. *Cognition, 32*, 65–97.

Pylyshyn, Z. W. (1994). Some primitive mechanisms of spatial attention. *Cognition, 50*, 363–384.

Pylyshyn, Z. W. (2001). Visual indexes, preconceptual objects, and situated vision. *Cognition*, this issue, *80*, 127–158.

Pylyshyn, Z. W., & Storm, R. W. (1988). Tracking multiple independent targets: evidence for a parallel tracking mechanism. *Spatial Vision, 3*, 179–197.

Quinlan, P. T. (1998). The recovery of identity and relative position from visual input: further evidence for the independence of processing of what and where. *Perception & Psychophysics, 60*, 303–318.

Rafal, R. D. (1997). Balint syndrome. In T. Feinberg, & M. Farah (Eds.), *Behavioral neurology and neuropsychology* (pp. 337–356). New York: McGraw-Hill.

Rafal, R. D. (1998). Neglect. In R. Parasuraman (Ed.), *The attentive brain* (pp. 489–525). Cambridge, MA: MIT Press.

Rensink, R. A. (2000a). The dynamic representation of scenes. *Visual Cognition, 7*, 17–42.

Rensink, R. A. (2000b). Seeing, sensing, and scrutinizing. *Vision Research, 40*, 1469–1487.

Rensink, R. A., O'Regan, J. K., & Clark, J. J. (1997). To see or not to see: the need for attention to perceive changes in scenes. *Psychological Science, 8* (5), 368–373.

Reuter-Lorenz, P., Drain, M., & Hardy-Morais, C. (1996). Object-centered attentional biases in the intact brain. *Journal of Cognitive Neuroscience, 8*, 540–550.

Robertson, I. & Marshall, J. (1993). *Unilateral neglect: clinical and experimental studies.* Hove: Erlbaum.

Robertson, L., Treisman, A., Friedman-Hill, S., & Grabowecky, M. (1997). The interaction of spatial and object pathways: evidence from Balint syndrome. *Journal of Cognitive Neuroscience, 9*, 295–317.

Sagi, D., & Julesz, B. (1985). What and where in vision. *Science, 228*, 1217–1219.

Scholl, B. J., & Leslie, A. M. (1999). Explaining the infant's object concept: beyond the perception/cognition dichotomy. In E. Lepore, & Z. Pylyshyn (Eds.), *What is cognitive science?* (pp. 26–73). Oxford: Blackwell.

Scholl, B. J., & Pylyshyn, Z. W. (1999). Tracking multiple items through occlusion: clues to visual objecthood. *Cognitive Psychology, 38*, 259–290.

Scholl, B. J., Pylyshyn, Z. W., & Feldman, J. (2001a). What is a visual object? Evidence from target merging in multi-element tracking. *Cognition*, this issue, *80*, 159–177.

Scholl, B. J., Pylyshyn, Z. W., & Franconeri, S. L. (2001b). The relationship between property-encoding and object-based attention: evidence from multiple object tracking. Manuscript submitted for publication.

Scholl, B. J., & Tremoulet, P. D. (2000). Perceptual causality and animacy. *Trends in Cognitive Sciences, 4* (8), 299–309.

Sears, C. R., & Pylyshyn, Z. W. (2000). Multiple object tracking and attentional processing. *Canadian Journal of Experimental Psychology, 54*, 1–14.

Simons, D. J. (1996). In sight, out of mind: when object representations fail. *Psychological Science, 7*, 301–305.

Simons, D. J., & Chabris, C. F. (1999). Gorillas in our midst: sustained inattentional blindness for dynamic events. *Perception, 28*, 1059–1074.

Simons, D. J., & Levin, D. T. (1997). Change blindness. *Trends in Cognitive Sciences, 1* (7), 261–267.

Singh, M., & Scholl, B. J. (2000). *Using attentional cueing to explore part structure.* Poster presented at the 2000 Pre-Psychonomies Object Perception and Memory meeting, New Orleans, LA.

Spelke, E. (1988a). The origins of physical knowledge. In L. Weiskrantz (Ed.), *Thought without language* (pp. 168–184). Oxford: Oxford Science.

Spelke, E. (1988b). Where perceiving ends and thinking begins: the apprehension of objects in infancy. In A. Yonas (Ed.), *Perceptual development in infancy* (pp. 197–234). Hillsdale, NJ: Erlbaum.

Spelke, E. (1994). Initial knowledge: six suggestions. *Cognition, 50*, 431–445.

Spelke, E., Gutheil, G., & Van de Walle, G. (1995). The development of object perception. In S. Kosslyn, & D. Osherson (Eds.), *Visual cognition. An invitation to cognitive science* (2nd ed. pp. 297–330). Cambridge, MA: MIT Press.

Stuart, G., Maruff, P., & Currie, J. (1997). Object-based visual attention in luminance increment detection? *Neuropsychologia, 35*, 843–853.

Styles, E. (1997). *The psychology of attention.* Hove: Psychology Press.

Subbiah, I., & Caramazza, A. (2000). Stimulus-centered neglect in reading and object-recognition. *Neurocase, 6*, 13–31.

Tipper, S., & Behrmann, M. (1996). Object-centered not scene-based visual neglect. *Journal of Experimental Psychology: Human Perception and Performance, 22*, 1261–1278.

Tipper, S., Brehaut, J., & Driver, J. (1990). Selection of moving and static objects for the control of spatially directed action. *Journal of Experimental Psychology: Human Perception and Performance, 16*, 492–504.

Tipper, S., Driver, J., & Weaver, B. (1991). Object-centered inhibition of return of visual attention. *Quarterly Journal of Experimental Psychology, 43A*, 289–298.

Tipper, S., Jordan, H., & Weaver, B. (1999). Scene-based and object-centered inhibition of return: evidence for dual orienting mechanisms. *Perception & Psychophysics, 61*, 50–60.

Treisman, A. (1988). Features and objects: the fourteenth Bartlett memorial lectures. *Quarterly Journal of Experimental Psychology, 40*, 201–237.

Treisman, A. (1993). The perception of features and objects. In A. Baddeley, & L. Weiskrantz (Eds.), *Attention: selection, awareness, and control* (pp. 5–35). Oxford: Clarendon Press.

Treisman, A., Kahneman, D., & Burkell, J. (1983). Perceptual objects and the cost of filtering. *Perception & Psychophysics, 33,* 527–532.

Ullman, S. (1984). Visual routines. *Cognition, 18,* 97–159.

Valdes-Sosa, M., Cobo, A., & Pinilla, T. (1998). Transparent motion and object-based attention. *Cognition, 66,* B13–B23.

Van de Walle, G., & Spelke, E. (1996). Spatiotemporal integration and object perception in infancy: perceiving unity vs. form. *Child Development, 67,* 2621–2640.

Van Lier, R., & Wagemans, J. (1998). Effects of physical connectivity on the representational unity of multi-part configurations. *Cognition, 69,* B1–B9.

Vecera, S. (1994). Grouped locations and object-based attention: comment on Egly, Driver, and Rafal (1994). *Journal of Experimental Psychology: General, 123,* 316–320.

Vecera, S., Behrmann, M., & Filapek, J. (in press). Attending to the parts of a single object: part-based selection limitations. *Perception & Psychophysics.*

Vecera, S., Behrmann, M., & McGoldrick, J. (2000). Selective attention to the parts of an object. *Psychonomic Bulletin & Review, 7,* 301–308.

Vecera, S., & Farah, M. (1994). Does visual attention select objects or locations? *Journal of Experimental Psychology: Human Perception and Performance, 23,* 1–14.

Viswanathan, L., & Mingolla, E. (in press). Dynamics of attention in depth: evidence from multi-element tracking. *Perception.*

Ward, R., Goodrich, S., & Driver, J. (1994). Grouping reduces visual extinction: neuropsychological evidence for weight-linkage in visual selection. *Visual Cognition, 1,* 101–129.

Warren, R. (1982). *Auditory perception: a new synthesis.* New York: Pergamon.

Warren, R., Obusek, C., & Ackroff, J. (1972). Auditory induction: perceptual synthesis of absent sounds. *Science, 176,* 1149–1151.

Watson, D., & Humphreys, G. (1998). Visual marking of moving objects: a role for top-down feature-based inhibition in selection. *Journal of Experimental Psychology: Human Perception and Performance, 24,* 946–962.

Watson, S., & Kramer, A. (1999). Object-based visual selective attention and perceptual organization. *Perception & Psychophysics, 61,* 31–49.

Watt, R. J. (1988). *Visual processing: computational, psychophysical, and cognitive research.* Hillsdale, NJ: Erlbaum.

Wheeler, M., & Treisman, A. (1999). *Aspects of time, space, and binding in visual working memory for simple objects.* Paper presented at the 1999 Pre-Psychonomics Object Perception and Memory meeting, Los Angeles, CA.

Wiggins, D. (1980). *Sameness and substance.* Oxford: Basic Blackwell.

Wiggins, D. (1997). Sortal concepts: a reply to Xu. *Mind & Language, 12,* 413–421.

Wright, R., & Ward, L. (1998). The control of visual attention. In R. Wright (Ed.), *Visual Attention* (pp. 132–186). New York: Oxford: University Press.

Wynn, K. (1998). Psychological foundations of number: numerical competence in human infants. *Trends in Cognitive Sciences, 2,* 296–303.

Xu, F. (1997). From Lot's wife to a pillar of salt: evidence that physical object is a sortal concept. *Mind & Language, 12,* 365–392.

Xu, F., & Carey, S. (1996). Infants' metaphysics: the case of numerical identity. *Cognitive Psychology, 30,* 111–153.

Xu, Y. (2001). Integrating color and shape in visual short-term memory for objects with parts. Manuscript submitted for publication.

Xu, Y. (2001). Limitations in object-based feature encoding in visual short-term memory. Manuscript submitted for publication.

Yantis, S. (1992). Multielement visual tracking: attention and perceptual organization. *Cognitive Psychology, 24,* 295–340.

Yantis, S. (1995). Perceived continuity of occluded visual objects. *Psychological Science, 6,* 182–186.

Yantis, S., & Hillstrom, A. (1994). Stimulus-driven attentional capture: evidence from equiluminant visual objects. *Journal of Experimental Psychology: Human Perception and Performance, 20,* 95–107.

2

Attention-based visual routines: sprites

Patrick Cavanagh[a],*, Angela T. Labianca[a], Ian M. Thornton[b,1]

[a]*Vision Sciences Laboratory, Department of Psychology, Harvard University, 33 Kirkland Street, Cambridge, MA 02138, USA*
[b]*Cambridge Basic Research, Nissan Research and Development Inc., Cambridge, MA 02142, USA*

Abstract

A central role of visual attention is to generate object descriptions that are not available from early vision. Simple examples are counting elements in a display or deciding whether a dot is inside or outside a closed contour (Ullman, *Cognition 18* (1984) 97). We are interested in the high-level descriptions of dynamic patterns – the motions that characterize familiar objects undergoing stereotypical action – such as a pencil bouncing on a table top, a butterfly in flight, or a closing door. We examine whether the perception of these action patterns is mediated by attention as a high-level animation or 'sprite'. We have studied the discrimination of displays made up of simple, rigidly linked sets of points in motion: either pairs of points in orbiting motion or 11 points in biological motion mimicking human walking. We find that discrimination of even the simplest dynamic patterns demands attention. © 2001 Elsevier Science B.V. All rights reserved.

Keywords: Attention; Tracking; Motion; Visual search

1. Introduction

Recognizing an item can call on much more than just an analysis of its static form. Something that moves on a street and makes motor sounds is probably a car or a truck (or maybe a 3-year-old boy). But in addition to characteristic sounds or properties, many objects have characteristic patterns of movement, revealed only over

* Corresponding author. Fax: +1-617-495-3764.
 E-mail address: patrick@wjh.harvard.edu (P. Cavanagh).
[1] Present address: Max-Planck-Institut fuer Biologische Kybernetik, Spemannstrasse 38, D-72076 Tuebingen, Germany.

some duration of time. Rubber balls bounce on floors, billiard balls bounce less, butterflies dance up and down, Frisbees fly straight, a pencil bouncing off the floor takes an end over end tumble, and doors swing slowly through an arc when opening and bang up against their endpoints. Many of these characteristic patterns of motion are so familiar as to be sufficient for recognition of the object. The case of biological motion is perhaps the strongest evidence for this. A human form is easily recognized from the motions of a set of lights attached to a person filmed while walking in the dark (Johansson, 1973; Neri, Morrone, & Burr, 1998).

How do we accomplish this seemingly effortless recognition of motion patterns? We are not aware of analyzing components of the motion and coming to intermediate decisions. The human walking just seems to pop out of the display. Johansson (1973) proposed that the analysis relied on an automatic and spontaneous extraction of mathematically lawful spatiotemporal relations. But is this act of recognition really effortless? And what about the continued perception of the motion, an analysis which continually adapts our impression of the walker's posture and progress to the moving points in the display. Can that also be as effortless as it seems?

We propose that these characteristic motions are analyzed and interpreted by a special set of operators that we will call 'sprites'. In this paper, we will only address the attentional demands of these operators but we will nevertheless sketch our view of their properties and the role they play. We consider a sprite to be the set of routines that is responsible for detecting the presence of a specific characteristic motion in the input array, for modeling or animating the object's changing configuration as it makes this stereotypical motion, and for filling in the predictable details of the motion over time and in the face of noisy or absent image details. Each different characteristic motion pattern would have its own 'sprite' that would be built up over many exposures to the pattern. These stored recognition and animation routines then allow sparse inputs to support rich dynamic percepts. Many others have stressed that regularities in the world can be captured by efficient, higher-order data structures such as chunks (Miller, 1956), schemata (Bartlett, 1932; Neisser, 1967), frames or scripts (Minsky, 1975; Schank & Abelson, 1977). Characteristic patterns of motion ought to lend themselves quite well to similarly efficient representations.

Separate instances of a characteristic motion are seldom exact repetitions, however. The path of a bouncing pencil can be quite chaotic, depending strongly on many factors (starting position, rotation, surface properties, etc.). The regularities of a bouncing pencil, or a butterfly's flight, or a walking human, lie at a higher level of description of the motion. Significant analysis of the motion pattern must precede any recognition of the regularity and significant computation is then required to use the knowledge of the regularity to predict or animate subsequent motions.

This procedural aspect of a sprite is closely related to the concept of 'visual routines' addressed by Ullman (1984). These routines act on the representations emerging from the initial stage of visual analysis to establish properties and relations that are not explicitly represented in the first stage. Ullman identified elemental processes such as counting, indexing, tracking, and region-filling which could be organized (compiled) into visual routines to perform a high-level task such as, for example, judging whether a point is inside or outside a complex closed curve.

Importantly, in the original work by Ullman (1984), he assigned the critical operation of shifting the focus of analysis to attentional processes so that his visual routines were exclusively attention-based. In our case, abstracting the high-level description of, say, a bouncing pencil or a point-light walker certainly calls on an analysis of similar or greater complexity than the spatial tasks that Ullman (1984) described. Nevertheless, whether or not these high-level motion descriptors – sprites – require attention remains an open question. It is the central question that we address in this paper.

In the two experiments reported below, we use visual search tasks to examine the attentional load required to perceive a dynamic motion pattern. The displays present one to four motion patterns and the subjects report the presence or absence of a target motion. The relation between reaction time and number of items in the display allows us to evaluate any increase in attentional load with each additional item. If, for example, point-light walkers are recognized effortlessly, then there should be no increase in reaction time as the number of walkers in the display increases from one to four.

Our first experiment examines simple configurations of two moving dots. Although these patterns of motion are relatively simple they are not highly familiar. If attention is required to discriminate between configurations, it may be because we do not have highly efficient routines, sprites, to handle them. Our second experiment examines highly familiar configurations involving human motion. The movements in these stimuli are more complex but extremely familiar. If any dynamic patterns can be discriminated without attentional load, we believe it should be these patterns.

2. Experiment 1

In the first experiment, observers had to discriminate between two different orbital motions. In each stimulus, two lights rotate around each other while moving around a central fixation point. We will describe the two stimuli briefly before examining the similarities between our displays and the classic wheel-generated motions studied in many previous articles (Duncker, 1937; Johansson, 1973; Proffitt, Cutting, & Stier, 1979; Wallach, 1965).

In our first stimulus (Fig. 1a), the motion is like that of a moon orbiting a planet where the planet itself orbits a central 'star' (the fixation point). The moon traces out a complex curve (of the cycloid family) around the central point whereas the planet traces a circle. If the smoothly moving light (the 'planet') is turned off, the complex nature of the moon's motion is immediately evident as a looping path of wildly varying velocity. With the smoothly moving 'planet' turned on, however, the erratic motion is no longer apparent as the first light is now seen to rotate smoothly at constant velocity around the 'planet'.

In the second stimulus (Fig. 1b), the two lights rotate around a common center and this central point rotates around the fixation point. In this case, both lights trace

a) Orbiting pair   b) Tumbling pair

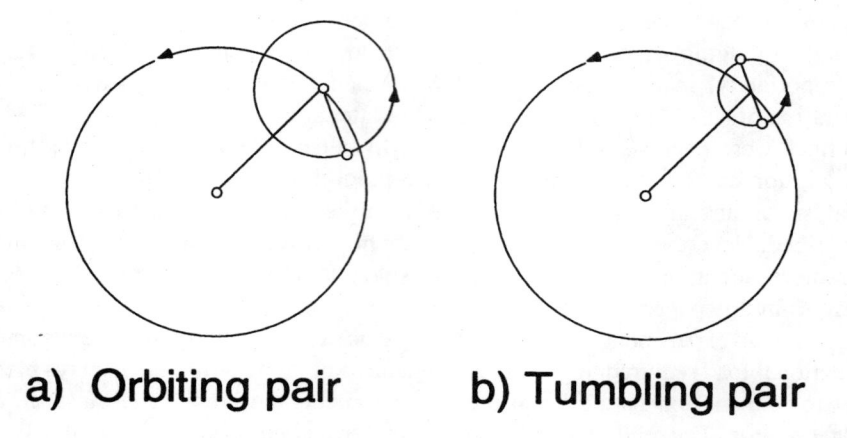

Fig. 1. Trajectories of the orbiting and tumbling motions for dot pairs. Both dot pairs are separated by the same distance and rotate around each other at the same rate. (a) The center of rotation for the orbiting pair is one of the dots so the motion is like that of a moon orbiting a planet which itself orbits the central point. (b) The center of rotation for the tumbling pair is the midpoint between the two dots.

similar intertwined curves (again both are of the cycloid family). Either light alone is seen as moving along a complex path of changing velocity. When the two are present together, however, they create a tumbling motion like that of a baton turning end over end as it moves around the circular path at a constant rate.

The two stimuli have very simple and distinctive motion patterns that might suggest automatic processing of their organization. To examine this question, we asked observers to distinguish between the orbiting and tumbling motions of the two stimuli when there were one or more pairs at different points around the circular path. We consider the tumbling and orbiting motions to be examples of quite familiar motion patterns. Rolling wheels, twirling batons, sticks thrown tumbling through the air, and objects spun around your head on a string fall in one or the other or both of these characteristic motion types. The motions may not have the compelling familiarity of a walking human but they are so simple that we assume that they are good candidates for encoding as characteristic motions or sprites.

Earlier research has looked in depth at a more basic version of these motions: the motions traced out by lights on a wheel rolling along a flat surface. Duncker (1937), for example, noticed that a single light on the rim of a rolling wheel traced out a curve similar to a semicircle (a cycloid). However, when he added a second light to the center of the wheel, the cycloid was no longer seen. Rather, the light on the rim was seen by many observers to rotate around the central light which itself moved in a straight line. Based on the paths of only these two lights (Fig. 2b), the observers 'saw' a wheel in motion even though neither of the motions alone seemed at all wheel-like. Further studies by Johansson (1973), Proffitt et al. (1979), and Wallach (1965) have examined, among other things, the importance of the number and placement of the lights on the wheel in supporting the recovery of the wheel's motion.

Attention-based visual routines: sprites

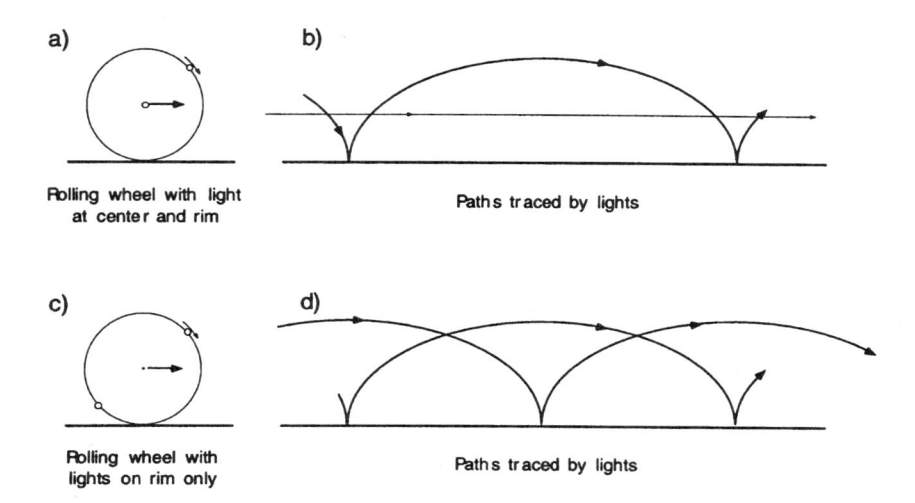

a) Rolling wheel with light at center and rim

b) Paths traced by lights

c) Rolling wheel with lights on rim only

d) Paths traced by lights

Fig. 2. Trajectories of lights on rolling wheels. (a) One light on the rim and one at the center. (b) Paths followed by the two lights. (c) Two lights on opposite sides of the rim. (d) Paths followed by the lights.

Our first stimulus is equivalent to a translating wheel display with one light on the rim and one in the center (Fig. 2a,b). Our second configuration is equivalent to two lights on the rim at opposite ends of a diameter of the wheel (Fig. 2c,d). According to Proffitt et al. (1979), both of these configurations give rise to equally strong impressions of wheel motion. With displays simulating lights on linearly translating wheels, observers are often drawn to follow the wheel with eye movements. The role of eye movements in recovering the wheel motion has been examined in the traditional wheel displays by Proffitt and Cutting (1979). They found no difference in judgments of wheel motion with or without eye movements. Nevertheless, in our task, we use a central fixation with light pairs orbiting around fixation specifically to avoid eye movements and their effects on reaction time in visual search.

Our two stimuli are constructed to be as similar as possible in terms of basic features and to differ most notably in their high-level organization: tumbling versus orbiting. For example, our tumbling configuration (Fig. 1b) cannot have the same 'wheel' diameter as the orbiting configuration (Fig. 1a). The two lights are on opposite sides of the wheel in the tumbling case but only separated by the radius of the wheel in the orbiting case. If the two 'wheels' had the same diameter, the two lights would be twice as far apart in the tumbling case as in the orbiting case, a difference that would be immediately obvious. To equate the separation of the two lights in both configurations, the radius of the tumbling motion is therefore half that of the orbiting motion. Despite the difference in diameters of the equivalent 'wheels', the rotation of the two lights about their respective midpoints is identical in both stimuli (the midpoints themselves follow different paths).

Our goal in this experiment was to have two easily identified, characteristic motions and determine how quickly each is processed. To do so, we displayed one, two, three, or four of the dot pairs moving in the same direction at the same rate around the fixation. On a target present trial, one of the pairs is following the target motion, say, tumbling, whereas the others are following the alternative motion, orbiting in this case. We recorded the reaction time to respond that the target was present or absent and analyzed the function relating the reaction time and the number of dot pairs present. If the reaction time did not increase with the number of dot pairs present, we would conclude that the extraction of the characteristic motions calls only minimally on central, attentional resources.

As a control, we also measured the reaction time with only one of the dots present in each pair. The target would then be the smoothly moving 'planet' among singleton tumbling dots or one singleton tumbling dot among smoothly moving planets. This gives a measure of the distinctiveness of the single dot motions that make up the characteristic motions of the pairs.

2.1. Methods

2.1.1. Observers

Twelve paid volunteers, with an average age of about 21 years and with normal or corrected-to-normal vision, participated in this experiment. All participants were naive to the purpose of the experiment and gave informed written consent before the experiments, which were approved by the F.A.S. Human Subjects Committee, Harvard University.

2.1.2. Stimuli

The display was presented on a 14 inch 67 Hz Macintosh display driven by a Macintosh 7500/100 programmed in Vision Shell. The two motion patterns we used are shown in Fig. 1. Between one and four of these orbiting or tumbling pairs were presented rotating around the central fixation. The distance from the fixation to the center of rotation of the pair was 4.3° of visual angle at a fixed viewing distance of 57 cm. The center–center separation of the two dots was 1° of visual angle. The dots themselves had a diameter of 0.4° of visual angle. The two dots made one full cycle around each other every 1.5 s while the pair made a full circuit around fixation every 7.5 s. The local and global rotations were always in opposite directions and the direction was set randomly on each trial. The stimuli, when there was more than one, were spaced evenly around the circular path. The initial position of each local rotation was set randomly at the beginning of each trial as was the starting location of the rotation around the circular path. The dots had a luminance of 70 cd/m^2, and were presented on a 20 cd/m^2 background. The temporal onset and offset of the motion pairs on each trial was a step function. The fixation mark was a single static dot at the center of the display. It was identical in size to the moving dots (0.4° of visual angle in diameter).

2.1.3. Procedure

In the control conditions, only one dot of each pair was shown. It was always the smoothly moving dot (the planet) in the orbiting configuration and either of the dots in the tumbling configuration. In the experimental conditions, both dots of each pair were shown. In half the sessions, an orbiting configuration was the target (with tumblers as distractors) and in the other half, a tumbling configuration was the target (with orbiters as distractors). Across observers, the order of targets and the order of control versus experimental conditions were counterbalanced.

Each set size of one to four motion pairs was presented equally often and half the trials had a target present; half had no target present. The order of presenting set sizes and target present or absent was random. Testing began with four short practice sessions of 16 trials each, followed by the four sessions for the two target types and control or experimental conditions. The order of control and experimental sessions was balanced across observers. Experimental sessions with dot pairs had 64 trials. Control sessions with dot singletons had 32 trials. In all, the testing lasted about 1 h.

Each trial began with a warning tone followed immediately by the presentation of the configurations of dots. Observers had up to 15 s to respond either present or absent by pressing a key. There was no feedback. The reaction time and errors were recorded. The inter-trial interval was 1 s. The observers were told to fixate the central dot at all times. At the start of each session, the target stimulus was identified. Observers were instructed to respond quickly and to avoid making errors.

2.2. Results

The overall error rate was 2.3% in the control conditions and 10.9% in the experimental conditions. The reaction times of correct responses were averaged across observers and are shown in Fig. 3. Linear regression was used to estimate the rate of processing of the moving configurations.

In the control conditions, the single wobbling dot was discovered among smoothly moving dots (Fig. 3a) very rapidly. The search slope for target present trials was about 4 ms per item. Deciding that there was no target present was notably slower with a slope of 173 ms per item. It was harder still to find the one smoothly moving dot among wobbling distractors (slopes of 393 and 658 ms per item for target present and absent, respectively).

In the experimental sessions, finding the tumbling pair among orbiting pairs was extremely slow and finding the orbiting pair among tumbling pairs was the slowest of all. The observers spent almost 1 s or more per item to decide whether it was tumbling or not. It is interesting to consider how long each dot pair was monitored before a decision on the type of motion was reached. For our rough estimate we will assume that search was serial and stopped once the target was found. Since on average only half the pairs need to be checked before finding the target, the slope of 474 ms per pair for the target present trials should be doubled to 948 ms to estimate the average time spent on each pair. The slope for the target absent trials also estimates the time per pair and its value is similar at 1059 ms. The dots complete one rotation around each other every 1.5 s so the approximately 1 s of inspection time is two-thirds of a cycle. Even if we subtract a small portion of that second to allow for attention to shift from pair to pair (Duncan, 1984), it is still the case that the dot pairs require extended monitoring before the representation of their motion is

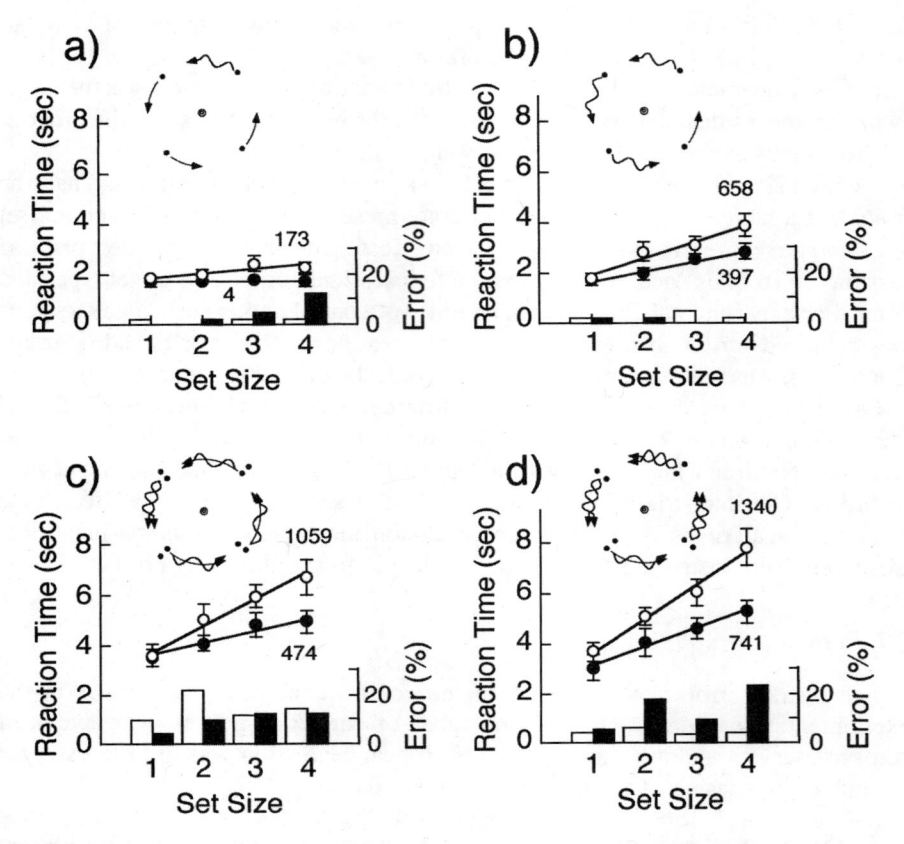

Fig. 3. Reaction time in seconds (left hand vertical axes) as a function of set size for the four search conditions. Target present responses are shown as filled symbols, and target absent responses are shown as outline symbols. Standard errors of the mean are shown as vertical bars when larger than the data symbols (±1 SE). The solid lines show the linear regressions for each data set and the numbers adjacent to the lines are the slopes of the linear regressions in milliseconds per item. Error rates (right hand vertical axes) are shown as histograms at the bottom of each panel with filled bars for target present, and outline bars for target absent trials. (a) Search for a singleton tumbling path among singleton planet paths. (b) Search for a singleton planet path among singleton tumbling paths. (c) Search for a tumbling pair among orbiting pairs. (d) Search for an orbiting pair among tumbling pairs. The data are averages for 12 observers.

settled. Our conclusion is that the perception of these motions is not supported by prepackaged operators specific to their trajectories. The analysis seems to require scrutiny and laborious 'on-line' construction of the links and their relative motions. Over many trials of building these constructed motion patterns, performance would undoubtedly improve and a more rapidly engaged operator might emerge that would permit rapid discrimination. No rapid discrimination was evident for the limited exposure offered in our experiments (fewer than 200 trials with dot pairs).

3. Experiment 2

In this experiment, we repeated the procedure of the first experiment but now we used point-light walkers, sets of dots in animation which generate a compelling impression of a human walking. Each walker has 11 moving points rather than just the two points of the stimuli in the previous experiment. Although the patterns of motion are also far more complex, they are so familiar that the stimuli are easily and rapidly seen as walking human forms. However, the ease of identifying the motion of a single walker does not tell us much about attentional requirements. The slope of the visual search function could be as steep for these stimuli as the slope for the dot pairs. Conversely, if our intuition about the ease of recognizing these figures is correct, the slopes may be flat – there may be no attentional load.

Thornton, Rensink, and Shiffrar (1999) examined the attention demands of point-light walkers using a dual task method. In the primary task, observers had to report the apparent direction of a point-light walker (leftward or rightward). In the second, observers monitored whether any of a set of rectangles changed orientation. The rectangles appeared at random locations within the same display area as the walker. When the walker was presented in a complex noise field – one designed to disrupt low-level motion integration – the introduction of the secondary task reduced the performance for biological motion to chance levels. They concluded that the perception of biological motion under some display conditions must be an active process, that is, one that is dependent on the availability of attentional resources (Cavanagh, 1992). Interestingly, when a simpler mask was used, the secondary task had little effect, suggesting that a biological motion stimulus might be processed automatically if it were not too degraded.

The attentional load reported by Thornton et al. (1999) may have resulted from the requirements of analyzing biological motion or it may have been due to the requirements of the task itself. The visual search task allows us to separate the overall task demands from the processing demands of each walker. Each additional walker may increase the attentional load, all the while keeping the task demands the same. We displayed one to four walkers simultaneously. On target present trials, one of the walkers was walking to the right and the distractors were walking to the left (the target and non-target directions were reversed for half of the observers). A control task was also run with walkers as targets among non-walking distractors (similar dot motions that did not appear to be a human walking) (Fig. 4). In all cases, observers maintained fixation at the center of the display and responded as quickly as possible whether or not a target walker was present.

3.1. Methods

3.1.1. Observers

Ten experienced observers, members of the Vision Sciences Laboratory, with normal or corrected-to-normal vision, participated in this experiment without reimbursement. All participants were naive to the purpose of the experiment and gave

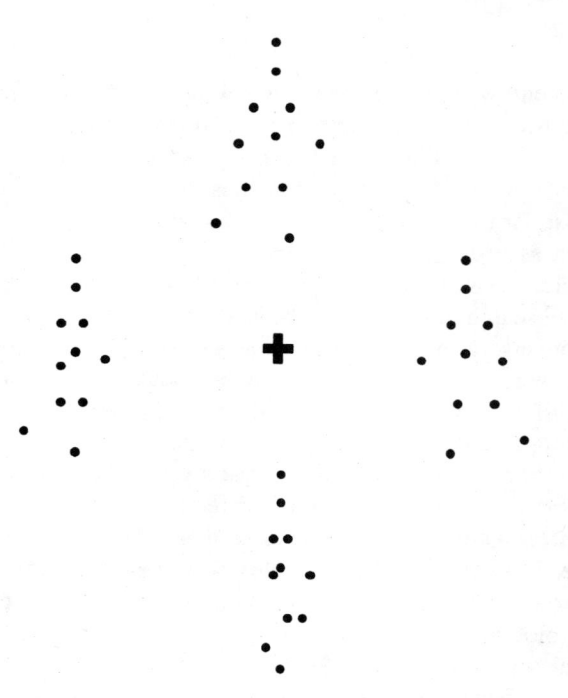

Fig. 4. A static frame from a display with four walkers. This depicts a trial where the target is a figure walking to the left, in this case, the figure at 3 o'clock.

informed written consent before the experiments, which were approved by the F.A.S. Human Subjects Committee, Harvard University.

3.1.2. Stimuli

The details of the displays were the same as in Experiment 1 with the following exceptions. The biological motion configuration was generated by modifying Cutting's classic point-light walker algorithm (Cutting, 1978). The set of 11 dots simulated a walker seen in profile with lights on the head, near shoulder, both elbows, both wrists, near hip, both knees and both ankles. The dots were always visible, and they did not disappear when they would be occluded by the walker's body. The walker did not move across the screen but walked in place with either left- or rightward gait. The distance from the fixation to the center dot of the walker subtended about 4° of visual angle, as did the height of the walker. The maximum stride width of a walker was about 2° of visual angle. The dots themselves had a diameter of 0.2° of visual angle. The walker's stride cycle took about 1.3 s, falling within the range of 0.8–2 s per stride reported for normal human walking (Inman, Ralston, & Todd, 1981). The walker's starting phase in its stride and position around the fixation point was selected randomly on each trial. When more than one walker was displayed, the starting phase of the stride for each was assigned randomly and spaced equally around fixation. The dots had a luminance of 0.1 cd/m^2, and were presented on a 2.12 cd/m² background. The fixation mark was a black cross at the center of the display subtending 0.5° of visual angle.

3.1.3. Procedure

The details of the procedures were the same as in Experiment 1 with the following exceptions. The target could be either a rightward gait or a leftward gait while the distractors had the opposite gait. The target was fixed for each observer but counterbalanced across observers. Each observer participated in two sessions of 80 trials. They had up to 5 s to respond either present or absent by pressing a key. No warning tone was used. In all, the testing lasted about 15 min. Sessions began with a few practice trials to familiarize the observers with the stimuli and responses.

3.2. Results

The overall error rate was 3.5%. The reaction times of correct responses were averaged across observers and are shown in Fig. 5. Linear regression was used to estimate the rate of processing of the walkers.

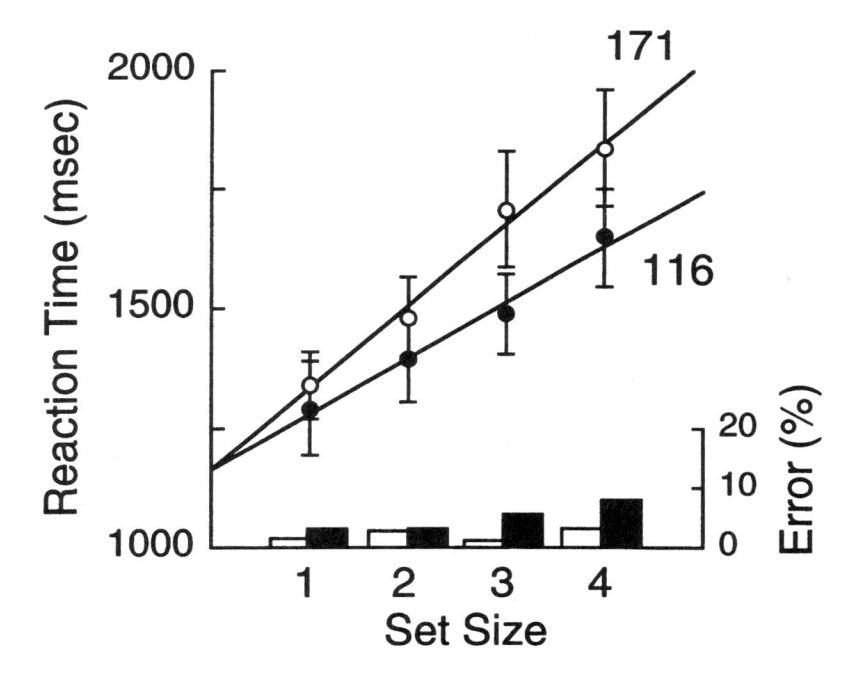

Fig. 5. Reaction time in seconds (left hand vertical axis) as a function of set size for the walker search task. Target present responses are shown as filled symbols, and target absent responses are shown as outline symbols. Standard errors of the mean are shown as vertical bars (±1 SE). The solid lines show the linear regressions for each data set and the numbers adjacent to the lines are the slopes of the linear regressions in milliseconds per item. Error rates (right hand vertical axis) are shown as histograms at the bottom of each panel with filled bars for target present, and outline bars for target absent trials. The data are averages for ten observers.

Finding the leftward gait among rightward distractors (or vice versa) was much faster than finding the tumbling or orbiting target in the previous experiment. Nevertheless, there was a significant slope in excess of 100 ms per walker. Although familiarity helped the search tremendously, search remained serial. There was no pop-out of the odd walker. Again we estimated how long each walker was monitored before a decision on gait direction was reached. The slope of 116 ms per walker is doubled to 232 ms to estimate the average time spent on each walker in the target present trials. The slope for the target absent trials suggests somewhat less at 171 ms per walker. The walkers complete one cycle of their stride every 1.3 s so even 232 ms is only one-fifth of a cycle. Once any time required for shifting attention from walker to walker is subtracted, it appears that even though the walkers must be scrutinized serially, the direction of the gait is determined very rapidly.

We were interested in whether left–right confusions might have contributed to the difficulty of the search. We ran a control condition with a standard walker as the target among impossible walkers (the dots comprising one arm and one leg were phase shifted relative to the rest of body, providing a very distinctive, non-rigid, non-human, skipping or dancing gait). The search rate here, averaged across four subjects, was even slower than for the left versus right task with slopes of about 160 ms per item (and higher still, 230 ms per item, for a non-walker target in walker distractors).

4. Conclusions

Distinguishing the tumbling from the orbiting motions in Experiment 1 was effortful. When several dot pairs were present, they all appeared to be tumbling. Only by attending to an orbiting pair did it become obvious that one of the dots was moving smoothly around the central dot and that the other was orbiting the first. The tumbling percept seemed to be the default that was seen with minimal attention for both of the motions; extracting the true relative motion required extended scrutiny. The estimated processing time per dot pair was about 1 s or more indicating that substantial processing was required.

Why were the dot pairs so difficult? Recall that in the control conditions a single tumbling target could be easily picked out from individual smoothly moving dots (without their orbiting moons). The highly distinctive motion of the individual dots was totally lost when an additional dot was added. It appeared that only the relative motion of the two dots was available and in terms of relative motion, both the tumbling and the orbiting pairs were constructed to be very similar. To distinguish the two, the observer must attend to the three-dot configuration including the central dot. Only then it is clear that one of the dots is always the same distance from the central point. This very slow process suggests that the subjects have no specialized analyzers that can rapidly identify these motion patterns – no sprites for tumbling or orbiting motions. The trajectories must be individually traced with attention to determine which pattern is governing each dot pair.

Moreover, it appears to be the dynamic aspect of the trajectory that makes it so difficult. Motion takes place over time and considerable time appears to be required to establish the trajectory of each pair. The static versions of the trajectories of our two motion patterns are much easier to distinguish. The orbiting pattern traces out something like a dollar sign and the tumbling pair something like a figure 8. When we simply presented these short trajectories as spatial patterns all at once, the discrimination was much more rapid (slope of less than 100 ms/item, averaged over four subjects). What makes the real motion case so difficult is that the configuration of dot motions needs to be made explicit, linking each dot to the next and then to the central dot. This is the only way to discover if one of the dots is actually maintaining a constant distance from the central dot.

These articulated links of constant length in tumbling and orbiting motion also form the basis of the structure for the point-light walkers where the light at each joint is separated from the next by a fixed distance. However, for the walkers in Experiment 2, the processing time was much faster at about 200 ms per walker (compared to about 1 s per dot pair). This rate is comparable to some estimates of the dwell time of attention (Duncan, 1984). This suggests that attention was required to notice the gait of each walker in turn but that little processing was required once each walker had been selected. This is evidence that the analysis of a very familiar motion pattern, despite its complexity, can be very rapid. We suggest that this rapid extraction of the motion pattern is the signature of the 'sprite' responsible for recognizing and animating the percept of a walking human form. Despite this rapid extraction, our data also show that only one walker at a time can be analyzed. The search rate was still substantial indicating that the operation of at least the 'walker' sprite requires attention.

The dual task results of Thornton et al. (1999) suggested that, in some cases, the perception of biological motion can be automatic. However, a search task is perhaps a more sensitive measure of attentional load because dual task interference only reveals an interaction between the two tasks if the combined load exceeds the available capacity. It cannot differentiate between no attentional demands and any combination that is less than the limit available.

If even familiar patterns of motion require attention to be discriminated, what can be the advantage of the routines that support the perception of the pattern? Clearly, it is the same advantage that is offered by any recognition of a familiar pattern. Once enough of the pattern is acquired to recognize it, the rest can be filled in from memory. Sparse inputs can support rich percepts and in the case of a moving object, filling in implies a prediction of likely motions and tracking them with less data than would be otherwise necessary. These advantages have formed the basis of many theories of perception from schemata and schema theory (Bartlett, 1932; Neisser, 1967) to frames and scripts (Minsky, 1975; Schank & Abelson, 1977).

To conclude, we suggest that the visual system acquires and uses stored motion patterns, sprites, which are characteristic of familiar events or objects: the motion of a wheel, the jump of a fish out of water, the way a pencil bounces on the floor when dropped, and the way a fresh egg does not. We use these stored patterns to recognize and then animate our perception of familiar events. Our experience of these animation routines might suggest that they are effortless but our study here shows that they are not. We claim that the animations are played out by attentive processes in the same way that we can animate a mental image. In the visual case, the input image data act like set points in the progress of the animation but the animation still requires the support of attentive processes.

Acknowledgements

Thanks to Pawan Sinha for helpful discussions of this work and to Jane Raymond for sharing her observations on Frisbees and butterflies. This research was supported by grant EY09258 to P.C.

References

Bartlett, S. F. (1932). *Remembering: a study in experimental and social psychology.* Cambridge: Cambridge University Press.
Cavanagh, P. (1992). Attention-based motion perception. *Science, 257,* 1563–1565.
Cutting, J. E. (1978). A program to generate synthetic walkers as dynamic point-light displays. *Behavioral Research Methods and Instrumentation, 10,* 91–94.
Duncan, J. (1984). Selective attention and the organization of visual information. *Journal of Experimental Psychology: General, 113,* 501–517.
Duncker, K. (1937). Induced motion. In W. D. Ellis (Ed.), *A sourcebook of Gestalt psychology.* London: Routledge and Kegan Paul.
Inman, V. T., Ralston, H., & Todd, J. T. (1981). *Human walking.* Baltimore, MD: Williams & Wilkins.
Johansson, G. (1973). Visual perception of biological motion and a model for its analysis. *Perception and Psychophysics, 14,* 201–211.
Miller, G. A. (1956). The magical number seven plus or minus two: some limits on our capacity for processing information. *Psychological Review, 63,* 81–97.
Minsky, M. (1975). A framework for representing knowledge. In P. H. Winston (Ed.). *The psychology of computer vision* (pp. 211–280). New York: McGraw-Hill.
Neisser, U. (1967). *Cognitive psychology.* New York: Appleton.
Neri, P., Morrone, M. C., & Burr, D. C. (1998). Seeing biological motion. *Nature, 395,* 894–896.
Proffitt, D. R., & Cutting, J. E. (1979). Perceiving the centroid of configurations on a rolling wheel. *Perception and Psychophysics, 25,* 389–398.
Proffitt, D. R., Cutting, J. E., & Stier, D. M. (1979). Perception of wheel-generated motions. *Journal of Experimental Psychology: Human Perception and Performance, 5,* 289–302.
Schank, R., & Abelson, R. (1977). *Scripts, plans, goals and understanding.* Hillsdale, NJ: Lawrence Erlbaum Associates.
Thornton, I. M., Rensink, R. A., & Shiffrar, M. (1999). Biological motion processing without attention. *Perception, 28* (Suppl), 51.
Ullman, S. (1984). Visual routines. *Cognition, 18,* 97–159.
Wallach, H. (1965). Visual perception of motion. In G. Keyes (Ed.), *The nature and the art of motion.* New York: George Braziller.

3

Segmentation, attention and phenomenal visual objects

Jon Driver[a,*], Greg Davis[b], Charlotte Russell[a], Massimo Turatto[c], Elliot Freeman[a]

[a]*Institute of Cognitive Neuroscience, University College London, 17 Queen Square, London WC1N 3AR, UK*
[b]*Birkbeck College, London, UK*
[c]*University of Padova, Padova, Italy*

Abstract

Issues concerning selective attention provoke new questions about visual segmentation, and vice-versa. We illustrate this by describing our recent work on grouping under conditions of inattention, on change blindness for background events and the residual processing of undetected background changes, on modal versus amodal completion in visual search, and the differential effects of these two forms of completion on attentional processes, and on attentional modulation of lateral interactions thought to arise in early visual cortex. Many of these results indicate that segmentation processes substantially constrain attentional processes, but the reverse influence is also apparent, suggesting an interactive architecture. We discuss how the 'proto-objects' revealed by studies of segmentation and attention (i.e. the segmented perceptual units which constrain selectivity) may relate to other object-based notions in cognitive science, and we wrestle with their relation to phenomenal visual awareness. © 2001 Elsevier Science B.V. All rights reserved.

Keywords: Segmentation; Attention Phenomenal visual objects

1. Introduction

The recent literature on so-called 'object-based' visual attention represents fertile new cross-talk between two traditionally separate research fields, one concerning visual segmentation and grouping processes, and the other concerning selective

* Corresponding author. Fax: +44-207-813-2835.
E-mail address: j.driver@ucl.ac.uk (J. Driver).

attention. We shall not provide an exhaustive summary of research on object-based visual attention here (for reviews see Driver & Baylis, 1998; Kanwisher & Driver, 1992; Scholl, 2001). Instead, we shall use selected examples from our own recent work, seeking to illustrate how research on visual segmentation and on selective attention can be complementary. When the two fields are considered together, new questions arise that neither research tradition would otherwise have considered. Moreover, methods from the two fields can be fruitfully used in combination.

2. Image segmentation

The 'objects' with which we will be concerned are segmented perceptual units. These might more properly be called 'proto-objects', since they need not correspond exactly with conceptual or recognizable objects. Instead, they reflect the visual system's segmentation of current visual input into candidate objects (i.e. grouping together those parts of the retinal input which are likely to correspond to parts of the same object in the real world, separately from those which are likely to belong to other objects). There is a long research tradition on visual segmentation, dating back to seminal work by the Gestaltists (e.g. Wertheimer, 1923). Image segmentation is traditionally viewed as a fundamental problem that the visual system must solve quite early (e.g. Marr, 1982; Nakayama, He, & Shimojo, 1995; Nakayama, Shimojo, & Silverman, 1989; Neisser, 1967; Rock, 1975), before proceeding to further processes such as object recognition (although see Peterson, 1994). Rock, Nijhawan, Palmer, and Tudor (1992, p. 779) state that "it is widely acknowledged that a precondition for the perception of the world of objects and events is an early process of organization in the visual system". Thus, a standard idea is that real-world objects can only be recognized appropriately if fragments of the retinal image are bundled together appropriately, before matching against long-term memories of known visual objects. For instance, when faced with an animal partly occluded behind a tree, the retinal fragments corresponding to the animal should ideally be bundled together for matching against representations of known objects in long-term memory, separately from those fragments corresponding to the tree. Trying to recognize a bundle of features which combined part of the animal with part of the tree would be unlikely to lead to an appropriate match with a single known object! From this perspective, appropriate image segmentation seems to be an essential first step, and so it has traditionally been attributed to quite early visual processes (although many current accounts refer to it as reflecting 'mid-level' vision, with this term implying an intermediate stage between initial description of raw image statistics, and subsequent matching against a knowledge base).

The starting point for much research on image segmentation was phenomenology, as in the Gestaltists' many demonstrations of grouping (e.g. Wertheimer, 1923) or figure-ground segmentation (e.g. Rubin, 1921). These demonstrations, reproduced in countless textbooks since, rely entirely on the phenomenology of the observer for their appeal. For instance, the reader may be asked to inspect an array of dots in order to confirm the introspection that subsets of these dots seem to go together (as when organized into columns or rows by principles such as proximity or similarity). Because of the theoretical perspective outlined above (on which image segmentation is typically considered as an essential first step for the visual system), it has commonly been assumed that the phenomenology of Gestalt grouping displays somehow affords a privileged view of quite early visual processes. However, it should be remembered that since the classic Gestalt demonstrations rely entirely on phenomenology, they may presumably tap into many stages of vision, or even reflect an end-product. Phenomenology is certainly a useful starting point for much research into perception, and the phenomenal appearance of visual displays remains one of the things that researchers must explain (and which we will wrestle with here). However, phenomenology can be a crude or even inappropriate tool for addressing some questions, especially those of the sort thrown up by the literature on selective attention.

3. Selective attention

Just as for image segmentation, there is a long but entirely separate research tradition on selective attention, our ability to process incoming information selectively. Again phenomenology provides one starting point, as many of the fundamental issues about selective attention can be prompted simply by phenomenal demonstrations that involve two streams of information (traditional examples include two concurrent spoken messages in audition, or two superimposed pictures in vision, e.g. Cherry, 1953; Neisser & Becklen, 1975; Rock & Gutman, 1981). People can simply be asked to confirm the introspection that they may concentrate on one or the other of the two streams at will, even when both streams are equally clear at the ear or eye. Phenomenologically, there is a much richer awareness of the attended stream. Moreover, objective tests confirm that there is little or no explicit knowledge of the unattended stream (e.g. Cherry, 1953; Mack & Rock, 1998; Neisser & Becklen, 1975; Rock & Gutman, 1981). Several issues are immediately prompted by the phenomenology of attention in such settings: for instance, on what basis can we attend to one stream versus the other, and what are the consequences for the two streams? Such questions have now been addressed with many objective measures.

Ever since the seminal account of Broadbent (1958), it has been traditional to contrast two hypothetical stages of perceptual processing, thought to be qualitatively distinct, for such situations. 'Preattentive' processing is traditionally thought to be automatic, parallel, and to extract relatively simple stimulus properties. This stage would operate for both streams of input in the examples above, regardless of which one the person attended at will. This 'preattentive' stage by definition is traditionally thought to precede a subsequent 'attentive' stage, with the latter by definition depending on the attentional state of the observer. The attentive stage would only operate for one of the two streams in the examples above, and has been variously characterized as serial or of limited capacity, and as extracting more complex stimulus properties (e.g. Broadbent, 1958; Treisman & Gelade, 1980), although there have been many subsequent qualifications of this (e.g. see Pashler, 1998).

Space limits preclude a full consideration of the substantial and complex literature motivated by this preattentive/attentive dichotomy. Suffice to say that while it remains influential, and has proved a useful heuristic for generating research, the dichotomy is clearly a gross oversimplification of biological reality. For instance, recent neuroscience studies of selective attention have shown, both with single-cell recording in animals (e.g. Desimone & Duncan, 1995) and with functional imaging in people (e.g. Kastner, Pinsk, De-Weerd, Desimone, & Ungerleider, 1999), that the attentional state of the observer can modulate *many* levels of perceptual processing, rather than kicking in only at one specific 'attentive' stage, following an initial 'preattentive' stage. It does remain roughly true that later stages of vision can show greater attentional modulation than earlier stages (e.g. Kastner et al., 1999), but even primary visual cortex can be modulated to some extent (e.g. Somers, Dale, Seiffert, & Tootell, 1999). Our own view is that 'attention' is best thought of as the umbrella-term for a general topic, subsuming a host of questions about selective processing, *not* as a single explanatory process, which affects just a single stage of perception. If we occasionally slip into referring to 'attention' as if this were a singular process, then we do so merely for expository convenience.

4. Attention and image segmentation

The kind of questions which an attention researcher might have about visual segmentation include the following. Does such-and-such a segmentation process occur 'automatically', regardless of the attentional state of an observer? Does it still proceed if the observer attends elsewhere to perform some other task, of low or high demand? Can it be strengthened by attending appropriately? Can it be weakened by attending in a different way? Does it constrain what an observer can efficiently select for judgement from a visual display (e.g. with better performance when judging two visual attributes if these two attributes are segmented together, rather than apart)? Does it constrain what an observer can ignore (e.g. are distractors more distracting when grouped together with a target)? These various questions differ in their specifics, but many relate to whether the visual task that an observer is currently performing, or is about to perform, can modify how an image gets segmented (i.e. can attention affect segmentation?). Conversely, many concern whether image segmentation constrains what can be efficiently selected in a particular visual task (i.e. does segmentation affect attention?).

The Gestaltists tended to view their grouping phenomena as an illustration of the perceiver imposing a seemingly arbitrary (albeit systematic) organization upon the stimuli (e.g. Wertheimer, 1923). Nowadays the more typical view of such grouping demonstrations would be that they reflect non-arbitrary properties within the stimuli (similarity, etc.), which the visual system exploits heuristically because these properties are likely to reflect divisions into distinct objects in the real world. The attentional questions about segmentation, as outlined above, provide a new framework for asking whether an observer can, at will, make a contribution to how a given display will be segmented, or whether instead, the influence works mainly in the opposite direction, with image segmentation constraining what an observer can attend at will.

The traditional view from attention research, within the preattentive/attentive dichotomy, emphasizes the latter direction of influence, with segmentation processes thought to arise preattentively, to yield 'proto-objects' (or feature-bundles) which may then be attended in turn for further processing (e.g. Driver & Baylis, 1998; Duncan, 1984; Neisser, 1967; Treisman, 1986). Palmer and Rock (1994, p. 37) went so far as to suggest that this may be a logical necessity, arguing that "...logic dictates that some amount of visual organization must occur at an early stage in visual processing and that it must occur preattentively. As Neisser (1967) and Treisman (1986) have put it, discrete perceptual elements of some sort must be present to serve as candidates for further element-based processing. Only after such elements are present can we attend selectively to one or another."

Note that although somewhat different language is used in this quotation (now gesturing towards the preattentive/attentive dichotomy), this line of argument accords with the traditional view within the segmentation literature as described earlier, on which segmentation is considered an essential first step of organizing the input into feature-bundles, before further processing of each bundle. Note also that many questions are begged when using attentional language to convey this general story. In particular, exactly which kinds of segmentation precede selective processing (note the 'some amount' in the above quotation), and for what kinds of selective processing, given that rather than modulating vision at just a single discrete stage of selectivity, attentional factors are now known to modulate visual processing at many stages (cf. the neuroscience evidence above)?

Despite these uncertainties, some of us have long been sympathetic (e.g. Driver & Baylis, 1989, 1998) to the general view that some forms of segmentation can precede attentional selectivity. In part, we sympathize with this because we consider it to be broadly consistent with the actual *phenomenology* of Gestalt grouping displays (see Driver & Baylis, 1998). As explained earlier, the phenomenology of Gestalt grouping is often naively taken to tap directly into early segmentation processes, but we suggest that it may reflect attentional processes also. Indeed, the introspection that a subset of dots in a Gestalt display 'belongs together' may arise precisely because when trying to pick out one of these dots, you tend to pick out also those dots which are grouped with it. In other words, they may seem to 'belong together' precisely because you tend to attend them together. This would fit the general story (Driver & Baylis, 1998; Neisser, 1967) that initial grouping processes constrain the perceptual units that can be attended. Thus, it may be hard to attend separate groups at the same time, and also hard to attend a single element within a group, without also selecting the other elements that are grouped with it. Much evidence from objective performance measures (see Driver & Baylis, 1998, for review) now supports this general account, in addition to it being broadly consistent with the phenomenology of grouping displays.

On the above perspective, phenomenology may reveal some useful facts about attentional issues, not merely about segmentation processes. Nevertheless, it is virtually impossible to address some of the more specific 'attentional' issues about segmentation that we raised above, using phenomenology alone. In particular, it is extremely awkward to assess whether a particular segmentation process still takes place when the observer does *not* wish it to do so, using mere phenomenology. The problem here is similar to that induced by asking someone *not* to think about spotted pink elephants! Asking people to introspect about whether a particular grouping phenomenon still arises, when they attend elsewhere, runs into the obvious problem that merely asking about the grouping phenomenon is likely to induce attention to the associated stimuli. This is a familiar methodological problem in the selective attention literature (i.e. how to measure unattended processing without turning it into attended processing) and many standard solutions have been developed (e.g. see Driver, in press; Pashler, 1998, for reviews), as described later. However, these have only recently been applied to attentional issues concerning segmentation processes.

The late Irvin Rock was one of the first researchers to note explicitly that the way a visual display gets segmented may depend on the question asked of an observer, and thus on what they 'attend' in this sense (e.g. Rock, 1975, 1983). He realized that the very act of asking observers to confirm an introspection (e.g. that certain arrays of dots appear to group into rows or columns, as in the standard Gestalt demonstrations) may well change how particular visual stimuli are processed. Together with Arian Mack and their collaborators, he developed a seemingly straightforward method of measuring whether traditional Gestalt grouping still takes place under conditions of true 'inattention'. In other words, under conditions where the observer has no specific intention with respect to the grouping display, being engaged with a different demanding visual task instead, which involves a completely separate visual stimulus at another location (e.g. Mack & Rock, 1998; Mack, Tang, Tuma, Kahn, & Rock, 1992; Rock, Linnett, Grant, & Mack, 1992). From the perspective of attention research, we think their studies posed exactly the right kind of question about segmentation processes. But as discussed below, we are less satisfied with the methods they used, and the conclusions reached. Nevertheless, some of their conclusions from their early studies were certainly provocative. Indeed, they appear to be in direct opposition to the position some of us had adopted in the past. Whereas Baylis and Driver (1992) argued that "visual attention is directed to groups derived from a preattentive segmentation of the scene according to Gestalt principles", in the same year Mack et al. (1992, p. 498) concluded that "no perception of either texture segregation of Gestalt grouping" takes place for unattended stimuli!

5. Gestalt grouping without attention: 'inattentional blindness' reconsidered

Mack et al. (1992) and Rock, Linnett et al. (1992) correctly noted that some of the paradigms traditionally thought to tap 'preattentive' processing may in fact involve diffuse attention, plus some intention by the observer to see particular visual properties (see also Joseph, Chun, & Nakayama, 1996). For instance, in visual search studies (e.g. Treisman, 1986), observers typically look for a specific target, and know that all locations on the screen may be task-relevant. Mack et al. (1992) suggested that in order to test whether segmentation processes can truly operate without attention, one needs a situation where the observer has no intention to perform the segmentation, being engaged in some other demanding visual task for another stimulus at a different location (see Joseph et al., 1996; Lavie, 1995, for arguments that the level of demand may be critical).

Mack et al. (1992) presented subjects with displays in which a central cross appeared, with a Gestalt grouping display (or texture segmentation display) as its surrounding background. The instructed task concerned the central cross (was its horizontal or vertical limb longer?), so the background display was initially irrelevant to the task. But after several trials, observers were suddenly asked surprise questions about the immediately preceding background display, concerning how it appeared to group. This actually represents one of the oldest ways to try and measure unattended processing, by asking surprise retrospective questions (e.g. Broadbent, 1958; Cherry, 1953). The basic finding, across several experiments (see Mack & Rock, 1998, for recent extensions), was that observers seemed to know surprisingly little about the segmentation of the background display, in response to the surprise question. From this basic result, plus various control observations, Mack et al. (1992) reached their radical conclusion that no Gestalt grouping takes place without attention.

The results of Mack et al. (1992) accord with many classic demonstrations that little is known about unattended stimuli on subsequent surprise questioning (e.g. Broadbent, 1958; Cherry, 1953). In the visual domain, such results are now often discussed under the general heading of 'inattentional blindness' (e.g. Mack & Rock, 1998). However, there is a standard objection to findings of little knowledge for unattended stimuli on surprise retrospective questioning, which dates back to the dawn of attention research (e.g. Cherry, 1953). The poor knowledge shown may reflect poor explicit memory, rather than the absence of on-line processing when the unattended stimulus was presented (i.e. inattentional 'amnesia' rather than inattentional 'blindness'; Holender, 1986; Wolfe, 1999). Although Mack et al. (1992) and also Mack and Rock (1998) do discuss this possibility, and attempt to reject it, the problem is intrinsic to the method of surprise retrospective questioning. But posing the direct questions in advance, or at the time of presentation, would clearly suffer from the 'spotted-pink-elephant' problem, being likely to make a supposedly unattended stimulus become task-relevant and thus attended. The traditional solution to this methodological problem, within mainstream attention research (e.g. Lewis, 1970; Stroop, 1935), has been to devise *indirect* on-line measures of unattended processing, which do not require the subject to explicitly judge or respond to the unattended information. In prototypical form, one measures instead whether unattended information can influence responses to attended information.

Moore and Egeth (1997) applied this general approach to the issue of whether Gestalt grouping can arise under 'inattention'. They took advantage of some standard geometric illusions (i.e. the Ponzo and Muller-Lyer illusions), manipulating whether background dots could be grouped (by similarity in contrast polarity) into appropriate inducers for biasing the perception of the horizontal line-length of two target lines via geometric illusions. In a task of judging the relative length of the two target lines, they found that the background organization could produce the conventional illusions for the target lines, even when subjects were unable to report this background organization retrospectively, as tested by the Mack et al. (1992) surprise retrospective questions. The implication is that some degree of background grouping by similarity in contrast polarity can still take place, even when the background is task-irrelevant.

This is an ingenious study, but the implications may be restricted in several respects. First, the effective 'grouping' of the very proximal dots by common contrast polarity may have been simply due to blurring in low spatial frequency channels, and so would represent only a very crude form of grouping at best. Indeed, it has often been suggested that the Ponzo and Muller-Lyer illusions can have a low spatial frequency basis (e.g. Rock, 1983). Second, many of the dots inducing the foreground illusion were very close to the target lines, and so a sceptic might argue that their effectiveness could have been due to their falling within an attended spatial area.

We (Driver, Russell, & Howlett, unpublished data) have recently developed a new method which can also provide an indirect on-line measure of whether grouping may still take place under 'inattention', but while avoiding these limitations. Unlike the Moore and Egeth (1997) study, the method is not tied to the requirements of a particular illusion. As in Mack et al. (1992), subjects are presented with displays that each comprise a central target (now a small square made up of random black or white pixels) plus a surrounding background Gestalt grouping display of dots (which can be arranged into regular columns or rows by common colour, or can have a random organization by the two equiluminant colours used within each display). Each trial comprises two successive displays of this kind (see Fig. 1), separated by 150 ms. The task is to judge as rapidly as possible whether the two successive central target squares are the same or different (when different, only a single pixel changes). Independently of whether these successive targets are the same or different, we also manipulate whether the background has the same organization between two successive displays (e.g. Fig. 1A) or a different organization (e.g. Fig. 1B). The two colours used for the dots in the two successive backgrounds always change (e.g. red and green dots in the first display, but yellow and blue in the second display), so that same versus different background organization can be unconfounded from same versus different colours for each dot between the two successive displays. We measure whether reaction time (RT) and errors in the same/different task for the central square are influenced by the background organization being the same or different over the pair of successive displays. Then, at the end of the experiment, we test for explicit knowledge of the immediately preceding background display, using the surprise retrospective questioning method of Mack et al. (1992).

In a series of studies of this kind, we have repeatedly found that the surprise retrospective questions at the end replicate the findings of Mack et al. (1992), from which they had concluded that no Gestalt grouping takes place under inattention. However, the RT and error data from the on-line same/different task (performed on

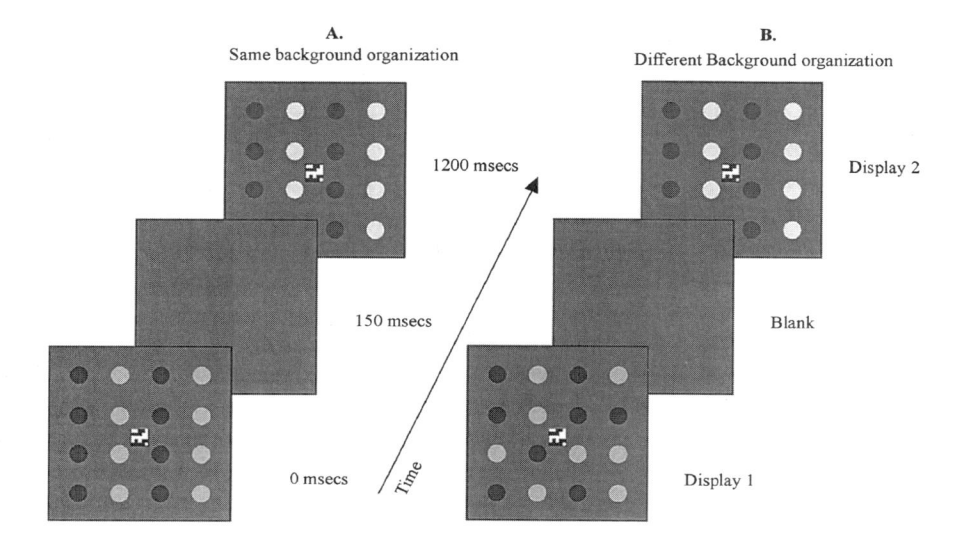

Fig. 1. Two examples of the display sequence for a single trail in the studies of Driver et al. (unpublished data). The task is to decide whether the central square matrix, comprising randomly black or white pixels, is the same or different for Display 1 and Display 2 (it is the same in both the example sequences shown). The surrounding grid of dots can be organized by common colour into columns, or into rows (not shown), or pseudo-randomly (e.g. see Display 1 at bottom right of B). This background organization can change (as in B) or be the same (as in A) across Display 1 and Display 2 within a trial, independently of whether the central target matrix changes or not. The two colours used for the background dots always changed between Display 1 and Display 2, so that colour change per se could be disentangled from changes in grouping by colour.

the central square matrix) suggest that some grouping of the background dots had in fact taken place. Subjects are faster and/or more accurate with their target-different judgements if the background organization also changes (e.g. from random into columnar; see Fig. 1B), and target-same judgements can also be faster and/or more accurate if the background organization stays the same. We find such results even if the critical change in background organization depends only on dots which are relatively far away from the central square target (e.g. those in the outer locations).

These data suggest that some degree of grouping by common colour can arise under conditions of 'inattention', as Mack et al. (1992) define this, contrary to the strong conclusion drawn in their original paper. In our experimental situation, the effective background grouping is irrelevant to the demanding central target task. It arises in a dimension (i.e. equiluminant colour) which is different from the relevant properties for the central task (which concerns luminance, and possibly shape). The effective background grouping can involve only elements which are some distance away from the central target. Finally, subjects cannot explicitly report the background organization, using Mack et al.'s (1992) surprise question method. This situation would therefore seem to fit Mack et al.'s definition of true 'inattention', and yet some evidence for Gestalt grouping is still found.

On the other hand, the nature of this evidence tells us little about phenomenology, which has traditionally been of considerable (often primary) interest in Gestalt demonstrations, as discussed above. The RT and error pattern we find in the same/different task implies that the background displays were grouped by common colour to some extent, despite the conditions being set up to induce 'inattention' for them. However, these data certainly do not imply that the subjects necessarily perceived the background grouping consciously, in the manner of a standard Gestalt demonstration. Indeed, on a Mack et al. (1992) interpretation of the results for the surprise direct questioning, one would conclude that subjects were not aware of the background grouping, even though it could evidently still influence their target judgements. Our results might therefore be reconciled with the idea of 'inattentional blindness' for Gestalt grouping, but only as regards conscious vision (see Mack & Rock, 1998), not in the sense of no Gestalt grouping taking place whatsoever, as Mack et al. (1992) had originally claimed. However, the retrospective nature of Mack et al.'s surprise questioning method can again be criticized, this time as an index of visual awareness, rather than of visual processing in general (i.e. responses to a surprise question after a display may underestimate what is consciously seen during a display).

6. 'Change blindness' reconsidered

The method depicted in Fig. 1 may relate to another paradigm which, like 'inattentional blindness', has recently been taken as evidence that our representation of the visual world can be surprisingly sparse. We refer here to the recent demonstrations of 'change blindness' in the flicker paradigm introduced by Rensink, O'Regan, and Clark (1997) (see Simons, 2000; Simons & Levin, 1997, for reviews). In the original version of this, subjects are presented with complex images of natural scenes. Successive displays show the same scene, separated by a substantial transient (a brief 'flicker') in which the whole screen goes blank, thus changing luminance and other properties everywhere. The subjects' task is typically to report whether anything has changed in the scene when it returns after the flicker, or to press a button when they detect this change. Often, two versions of the same scene, differing in one aspect (e.g. deletion of an object), may be cycled repeatedly with a flicker separating them, until the change to the scene is reported.

The basic finding (Rensink et al., 1997) is that it can take a remarkably long time (i.e. many cycles) before the change to the scene is noticed, even for quite substantial changes (e.g. a large object disappearing and reappearing). Of course this depends on the flicker which separates the successive versions of the scene, as this provides a large global transient to obscure the local transient that the change to the scene would otherwise produce. Nevertheless, when the change is detected, subjects can hardly believe it went undetected for so long; once detected, the change seems absurdly salient across subsequent repeated cycles. We (Russell & Driver, unpublished data) have confirmed that similar phenomena remain when eye-position is held fixed, and that an otherwise undetectable change becomes noticeable as soon as its location is cued, even without saccades.

Such 'change blindness' has been interpreted as strong evidence for surprisingly sparse internal representations of visual scenes, similarly to 'inattentional blindness' claims, but now primarily concerning the issue of what is brought forward across successive displays, rather than what is extracted from a single display. It has been interpreted (see O'Regan, Rensink, & Clark, 1999; Simons & Levin, 1997) as suggesting that standard introspections of perceiving a rich visual world are an 'illusion'. We agree that change blindness provides a particularly compelling example of the influence that attentional factors can have on phenomenal visual experience, as when a previously undetectable change becomes overwhelmingly salient once its location is cued. However, we are more sceptical about some of the radical conclusions that have been drawn from change blindness. In particular, one may question whether it really implies exceptionally sparse representation, or a total failure to bring visual information forward across successive samples. The method depicted in Fig. 1 could be usefully adapted to test whether various undetected changes in the flicker paradigm might still be extracted unconsciously by the visual system (see Fernandez-Duque & Thornton, 2000; Rensink, 2000; Smilek, Eastwood, & Merikle, 2000). This could be revealed by any effects of background changes on RT or accuracy for same/different judgements to central targets, similar to those we have already observed for changes in background grouping.

We have already found some initial evidence (Turatto, Russell, & Driver, unpublished data) that unseen changes may nevertheless be extracted in the flicker paradigm. We used displays (see examples in Fig. 2) comprising dots on a background of vertical stripes. As in the standard flicker paradigm (e.g. Rensink et al., 1997), successive displays were separated by an intervening blank (of intermediate grey), and subjects had to report simply whether anything changed (and if so what) between successive displays. In fact, only two types of change were possible. Either one or more of the grey dots could change luminance (from dark grey to light grey, or vice-versa; e.g. Fig. 2A), or all the background stripes could change their luminance (from dark to light, or vice-versa; e.g. Fig. 2B). Even though the latter change was physically much more substantial (in terms of actual luminance change and spatial area affected) than any change to the dots within the same luminance domain, we found that subjects typically reported virtually all the dot changes, yet none of the background changes.

This appears to confirm that change blindness in the flicker paradigm is indeed more pronounced for background than foreground changes (see Rensink et al., 1997), even when the background change is physically stronger. As soon as the possibility of background changes was pointed out to subjects, they actually became faster at detecting those than for changes to the foreground dots, consistent with the larger physical signal for the background stripes. The initial failure to detect any background changes may relate both to a default tendency to attend foreground items, and also to the Gestalt psychologists' proposals that foregrounds are more phenomenally compelling than backgrounds (e.g. Rubin, 1921). Indeed, attentional factors may conceivably provide part of the explanation for the latter phenomenology.

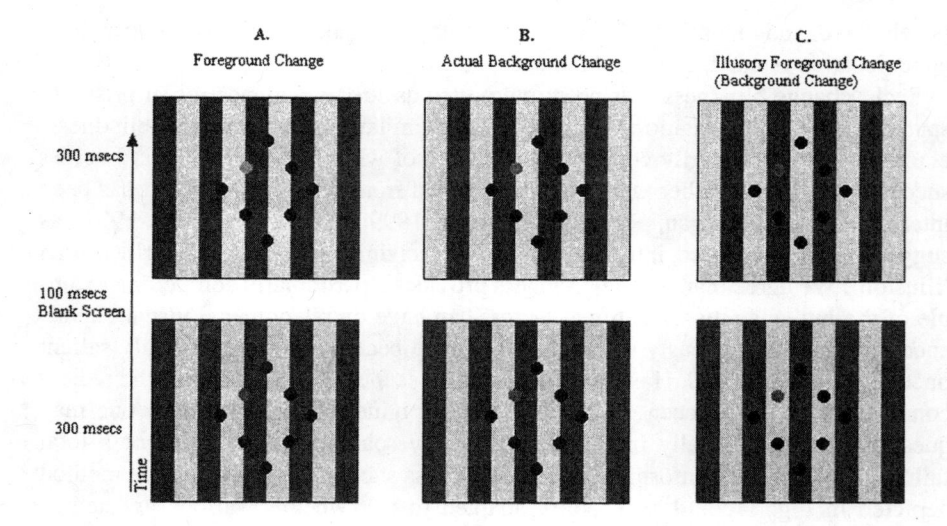

Fig. 2. Three examples of two successive displays, which were separated by a brief blank screen, in the change blindness study of Turatto et al. (unpublished data). Time runs from bottom to top. (A) The grey circle in the second display brightened; such changes were reported by naive observers. (B) The background stripes reversed contrast; such changes were not noticed until pointed out to naive observers, even though the luminance change was larger than for the circle in (A). Note that in (A) and (B), each circle falls half on a light stripe and half on a dark stripe. (C) Each circle now falls on a single stripe. When the background stripes reversed contrast, illusory changes in the brightness of the grey circle (due to simultaneous contrast with the surrounding stripe) were reported, though the background change itself went unseen again.

The second question we addressed in our study was whether unseen background changes might nevertheless still be coded by the visual system. We addressed this by exploiting a well known simultaneous contrast illusion (see Rock, 1975). When a grey dot appears with a darker stripe as its surrounding background, it appears lighter than when appearing against a light background. Some of our displays were arranged such that the background change altered whether a given grey dot appeared on a dark stripe or on a light stripe between the two successive displays (see Fig. 2C). In such cases, naive observers always reported any change as concerning the brightness of the foreground grey dot, not as the alteration of the background stripes which took place physically. They did so even though the stripes went from dark to light (or vice-versa) physically, while the dot only underwent an illusory change in lightness that was entirely due to the change in the background stripes. This shows that unseen background changes can produce illusory phenomenal foreground changes in the flicker paradigm, which would seem to indicate that some of the unseen background changes must still be extracted (and the changed properties 'brought forward') by the visual system. We are currently adapting this paradigm to test whether several particular Gestalt grouping processes can operate in the guise of unseen background changes that produce foreground illusions.

7. Studying specific forms of segmentation in relation to attention: modal and amodal completion

The extensive literature on 'object-based' attention (see Driver & Baylis, 1998; Kanwisher & Driver, 1992; Scholl, 2001, for reviews) has tended to lump all image segmentation processes together. However, there is no guarantee that all forms of image segmentation (e.g. by different static Gestalt factors, by stereo cues, by dynamic motion cues, etc.) will have exactly the same relation to attentional processes. A more productive strategy may be to examine individual segmentation processes in particular, in relation to specific attentional issues. In this way, attention researchers might exploit many of the advances which have been made by the vision research literature in understanding specific forms of image segmentation (e.g. Nakayama et al., 1989, 1995; Palmer & Rock, 1994; Pomerantz & Kubovy, 1986).

Kanizsa subjective figures (e.g. Fig. 3A) provide one of the most intensively investigated examples of human image segmentation. Not only are they phenomenally intriguing (Kanizsa, 1979), but they are by now relatively well understood (see Lesher, 1995; Petry & Meyer, 1987). Moreover, they are often considered (e.g. Fahle & Koch, 1995) to represent a prototypical case of the visual system binding together separate elements in the image (such as the 'pacmen' inducers in Fig. 3A) to produce a single subjective object. They certainly illustrate several principles of image segmentation. These include edge assignment (e.g. the straight edges on the pacmen inducers in Fig. 3A,B typically get assigned to the subjective square, not to the pacmen) plus several completion processes, as follows. When a subjective figure is seen, the inducing pacmen are typically seen as 'amodally' complete circles (i.e. complete circles that are partially occluded; see Fig. 3C), while the subjective square is 'modally' completed (i.e. with accompanying illusory colour and/or brightness in the completed region). Such figures thus also provide compelling examples of subjective 'filling-in' of illusory colour and brightness (as for the seemingly grey and transparent regions near the central cross in Fig. 3B, which are actually white).

There have been many experimental studies of such subjective figures. One enduring issue has been whether they are best thought of as reflecting the operation of relatively 'low-level' processes (e.g. blurring at low-spatial frequencies), or of much 'higher-level' processes (e.g. the inference of a superimposed figure). Space constraints preclude a full review of this debate. Suffice to say that there is now substantial evidence that low-level properties of the stimulus can strongly affect the subjective strength of the subjective figure, but also that seemingly higher-level factors, such as set or knowledge, can affect the percept to some extent (see Lesher, 1995; Petry & Meyer, 1987, for reviews). In other words, several different levels of processing may contribute to the final subjective percept. Below, we consider the possible influence of attentional factors on subjective figures, and vice-versa.

8. Phenomenology and its limits once again

The overwhelming majority of previous studies on subjective figures have relied

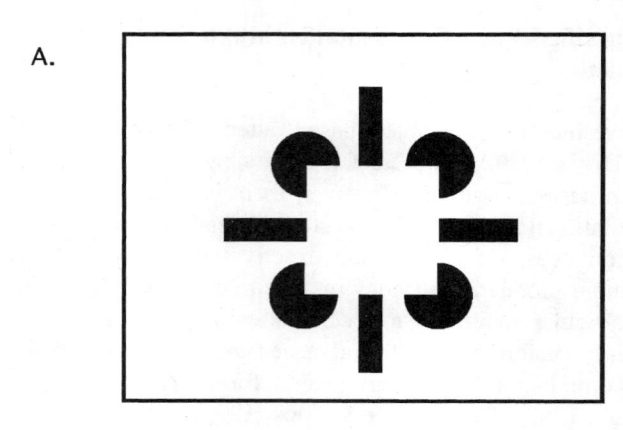

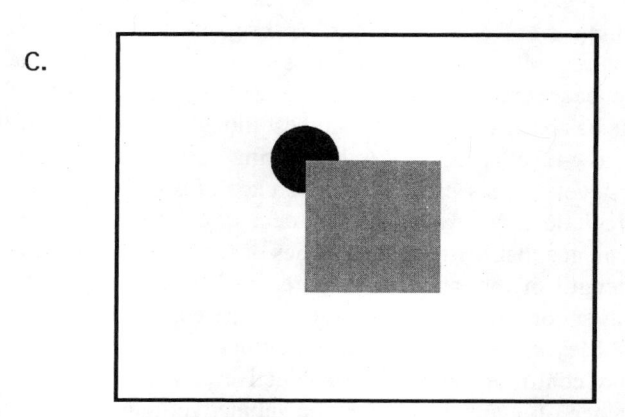

Fig. 3. (A) Example of a Kanizsa subjective square. (B) Example of an apparently transparent Kanizsa subjective square. The central region between inducing circles and the cross appears infused with transparent grey, although it is actually white. This is one example of 'modal' completion. (C) Illustration of 'amodal' completion of a shape which appears to be partly occluded, in this case the circle with the quadrant that appears occluded by the square. Note that no illusory properties are seen in the completed region of the circle.

on phenomenal measures (e.g. rating the strength of the subjective figure, as in Warm, Dember, Padich, Beckner, & Jones, 1987; though see Dresp & Bonnet, 1995; Rubin, Nakayama, & Shapley, 1996, for more objective measures). Moreover, most studies have taken such phenomenal measures while presenting just a single subjective figure display to the observer, often for unspeeded visual inspection and self-rating. Such methods are clearly unsuitable for addressing the many attentional questions one can ask about image segmentation in general, and about subjective figures in particular. For instance, how could an observer possibly ignore a subjective figure while rating its supposedly 'unattended' phenomenal strength? This seems a clear case of the spotted-pink-elephant problem. Such unspeeded phenomenal methods will presumably also increase the likelihood of many different levels of processing contributing to the final report.

The restrictions that arise when relying too much upon phenomenology may apply to other recent work on grouping processes also. Just as it is tempting to ask whether subjective figures reflect relatively 'early' or 'late' processes in vision, one may ask whether segmentation processes in general arise early (as traditionally thought), or might also involve higher-level processes. Rock and Palmer have raised this general question for Gestalt grouping displays in a series of studies with their collaborators (e.g. Palmer, Neff, & Beck, 1997; Palmer & Nelson, in press; Palmer & Rock, 1994; Rock, Nijhawan et al., 1992). More specifically, they asked whether grouping might operate before or after various perceptual constancy mechanisms and various completion mechanisms. A typical experiment used grids of elements, rather like the Wertheimer (1923) grouping demonstrations. The elements on one side of the grid would be of a uniform type, and the elements on the other side would be of a different uniform type. The central column comprised elements of the critical experimental type; the question was whether these would group phenomenally with the type of elements on the left or on the right. Observers judged this explicitly (i.e. making leftwards versus rightwards grouping judgements) in an unspeeded manner with free vision.

Using such a method, Rock, Nijhawan et al. (1992) found that grouping by similarity in achromatic colour apparently takes place only *after* the operation of lightness constancy (they exploited cast shadows or translucent overlays on the central column to decouple retinal luminance and perceived lightness). In forced-choice decisions, observers reported that the central column appeared to belong with other elements that matched in phenomenal lightness, rather than in retinal luminance. Palmer et al. (1997) used a similar method to argue that grouping by similarity in shape may take place after amodal completion of apparently occluded shapes has taken place. More recent studies by Palmer and Nelson (in press) have extended this to the case of modal completion for subjective figures.

Palmer and Rock have taken such results to indicate that 'grouping is later than you think', being based on quite sophisticated visual properties, which are closer to the phenomenal percept than to the retinal image. However, one can query the method used, and wonder whether instead grouping might be 'later only *when you think*'! Given the unspeeded viewing conditions, subjects had ample time to inspect (and even think about) each element of the stimulus in turn. Moreover, given the forced-choice task (i.e. does the central column group with the left or right?) there may even have been no true grouping at all, with observers simply using their response to indicate which stimuli looked most similar phenomenally. We already know which stimulus pairs these would be: perceived brightness for individually inspected stimuli depends on lightness constancy, partly-occluded shapes usually get amodally completed, and the appropriate inducing stimuli will form subjective figures.

In other words, while Palmer, Rock and their colleagues have asked an extremely pertinent question about the level(s) at which grouping processes can arise, their actual method may only tell us what we already know from introspection (i.e. what the particular stimuli look like, phenomenally, with unspeeded viewing). Methods from the attention literature such as those reviewed here may provide better handles on the level(s) at which particular segmentation processes arise, and on whether the observer can modulate these at will. Below, we address modal and amodal completion from this perspective.

9. Visual search studies of modal and amodal completion

Several recent studies have examined the roles of amodal completion for partly-occluded objects (e.g. Davis & Driver, 1998; He & Nakayama, 1992; Rensink & Enns, 1998) and of modal completion for subjective figures (e.g. Davis & Driver, 1998) in visual search tasks. In such tasks, the observer must typically determine the presence or absence of a prespecified target among a varied number of non-targets as fast as possible. This task has traditionally been used with the aim of distinguishing those visual properties extracted 'preattentively' (i.e. efficiently in parallel, regardless of the number of items in the display) from those extracted only 'attentively' (classically, these were thought to require strictly serial processing, leading to linear increases of search time with the number of items to be searched; e.g. Treisman, 1986; Treisman & Gelade, 1980). It is now well known that many caveats must be placed on such interpretations of search data (e.g. see Wolfe, 1998, for review), just as many caveats must be placed on any simplistic preattentive/attentive dichotomy. Nevertheless, the visual search task still remains very useful as one way of addressing attentional issues for specific processes. Moreover, with appropriate tweaking, it can get around the spotted-pink-elephant methodological problem that was described earlier.

As one example of this, Rensink and Enns (1998) examined the search for notched target shapes among complete (i.e. un-notched) non-targets in 2D displays (see Fig. 4 for schematic examples that have been adapted for our present purposes). In control conditions this was an easy task, yielding a 'parallel' search outcome (i.e. little or no increase in search time with set-size). In the critical experimental conditions, the same notched target (a notched circle in our example; see Fig. 4A) was placed so that pictorially it appeared to be occluded by an abutting shape in the region corresponding to the notch. Hence, with unrestricted viewing, it would tend to be amodally completed as a partly-occluded version of the same complete shape

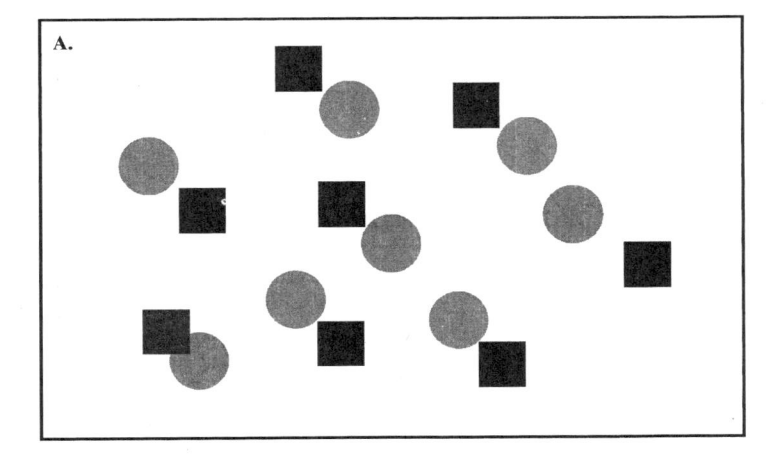

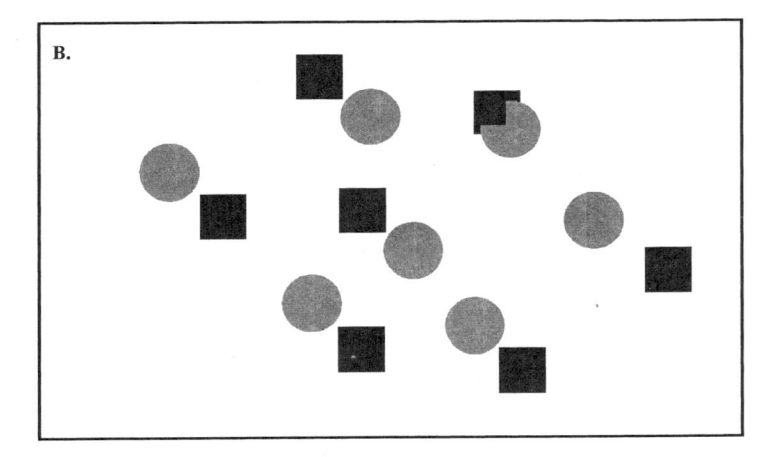

Fig. 4. Search displays analogous to some of those used by Rensink and Enns (1998). The task for these examples would be to determine the presence or absence of a notched circle. Note that this seems much harder in (A) (where the notched circle appears to be partly occluded in the notched region by the abutting square) than in (B).

as the (circular) non-targets. The critical question was how such an apparently occluded target would behave in the search task. Would it act like the notched target (whose shape it still had in the retinal 'mosaic') that was previously so easy to find, or like a completed shape, in which case it should presumably now be hard to find (given the presence of many physically complete versions of this shape among the non-targets)? The results clearly showed that the search became very hard, now showing a classic 'serial' pattern, with a steep increase in search time against the number of items in the display. He and Nakayama (1992) had previously found a very similar result in a study which used stereoscopic depth to determine whether amodal completion should take place.

These results have several implications. They imply that amodal completion may arise in so-called 'parallel' vision (i.e. efficiently for all items at once, without serial inspection of each item in turn). They also imply that amodal completion may still arise even when counter to the observer's current intentions. Although amodal completion of partly-occluded objects may be very useful for many real-world visual tasks (see Nakayama et al., 1989), it could only be detrimental to performance in the visual search task, as shown by the impaired search performance when such completion arose. This implies that amodal completion (or at least, assignment of the notched edges to the apparent occluder, rather than to the target shape) may arise even against the observer's will, despite many hundreds of trials attempting to see the notched target in terms of just its retinal shape. Note that in reaching this conclusion, the spotted-pink-elephant problem was neatly side-stepped. The observers never had to be asked directly about whether they saw the target as amodally completed or not; its coding by their visual system was simply inferred from their objective search performance. The only downside of this is that the results tell us little, directly, about phenomenological visual appearance. On the other hand, they do tell us something quite specific about the nature of amodal completion processes, which are presumed to have some ultimate influence on phenomenal vision.

We (Davis & Driver, 1998) recently adapted the basic methods of He and Nakayama (1992) and Rensink and Enns (1998) to examine whether *modal* completion (i.e. as in Kanizsa subjective figures) might similarly arise within 'parallel' vision in search tasks, even when this could only be detrimental to objective performance. Essentially, we asked whether a subjective figure might act as an occluder to induce unwanted amodal completion of an abutting notched target, just as the real squares do in Fig. 4. Similarly to the search displays in Fig. 4, observers again searched for a notched circle among complete circles. Smaller 'pacmen' stimuli were now arranged so as to produce possible subjective squares, which might serve as occluders in the critical conditions (see Fig. 5). The search for the notched circle among full circles was very slow and inefficient when these appeared (see Fig. 5A) stereoscopically *behind* the potential subjective surfaces (yielding a classic 'serial' search outcome), but was fast and efficiently parallel when they appeared in front (Fig. 5B). Various control conditions confirmed that the search difficulty was specific to apparent occlusion of the notched target by a subjective surface, rather than simply to searching in the back plane. Moreover, these control conditions also ruled out trivial accounts of the effect from the subjective surface in terms of low spatial frequency blurring, or the mere alignment of inducing edges with the notched circle target.

As with the results of He and Nakayama (1992) and Rensink and Enns (1998), these results imply that amodal completion (of the notched target) may arise in 'parallel' vision, and may do so even when counter to the observer's intentions. The data of Davis and Driver (1998) further indicate that both these assertions also apply to the formation of subjective surfaces via modal completion. Such surfaces are evidently treated in parallel vision as occluding regions which cannot be seen through, even though they are entirely 'subjective' creations of the visual system, as no physical occluder is actually present.

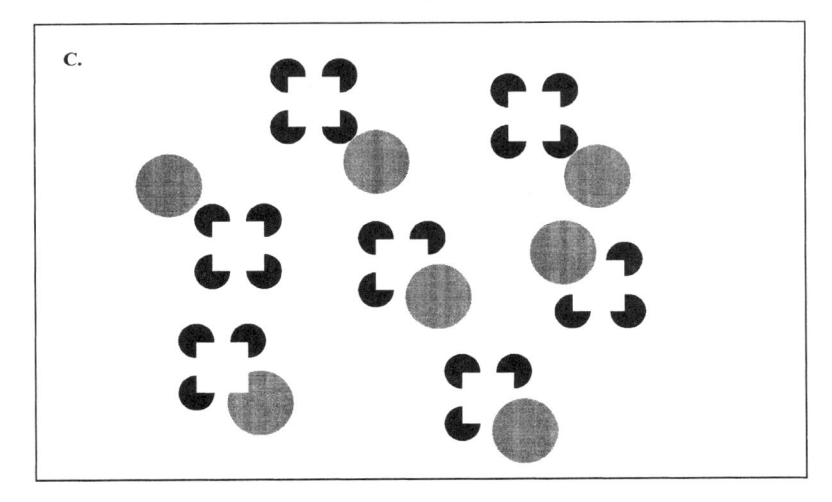

Segmentation, attention and phenomenal visual objects 79

Fig. 5. Schematic depiction of target stimuli (A,B) or a typical search display (C) from Davis and Driver (1998). For a search display like (C), the task would be to determine the presence or absence of a large notched grey circle. Note that this appears difficult, due to apparent occlusion (and associated amodal completion) by the Kanizsa subjective square. In the actual experiment, the large pacmen and small pacmen were in different stereoscopic depth planes (see cartoons of this for one cluster of stimuli in A and B). When the small inducers of the subjective square lay in the front plane (as in A), the search for the large notched circle was very difficult. But when the latter target lay in front instead (see B), so that the subjective square could no longer appear to occlude it, the search became efficient.

10. Distinguishing modal versus amodal completion in visual search: the Metelli rule

The recent evidence from visual search reviewed above suggests that modal and amodal completion may operate similarly in visual search tasks, both arising in parallel, and in an apparently obligatory manner. This can be added to a long list of similarities between the two forms of completion, as previously articulated by Kellman and Shipley (1991). Indeed, Ramachandran (1995) has gone so far as to suggest that modal and amodal completion may not be differentiated until very late in the visual system. However, despite their commonalities, modal and amodal completion do differ in a crucial phenomenological respect. As noted earlier, in the case of subjective figures, completion is 'modal' in the sense that illusions specific to the visual modality (i.e. filling-in of illusory colour and/or brightness) take place within the completed region (e.g. see Fig. 3B). No such illusions of colour and brightness arise for amodally-completed regions, which are seen as lying behind apparently occluding surfaces (e.g. Fig. 3C). We (e.g. Davis & Driver, 1997, 1998) have examined whether this filling-in of illusory colour and/or brightness, for the case of modal completion only, might be of functional as well as phenomenal significance, as described below. In more recent studies, we have also begun to address whether modal and amodal completion may behave differently within visual search tasks. Our search experiments took advantage of one well established subjective difference between modal and amodal completion, which relates to the perception of transparency.

Kanizsa (1979) and Van Tuijl and de Weert (1979) demonstrated that for simple patterns comprising three luminance levels, modal completion of transparent subjective figures is constrained by the luminance profile of the inducing stimuli in a way that amodal completion is not (see also Nakayama & Shimojo, 1992). We will refer to this constraint as the 'Metelli rule', since it stems from the description by Metelli (1974) of the luminance conditions constraining transparency perception. In order for the elements of an inducing stimulus to form part of a transparent, modally-completed surface, the luminance of these inducing elements must fall between the luminance of the surround and the luminance of the inner region over which the subjective figure is formed. For example, the stimulus in Fig. 6A satisfies these constraints. The luminance of the four small grey sectors on the otherwise black circles falls between that of the white inner region and the black surround of the circles. These grey sectors can therefore be seen to form part of a transparent, modally-completed surface. However, the stimulus in Fig. 6B fails to satisfy the Metelli rule prescription for the luminance relations. The luminance of the small dark sectors on the otherwise grey circles does *not* fall between the luminance level of the grey surrounding regions and the white inner region, being less than both. Thus, the dark sectors cannot form parts of a modally-completed surface.

This dependence of modal completion upon the luminance profile of the stimulus makes functional sense when one considers the optics of transparent surfaces (see Metelli, 1974), and also that modal completion processes may serve to encode partly-camouflaged surfaces (e.g. Davis & Driver, 1994; Ramachandran, 1987). If the grey regions of Fig. 6A did indeed belong to a uniform transparent surface, that surface must be rather light, since it apparently causes the black circles to appear lighter where it overlaps with them. Such a light surface could conceivably become invisible in the current retinal image at regions where it overlapped with a lighter background. This luminance configuration is therefore at least consistent with the presence of a partly-camouflaged transparent surface. It might therefore be adaptive for modal completion mechanisms to code a partly-camouflaged but complete transparent surface under these circumstances.

By contrast, if the small dark sectors in Fig. 6B actually formed part of a larger

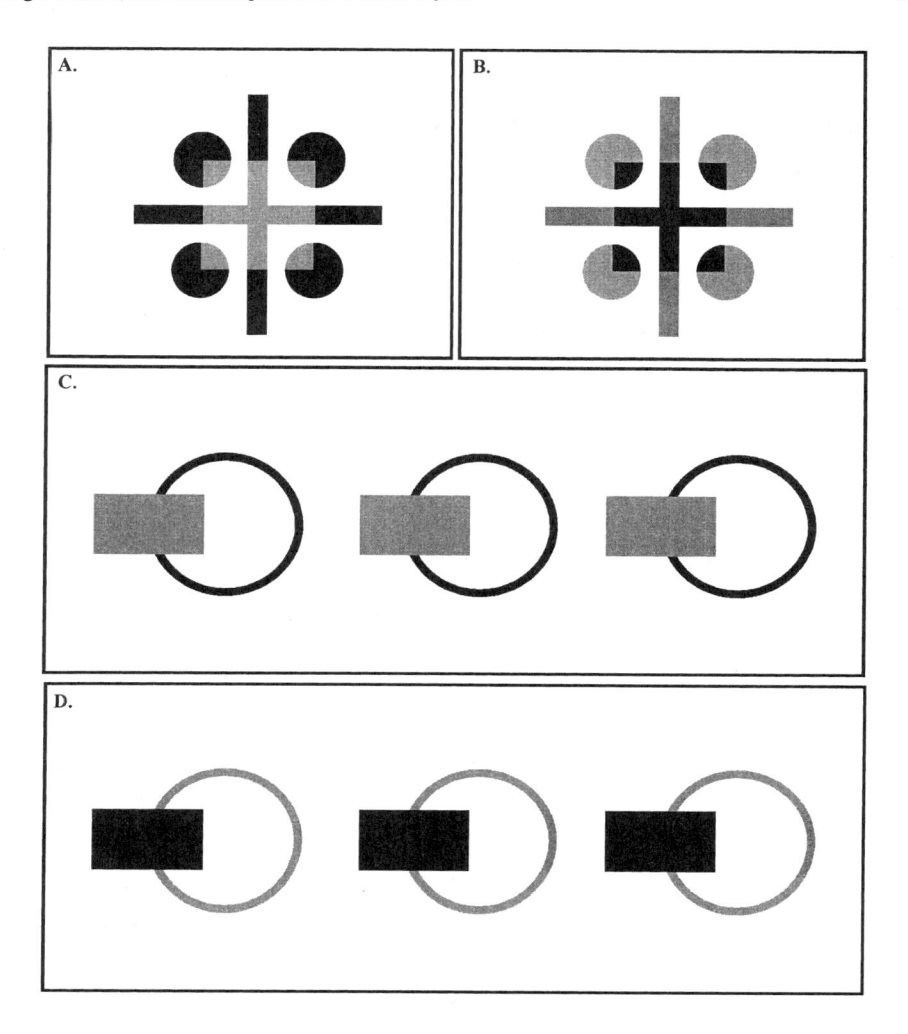

Fig. 6. (A) Transparent Kanizsa square. Note that the grey of the inducing quarter-segments on the four circles and of the central region on the cross has a luminance which is intermediate between the surrounding black and the white over which modal completion takes place. This luminance profile is consistent with the Metelli rule. (B) The same display layout, but now with luminance levels that do *not* fit the Metelli rule. Note that now no subjective figure is formed. (C,D) Example displays that with free fusion illustrate the change from modal to amodal completion with a reversal in depth, and the dependence of completion on the Metelli rule only for the case of modal completion (i.e. only when the circular element appears in front of the abutting rectangle, as with uncrossed free fusion of left and centre columns; uncrossed fusion of right and centre columns should place the circle at the back plane). (C) is inconsistent with the Metelli rule and (D) is consistent.

uniform transparent surface, this would have to be a dark surface, since it causes the otherwise grey circles to appear darker where it overlaps in front of them. It is unlikely that such a dark surface could be invisible where it passes in front of a white background. Such a luminance configuration is therefore inconsistent with the presence of a partly-camouflaged, transparent surface, and hence modal completion mechanisms should not operate. Of course, we would not suggest that the visual system literally undertakes the kind of inferential procedure we have outlined here, in explaining why the Metelli rule makes reasonable sense. Nakayama and Shimojo (1992) provide one biologically plausible account of how the visual system could come to obey such constraints.

The dependence of modal completion upon the luminance configuration of the inducing stimuli can be experienced by free-fusing the *left* and centre patterns in Fig. 6C with uncrossed fusion. This procedure should yield the impression of a notched ring element at a nearer plane than the rectangle it abuts. Note that the notched ring is *not* modally completed to form a complete, transparent ring, because its luminance does not fall between that of the rectangle and the background (i.e. the luminance profile is inconsistent with modal completion in terms of the Metelli rule). However, when the luminance profile of the elements is reversed, as in Fig. 6D, it now becomes consistent with modal completion of a transparent surface in terms of the Metelli rule. When the *left* and centre patterns in this figure are free-fused (uncrossed), the grey notched ring element should now appear modally complete, as a transparent subjective surface (a complete ring) lying in front of the abutting black rectangle.

The Metelli transparency constraints apply to modal completion, because modally-completed surfaces appear to pass *in front of* the surfaces they overlap with (and transparent surfaces lying in front of other surfaces can alter the amount of light reaching the retina from the latter surfaces). However, this does not apply to *occluded* regions of surfaces, such as those generated by amodal completion. Occluded regions generally cannot prevent light from other objects reaching the observer. Hence, the luminance constraints that apply to modal completion do not apply to amodal completion. Indeed, several studies have found no modulation of amodal completion by the luminance profile of the inducing stimuli (e.g. Kanizsa, 1979; Nakayama & Shimojo, 1992). This can be experienced by free-fusing the centre and *right* patterns of Fig. 6C,D. The stimulus should now appear as a ring that is further away than the abutting rectangle. Note that the notched ring becomes amodally completed to form an apparently complete but partly-occluded ring in both cases (i.e. even when its luminance does not fall between that of the rectangle and the background (Fig. 6C), because the Metelli constraint does not apply to cases of partial occlusion).

We (Davis, Russell, & Driver, unpublished data) recently tested whether these constraints apply within the 'parallel vision' tapped by appropriate search tasks, and whether they do so even when any completion can only be detrimental to performance. Subjects searched for notched rings (i.e. like those in Fig. 6C,D) among physically complete rings in four different search conditions. The luminance profile of the displays was either consistent or inconsistent with the Metelli rule; orthogonally to this, stereo disparity was arranged so that all the rings either lay in the back plane (behind the rectangles) or in the front plane (as when viewing Fig. 6C,D with the appropriate free fusion). The results showed efficient parallel search only when the rings lay in the front plane, with a luminance profile that was *inconsistent* with the Metelli rule. In all the other three conditions, a classic 'serial' search pattern was found. The implication is once again that in these three conditions, completion of the notched target arose in parallel vision (thus making it hard to distinguish from the physically complete non-targets) even though this was highly detrimental to performance, and thus counter to the observer's intentions. Amodal completion (of notched circles apparently lying behind the abutting rectangles) was unaffected by the Metelli constraints. By contrast, modal completion (i.e. of notched circles lying in front of the abutting rectangles) was highly dependent on the Metelli rule, taking place only when the luminance profile was consistent with the constraints on perception of a subjective transparent surface. When the Metelli rule was broken, no modal completion took place, and so the target 'popped out' as the only incomplete circle in the display. Note that these results cannot be explained by the luminance relations alone, because the effect of these depended on depth relations, in a manner consistent with the Metelli rule applying to modal but not amodal completion.

This shows that the Metelli rule for the perception of transparency, which relates to the real-world optics of transparent surfaces, can operate within parallel vision as tapped by appropriate visual search tasks. Moreover, it also suggests that cases of modal and amodal completion are treated differentially within such parallel vision, in a manner consistent with their very different phenomenology, and with the differential impact of the Metelli rule that is apparent when each item is inspected with free vision (see Fig. 6).

11. Differential effects of modal versus amodal completion upon attentional processes

The conventional interpretation of the above search results would be that both modal and amodal completion can arise, and be distinguished, within 'preattentive' vision. In further research, we have gone on to examine whether modal and amodal completion may have different effects upon attentional processes (Davis & Driver, 1997, 1998). These studies used displays like Fig. 7A, comprising two segments of a grey ellipse separated by a vertical white bar. When stereo disparity placed the bar in front of the ellipse segments, the latter were amodally completed, to give the appearance of a continuous ellipse occluded centrally by the white bar (much as it appears in Fig. 7A). But when stereo disparity placed the bar behind the grey segments, these were now modally completed as a continuous transparent grey surface in front of the bar, with illusory grey 'filling-in' of the central region (much like the cartoon in Fig. 7B; note that the luminance profile of the inducing stimulus was consistent with the Metelli rule, as in Fig. 7A).

In two series of studies, we examined whether modal versus amodal completion might have differential effects on the 'spreading of attention' (as shown by distractor or cueing effects), consistent with the differential phenomenology for the central region (which is filled-in with illusory colour for the modal case only). In one series (Davis & Driver, 1997), we placed a target character on the central bar, and distrac-

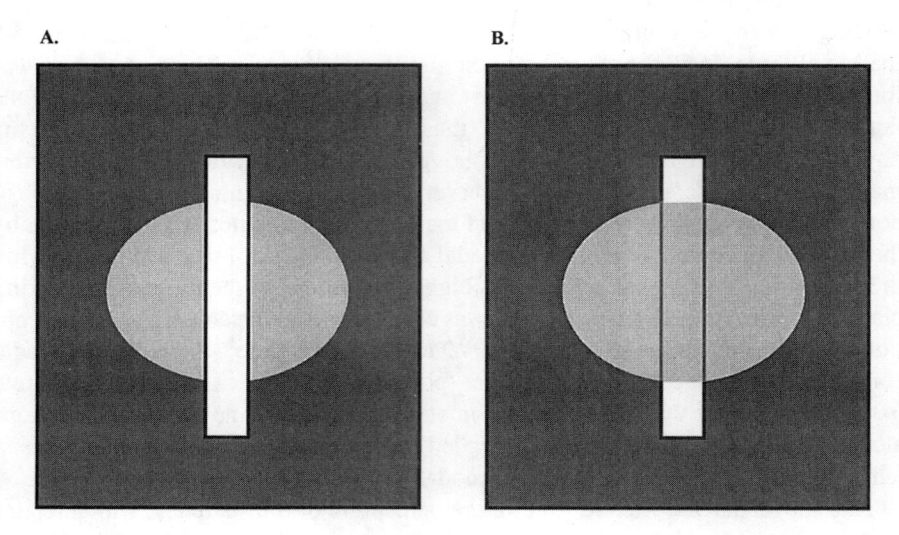

Fig. 7. (A) Example of the displays used by Davis and Driver (1997, 1998). In some conditions the central white bar was placed stereoscopically in front of the flanking grey regions; this led to the percept of an amodally-complete grey ellipse passing behind the white bar. In other conditions, the white bar was placed stereoscopically behind instead. This led to the percept of a modally-complete, transparent grey ellipse passing in front of the central bar, with illusory grey being 'filled-in' where it appeared to overlap the white bar, as cartooned in (B).

tor characters on the outer segments of the ellipse (or vice-versa). The efficiency of distractor rejection was measured (via compatibility effects on RT to the target). We found that distractors produced more interference in the modal completion condition than in the amodal completion condition. We took this to show that when observers attempted to select just one region of the display (e.g. just a central region, or just one outer region of the ellipse), they tended instead to select the entire modally-completed object in the modal completion situation. Thus, their 'attention' (i.e. their selective intake of information) tended to spread from modally-completed regions to include their inducers, and vice-versa, in a manner that did not apply for amodally-completed regions and their inducers. This objective performance result is, of course, consistent with the phenomenology here. The central region of the display (see Fig. 7) appears to include a visible surface that 'belongs' to the outer inducers of the ellipse only in the modal completion condition (i.e. where a subjectively complete ellipse becomes filled-in with illusory grey at the centre). This does not apply to the amodal completion condition (where although a complete ellipse is perceived, it appears to be occluded by the bar in the central region).

In another set of studies (Davis & Driver, 1998), we made a similar point but with a different attentional measure. We 'cued' the bar, or the outer segments of the ellipse, by transiently altering their vertical extent. We then measured the effect of this cueing on RT to subsequent target characters, which could be presented either on the bar or on the outer (physically present) segments of the ellipse. In the modal completion condition, cueing the outer segments of the ellipse appeared to attract attention to the central region as well as to the outer regions, whereas in the amodal completion this did not arise.

Again, this objective performance result seems consistent with the phenomenology of the displays, as the central region of the displays appears to include a visible surface that 'belongs' to the ellipse only in the modal completion condition, where it becomes 'filled-in' with illusory transparent grey. Indeed, we went so far as to suggest that such filling-in may take place precisely in order to indicate a potentially visible surface, which may then lead to appropriate attraction of attention (or spreading of attention across the entire surface), just as for physically present surfaces. In other words, 'filling-in' may serve functional as well as phenomenal purposes, and indeed these may be closely related. These studies appear to provide examples of 'object-based' visual attention, in which the critical object depends on a subjective illusion. Of course, in all the cases we have discussed (i.e. even for the experiments which did not directly concern subjective figures), the effective groups or objects are similarly the products of segmentation processes in the visual system, given the stimulus input.

The studies described so far seem broadly consistent with traditional views (e.g. Neisser, 1967; Duncan, 1984; Driver & Baylis, 1989, 1998), within the simplifying preattentive/attentive dichotomy, that much image segmentation can precede and constrain attentional selectivity. We have suggested here that Gestalt grouping can still arise under conditions of 'inattention', that undetected background changes in the flicker paradigm may still be extracted by the visual system, and can even influence the phenomenology of foreground elements, and that modal and amodal completion may arise and be differentiated by parallel vision within visual search, incorporating relatively sophisticated constraints such as the Metelli rule. Finally, we have suggested that modal and amodal completion may impose differential constraints on attentional processes, in accord with their very different phenomenology.

All this seems consistent with the traditional view of segmentation processes largely preceding attentional processes. However, we think that under appropriate conditions, the influence can also work in the other direction (see Farah, Wallace, & Vercera, 1993; Humphreys, Olson, Romani, & Riddoch, 1996), with attentional processes modulating segmentation processes to some extent. In our final experimental section, we give a recent example of this possibility from our own work.

12. Possible attentional modulation of very early visual segmentation

Here we exploited a particularly well understood form of primitive image segmentation, which is thought to reflect interactions between interconnected neurons in primary visual cortex (Polat & Sagi, 1993, 1994). Contrast thresholds for detecting a central Gabor patch stimulus (i.e. a cosine grating convolved with a Gaussian filter; see Fig. 8) can be systematically affected by flanking Gabor patches. Such Gabor stimuli are experimentally useful, not only because of their precise

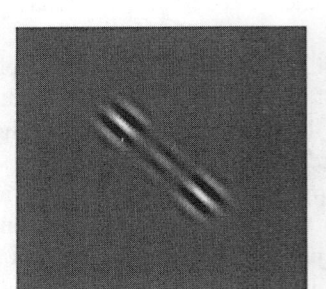

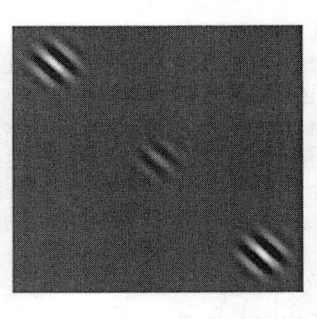

Fig. 8. (A) Central Gabor patch with high-contrast and collinear flankers separated from the central target by only three Gabor wavelengths. In such conditions, the flankers lower contrast thresholds for detecting the central target. This facilitatory effect falls off with increasing separation, being reduced at the eight-wavelength separation shown in (B).

physical characteristics, but also because they are thought to stimulate highly specific populations of cells in primary visual cortex.

It is now well established that thresholds for a central target patch are affected by the presence and nature of flanking patches (e.g. Polat & Sagi, 1993, 1994), reflecting highly systematic lateral interactions. Target detection is maximally facilitated for a central patch that is iso-oriented and aligned with flanking patches of the same spatial frequency at separations of around three Gabor wavelengths (see Fig. 8A). Suppression is found at lower separations, while the facilitation gradually declines at higher separations (e.g. Fig. 8B). Global configuration is critical; non-collinear arrangements of iso-oriented patches produce suppression instead of facilitation (Zenger & Sagi, 1996). Further properties of the lateral interactions between target and flankers are also well characterized; they are invariant over magnification and independent of relative phase above critical separations, and flankers with orthogonal local orientation to the target have no influence (e.g. Field, Hayes, & Hess, 1993; Polat & Sagi, 1993).

These lateral interactions between Gabor patches have been modelled by an array of detectors akin to V1 neurons (e.g. Polat, 1999; Usher, Bonneh, Sagi, & Herrmann, 1999), with neighbouring units reinforcing or suppressing each other via lateral connections, similar to those actually observed in primary visual cortex (e.g. Spillmann & Werner, 1996). More importantly for our current topic, these lateral interactions may reflect a very early form of segmentation involved in contour integration and texture segmentation (e.g. Polat, 1999). For example, note that when viewing Fig. 8A, a virtual contour may appear to be formed, linking the central patch and the aligned flankers, while this applies less at the greater separation in Fig. 8B. Given the suspected substrate in primary visual cortex, lateral interactions between flanking Gabor patches may tap into the very first cortical stage of image segmentation.

We wondered whether these lateral interactions and the associated formation of virtual contours might depend on the flankers being attended. To address this, one of us (E.F.) instigated a novel variant of the lateral interactions paradigm (see Fig. 9),

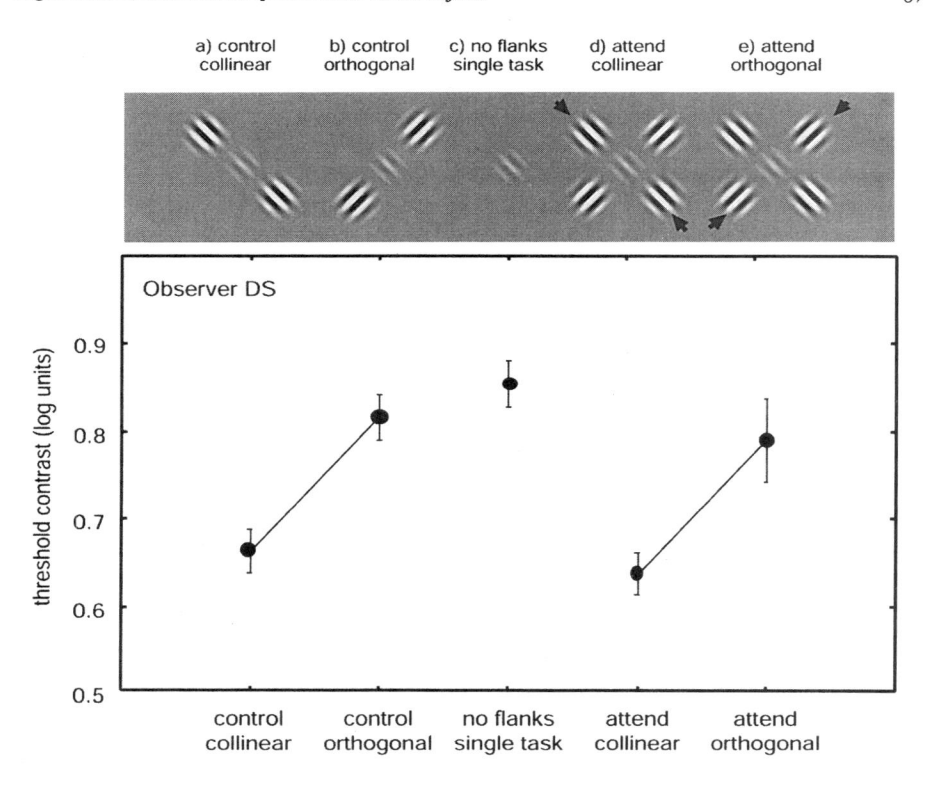

Fig. 9. The upper panel shows example displays from the preliminary study by Freeman, Sagi, and Driver, as described in the text (the arrows in D and E were not physically present, and are shown only to indicate which flankers were attended for the secondary task). The lower panel plots contrast thresholds for detecting the central target in each of the conditions shown above. Data from one experienced observer (D.S.) with standard error are shown.

which we have since pursued in collaboration with Dov Sagi (Freeman, Sagi, & Driver, unpublished data). In this new version, contrast thresholds for detecting a central target Gabor patch are measured not only in the context of one pair of flankers (as is conventional; see Fig. 9A,B), but also with *two* pairs of flankers, which have orthogonal global and local orientations (see Fig. 9D,E). Thus, in any given display of four flankers, two of them will be collinear with the target (those along one diagonal), while the other two will not (those on the other diagonal). We manipulate which pair of flankers (i.e. which diagonal) is attended for a secondary task performed in addition to central target detection.

In the study illustrated by Fig. 9, this secondary task was vernier acuity (i.e. judging the direction of a small offset for the two flankers along one diagonal). On each trial, there were two successive displays. Observers then made unspeeded, independent decisions concerning which of the two intervals contained (a) a central target, and (b) a particular direction of vernier offset for the relevant two flankers. In some blocks of trials (see Fig. 9A,B) only two flankers were present, which could be collinear or non-collinear with the target. Observers performed both the central detection task and the vernier task for the flankers. In other blocks (see Fig. 9D,E) four flankers were presented, with observers performing the secondary vernier task for only one relevant pair (i.e. those indicated by arrows in Fig. 9, although no arrows were actually present in the study). Finally, baseline blocks (Fig. 9C) presented no flankers, with observers performing only the central target detection task. Any flankers were separated from the central target by four Gabor wavelengths, a separation where facilitation of target detection thresholds by collinear flankers is usually found, while orthogonal flankers have no effect.

Contrast thresholds for one experienced psychophysical observer (an initially sceptical Dov Sagi!) are shown in the lower panel of Fig. 9 underneath the corresponding display type from the upper panel. A second experienced observer, E.F., produced a very similar pattern. With a single pair of flankers (leftmost two points in the graph), the usual lowering of target threshold was found when the flankers were collinear rather than orthogonal. With two pairs of flankers (rightmost two points in the graph), central target detection depended heavily on which pair was attended for the secondary vernier task, with lower central thresholds when the pair that was collinear with the target was attended. Indeed, with four flankers present, the central thresholds behaved as if the currently ignored pair of high-contrast flankers was simply absent (compare leftmost two datapoints with rightmost two datapoints in the graph of Fig. 9).

These initial results provide preliminary evidence for attentional modulation of lateral interactions between Gabor patches, which had previously been attributed to hard-wired lateral connections within primary visual cortex (e.g. Polat & Sagi, 1993; Usher et al., 1999), that may subserve contour integration and texture segmentation. We shall exploit this apparent attentional modulation in further psychophysical studies to determine exactly how the lateral interactions are influenced by attentional set in terms of existing V1 models (e.g. Li, 1998; Zenger & Sagi, 1996). These models suggest various possibilities. For instance, attending to specific flankers for the secondary task might simply boost activity in cells responding to those flankers, alter their dynamic range, or affect the strength of connections between cells responding to the flankers, and those responding to the target. Models of primary visual cortex are now sufficiently advanced that these different possibilities for the underlying mechanism of the attentional modulation can lead to different psychophysical predictions.

This study provides an apparent case of attentional factors modulating a very early and primitive form of image segmentation, namely lateral interactions between detectors for specific spatial frequencies and orientations, which relate to contour integration. In this example, attention seems able to influence segmentation processes, rather than the influence being only in the reverse direction. Nevertheless, various further questions from the literature on 'object-based' visual attention still arise, even for this situation. For instance, is the effect of attending to one pair of flankers rather than the other (upon central target thresholds) only found when the secondary task for these relevant flankers concerns their *spatial* alignment (as in the vernier task, which may have encouraged a specifically spatial strategy of judging the virtual contour formed by central target and collinear flankers together; see Fig. 9)? Or is it still found even when observers judge entirely non-spatial properties for the relevant flankers? The latter outcome might be predicted by some 'object-based' accounts of attention (e.g. Duncan, 1984), which propose that whenever one property of an item is judged, all of its other properties (e.g. spatial frequency and orientation) may also be extracted.

13. Mutual constraints between segmentation and attention

We hope the studies we have described illustrate that attentional issues can provoke new questions about visual segmentation, and vice-versa. Our description may also have illustrated the intimate but vexing relation with phenomenology which characterizes much research on perception and attention. Phenomenology provides a useful starting point for many questions, and is also part of what must be explained, yet it is clearly inadequate for resolving many of the questions that an attentional perspective raises. This is not only because of the spotted-pink-elephant methodological problem, but also because our phenomenal visual experience represents only some aspects of the underlying visual processing. Indeed, the study of attention is largely motivated by the selective nature of perceptual awareness.

As noted earlier, much of the evidence we have described (e.g. on grouping under inattention, visual search in relation to modal versus amodal completion, and the differential effects of these forms of completion on distractor interference, or on cueing effects) is broadly consistent with the traditional story that many segmentation processes constrain attentional selectivity (e.g. Driver & Baylis, 1998; Duncan, 1984; Neisser, 1967). Our results suggest that such segmentation processes can include cases as sophisticated as modal or amodal completion, and incorporate constraints as subtle as the Metelli rule, concerning the optics of transparent surfaces. On the other hand, the final study described here (on detection of Gabor patches) indicates that some aspects of attention (here, the task-relevance of one pair of flankers versus the other) can modulate very early segmentation processes (perhaps even the very first cortical stage of image segmentation).

If approached within the conventional preattentive/attentive dichotomy, this combination of results (i.e. cases where segmentation influences attention, but also cases of the reverse) would seem paradoxical. However, this seeming paradox only arises because the conventional preattentive/attentive view assumes a strictly serial succession of (just two!) distinct stages. It is now well known that human vision incorporates many more than just two levels of processing, and that back projections are at least as numerous as forward projections. Moreover, as we have emphasized, attention is best thought of as an umbrella-term for several selective processes, not as a single process with a single modulatory influence. In any case, 'interactive activation' models, incorporating back projections, have long been able to resolve apparent paradoxes of the kind raised here, whereby seemingly 'later' processes can influence apparently 'early' processes (e.g. McClelland & Rumelhart,

1986). We would suggest that the relation between various forms of segmentation, and of attention, has this mutually constraining nature.

The phenomenology of many grouping displays is also consistent with such mutual influences, whereby segmentation can constrain selective attention, but the reverse influence is also possible. While grouping can certainly restrict which units you can pick out subjectively, you can also modulate subjective grouping at will to some extent in many grouping displays, especially when the stimulus factors are relatively subtle. Finally, the burgeoning neuroscience evidence also suggests that many forms of attentional selectivity and grouping are implemented in the brain by interactions between multiple levels of processing (e.g. Desimone & Duncan, 1995; Driver & Frith, in press; Kastner et al., 1999), and not in the strictly feed-forward manner envisaged by the traditional preattentive-then-attentive dichotomy.

We consider such an interactive architecture to be a plausible explanation for the mutual constraints between segmentation and attention. However, some of the apparent conflicts in attention research may arise for other reasons. For instance, it has been proposed (Lavie, 1995) that one critical factor may be attentional load, which often varies in an uncontrolled manner across different experiments, or is not manipulated across the entire possible range (i.e. may not include situations where attention reaches 'absolute zero'; Nakayama & Josephs, 1998). We are sympathetic to this general point, and concede that it may apply to some of the observations we have discussed. For instance, the evidence for implicit grouping of unattended displays, found with the method shown in Fig. 1, might subsequently be shown to vary with the load of the central task. However, on its own, the absolute-zero point does not satisfactorily resolve why in some cases segmentation processes can be modulated by attention, whereas in other cases segmentation clearly constrains attentional selectivity. The absolute-zero approach essentially claims only that many apparently 'preattentive' processes might in fact prove subject to some attentional limitations if the latter were pushed far enough (e.g. Joseph et al., 1996). This emphasizes only one direction of influence (i.e. attention affecting segmentation), saying nothing about the many cases where segmentation constrains selectivity.

14. Relation to other 'object-based' notions in cognitive science

Throughout this paper, we have rarely used the term 'object', despite the stated theme of this volume. Typically, we have referred to 'segmentation' or 'grouping' instead, quite intentionally. We did so because we consider 'object' to be an unfortunately vague and intuitive term in our particular context, which might nevertheless be mistaken to have a highly specific meaning by some readers. In our view, most (perhaps all) of the literature on 'object-based' attention is in fact concerned with how segmentation processes constrain attentional processes, and vice-versa (see also Driver, 1999, for a similar account of the extensive neuropsychological literature on so-called 'object-centred neglect'). We did not have space to describe all the variations on the object-based attention theme here (see Scholl, 2001, for review). For instance, some of this literature is concerned with how segmentation into distinct feature-bundles may unfold or be maintained over time in dynamic displays (e.g. Kahneman, Treisman, & Gibbs, 1992; Pylyshyn & Storm, 1988; Scholl, Pylyshyn, & Feldman, 2001). Other papers are concerned with how different dimensions (e.g. colour and shape) may be bound together at a particular location to construct multi-dimensional objects (e.g. Luck & Vogel, 1997; Treisman & Gelade, 1980). But in our view, these are all variations on a more general question concerning the relation between attention and segmentation (which pieces of information should be bound together, be this over space or over time).

Despite our present reluctance to use the term 'object', it seems clear that a major role of segmentation processes is to distinguish between those parts of the sensory input that are heuristically likely, on the basis of segmentation factors, to correspond to distinct objects (or separate image sources) in the real world, thus constituting 'proto-objects'. As described above (and more extensively by Driver & Baylis, 1998), image segmentation often constrains our ability to attend selectively, so that we may tend to select all or most of one 'proto-object', even when we try to select just part of it (as in our study (Davis & Driver, 1997) of distraction in the context of modal versus amodal completion; see Fig. 7). Similarly, image segmentation can constrain what we may efficiently search for. For example, the search studies of modal and amodal completion suggest that we cannot obtain direct access to the retinal shape of stimuli, as completion processes operate to some extent even against our will, yielding proto-objects which go beyond the various shapes in the retinal mosaic.

Such proto-objects produced by the various image segmentation processes may often be more primitive than the conceptual objects, or real-world objects, which we discuss verbally in daily life. As the term 'mid-level' vision implies, they typically reflect bundles of visual information which are packaged on the basis of properties that go beyond raw image statistics (or primitive 'features'), yet which fall short of conceptually recognized entities. Nevertheless, they may bear a fairly close correspondence to the distinction between separate visual 'objects' which we experience phenomenally (as for the modally-completed ellipse with its filled-in colour that is cartooned in Fig. 7B versus the white bar which it appears to occlude). Moreover, the proto-objects produced by image segmentation processes, and the constraints they impose on various attentional processes, may provide an essential precursor for learning more conceptual distinctions between separate types of objects, as in the developing child (e.g. see Carey & Xu, 2001).

Despite these possible links to other object-based concepts in cognitive science, we still prefer to refer to the processes we have studied in terms of image segmentation rather than 'objects', as we think this encourages the right way of thinking about them. It leads to questions about the various visual processes which construct the effective 'proto-objects', rather than simply assuming separate objects as givens. In this respect, we think that the various manifestos proclaiming visual attention to be 'object-based' (see Scholl, 2001, for review) may now have served their useful purpose. They have focused research on the perceptual units which attentional processes operate upon, and thus moved attention research beyond the simplistic spatial spotlight metaphors which dominated much previous work, to trigger new questions about segmentation and binding. We think that further progress in visual attention research will now stem from examining specific visual processes, such as particular forms of segmentation, in more detail. Many such segmentation processes have already been well characterized in previous vision research (as for lateral interactions between Gabor patches, or modal versus amodal completion), but with little previous consideration of attentional issues. We hope to have illustrated here that perception research and attention research can be complementary on such issues, with the two previously separate research traditions being strengthened when combined.

Acknowledgements

The experimental work described here was supported by project grants from the Economic and Social Research Council (UK), and the Biology and Biotechnology Research Council (UK) to J.D. Our thanks to Gordon Baylis, Diane Beck, Henry Howlett, Brian Scholl, and the late Irvin Rock.

References

Baylis, G. C., & Driver, J. (1992). Visual parsing and response competition: the effect of grouping factors. *Perception & Psychophysics, 51* (2), 145–162.
Broadbent, D. E. (1958). *Perception and communication*. Oxford: Oxford University Press.
Carey, S., & Xu, F. (2001). Infant knowledge of objects: beyond object files and object tracking. *Cognition*, this issue, 80, 179–213.
Cherry, E. C. (1953). Some experiments on the recognition of speech, with one and with two ears. *Journal of the Acoustical Society of America, 25*, 975–979.
Davis, G., & Driver, J. (1994). Parallel detection of Kanizsa subjective figures in the human visual system. *Nature, 371* (6500), 791–793.
Davis, G., & Driver, J. (1997). A functional role for illusory colour spreading in the control of focused visual attention. *Perception, 26* (11), 1397–1411.
Davis, G., & Driver, J. (1998). Kanizsa subjective figures can act as occluding surfaces at parallel stages of visual search. *Journal of Experimental Psychology: Human Perception and Performance, 24* (1), 169–184.
Desimone, R., & Duncan, J. (1995). Neural mechanisms of selective visual attention. *Annual Review of Neuroscience, 18*, 193–222.
Dresp, B., & Bonnet, C. (1995). Subthreshold summation with illusory contours. *Vision Research, 35* (8), 1071–1078.
Driver, J. (1999). Egocentric and object-based visual neglect. In N. Burgess, K. J. Jeffery, & J. O'Keefe (Eds.), *The hippocampal and parietal foundations of spatial cognition* (pp. 67–89). Oxford: Oxford University Press.
Driver, J. (in press). A selective review of selective attention research from the past century. *British Journal of Psychology*.
Driver, J., & Baylis, G. C. (1989). Movement and visual attention: the spotlight metaphor breaks down. *Journal of Experimental Psychology: Human Perception and Performance, 15* (3), 448–456.
Driver, J., & Baylis, G. C. (1998). Attention and visual object segmentation. In R. Parasuraman (Ed.), *The attentive brain* (pp. 299–325). Cambridge, MA: MIT Press.
Driver, J., & Frith, C. (in press). Shifting baselines in attention research. *Nature Reviews Neuroscience*.
Duncan, J. (1984). Selective attention and the organization of visual information. *Journal of Experimental Psychology: General, 113* (4), 501–517.

Fahle, M., & Koch, C. (1995). Spatial displacement, but not temporal asynchrony, destroys figural binding. *Vision Research, 35* (4), 491–494.

Farah, M. J., Wallace, M. A., & Vercera, S. P. (1993). 'What' and 'where' in visual attention: evidence from the neglect syndrome. In I. H. Robertson, & J. C. Marshall (Eds.), *Unilateral neglect: clinical and experimental studies* (pp. 123–138). Hillsdale, NJ: Erlbaum.

Fernandez-Duque, D., & Thornton, I. M. (2000). Change detection without awareness: do explicit reports underestimate the detection of change in the visual system? *Visual Cognition, 7,* 323–344.

Field, D. J., Hayes, S., & Hess, R. F. (1993). Contour integration by the human visual system: evidence for a local "association field". *Vision Research, 33* (2), 173–193.

He, Z. J., & Nakayama, K. (1992). Surfaces versus features in visual search. *Nature, 359* (6392), 231–233.

Holender, D. (1986). Semantic activation without conscious activation in dichotic listening, parafoveal vision, and visual masking: a survey and appraisal. *Behavioural and Brain Sciences, 9,* 1–23.

Humphreys, G. W., Olson, A., Romani, C., & Riddoch, M. J. (1996). Competitive mechanisms of selection by space and object: a neuropsychological approach. In A. F. Kramer, M. G. H. Coles, & G. D. Logan (Eds.), *Converging operations in the study of visual selective attention* (pp. 365–393). Washington, DC: APA Press.

Joseph, J. S., Chun, M. M., & Nakayama, K. (1996). Attentional requirements in a "preattentive" feature search task. *Nature, 379,* 805–807.

Kahneman, D., Treisman, A., & Gibbs, B. J. (1992). The reviewing of object files: object-specific integration of information. *Cognitive Psychology, 24* (2), 175–219.

Kanizsa, G. (1979). *Organization in vision: essays on Gestalt perception.* New York: Praeger.

Kanwisher, N., & Driver, J. (1992). Objects, attributes and visual attention: which, what and where. *Current Directions in Psychological Science, 1* (1), 26–31.

Kastner, S., Pinsk, M. A., De-Weerd, P., Desimone, R., & Ungerleider, L. G. (1999). Increased activity in human visual cortex during directed attention in the absence of visual stimulation. *Neuron, 22* (4), 751–761.

Kellman, P. J., & Shipley, T. F. (1991). A theory of visual interpolation in object perception. *Cognitive Psychology, 23* (2), 141–221.

Lavie, N. (1995). Perceptual load as a necessary condition for selective attention. *Journal of Experimental Psychology: Human Perception and Performance, 21,* 451–468.

Lesher, G. W. (1995). Illusory contours: toward a neurally based perceptual theory. *Psychonomic Bulletin & Review, 2* (3), 279–321.

Lewis, J. (1970). Semantic processing of unattended messages using dichotic listening. *Journal of Experimental Psychology, 85,* 225–228.

Li, Z. (1998). A neural model of contour integration in the primary visual cortex. *Neural Computation, 10* (4), 903–940.

Luck, S. J., & Vogel, E. K. (1997). The capacity of visual working memory for features and conjunctions. *Nature, 390* (6657), 279–281.

Mack, A., & Rock, I. (1998). *Inattentional blindness.* Cambridge, MA: MIT Press.

Mack, A., Tang, B., Tuma, R., Kahn, S., & Rock, I. (1992). Perceptual organization and attention. *Cognitive Psychology, 24* (4), 475–501.

Marr, D. (1982). *Vision: a computational investigation into the human representation and processing of visual information.* San Francisco, CA: W.H. Freeman.

McClelland, J. L., & Rumelhart, D. E. (1986). *Parallel distributed processing: explorations in the microstructure of cognition.* Cambridge, MA: MIT Press.

Metelli, F. (1974). The perception of transparency. *Scientific American, 230* (4), 90–98.

Moore, C. M., & Egeth, H. (1997). Perception without attention: evidence of grouping under conditions of inattention. *Journal of Experimental Psychology: Human Perception and Performance, 23* (2), 339–352.

Nakayama, K., He, Z., & Shimojo, S. (1995). Visual surface representation: a critical link between lower-level and higher-level vision. In S. M. Kosslyn, & D. Osherson (Eds.), *Visual cognition. An invitation to cognitive science* (2nd ed., Vol. 2, pp. 1–70). Cambridge, MA: MIT Press.

Nakayama, K., & Josephs, J. S. (1998). Attention, pattern recognition, and pop-out in visual search. In R. Parasuraman (Ed.), *The attentive brain* (pp. 279–298). Cambridge, MA: MIT Press.

Nakayama, K., & Shimojo, S. (1992). Experiencing and perceiving visual surfaces. *Science*, *257* (5075), 1357–1363.

Nakayama, K., Shimojo, S., & Silverman, G. H. (1989). Stereoscopic depth: its relation to image segmentation, grouping, and the recognition of occluded objects. *Perception*, *18* (1), 55–68.

Neisser, U. (1967). *Cognitive psychology*. New York: Appleton.

Neisser, U., & Becklen, R. (1975). Selective looking: attending to visually specified events. *Cognitive Psychology*, *7*, 480–494.

O'Regan, J. K., Rensink, R. A., & Clark, J. J. (1999). Change-blindness as a result of 'mudsplashes'. *Nature*, *398* (6722), 34.

Palmer, S. E., Neff, J., & Beck, D. (1997). Grouping and amodal completion. In I. Rock (Ed.), *Indirect perception* (pp. 63–75). Cambridge, MA: MIT Press.

Palmer, S. E., & Nelson, R. (in press). Late influences on perceptual grouping: illusory contours. *Perception & Psychophysics*.

Palmer, S., & Rock, I. (1994). Rethinking perceptual organization: the role of uniform connectedness. *Psychonomic Bulletin & Review*, *1* (1), 29–55.

Pashler, H. (1998). *The psychology of attention*. Cambridge, MA: MIT Press.

Peterson, M. A. (1994). Object recognition processes can and do operate before figure-ground organization. *Current Directions in Psychological Science*, *3*, 105–111.

Petry, S., & Meyer, G. E. (1987). *The perception of illusory contours*. New York: Springer-Verlag.

Polat, U. (1999). Functional architecture of long-range perceptual interactions. *Spatial Vision*, *12* (2), 143–162.

Polat, U., & Sagi, D. (1993). Lateral interactions between spatial channels: suppression and facilitation revealed by lateral masking experiments. *Vision Research*, *33* (7), 993–999.

Polat, U., & Sagi, D. (1994). The architecture of perceptual spatial interactions. *Vision Research*, *34* (1), 73–78.

Pomerantz, J. R., & Kubovy, M. (1986). Theoretical approaches to perceptual organization: simplicity and likelihood principles. In K. R. Boff, L. Kaufman, & J. P. Thomas (Eds.), *Cognitive processes and performance. Handbook of perception and human performance* (Vol. 2, pp. 1–46). New York: Wiley.

Pylyshyn, Z. W., & Storm, R. W. (1988). Tracking multiple independent targets: evidence for a parallel tracking mechanism. *Spatial Vision*, *3*, 179–197.

Ramachandran, I. (1987). Visual perception of surfaces: a biological theory. In S. Petry, & S. E. Meyer (Eds.), *The perception of illusory contours*. New York: Springer-Verlag.

Ramachandran, V. S. (1995). Filling in the gaps in logic: reply to Durgin et al. *Perception*, *24*, 841–843.

Rensink, R. A. (2000). Seeing, sensing, and scrutinizing. *Vision Research*, *40*, 1469–1487.

Rensink, R. A., & Enns, J. T. (1998). Early completion of occluded objects. *Vision Research*, *38*, 2489–2505.

Rensink, R. A., O'Regan, J. K., & Clark, J. (1997). To see or not to see: the need for attention to perceive changes in scenes. *Psychological Science*, *8* (5), 368–373.

Rock, I. (1975). *An introduction to perception*. New York: Macmillan.

Rock, I. (1983). *The logic of perception*. Cambridge, MA: MIT Press.

Rock, I., & Gutman, D. (1981). The effect of inattention on form perception. *Journal of Experimental Psychology: Human Perception and Performance*, *7* (2), 275–285.

Rock, I., Linnett, C. M., Grant, P., & Mack, A. (1992). Perception without attention: results of a new method. *Cognitive Psychology*, *24*, 502–534.

Rock, I., Nijhawan, R., Palmer, S., & Tudor, L. (1992). Grouping based on phenomenal similarity of achromatic colour. *Perception*, *21* (6), 779–789.

Rubin, E. (1921). *Visuell Wahrgenommene Figuren*. Kobenhaven: Glydenalske Boghandel.

Rubin, N., Nakayama, K., & Shapley, R. (1996). Enhanced perception of illusory contours in the lower versus upper visual hemifields. *Science*, *271* (5249), 651–653.

Scholl, B. J. (2001). Objects and attention: the state of the art. *Cognition*, this issue, *80*, 1–46.

Scholl, B. J., Pylyshyn, Z. W., & Feldman, J. (2001). What is a visual object? Evidence from target merging in multi-element tracking. *Cognition*, this issue, *80*, 159–177.

Simons, D. J. (2000). Current approaches to change blindness. *Visual Cognition*, *7*, 1–16.

Simons, D. J., & Levin, D. T. (1997). Change blindness. *Trends in Cognitive Sciences*, *1* (7), 261–267.

Smilek, D., Eastwood, J. D., & Merikle, P. M. (2000). Does unattended information facilitate change detection? *Journal of Experimental Psychology: Human Perception and Performance, 26,* 480–487.

Somers, D. C., Dale, A. M., Seiffert, A. E., & Tootell, R. B. (1999). Functional MRI reveals spatially specific attentional modulation in human primary visual cortex. *Proceedings of the National Academy of Sciences USA, 96* (4), 1663–1668.

Spillmann, L., & Werner, J. S. (1996). Long-range interactions in visual perception. *Trends in Neuroscience, 19* (10), 428–434.

Stroop, J. R. (1935). Studies of interference in serial verbal reactions. *Journal of Experimental Psychology, 18,* 643–662.

Treisman, A. (1986). Features and objects in visual processing. *Scientific American, 255* (5), 114B–125B.

Treisman, A. M., & Gelade, G. (1980). A feature integration theory of attention. *Cognitive Psychology, 12* (1), 97–136.

Usher, M., Bonneh, Y., Sagi, D., & Herrmann, M. (1999). Mechanisms for spatial integration in visual detection: a model based on lateral interactions. *Spatial Vision, 12* (2), 187–209.

Van Tuijl, H. F., & de Weert, C. M. (1979). Sensory conditions for the occurrence of the neon spreading illusion. *Perception, 8* (2), 211–215.

Warm, J. S., Dember, W. N., Padich, R. A., Beckner, W. N., & Jones, S. (1987). The role of illumination level in the strength of subjective contours. In S. Petry, & G. E. Meyer (Eds.), *The perception of illusory contours* New York: Springer-Verlag.

Wertheimer, M. (1923). Untersuchungen zur Lehre von Gestalt. *Psycholgishe Furschung, 4,* 301–350.

Wolfe, J. M. (1998). Visual search. In H. Pashler (Ed.), *The psychology of attention.* Hove: Psychology Press.

Wolfe, J. M. (1999). Inattentional amnesia. In V. Coltheart, *Fleeting memories: cognition of brief visual stimuli* (pp. 71–94). Cambridge, MA: MIT Press.

Zenger, B., & Sagi, D. (1996). Isolating excitatory and inhibitory nonlinear spatial interactions involved in contrast detection. *Vision Research, 36* (16), 2497–2513.

4

Auditory and visual objects

Michael Kubovy[*], David Van Valkenburg

University of Virginia, Charlottesville, VA, USA

Abstract

Notions of objecthood have traditionally been cast in visuocentric terminology. As a result, theories of auditory and cross-modal perception have focused more on the differences between modalities than on the similarities. In this paper we re-examine the concept of an object in a way that overcomes the limitations of the traditional perspective. We propose a new, cross-modal conception of objecthood which focuses on the similarities between modalities instead of the differences. Further, we propose that the auditory system might consist of two parallel streams of processing (the 'what' and 'where' subsystems) in a manner analogous to current conceptions of the visual system. We suggest that the 'what' subsystems in each modality are concerned with objecthood. Finally, we present evidence for – and elaborate on – the hypothesis that the auditory 'where' subsystem is in the service of the visual-motor 'where' subsystem. © 2001 Elsevier Science B.V. All rights reserved.

Keywords: Auditory; Visual; Objecthood

---

1. Introduction

In this article we argue for the concept of an *auditory object*. Although some have found such a concept so strange that they avoid the term altogether in favor of 'auditory event' (Blauert, 1997, p. 2), we are convinced that it is both a useful and important concept. To clarify it, we offer a distinction between an auditory 'what' subsystem and an auditory 'where' subsystem (in a manner analogous to

---

[*] Corresponding author. Department of Psychology, P.O. Box 400400, University of Virginia, Charlottesville, VA 22904-4400, USA. Fax: +1-804-982-4766.

E-mail addresses: kubovy@virginia.edu (M. Kubovy), dlv6b@virginia.edu (D. Van Valkenburg).

Milner & Goodale, 1995), and argue that the 'what' subsystem forms auditory objects, and that the 'where' subsystem is in the service of vision.

The bias against the idea of auditory objecthood is embedded in folk ontology. Language itself[1] may lead us to believe that objects are visible by definition. For example, according to the *Oxford English Dictionary*, *object* means "Something placed before the eyes, or presented to the sight or other sense; an individual thing seen or perceived, or that may be seen or perceived; a material thing" (Object, 1993). The etymology of the word *object* explains the visuocentric connotation of the word: it derives from the Latin *ob-*, 'before' or 'toward', and *iacere*, 'to throw'. It used to mean, "Something 'thrown' or put in the way, so as to interrupt or obstruct the course of a person or thing; an obstacle, a hindrance" (Object, 1993). Indeed, most visible things are obstacles or a hindrance to sight; they prevent you from seeing something that lies behind them because they are opaque.[2]

In this paper we will deviate from our everyday notion of object in order to extend it to audition. We will do this by finding a different criterion for objecthood, one that does not rely on the notion of opacity. We must do this because the notion of opacity simply does not apply to auditory perception. Material things can of course be opaque to sound (Beranek, 1988, Chapter 3). But we do not listen to *material* things, we listen to *vibrating* things – *audible sources*. One sound source does not in general prevent you from hearing another: many natural sounds, especially biological ones, are composed of a fundamental frequency and discrete harmonics – i.e. they are sparse, like fences. Furthermore, masking is rare in nature because the masking sound must be considerably louder than the masked one (e.g. it takes the sound of a waterfall or thunder to mask our voices).

Although one sound can mask another, Bregman (1990), in his discussion of the auditory continuity illusion, shows that audible sources do not offer a natural analog to opacity. The auditory continuity illusion is created when one deletes part of a signal and replaces it with a louder sound: the signal is perceived to continue uninterrupted 'behind' the sound. Bregman compares this illusion with the visual experience of continuity behind an occluder (Fig. 1): "Let us designate the interrupted sound or visual surface as A, and consider it to be divided into A1 and A2 by B, the interrupting entity... [In vision one] object's surface must end exactly where the other begins and the contours of A must reach dead ends where they visually meet the outline of B. In the auditory modality, the evidence for the continuity occurs in the properties of B itself as well as in A1 and A2; B must give rise to a set of neural properties that contain those of the missing part of A. In vision, on the other hand, if objects are opaque, there is no hint of the properties of A in the visual region occupied by B" (p. 383).

We pointed out earlier that we do not listen to material things, but to audible sources. The auditory system is generally concerned with *sources* of sound (such as speech or music), not with *surfaces* that reflect the sound (Bregman, 1990, pp. 36–

---

[1] Indo-European languages in particular.

[2] There are two exceptions: things that are transparent and things that are sparse. There are two kinds of sparse things: things with holes in them (e.g. fences) and things that branch (e.g. plants).

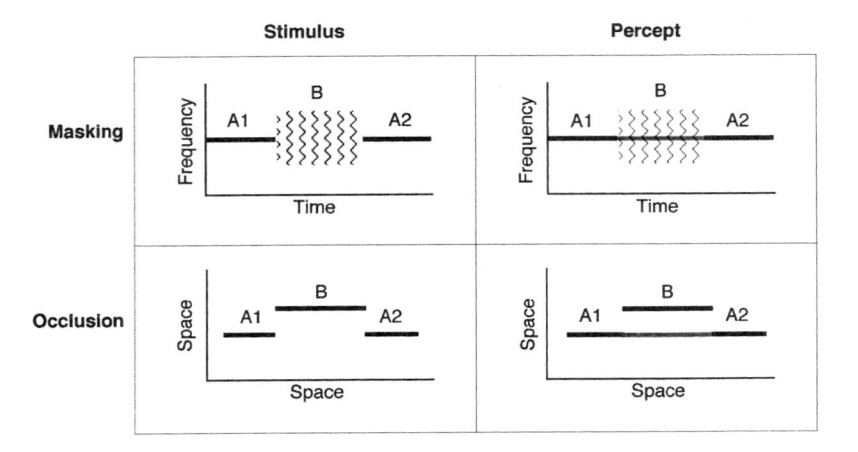

Fig. 1. The auditory continuity illusion (top) compared to the visual effect of continuity behind an occluder (bottom).

38). In a series of experiments, Watkins (Watkins, 1991, 1998, 1999; Watkins & Makin, 1996) has explored how the auditory system compensates for the distortion of spectral envelope (the major determinant of the perceived identity of many sounds) caused by factors such as room reverberation.

For the visual system just the opposite is true: it is generally concerned with *surfaces* of objects, not with the *sources* that illuminate them. As Mollon (1995) points out (giving credit to Monge, 1789):

> our visual system is built to recognise ... permanent properties of objects, their spectral reflectances, ... not ... the spectral flux ... (pp. 148–149).

These differences are summarized in Table 1.

For these reasons, we believe that to understand auditory objects we will have to rethink certain commonly accepted analogies between visual and auditory perception. In particular, we will show that both modalities are endowed with 'what' and 'where' subsystems, but that the relation between these four subsystems is complex. Obviously it is the 'what' subsystem of each modality that deals with objects, and so we will devote considerable attention to the auditory 'what' subsystem. But before we do, we must attend to the evidence connecting the auditory 'where' subsystem and the visuomotor orienting subsystem. We will claim that auditory localization is in the service of visual localization. This assertion is one of the cornerstones of our argument that space is not central to the formation of auditory objects.

Table 1
Comparison of vision and audition

Source of information	Vision	Audition
Primary	Surfaces	Sources
Secondary	Location and color of sources	Surfaces

2. Auditory 'where' in the service of visual 'where'

When two auditory sources appear to come from different spatial locations, shouldn't we say that they constitute different auditory objects, as do Wightman and Jenison (1995, pp. 371–372)? We prefer not to, because we believe that auditory localization is in the service of visual orienting, a hypothesis first formulated at the turn of the twentieth century by Angell: auditory "localisation occurs in the space world of vision–touch–movement... Most persons seem to make their localisation of sounds either in the form of visual imagery, or in the form of quasi-reflex localising movements of head and eye" (Angell, 1906, pp. 154–155). In this section we review the evidence supporting Angell's hypothesis.

The earliest sign of directional discrimination of sound in the human newborn is head orientation (Clifton, 1992), which suggests that the newborn is optimizing its head orientation to see the source.

Auditory localization is malleable, and can be influenced by the spatial location of a simultaneous visual stimulus. Bertelson and Aschersleben (1998) asked observers to judge whether the source of a sound was to the left or right of the median sagittal plane. When they presented the sound synchronously with an off-center flash, the sound appeared to be shifted in the direction of the light flash.

Sound localization itself is influenced by the act of visual orienting. Rorden and Driver (1999) presented observers with a noise burst from one of four speakers arranged in a fronto-parallel square array, and asked them to indicate whether the sound came from above or below their head. Before the noise was played, the observers were given a signal instructing them to move their eyes to the left or to the right. Reaction times (RTs) for correct up/down decisions were shorter when the direction of the intended eye movement was ipsilateral with the source of the noise than when it was contralateral to the source of the noise (regardless of whether the noise was heard before or after the eye movement was initiated).

Even clearer evidence of the role of auditory localization in visuomotor orientation is provided by Goldring, Dorris, Corneil, Balantyne, and Munoz (1996). On each trial they presented (for 1 s) either a visual target (an LED), an auditory target (broadband noise), or both, from a variety of azimuths. The participants' task was to turn their gaze towards the target as quickly as possible. When the targets were unimodal the relative eye–head latency depended on the eccentricity of the target: if eccentricity was less than 20° visual angle (dva), visual targets elicited a lower latency than auditory targets; beyond 20 dva, this order was reversed. For our purposes this result has one major implication: auditory localization is in the service of visual orientation where vision is weakest. (See also, Hughes, Nelson, and Aronchick (1998) who develop these findings further.)

To say that auditory localization is in the service of vision does *not* imply that auditory cueing is the most effective way to orient the visual system. Indeed, Jay and Sparks (1990) have shown that auditory-induced saccades are generally slower and less accurate than visually-induced saccades. Moreover, we are not arguing that auditory localization is equivalent to visual localization.

There is evidence of a one-way dependence of the visual modality on the auditory modality from studies of multimodal cueing. Spence and Driver (1997) presented observers with a light or sound (the target) from one of four positions in a fronto-parallel square array, and asked them to indicate whether the sound came from above or below their head. Some ISI before the target, observers were presented with an uninformative exogenous visual or auditory cue from either the left or right side. RTs for correct localization were compared across conditions. The results showed short-lived (ISI ≤ 200 ms) facilitated performance for valid auditory cues when the target was either visual or auditory. Visual cues, however, facilitated performance only for visual targets. Spence and Driver have since replicated this effect numerous times; they interpret their results as evidence for auditory localization in the service of vision: audition influences visual localization but *not* vice-versa (Spence & Driver, 1999).

The dominance of vision over audition is confirmed in a case of left visual neglect, i.e. a derangement of visual space representation (Ladavas & Pavani, 1998). The patient was asked to point to left, center or right acoustic stimuli under visual control or blindfolded. Her pointing to left auditory stimuli was influenced by visual spatial information, i.e. she manifested left neglect. But when she was blindfolded, she pointed to the previously ignored left space.

In macaque monkeys, Jay and Sparks (1984) found that the auditory receptive fields shifted with changes in eye position, allowing the auditory and visual maps to remain in register. Even in the barn owl, for which auditory localization is of primary importance in predation, Brainard and Knudsen (1993) found that individuals reared wearing prisms undergo visually-induced changes in the tuning for sound localization cues in the tectum and in the external nucleus of the inferior colliculus (see also Aitkin, 1990; Aronson & Rosenbloom, 1971; Stryker, 1999; Zheng & Knudsen, 1999).

If an auditory 'where' subsystem exists, it would have to combine spatial and somatosensory information. Young, Spirou, Rice, and Voigt (1992) have produced intriguing evidence on this matter. They suggested that the dorsal cochlear nucleus in the cat DGN is responsible for early analysis of sound source location on the basis of two observations: (1) the "DGN principal cells are exquisitely sensitive to spectral features of stimuli that carry sound localization information...", and (2) there is a somatosensory input to the DGN which may be providing information about the orientation of the cat's mobile pinnae, and thus allowing the DGN to integrate pinna-position information with sound localization cues. In humans, there are numerous subcortical areas that are believed to be responsible for cross-modal integration, and which possibly contain a supramodal representation of space (Andersen, Snyder, Bradley, & Xing, 1997; Stein & Meredith, 1993). Audio-visual speech integration studies using fMRI (Calvert, Campbell, & Brammer, 2000) as well as PET studies examining visual-tactile integration (Banati, Goerres, Tjoa, Aggleton, & Grasby, 2000; Macaluso, Frith, & Driver, 2000) provide converging evidence that the superior colliculus, as well as portions of the heteromodal cortex, are likely candidate areas. (See Spence and Driver (1997) for a more complete review of the neurological evidence supporting this idea.)

Let us summarize our argument to this point: (a) sound appears to inform us about

●●●　●●●　●●●　●●●　●●●

Fig. 2. Grouping by proximity (after Wertheimer, 1923/1938).

○ ○ ● ●　○ ○ ● ●　○ ○ ● ●　○ ○ ● ●　○ ○ ● ●

Fig. 3. Grouping by similarity (after Wertheimer, 1923/1938).

sources and events rather than surfaces and material objects; (b) our language suggests to us that objects are visual; and (c) the visual objects we see have considerable control over what we hear. Wightman and Jenison (1995, pp. 371–372) distinguish between *concrete* auditory objects "formed by sounds emitted by real objects in the environment" (i.e. an orchestra) and *abstract* auditory objects, which "do not often correspond to real environmental objects" (i.e. a melody). We differentiate the auditory subsystem that processes these 'concrete' objects – the 'where' subsystem – from the auditory subsystem that processes 'abstract' auditory objects – the 'what' subsystem. To understand the auditory 'what' subsystem, we must abandon visuocentric notions of objecthood and offer a more general definition of perceptual object, be it visual or auditory.

3. 'What' subsystems: objects, grouping, figure-ground, and edges

A *perceptual object* is that which is susceptible to figure-ground segregation. This definition will allow us to develop a useful concept of auditory object. A critic who *defines* figure-ground segregation as a process applied to objects might claim that our definition is circular. But we believe that the benefit of the new definition outweighs the cost of abandoning the definition of figure-ground segregation in terms of objects. We believe that the process of grouping and most forms of feature integration are pre-attentive (Kubovy, Cohen, & Hollier, 1999; see also Bregman, 1990, pp. 206–209). We propose the following view of the relation between early processing, grouping, figure-ground segregation and attention. Early processing produces elements that require grouping. Grouping occurs following the principles described by the Gestalt psychologists (Figs. 2 and 3, from Wertheimer, 1923/1938, further developed by Kubovy, Holcombe, & Wagemans, 1998); it produces Gestalts, or perceptual organizations, which are also putative perceptual objects. Attention selects one putative object (or a small set of them) to become figure (Fig. 4) (Peterson & Gibson, 1994) and relegates all other information to ground (Fig. 5). The putative objects that become figure are perceptual objects, whereas the ground remains undifferentiated information (see Brochard, Drake, Botte, & McAdams, 1999 for evidence that the ground remains undifferentiated in audition).

There is little doubt that grouping and figure-ground segregation describe processes that are meaningful for auditory perception. Grouping is a well-estab-

Fig. 4. Rubin vase/face.

lished auditory phenomenon. In particular, auditory stream formation – the auditory analog of visual grouping – has been studied in depth (Bregman, 1990; Handel, 1989, Chapter 7).

Figure-ground segregation is mentioned less frequently.[3] Nevertheless, in studies of streaming it has often been observed that when an auditory sequence breaks into two streams, we cannot pay attention to more than one of them at a time. For example, Bregman and Campbell (1971) presented observers with a repeating sequence of three high pitch notes (ABC) and three low pitch notes (123) in the order A–1–B–2–C–3. Observers typically reported the order of notes as A–B–C–1–2–3 or 1–2–3–A–B–C; they were able to attend to one stream or the other, but not both streams simultaneously. As in vision, whichever stream is being attended becomes the figure and the other the ground.

3.1. Plensensory functions and edges

Another phenomenon characterizes visual objects: the formation and assignment of edges. When the faces in Fig. 4 are seen in the foreground, they take ownership of

---

[3] Many forms of music use a drone, a low-pitched sustained tone that serves as an auditory background for music played at a higher pitch. The word suggests that a musical drone resembles the hum produced by bees. Drones were common in antiquity; today they appear in the music of the Balkans, Sardinia, Appalachia, and India, to name just a few.

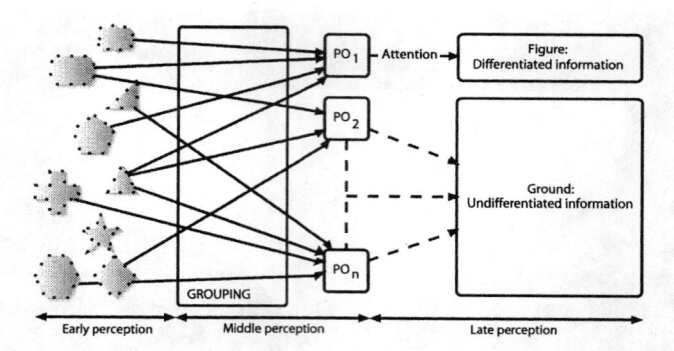

Fig. 5. A conservative view of the formation of perceptual objects. Early processing produces elements that undergo grouping to produce $PO_1, PO_2, ..., PO_n$, a set of perceptual organizations (or putative objects – recall that we have defined an object as the result of figure-ground segregation; therefore, these elements are merely *candidates* for objecthood). Attention is required to produce figure-ground segregation, which allocates processing capacity to the figure and leaves the ground relatively undifferentiated.

the two edges and the background appears to continue behind them. Let us suppose that *any object, be it visual or auditory, must have an edge or a boundary*.

What kinds of edges can be found in optic and acoustic information? To answer this question for vision, Adelson and Bergen (1991) developed the *plenoptic function*, which allows us to characterize edges in the optic information available at every point in space and time. But, as we will see, as soon as we try to construct an analogous *plenacoustic function*, we will face difficult theoretical questions, which we will try to answer in the course of this paper.

The plenoptic function (Fig. 6) is a formalized answer to the question, What can potentially be seen? It is the culmination of a line of thought that began with Leonardo da Vinci that was introduced into the study of perception by Gibson (1979) and further explored by Johansson and Orjesson (1989), who put the idea as follows:

> The central concept of ecological optics is the ambient optic array at a point of observation. To be an *array* means to have an arrangement, and to be *ambient at a point* means to surround a position in the environment that could be occupied by an observer. The position may or may not be occupied; for the present let us treat it as if it were not.[4] (p. 65)

The construction of the plenoptic function starts with a viewpoint, $V(x,y,z)$. We place a box with a pinhole (called a *pinhole camera*) at V, pointing in the direction (ϕ,θ)

---

[4] In this sense, our figures are slightly misleading because we have inserted pictures of eyes at points of observation in space.

Fig. 6. Two points of the plenoptic function for viewpoints V_1 and V_2. Each arrow, light or dark, corresponds to a pencil of rays in direction (θ,ϕ). The dark arrows correspond to what might be seen by eyes at V_1 and V_2. (Slightly modified and redrawn from Fig. 1.3 in Adelson and Bergen (1991).)

(Fig. 7).[5] At the back of the camera is a spectrograph. We obtain a record of the intensity of light as a function of two variables: wavelength, λ, and time, t. Since we can change the viewpoint and rotate the camera in any direction, what can potentially be seen of a scene from any position is the plenoptic function, $P(\phi,\theta,\lambda,t,x,y,z)$.

Objects that reflect light readily create discontinuities in the plenoptic function: edges. By slicing the plenoptic function along various planes, as in Fig. 8, we can see how edges in these planes correspond to familiar features of the visual world. For example, Fig. 8a shows an edge that does not change in azimuth (ϕ); it is therefore vertical, whereas in Fig. 8b it does not change in tilt (θ), and it is therefore horizontal. Fig. 8h describes the effect of a horizontal movement of the viewpoint without changing either ϕ or θ.

We now turn to the plenacoustic function, in the hope that it will help us think about acoustic edges. But we encounter difficulties from the very outset. We are not sure how to illustrate it. Can we use Fig. 6, except that we replace the eyes with ears but leave the ecology (here, a tree) unchanged? That cannot be right. Even students of auditory navigation (Arias, Curet, Moyano, Joekes, & Blanch, 1993; Ashmead & Wall, 1999; Ashmead et al., 1998; Stoffregen & Pittenger, 1995) do not claim that a tree is a natural object of auditory perception. So we are reminded that the acoustic ecology differs from the optic ecology: as we pointed out earlier, auditory perception is more concerned with sources than with surfaces.

Should we then start from an illustration like Fig. 9? We think that even this

---

[5] We adopt the convention of Euler angles (Goldstein, 1980) according to which ϕ (azimuth) and θ (pitch or tilt) are successive counterclockwise rotations of the camera: ϕ is a rotation about the z-axis, and θ is a rotation about the ξ-axis of the camera in the xy plane.

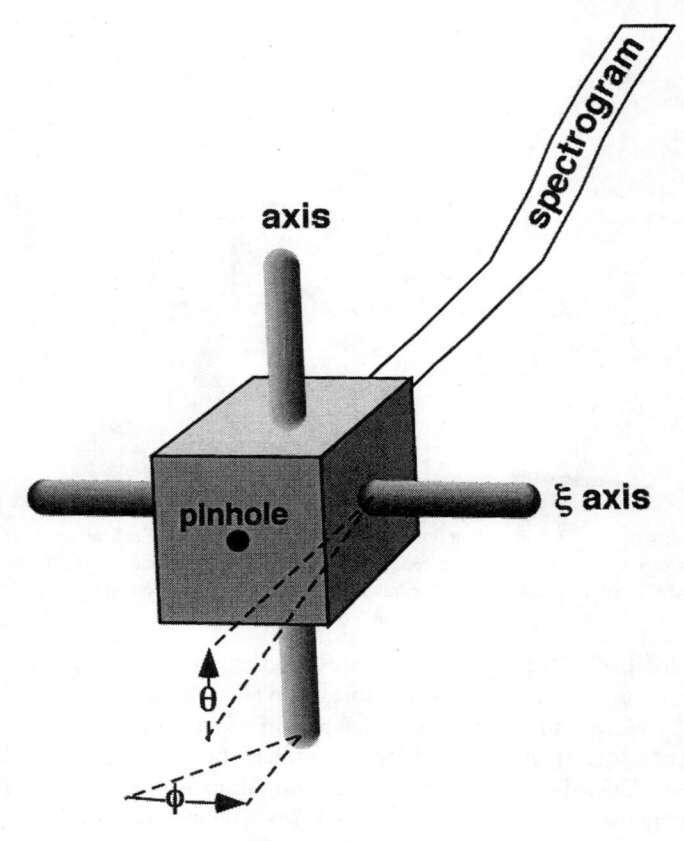

Fig. 7. The pinhole camera.

illustration is misleading, albeit subtly. It draws our attention to the 'where' aspect of audition: *Where* is the screaming boy? *Where* is the crying girl?

Before we can construct a plenacoustic function, we must think through the 'what' aspect of auditory perception. The Kubovy (1981) theory of indispensable attributes (TIA) will prove to be a useful tool in this endeavor.

3.2. *Indispensable attributes, emergent properties, and grouping*

Plensensory functions would suggest to us where edges might occur in the information available to an observer. Here we move beyond the perceptual ecology to examine the evidence that auditory objects are formed in pitch-time, whereas visual objects are formed in space-time. We begin with a series of thought experiments proposed by Kubovy to illustrate his TIA, after which we will present empirical evidence in support of this theory.

The TIA focuses on an important aspect of object formation: the aggregation of elements to form an emergent object. An emergent property is a property of an aggregate that is not present in the aggregated elements. For example, at room

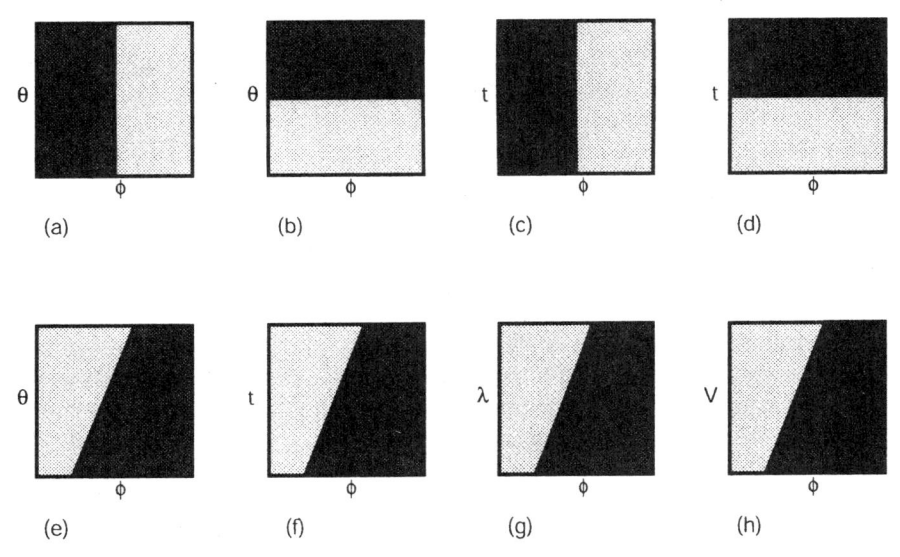

Fig. 8. Some edge-like structures that might be found along particular planes within the plenoptic function (note the varying axes, as labeled on each panel): (a) a vertical edge; (b) a horizontal edge; (c) a stationary edge; (d) a full-field brightening; (e) a tilting edge; (f) a moving edge; (g) a color sweep; (h) an edge with horizontal binocular parallax. (Slightly modified from Fig. 1.4 in Adelson and Bergen (1991).)

Fig. 9. Two points of the plenacoustic function for hearpoints H_1 and H_2. The dark arrows correspond to the sounds that might be least attenuated by the shadow of the head at H_1 and H_2.

temperature, water is a liquid, but the elements that compose it are both gasses. Thus, at room temperature, the property *liquid* is an emergent property of water. There are two kind of emergent properties: *eliminative* and *preservative*. When hydrogen and oxygen combine to form water, the properties of the elements (being gasses) are not observable; they are eliminated by the process of aggregation. In the human sciences such eliminative emergent properties are also common: we can mix two colored lights (say, red and yellow), and observers will not be able to tell whether the orange they see is a spectral orange or a mixture. Thus, color mixture is an eliminative emergent property. Preservative emergent properties were first noticed by Ehrenfels (1890/1988), who described a *melody* as being an emergent property of the set of notes comprising it. The notes can be heard; indeed they *must* be heard for the melody to be recognized. In a melody the elements are preserved in the process of aggregation; in fact the emergence of the melody is conditional upon the audibility of the elements.

The TIA offers a heuristic argument that suggests the conditions under which a perceptual aggregate will preserve the individuality of its elements. More simply, what are the features of stimuli that enable a perceptual system to determine that there is more than one entity in the environment? An attribute (or dimension) is defined as indispensable if and only if it is a prerequisite of perceptual numerosity. As we will show, these attributes are different for vision and for audition.

Spatial separation is an indispensable attribute for vision. Imagine presenting to an observer two spots of light on a surface (Fig. 10a). Both of them are yellow and they coincide; the observer will report one light. Now suppose we change the color of the lights, so that one spot is blue and the other is yellow, but they still coincide (Fig. 10b); the observer will report one white light. For the observer to see more than one light, they must occupy different spatial locations (Fig. 10c).

Pitch separation is an indispensable attribute for sound. Imagine simultaneously playing two 440 Hz sounds for a listener (Fig. 11a). Both of them are played over the same loudspeaker; the listener will report hearing one sound. Now suppose we play these two sounds over two loudspeakers (Fig. 11b); the listener will still report hearing one sound. For the listener to report more than one sound, they must be separated in frequency (Fig. 11c).

By analogous argument, time is an indispensable attribute for both vision and audition. Time thus takes on the role of a common indispensable attribute.

We would like to head off several possible misinterpretations of the TIA. (a) We do *not* claim that auditory spatial cueing is ineffective. On the contrary, we have no doubt that auditory spatial cueing gives rise to costs and benefits (Scharf, 1998). Our claim is that although spatial cueing may be sufficient to draw attention to a pitch, attention is allocated to the *pitch*, not to its *location*. (b) We do not claim that indispensable attributes are prerequisites of perceptual numerosity at every point. For example, consider Fig. 12. It would be foolish of us to claim that we do not see two planes at X. Rather, we see two overlapping objects, and we see them occupying different extensions in space. In audition, an analogous case is homophonic induction (Warren, 1982). Homophonic induction occurs when observers are played a long pure tone with periodic amplitude increases: we hear one continuous tone and a

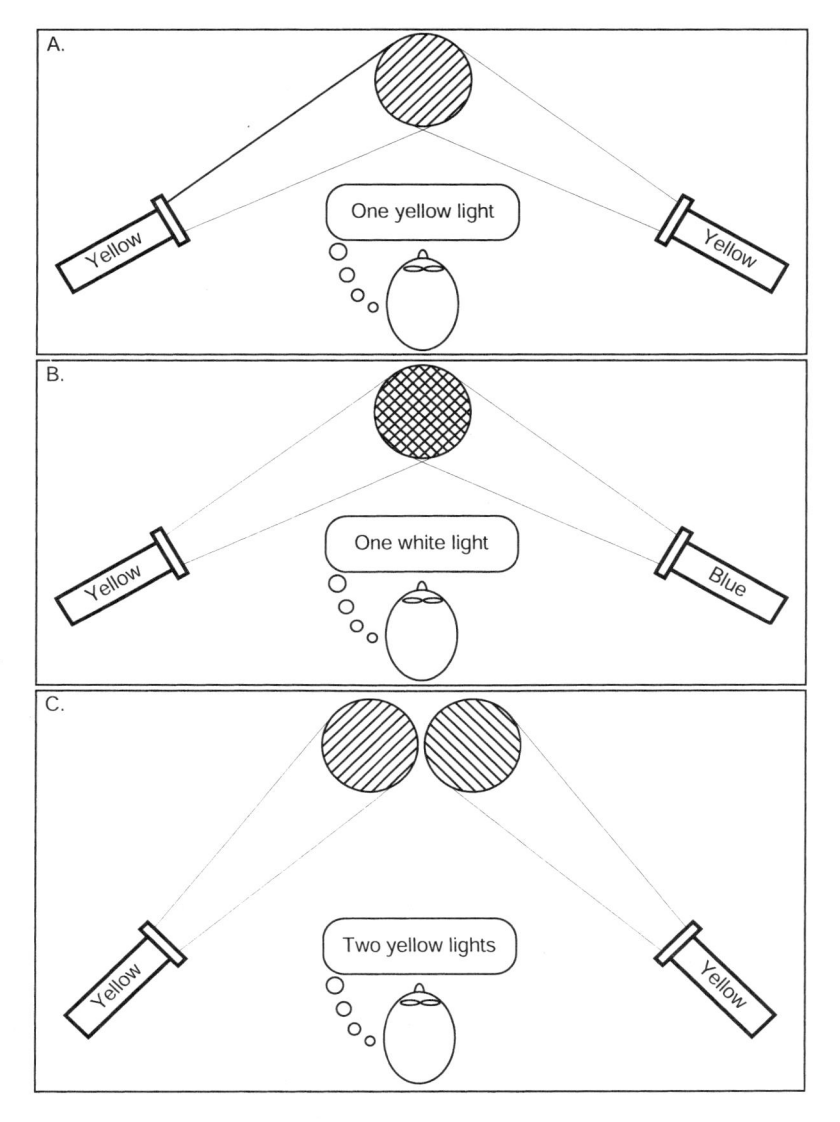

Fig. 10. (a) Two yellow spotlights create coincident spots. The observer sees one yellow spot. (b) One yellow spotlight and one blue spotlight create coincident spots. The observer sees one white spot. (c) Two spotlights create separate spots. Regardless of their color, the observer sees two spots.

second intermittent tone of the same pitch. Thus, we hear two overlapping objects, and we hear them occupying different extensions in time.

We draw the following conclusions from our thought experiments. (a) In vision space is an indispensable attribute for perceptual numerosity; color is not. (b) In audition frequency is an indispensable attribute for perceptual numerosity; space is not. (c) In both, time is an indispensable attribute.

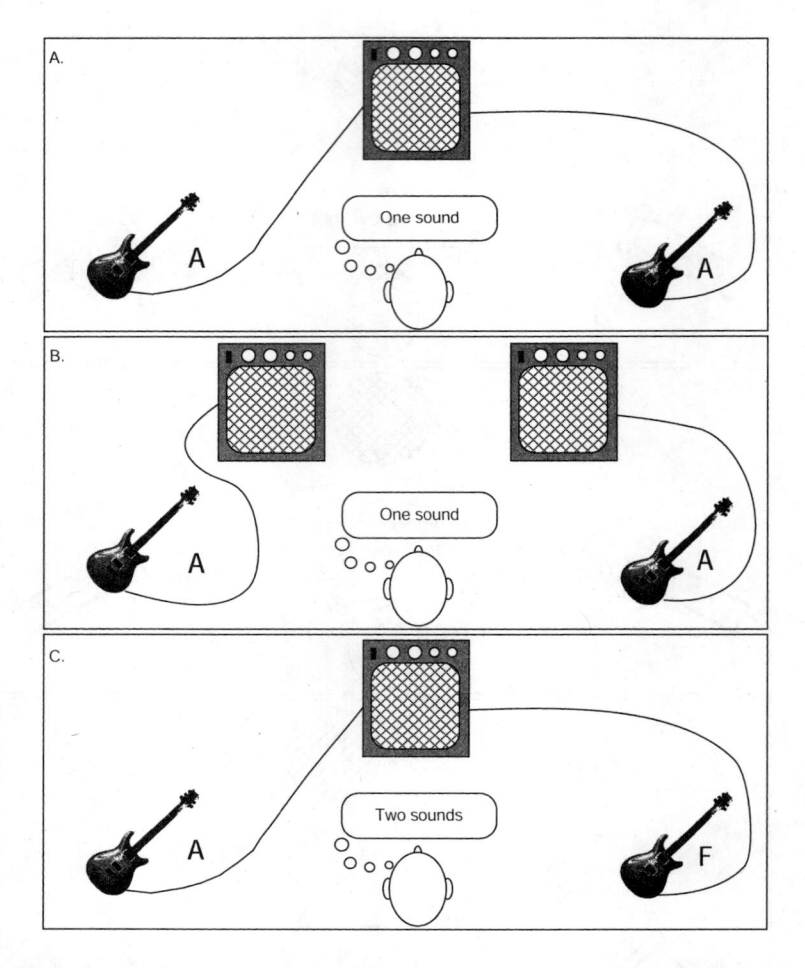

Fig. 11. (a) One loudspeaker plays two *A*s. The listener hears one *A* sound. (b) One loudspeaker plays an *A* while another speaker plays an *A*. The listener hears one *A* sound. (c) An *A* and an *F* are played. Regardless of whether they are played over one loudspeaker or two, the listener hears two sounds, an *A* and an *F*.

3.3. Indispensable attributes and edges

Earlier we could not construct a plenacoustic function because we did not know enough to map optics onto acoustics. With the TIA in hand, we can conjecture that we will find contours in the indispensable attributes of each modality. Looking back at Fig. 8 we observe that in each of the eight panels, one of the axes of the plane is spatial or temporal.

Likewise, in audition, we find edges in pitch, and edges in time, but not in space. The claim that there are edges in pitch may seem strange, but a moment's thought will show that the idea is quite natural. A biologically important source is periodic, at least over short periods of time. Therefore, it is characterized by a *fundamental frequency* that can be thought of as its lower edge in pitch. As we mentioned earlier,

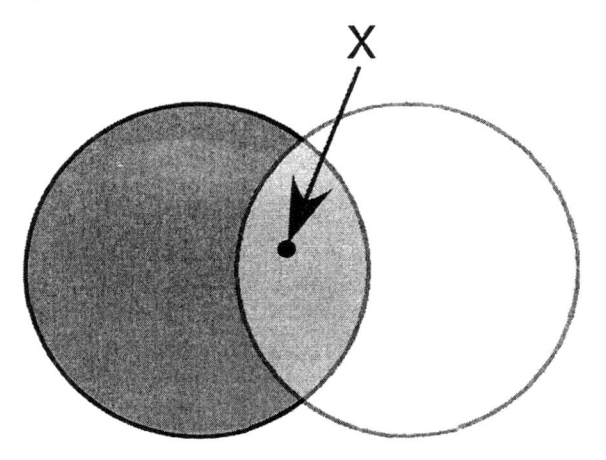

Fig. 12. Transparency: observers perceive two planes at X.

the object delimited can be schematically represented by its spectrum, as shown in Fig. 13. It is further characterized by the shape of its leading edge in pitch-time, its *attack*, and its trailing edge in pitch-time, its *decay*.

3.4. Interim conclusions

Up to here we have done two things. (a) We have argued in favor of an auditory 'where' subsystem that is linked to visuomotor orientation. (b) We have offered a new definition of perceptual objecthood, and we have shown that it implies a new way of thinking about auditory objects. We also made an assumption: in perceptual systems that have separate 'what' and 'where' subsystems, the 'what' subsystems are responsible for the generation of perceptual objects. We now turn to a fundamental question: what is the evidence for two auditory subsystems?

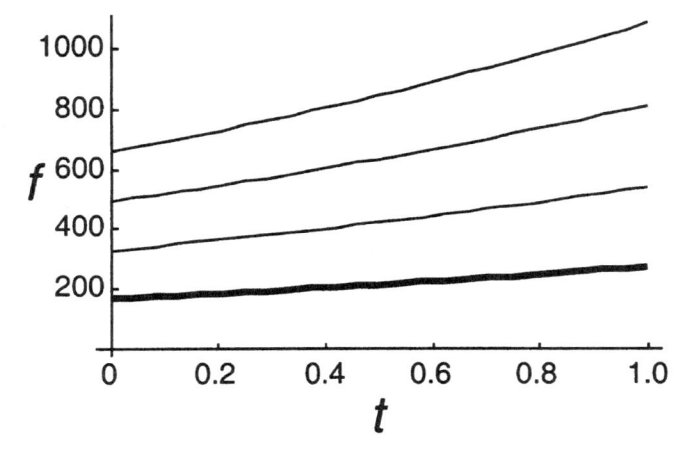

Fig. 13. An example of an auditory object. The first four harmonics of a tone gliding from 165 to 272 Hz over 1 s. The fundamental (the thick line) is the edge of the object.

4. Evidence for two auditory subsystems

The idea of a parallel between the two visual subsystems and two auditory subsystems is gaining favor (Cisek & Turgeon, 1999). Unfortunately, the evidence for a separation of streams in the auditory system is scattered in the literature and may not be sufficiently strong to be conclusive. We turn first to behavioral evidence, and then present neurophysiological evidence.

It is possible to create an auditory illusion in which the 'what' of a stimulus is perceived correctly, but the 'where' is perceived incorrectly. Deustch and Roll (1976) created a stimulus that consists of a sequence of five pairs of concurrent dichotic tones. Let us denote by A a 400 Hz tone lasting 250 ms, and by B an 800 Hz tone of the same duration. The right ear receives *AAABB* (with 250 ms pauses between tones) and the other receives *BBBAA*. Right-handed listeners report hearing *AAABB*, but they hear the first three tones as if they came to the right ear and the remaining two as if they came to the left. Thus, they dissociated the two subsystems, because the dominant ear determines 'what' is heard, but the localization of the sounds (the 'where') is illusory.

Under some conditions, adaptation affects localization but not pitch perception. Hafter (1997) studied adaptation to trains of high-frequency clicks. He presented click trains in which the clicks had an inter-aural time disparity (ITD), so that listeners heard the clicks localized to the right or to the left. The listeners showed *binaural adaptation*: the effectiveness of the inter-aural information in the click train gradually diminished. He then presented listeners with trains of clicks that give rise to *periodicity pitch*, which is controlled by the inter-click interval (ICI). He asked listeners to discriminate changes in the pitch they heard when he changed the ICI. He found that the listeners suffered no adaptation in the performance of this task.

A somewhat indirect piece of behavioral evidence in favor of two auditory subsystems comes from experiments on the distribution of auditory response times. Wynn (1977) collected more than 300 000 response times from observers who were asked to tap in synchrony with a visual or auditory pulse. The distribution of RTs to visual pulses was unimodal. But the distribution of RTs to auditory pulses was bimodal, with many more fast responses than slow ones. As he increased the intensity of the sounds, three phenomena emerged: (a) the modes did not shift; (b) the humps became narrower; and (c) the mode of slow RTs diminished. From this Wynn concludes that there are two pathways in audition: one 'slow' and one 'fast'.

There also is neurophysiological evidence in favor of our hypothesis. On the basis of single-unit and tracer studies in cats and macaques as well as results from PET and fMRI experiments on humans, Rauschecker (1997, 1998a,b) argues that the auditory system has a dorsal 'where' stream and a ventral 'what' stream. Vocal communication sounds – presumably processed by a 'what' subsystem – project into areas of the lateral belt (and parabelt) of the superior temporal cortex. Auditory spatial information – presumably processed by a 'where' subsystem – projects into parietal areas. Studies of human patients with left hemispheric lesions provide a double dissociation between the two subsystems (Clarke, Bellmann, Meuli, Assal, & Steck, 2000). Patients with lesions in the medial, posterior auditory cortex (which Clarke et al., 2000 call the 'putative spatial pathway') exhibit localization deficits, whereas more lateral lesions (in the 'putative recognition pathway') cause recognition deficits.

5. Relations between 'what' and 'where' in vision and audition

We have suggested that the auditory 'where' subsystem is probably in the service of the visuomotor subsystem. The visual 'where' subsystem provides us with spatial information about the world in egocentric terms (Milner & Goodale, 1995). We believe the same to be true about the auditory 'where' subsystem. In other words, both the visual and the auditory 'where' subsystems may be thought of as being in the service of action.

It is harder to describe the relation between the visual and the auditory 'what' subsystems. We suggested earlier that they both are concerned with the segregation of figure from ground and the grouping of elements into objects. In vision this conception does not create a disjunction between the products of the 'what' and the 'where' subsystems, although the mechanisms are dissociable. Visual objects are extended in space, and they are located in space. So in vision the two subsystems seem to work to the same end: collecting information about a unified spatiotemporal reality.

In audition, however, distinguishing between the two subsystems creates what might be called an ontological chasm. The kinds of objects the auditory 'what' subsystem constructs need not be located in space, nor do they need to be defined in spatial terms. Nevertheless, if we surmise that the origin of the auditory 'what' subsystem is in vocal communication, then its non-spatiality becomes somewhat less puzzling.

The problem we encountered earlier, when we were considering the possibility of constructing a plenacoustic function, may be called the *dimension mapping question*: which dimensions of the optical input are analogous to which dimensions of the acoustic input? *The answer depends on our view of these inputs.* If we think of them in spatiotemporal terms, then the spatial and temporal dimensions in the two inputs will correspond to each other. Thus, six dimensions of the plenoptic function, $\phi, \theta, t, V_x, V_y, V_z$, map onto six dimensions of a putative plenacoustic function, $\phi, \theta, t, H_x, H_y, H_z$. We call this the *spatiotemporal mapping*. If, on the other hand, we think of the plensensory functions in terms of object formation, then the analogous dimensions in the two functions are those that allow for the formation of edges in the plenoptic and the plenacoustic functions. We call this mapping the *indispensable attributes mapping*.

5.1. The spatiotemporal mapping

Under the spatiotemporal mapping visual space and time are mapped onto auditory space and time. This is a natural view to take in the light of the assumptions made by Newton (1726/1999): "Absolute, true, and mathematical time, in and of itself and of its own nature, without reference to anything external, flows uniformly... Absolute space, of its own nature without reference to anything external, always remains homogeneous and immovable ... times and spaces are, as it were, the places of themselves and of all things" (pp. 408–410). In his *Critique of Pure Reason*, Kant (1787/1996) took Newton's idea further: "Space is not an empirical concept that has been abstracted from outer experiences. For the presentation of space must already lie at the basis in order for certain sensations to be referred to something outside of me..." (p. 77, B 38).[6] "Time is not an empirical concept that has been abstracted from any experience. For simultaneity or succession would not even enter our perception if the presentation of time did not underlie them a priori" (p. 85, B 46).

Newton and Kant were powerful influences. It was natural for early psychologists to adopt the spatiotemporal mapping. From this mapping they concluded that color gets mapped onto pitch, since they are non-spatial and non-temporal, and since they are both caused by waves. For example, we read a footnote by A.J. Ellis, translator of *Sensations of Tone* by Helmholtz (1885/1954):

> Assuming the undulatory theory, which attributes the sensation of light to the vibration of a supposed luminous 'ether', resembling air but more delicate and mobile, then the phenomena of 'interference' enables us to calculate the lengths of waves of light in empty space, &c., hence the numbers of vibrations in a second, and consequently the ratios of these numbers, which will then clearly resemble the ratios of pitch numbers that measure musical intervals. Assuming, then, that the yellow of the spectrum answers to the tenor c in music, and Fraunhaufer's 'line A' corresponds to the G below it, Prof. Helmholtz, in his *Physiological Optics* (*Handbuch der Physiologischen Optik*, 1867, p. 237), gives the following analogies between the notes of the piano and the colors of the spectrum:
>
> G, Red,
> $G\#$, Red,
> A, Red
> $A\#$, Orange-red,
> B, Orange,
> c, Yellow,
> $c\#$, Green,
> d, Greenish-blue,
> $d\#$, Cyanogen-blue
> e, Indigo-blue,
> f, Violet,
>
> g, Ultra-violet,
> $g\#$, Ultra-violet,
> a, Ultra-violet,
> $a\#$, Ultra-violet,
> b, end of the solar spectrum.
> The scale therefore extends to about a Fourth beyond the octave.
>
> (p. 18)

---

[6] This is the traditional way to denote p. 38 in the second edition of the *Critique*.

As profound differences between light and sound became clear in the twentieth century, psychologists abandoned the exploration of parallels between pitch and color. But the rest of the spatiotemporal mapping has been retained. Research on the 'cocktail party problem' is an excellent example. How do we segregate a speaker's voice from the voices of other concurrent speakers at a cocktail party? To Cherry (1959), who coined the term, the problem was a spatial one. All of his experiments involved dichotic listening: the listener hears a different message in each ear and has to report something from one or both. The assumption of the primacy of space in audition is even clearer in Broadbent (1958): "Sounds reaching the two ears are of course often perceived as coming from different directions ... and such sounds we will regard as arriving by different 'channels'" (p. 15). In this context the auditory system was considered to be a 'where' system, and auditory segregation was thought to be spatial in nature.

The implicit assumption of the auditory system as a 'where' system persists. For example, Handel (1988) criticized the original formulation of the TIA (Kubovy, 1981) for this very reason (for a reply, see Kubovy, 1988): "The auditory and visual worlds are inherently both temporal and spatial" (p. 315). For this reason, Handel opposed Kubovy's commitment to the TIA mapping and claimed that all mappings are possible and relevant, depending on the context. Although we have come somewhat closer to Handel's position by proposing two mappings, we are making a more specific claim. For the 'where' subsystems the spatiotemporal mapping is appropriate; for the 'what' subsystems the TIA mapping is appropriate.

5.2. The indispensable attributes mapping

We believe that the TIA mapping will allow researchers to formulate testable hypotheses about the nature of auditory objects and auditory object perception. The TIA is a heuristic tool for extending theories of visual perception into the domain of auditory perception (and perhaps vice-versa). Note that such extensions have been done in the past with considerable success. For example, Bregman (1990) has shown the similarities between the Gestalt principles in vision and in audition. Just as grouping by proximity functions in visual space (Kubovy et al., 1998), it also operates in auditory pitch (Bregman, 1990). McPherson, Ciocca, and Bregman (1994) have shown that good continuation operates in audition in an analogous way to vision. The concept of amodal completion as it is used in vision (Kanizsa, 1979) has been given a number of different names in audition: the acoustic tunnel effect (Vicario, 1960), perceptual restoration (Warren, 1970, 1984), the continuity effect (Bregman, 1990), and the phonemic restoration effect (Samuel, 1991). Since all of these phenomena abide by the same laws of grouping and organization, a desirable goal would be to have a theoretical framework which can account for this. The TIA is such a framework.

5.3. Implications for theories of attention

An attentional counterpart of TIA – which we will abbreviate to ATIA – could come in two versions: *strong* and *weak*. According to a strong ATIA, selective attention can *only* be directed to indispensable attributes, and not to other stimulus attributes. For example, the strong ATIA predicts that in vision you can pay attention to a region of space (or to an object defined by its spatial boundaries), but not to a part of color space. The work of Shih and Sperling (1996) favors such a position. They have shown that visual selective attention can be directed to space but not to color or size. On each trial of the experiment they presented a series of briefly presented frames (typically 27 of them). In each frame six letters were presented, equidistant from a fixation point. The characters in a frame were uniformly colored red or green. In one of these frames one letter was replaced with a digit. The observer's task was to report the digit's name, location, and color. The dependent variable was the observer's report accuracy. Before each trial the observer was given information (not always valid) about the color of the digit. The main result was this: the observers' accuracy was not affected by the validity of the cue. In a second experiment the color of the digit differed from the color of the letters, and observers did show a cost or benefit that depended on the validity of the cue. Thus, color can *draw* our attention to spatial locations, we cannot selectively attend to color – only to spatial locations.

According to a weak ATIA selective attention is generally directed towards indispensable attributes, but *can* be directed towards other attributes. For example, color is not an indispensable attribute, yet color-based inhibition of return (IOR) has been reported. Law, Pratt, and Abrams (1995) showed observers two successive color patches in the center of a monitor, with an ISI of 900 ms. They asked observers to respond as soon as they detected the second patch. When the two colors were the same, RTs were ≈ 5.5 ms longer than when the colors were different. We note, however, that the magnitude of the inhibition observed in this experiment is much lower than the effects observed with space-based IOR. The authors themselves acknowledge that "the color-based inhibition of return that we observed might be reduced or eliminated in situations with spatial uncertainty" (p. 407). We therefore await further progress on this topic before we retreat from the strong ATIA.

5.4. Costs of not adhering to indispensable attributes

The spatiotemporal mapping implies that space holds the same status in audition as it does in vision. Culling and Summerfield (1995) have argued the contrary: "the introspective impression that one can concentrate on a particular direction in order to pick out an attended voice from an interfering babble may be misleading. ...there is evidence that localization occurs after concurrent sounds have been separated by other processes" (p. 796). In other words, auditory objects are *not* formed in space. This assertion is supported by three experiments in which Culling and Summerfield explored the role of within-channel and across-channel processes in the perceptual separation of competing sounds that had different inter-aural phase spectra. A similar position is adopted by Darwin and Hukin (1999) in regards to speech sounds. They claim (on p. 622, illustrated in their Fig. 3, right-hand panel) that auditory objects are the result of non-spatial grouping processes (e.g. harmonicity and onset time). Once an object is formed, listeners can direct their attention to it, and even attend to its direction. This is precisely what we have been arguing.

Reliance on the spatiotemporal mapping may have led researchers to the erroneous conclusion that attention operates differently in vision and in audition. For example, Posner (1978) attempted to obtain spatial cueing effects in a variety of tasks, using endogenous, or top-down, cues. Even though his attempt failed, Spence and Driver (1994) determined that "it is clear that endogenous mechanisms of spatial auditory attention must exist at some level of processing: otherwise we could not achieve such textbook feats, such as selectively shadowing a message from one location while ignoring a message from a different location" (p. 557). So Spence and Driver do not believe Posner's data because they are not consistent with the spatio-temporal mapping. Butchel and Butter (1988) used exogenous spatial cues and found spatial cueing effects in vision but not in audition. They argue that due to the lack of a 'fovea-like' area in audition, there is no spatial attention in audition.

According to Spence and Driver (1994) there may be several reasons why Butchel and Butter (1988), Posner (1978), and Scharf, Quigley, Aoki, Peachey, and Reeves (1987) failed to find an auditory IOR. (a) Audition is poorer than vision with respect to spatial localization, and so maybe past experimenters failed to utilize sufficient angular separation. (b) The intensity of the peripheral cues may have been insufficient to draw attention. (c) Because RTs in auditory detection/discrimination tasks are generally faster than in vision, the auditory response speeds may have been at ceiling because the tasks may not have been sufficiently demanding. (d) Perhaps the previous tasks were performed without engaging the spatial aspects of audition. In an extensive set of experiments, Spence and Driver showed that when the auditory spatial localization subsystem is engaged by the task, attentional effects appear. Observers were given exogenous cues at the lateral midline from either the left or the right with a sound that they were to ignore and which did not predict the lateralization of the target. Later observers were presented with a target sound on either the same side or the opposite side as the cue. Their task was to press one of two buttons as quickly as possible to indicate where the target was located. Targets were presented either in front of/behind (Experiment 1) or above/below the lateral midline (Experiment 2). They found an advantage for valid cues at ISI = 100 ms, but not at ISI = 400 ms or ISI = 1000 ms. There was no IOR. This was interpreted by Spence and Driver as being evidence for a short-lived advantage due to exogenous orientation. When the observers were required to make a frequency discrimination instead of a localization judgement (Experiment 3) the advantage on the cued side disappeared. Spence and Driver concluded that when the task demands are not based on localization, there is no attentional effect of spatial cueing in audition.

In a subsequent report, Spence and Driver (1998) argue that IOR operates differently in vision and audition. They showed that auditory RT *was not* affected by the location of the auditory target that appeared on the preceding trial, whereas visual detection RT *was* affected by the location of the visual target on the preceding trial. Only when targets were unpredictably auditory or visual did this effect occur between auditory targets presented on successive trials. Quinlan and Hill (1999) explained the auditory IOR in the modality-uncertain condition of Spence and Driver (1998) as a 'modality' switching effect. In a series of three experiments, observers made left/right localization judgments to either visual or auditory signals. In the first two experiments, observers were given a cue indicating the signal's modality, whereas in the third experiment the observers were not cued. The difference between the first and second experiments was the ISI between the modality cue and the subsequent presentation. The results of Experiment 1 (ISI = 50 ms) show that there is a cost to switching between modalities between trials. Observers were significantly slower when the modality changed between experimental trials. In Experiment 2 (ISI = 500 ms), where observers had time to prepare for the switch between modalities, the effect disappeared. Quinlan and Hill interpreted this result as an indication that the costs seen in Experiment 1 were due to the modality switching, and further, that modality switching requires attention. Finally, in Experiment 3, Quinlan and Hill showed that when there is no modality preparatory signal and ISI = 500 ms, the costs associated with modality switching re-emerge. They concluded that the effects seen in this and in Spence and Driver (1998) were the result of modality switching, not IOR. We believe that the above studies examined the 'where' component of the auditory system. Many researchers have hypothesized that this link occurs in the superior colliculus (Abrams & Dobkin, 1994; Goldring et al., 1996; Hughes et al., 1998; Spence & Driver, 1994; Tipper, Weaver, Jerreat, & Burak, 1994).

A TIA viewpoint would lead to a different experiment: instead of having tones vary in location, they would vary in pitch. Under *these* circumstances, we would expect to observe auditory IOR. (We are puzzled by the results of Mondor and Breau (1999) and Mondor, Breau, and Milliken (1998), who found frequency-based IOR, but also localization-based IOR. We are currently replicating their work.)

5.5. Benefits of indispensable attributes

When the TIA mapping is used, further analogies as well as an interesting separation between the auditory and the visual 'what' subsystems emerge. Duncan, Martens, and Ward (1997) report on experiments in which observers were asked to identify a stimulus shortly after they had deployed their attention to another stimulus (to study the so-called 'attentional blink', AB). In one experiment the stimuli were visual: they consisted of two streams of written trigrams ('xxx', 150 ms long, separated by an ISI of 100 ms). One stream consisted of a pair of trigrams above and below a fixation cross; the other consisted of a pair of trigrams to the right and the left of the fixation cross. One stream lagged behind the other by 125 ms. Each stream contained one target trigram ('nap', 'nab', 'cod', or 'cot'). The participants were asked to report which target trigrams they had seen. When the two target trigrams were 125 or 375 ms apart, the identification of the later trigram was depressed, i.e. an AB was observed. In a second experiment the stimuli were auditory: they consisted of two streams (one high-pitched, the other low-pitched) of spoken syllables ('guh', 150 ms long, separated by an ISI of 100 ms). One stream lagged behind the other by 125 ms. Each stream contained one target syllable ('nap', 'nab', 'cod', or 'cot'). The listeners were asked to report which target syllables they heard. If the two target syllables were 125 or 375 ms apart, the identification of the later syllable was depressed, i.e. an AB was observed. The auditory and the visual results were remarkably similar. In a third experiment one stream was visual and the other was auditory. No AB was observed. This result does not only fit what we would expect, given the TIA mapping, it also shows that the two 'what' subsystems are not linked. Despite these results, some research has shown that cross-modal AB can be elicited under certain circumstances (Arnell & Jolicoeur, 1999; Potter, Chun, Banks, & Muckenhoupt, 1998) – therefore tending to favor a weaker version of the ATIA. Arnell and Jolicoeur (1999), for example, have shown that if the target presentation rate is under 120 ms/item, then cross-modal AB is observable. Arnell and Jolicoeur argue that this cross-modal AB occurs because of a central processing limitation.

According to Treisman and Gelade (1980), if a target differs in one feature from a set of distracters (e.g. an O among Xs or a red O among green Os) the RT to find the target is independent of the number of distracters. If a difference between the target and the distracters is a conjunction of features (e.g. a green O among green Xs and red Os) then the RT varies with the number of distracters. It is as if targets in the single feature condition spontaneously segregated themselves from the other elements, but failed to do so when they were defined by a conjunction. An analogous phenomenon has been demonstrated by Lenoble (1986). Her work built upon a demonstration of concurrent-pitch segregation by Kubovy, Cutting, and McGuire (1974), in which listeners heard seven equal-intensity binaural tones. When the ITD of individual tones was manipulated, listeners were able to hear a melody segregated from the complex even though it was not audible in either ear alone. When Lenoble (1986) presented observers with tone complexes in which target tones were defined by a conjunction of ITD and amplitude or frequency modulation, concurrent-pitch segregation did not occur.

An interesting (and testable) hypothesis is that observers are only able to allocate voluntary attention to indispensable attributes. The Shih and Sperling (1996) results indicate that observers are able to voluntarily devote attention to space, but that only space could be attended to in this way. This would mean that in audition, observers would only be able to allocate attention to particular frequencies or pitch space and not to other features such as rise time, intensity, or space. While to our knowledge a critical test of this hypothesis has not been made, there are results which suggest that this may indeed be the case. Mondor and Terrio (1998) conducted a series of five experiments designed to examine the role of selective attention and pattern structure in audition. They presented observers with a sequence of ascending or descending tones and the observer was to make a speeded response to a target tone that differed from the non-targets in duration, rise time, or intensity, or the target tone contained a 1 ms gap. Target tones could be consistent with the overall pattern structure or inconsistent (in frequency). When targets fell on tones that were consistent with the overall pattern structure observers were not more sensitive or faster to make a response. When targets fell on tones inconsistent with the overall pattern structure, however, observers remained equally sensitive (as measured by d') but were significantly faster to detect the targets. Deviations in frequency from an established pattern were sufficient to draw attention and thus enhance the detection of these features when they fell on an inconsistent target. The implication of these studies is that frequency is more important than duration, rise time, intensity, or the presence of a gap for auditory selective attention mechanisms (although we acknowledge that the evidence would be stronger had Mondor and Terrio (1998) tested the analogous case – where pattern inconsistency is defined by, for example, duration or rise time).

The following experiment could serve as a critical test of the hypothesis that observers can only voluntarily allocate attention to indispensable attributes. We would place listeners in front of a linear array of four loudspeakers (i.e. two on each side of the observer's midline). We would use five different instrumental sounds: a target (i.e. a bassoon) and four distracters (i.e. a flute, a guitar, a piano, and a trumpet), chosen so that they are easily distinguishable. On each trial, we would play a series of brief 'frames' of sound, each of which would comprise the four distracter instruments. Each of the instruments would be played from a different speaker and at a different frequency. In one of the frames we would replace one of the distracters with the target instrument (the bassoon). We would ask the listeners to determine which frame contained the target. Before each trial we would give the listeners one of two types of cues: (a) a spatial cue (e.g. informing them that the target is 80% likely to come from the left), or (b) a pitch cue (e.g. informing them that the target is 80% likely to be high-pitched). According to the TIA there should be no cost or benefit from spatial cues, because listeners cannot allocate attention to a spatial location, but there should be costs and benefits associated with pitch cues.

6. Overview

In summary, consider Fig. 14. On the left side of the diagram we have set out the characteristics of audition, and on the right we have done so for vision. Each of the modalities is represented by two pathways, one labeled 'what' and the other labeled 'where'. We should stress that we are using the term 'where' as shorthand for the sense of Milner and Goodale (1995), i.e. a subsystem that maintains spatial information in egocentric coordinates for the purpose of controlling action. That is why we sometimes refer to it in this paper as a visuo*motor* system.

In the center of the diagram we show that the auditory and the visual 'where' subsystems are tightly linked. This is because of the evidence (see Section 2) that the auditory 'where' subsystem is in the service of the visual 'where' subsystem. We connected these two subsystems with a thick line to indicate their linkage, and added an arrow to this line to indicate the asymmetric relation between them (one is in the service of the other). The two subsystems are mapped onto each other with the traditional spatiotemporal mapping.

To either side of the 'where' subsystem(s) we represent the 'what' subsystems.

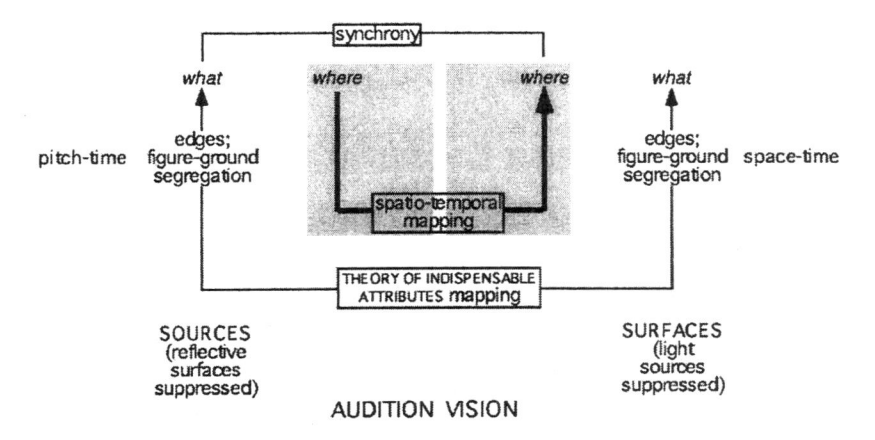

Fig. 14. Summary of the theory.

Here we show that the key operation of both the visual and the auditory 'what' subsystems is figure-ground segregation and edge formation (see Section 3.1). We also indicate that the auditory operation occurs in pitch-time, whereas the visual operation occurs in space-time (see Section 3.2). We connected these two subsystems with a thin line to indicate that they are analogous, and that the heuristic we offer to draw analogies between the two is the TIA. When we use the term 'analogy' we do not wish to take a stand on whether they are *merely* analogous, i.e. that they evolved separately, or whether they might be *homologous*, i.e. they have some common evolutionary origin.

We also note a link between the visual 'where' and auditory 'what' which represents the ventriloquism effect, in which synchronous visual and auditory events can determine the auditory localization.

Finally, we remind the reader (in the lower left and right corners of the auditory and visual boxes) of a fundamental difference between the two subsystems (summarized in Table 1).

7. Conclusion

The human cortex contains 10^{10} neurons. Up to half of these may be involved in visual function (Palmer, 1999, p. 24); the auditory system is much smaller. This seems to confirm that reality unfolds in space and time and that understanding is visual. But we believe that the main source of resistance to a non-visuocentric view of perception is the 'Knowing is Seeing' metaphor. According to Lakoff and Johnson (1999, Table 4.1, pp. 53–54) this metaphor (summarized in Table 2) is a tool all of us use to understand the idea of knowing.

We hope that our analysis will enable us to hear more clearly the polyphony between the two voices in the complex counterpoint between vision and audition.

Table 2
The Knowing is Seeing primary metaphor (Lakoff & Johnson, 1999, pp. 393–394)

Visual domain	Knowledge domain
Object seen	→ Idea
Seeing an object clearly	→ Knowing an idea
Person who sees	→ Person who knows
Light	→ 'Light' of reason
Visual focusing	→ Mental attention
Visual acuity	→ Intellectual acuity
Physical viewpoint	→ Mental viewpoint
Visual obstruction	→ Impediment to knowing

Acknowledgements

We wish to thank B.J. Scholl and J. Mehler for their superb editorial work on this paper. We are also grateful to those who contributed in various ways to this paper: A. Bregman, R.S. Bolia, C. Spence, S. Handel, C.L. Krumhansl, J.G. Neuhoff, B. Repp, M. Turgéon, and A.J. Watkins. Our work is supported by NEI grant No. R01 EY 12926-06.

References

Abrams, R. A., & Dobkin, R. S. (1994). Inhibition of return: effects of attentional cuing on eye movement latencies. *Journal of Experimental Psychology: Human Perception and Performance, 20* (3), 467–477.

Adelson, E. H., & Bergen, J. R. (1991). The plenoptic function and the elements of early vision. In M. S. Landy, & J. A. Movshon (Eds.), *Computational models of visual processing* (pp. 3–20). Cambridge, MA: MIT Press.

Aitkin, L. (1990). Coding for auditory space. In M. J. Rowe, & L. Aitkin (Eds.), *Information processing in mammalian auditory and tactile systems* (pp. 169–178). New York: Wiley-Liss.

Andersen, R. A., Snyder, L. H., Bradley, D. C., & Xing, J. (1997). Multimodal representation of space in the posterior parietal cortex and its use in planning movements. *Annual Review of Neuroscience, 20*, 303–330.

Angell, J. R. (1906). *Psychology: an introductory study of the structure and function of human conscious* (3rd ed., pp. 141–160). New York: Henry Holt.

Arias, C., Curet, C. A., Moyano, H. F., Joekes, S., & Blanch, N. (1993). Echolacation: a study of auditory functioning in blind and sighted subjects. *Journal of Visual Impairment & Blindness, 87*, 73–77.

Arnell, K. A., & Jolicoeur, P. (1999). The attentional blink across stimulus modalities: evidence for central processing limitations. *Journal of Experimental Psychology: Human Perception and Performance, 25* (3), 630–648.

Aronson, E., & Rosenbloom, S. (1971). Space perception in early infancy: perception within a common auditory-visual space. *Science, 172*, 1161–1163.

Ashmead, D. H., & Wall, R. S. (1999). Auditory perception of walls via spectral variations in the ambient sound field. *Journal of Rehabilitation Research and Development, 36*, 313–322.

Ashmead, D. H., Wall, R. S., Eaton, S. B., Ebinger, K. A., Snook-Hill, M.-M., Guth, D. A., & Yang, X. (1998). Echolocation reconsidered: using spatial variations in the ambient sound field to guide locomotion. *Journal of Visual Impairment & Blindness, 92*, 615–632.

Banati, R. B., Goerres, G. W., Tjoa, C., Aggleton, J. P., & Grasby, P. (2000). The functional anatomy of visuo-tactile integration in man: a study using pet. *Neuropsychologia, 38*, 115–124.

Beranek, L. L. (1988). *Acoustical measurements* (Rev. ed.). Woodbury, NY: American Institute of Physics.

Bertelson, P., & Aschersleben, G. (1998). Automatic visual bias of perceived auditory location. *Psychonomic Bulletin & Review*, 5 (3), 482–489.

Blauert, J. (1997). *Spatial hearing: the psychophysics of human sound localization* (Rev. ed.). Cambridge, MA: MIT Press.

Brainard, M. S., & Knudsen, E. I. (1993). Experience-dependent plasticity in the inferior colliculus: a site for visual calibration of the neural representation of auditory space in the barn owl. *Journal of Neuroscience*, 13, 4589–4608.

Bregman, A. (1990). *Auditory scene analysis: the perceptual organization of sound*. Cambridge, MA: MIT Press.

Bregman, A. S., & Campbell, J. (1971). Primary auditory stream segregation and perception of order in rapid sequences of tones. *Journal of Experimental Psychology*, 89, 244–249.

Broadbent, D. E. (1958). *Perception and communication*. New York: Pergamon Press.

Brochard, R., Drake, C., Botte, M., & McAdams, S. (1999). Perceptual organization of complex auditory sequences: effects of number of simultaneous subsequences and frequency separation. *Journal of Experimental Psychology: Human Perception and Performance*, 25 (6), 1742–1759.

Butchel, H. A., & Butter, C. M. (1988). Spatial attentional shifts: implications for the role of polysensory mechanisms. *Neuropsychologia*, 26, 499–509.

Calvert, G. A., Campbell, R., & Brammer, M. J. (2000). Evidence from functional magnetic resonance imaging of crossmodal binding in human heteromodal cortex. *Current Biology*, 10, 649–657.

Cherry, C. (1959). *On human communication*. Cambridge, MA: MIT Press.

Cisek, P., & Turgeon, M. (1999). 'Binding through the fovea', a tale of perception in the service of action. *Psyche*, 5 http://psyche.cs.monash.edu.au/v5/psyche-5-34-cisek.html, accessed January 2000.

Clarke, S., Bellmann, A., Meuli, R. A., Assal, G., & Steck, A. J. (2000). Auditory agnosia and spatial deficits following left hemispheric lesions: evidence for distinct processing pathways. *Neuropsychologia*, 38, 797–807.

Clifton, R. K. (1992). The development of spatial hearing in human infants. In L. A. Werner, & E. W. Rubel (Eds.), *Developmental psychoacoustics* (pp. 135–157). Washington, DC: APA Press.

Culling, J. F., & Summerfield, Q. (1995). Perceptual separation of concurrent speech sounds: absence of across-frequency grouping by common interaural delay. *Journal of the Acoustical Society of America*, 98 (2), 785–797.

Darwin, C. J., & Hukin, R. W. (1999). Auditory objects of attention: the role of interaural time differences. *Journal of Experimental Psychology: Human Perception and Performance*, 25 (3), 617–629.

Deustch, D., & Roll, P. (1976). Separate "what" and "where" decision mechanisms in processing a dichotic tonal sequence. *Journal of Experimental Psychology: Human Perception and Performance*, 2 (1), 23–29.

Duncan, J., Martens, S., & Ward, R. (1997). Restricted attentional capacity within but not between sensory modalities. *Nature*, 387, 808–809.

Ehrenfels, C. von (1988). On 'gestalt qualities'. In B. Smith (Ed.), *Foundations of gestalt theory* (pp. 82–117). Munich, Germany: Philosophia Verlag. (Original work published 1890)

Gibson, J. J. (1979). *The ecological approach to visual perception*. Hillsdale, NJ: Lawrence Erlbaum.

Goldring, J., Dorris, M., Corneil, B., Balantyne, P., & Munoz, D. (1996). Combined eye-head gaze shifts to visual and auditory targets in humans. *Experimental Brain Research*, 111, 68–73.

Goldstein, H. (1980). *Classical mechanics* (2nd ed.). Reading, MA: Addison-Wesley.

Hafter, E. R. (1997). Binaural adaptation and the effectiveness of a stimulus beyond its onset. In R. H. Gilkey, & T. R. Anderson (Eds.), *Binaural and spatial hearing in real and virtual environments* (pp. 211–232). Mahwah, NJ: Lawrence Erlbaum.

Handel, S. (1988). Space is to time as vision is to audition: seductive but misleading. *Journal of Experimental Psychology: Human Perception and Performance*, 14, 315–317.

Handel, S. (1989). *Listening: an introduction to the perception of auditory events*. Cambridge, MA: MIT Press.

Helmholtz, H. L. F. (1954). *On the sensations of tone as a physiological basis for the theory of music* (2nd ed., A. J. Ellis, Trans.). New York: Dover. (Original work published 1885)

Hughes, H., Nelson, M., & Aronchick, D. (1998). Spatial characteristics of visual-auditory summation in human saccades. *Vision Research, 38,* 3955–3963.

Jay, M. F., & Sparks, D. L. (1984). Auditory receptive fields in primate superior colliculus shift with changes in eye position. *Nature, 309,* 345–347.

Jay, M. F., & Sparks, D. L. (1990). Localization of auditory and visual targets for the initialization of saccadic eye movements. In M. A. Berkley, & W. C. Stebbins (Eds.), *Comparative perception. Basic mechanisms*: Vol. 1. (pp. 351–374). New York: Wiley.

Johansson, G., & Orjesson, E. B. (1989). Toward a new theory of vision. Studies in wide-angle space perception. *Ecological Psychology, 1,* 301–331.

Kanizsa, G. (1979). *Organization in vision: essays on Gestalt perception.* New York: Praeger.

Kant, I. (1996). *Critique of pure reason* (W. S. Pluhar, Trans.). Indianapolis, IN: Hackett. (Original work published 1787)

Kubovy, M. (1981). Concurrent-pitch segregation and the theory of indispensable attributes. In M. Kubovy, & J. Pomerantz (Eds.), *Perceptual organization* (pp. 55–99). Hillsdale, NJ: Lawrence Erlbaum.

Kubovy, M. (1988). Should we resist the seductiveness of the space:time:vision:audition analogy? *Journal of Experimental Psychology: Human Perception and Performance, 14,* 318–320.

Kubovy, M., Cohen, D., & Hollier, J. (1999). Feature integration that routinely occurs without focal attention. *Psychonomic Bulletin & Review, 6,* 183–203.

Kubovy, M., Cutting, J. E., & McGuire, R. M. (1974). Hearing with the third ear: dichotic perception of a melody without monaural familiarity cues. *Science, 186,* 272–274.

Kubovy, M., Holcombe, A., & Wagemans, J. (1998). On the lawfulness of grouping by proximity. *Cognitive Psychology, 35,* 71–98.

Ladavas, E., & Pavani, F. (1998). Neuropsychological evidence of the functional integration of visual, auditory and proprioceptive spatial maps. *NeuroReport: an International Journal for the Rapid Communication of Research in Neuroscience, 9,* 1195–1200.

Lakoff, G., & Johnson, M. (1999). *Philosophy in the flesh: the embodied mind and its challenge to western thought.* New York: Basic Books.

Law, M. B., Pratt, J., & Abrams, R. A. (1995). Color-based inhibition of return. *Perception & Psychophysics, 57* (3), 402–408.

Lenoble, J. S. (1986). Feature conjunctions and the perceptual grouping of concurrent tones (Unpublished doctoral dissertation, Rutgers – The State University of New Jersey, New Brunswick, NJ, 1986). *Dissertation Abstracts International, 47-06B,* 2654.

Macaluso, E., Frith, C., & Driver, J. (2000). Selective spatial attention in vision and touch: unimodal and multimodal mechanisms revealed by PET. *Journal of Neurophysiology, 83,* 3062–3075.

McPherson, L., Ciocca, V., & Bregman, A. (1994). Organization in audition by similarity in rate of change: evidence from tracking individual frequency glides in mixtures. *Perception & Psychophysics, 55* (3), 269–278.

Milner, A. D., & Goodale, M. A. (1995). *The visual brain in action.* Oxford: Oxford University Press.

Mollon, J. (1995). Seeing colour. In T. Lamb, & J. Bourriau (Eds.), *Colour: art & science* (pp. 127–150). Cambridge: Cambridge University Press.

Mondor, T. A., & Breau, L. M. (1999). Facilitative and inhibitory effects of location and frequency cues: evidence of a modulation in perceptual sensitivity. *Perception & Psychophysics, 61* (3), 438–444.

Mondor, T. A., Breau, L. M., & Milliken, B. (1998). Inhibitory processes in auditory selective attention: evidence of location-based and frequency-based inhibition of return. *Perception & Psychophysics, 60* (2), 296–302.

Mondor, T. A., & Terrio, N. A. (1998). Mechanisms of perceptual organization and auditory selective attention: the role of pattern structure. *Journal of Experimental Psychology: Human Perception and Performance, 24* (6), 1628–1641.

Monge, G. (1789). Mémoire sure quelques phénomènes de la vision. *Annales de Chimie, 3,* 131–147.

Newton, I. (1999). *Mathematical principle of natural philosophy* (I. B. Cohen & A. Whitman, Trans.). Berkeley, CA: University of California Press. (Original work published 1726)

Object (1993). In *Oxford English Dictionary* (2nd ed.). (http://etext.lib.virginia.edu/etcbin/oedbin/

oed2www?specfile = /web/data/oed/oed.o2w&act = text&offset = 287948343&textreg = 0&query = object, retrieved 1 October 1999)

Palmer, S. E. (1999). *Vision science: photons to phenomenology.* Cambridge, MA: MIT Press.

Peterson, M. A., & Gibson, B. S. (1994). Must figure-ground organization precede object recognition? An assumption in peril. *Psychological Science, 5,* 253–259.

Posner, M. I. (1978). *Chronometric explorations of the mind.* Hillsdale, NJ: Erlbaum.

Potter, M. C., Chun, M. M., Banks, B. S., & Muckenhoupt, M. (1998). Two attentional deficits in serial target search: the visual attentional blink and an amodal task-switch deficit. *Journal of Experimental Psychology: Learning, Memory and Cognition, 24* (4), 979–992.

Quinlan, P. T., & Hill, N. I. (1999). Sequential effects in rudimentary auditory and visual tasks. *Perception & Psychophysics, 61* (2), 375–384.

Rauschecker, J. P. (1997). Processing of complex sounds in the auditory cortex of cat, monkey, and man. *Acta Oto-Laryngologica – Supplement, 532,* 34–38.

Rauschecker, J. P. (1998a). Cortical processing of complex sounds. *Current Opinions in Neurobiology, 288,* 516–521.

Rauschecker, J. P. (1998b). Parallel processing in the auditory cortex of primates. *Audiology and Neurootology, 3,* 86–103.

Rorden, C., & Driver, J. (1999). Does auditory attention shift in the direction of an upcoming saccade? *Neuropsychologia, 37,* 357–377.

Samuel, A. G. (1991). A further examination of attentional effects in the phonemic restoration illusion. *Quarterly Journal of Experimental Psychology, 43A* (3), 679–699.

Scharf, B. (1998). Auditory attention: the psychoacoustical approach. In H. Pashler (Ed.), *Attention* (pp. 75–113). Hove: Psychology Press.

Scharf, B., Quigley, S., Aoki, C., Peachey, N., & Reeves, A. (1987). Focused auditory attention and frequency selectivity. *Perception & Psychophysics, 42,* 215–223.

Shih, S., & Sperling, G. (1996). Is there feature-based attentional selection in visual search? *Journal of Experimental Psychology: Human Perception and Performance, 22* (3), 758–779.

Spence, C., & Driver, J. (1994). Covert spatial orienting in audition: exogenous and endogenous mechanisms. *Journal of Experimental Psychology: Human Perception and Performance, 20* (3), 555–574.

Spence, C., & Driver, J. (1997). Audiovisual links in exogenous overt spatial orienting. *Perception & Psychophysics, 59* (1), 1–22.

Spence, C., & Driver, J. (1998). Auditory and audiovisual inhibition of return. *Perception & Psychophysics, 60* (1), 125–139.

Spence, C., & Driver, J. (1999). Cross-modal attention. In G. W. Humphreys, & A. Treisman (Eds.), *Attention, space, and action* (pp. 130–149). New York: Oxford University Press.

Stein, B. E., & Meredith, M. A. (1993). *The merging of the senses.* Cambridge, MA: MIT Press.

Stoffregen, T. A., & Pittenger, J. B. (1995). Human echolation as a basic form of perception and action. *Ecological Psychology, 7,* 181–216.

Stryker, M. P. (1999). Sensory maps on the move. *Science, 284,* 925–926.

Tipper, S. P., Weaver, B., Jerreat, L. M., & Burak, A. L. (1994). Object-based and environment-based inhibition of return of visual attention. *Journal of Experimental Psychology: Human Perception and Performance, 20* (3), 478–499.

Treisman, A. M., & Gelade, G. (1980). A feature-integration theory of attention. *Cognitive Psychology, 12,* 97–136.

Vicario, G. (1960). The acoustic tunnel effect. *Rivista da Psicologia, 54,* 41–52.

Warren, R. M. (1970). Perceptual restoration of missing speech sounds. *Science, 167,* 392–393.

Warren, R. M. (1982). *Auditory perception: a new synthesis.* New York: Pergamon Press.

Warren, R. M. (1984). Perceptual restoration of obliterated sounds. *Psychological Bulletin, 96,* 371–383.

Watkins, A. J. (1991). Central, auditory mechanisms of perceptual compensation for spectral-envelope distortion. *Journal of the Acoustical Society of America, 90,* 2942–2955.

Watkins, A. J. (1998). The precedence effect and perceptual compensation for spectral envelope distortion. In A. Palmer, A. Rees, A. Q. Summerfield, & R. Meddis (Eds.), *Psychophysical and physiological advances in hearing* (pp. 336–343). London: Whurr.

Watkins, A. J. (1999). The influence of early reflections on the identification and lateralization of vowels. *Journal of the Acoustical Society of America, 106*, 2933–2944.

Watkins, A. J., & Makin, S. J. (1996). Effects of spectral contrast on perceptual compensation for spectral-envelope distortion. *Journal of the Acoustical Society of America, 99*, 3749–3757.

Wertheimer, M. (1938). Laws of organization in perceptual forms. In W. Ellis (Ed.), *A source book of Gestalt psychology* (pp. 71–88). London: Routledge & Kegan Paul. (Original work published 1923)

Wightman, F. L., & Jenison, R. (1995). Auditory spatial layout. In W. Epstein, & S. J. Rogers (Eds.), *Perception of space and motion* (2nd ed. pp. 365–400). San Diego, CA: Academic Press.

Wynn, V. T. (1977). Simple reaction time – evidence for two auditory pathways to the brain. *Journal of Auditory Research, 17*, 175–181.

Young, E. D., Spirou, G. A., Rice, J. J., & Voigt, H. F. (1992). Neural organization and responses to complex stimuli in the dorsal cochlear nucleus. *Philosophical Transactions of the Royal Society of London, Series B, 336*, 407–413.

Zheng, W., & Knudsen, E. I. (1999). Functional selection of adaptive auditory space map by $GABA_A$-mediated inhibition. *Science, 284*, 962–965.

5

Visual indexes, preconceptual objects, and situated vision

Zenon W. Pylyshyn[*]

Rutgers Center for Cognitive Science, Rutgers University, Psychology Building, New Wing, Busch Campus, New Brunswick, NJ 08903, USA

Abstract

This paper argues that a theory of *situated vision*, suited for the dual purposes of object recognition and the control of action, will have to provide something more than a system that constructs a conceptual representation from visual stimuli: it will also need to provide a special kind of direct (preconceptual, unmediated) connection between elements of a visual representation and certain elements in the world. Like natural language demonstratives (such as 'this' or 'that') this direct connection allows entities to be referred to without being categorized or conceptualized. Several reasons are given for why we need such a preconceptual mechanism which individuates and keeps track of several individual objects in the world. One is that early vision must pick out and compute the relation among several individual objects while ignoring their properties. Another is that incrementally computing and updating representations of a dynamic scene requires keeping track of token individuals despite changes in their properties or locations. It is then noted that a mechanism meeting these requirements has already been proposed in order to account for a number of disparate empirical phenomena, including subitizing, search-subset selection and multiple object tracking (Pylyshyn et al., *Canadian Journal of Experimental Psychology* 48(2) (1994) 260). This mechanism, called a *visual index* or FINST, is briefly discussed and it is argued that viewing it as performing a demonstrative or preconceptual reference function has far-reaching implications not only for a theory of situated vision, but also for suggesting a new way to look at why the primitive individuation of visual objects, or proto-objects, is so central in computing visual representations. Indexing visual objects is also, according to this view, the primary means for grounding visual concepts and is a potentially fruitful way to look at the problem of visual integration across time and across saccades, as well as to explain how infants' numerical capacity might arise. © 2001 Elsevier Science B.V. All rights reserved.

---

[*] Fax: +1-908-445-0634.
E-mail address: zenon@ruccs.rutgers.edu (Z. Pylyshyn).

Keywords: Early vision; Visual attention; Visual indexing; Multiple object tracking; Object-based attention; Visual representation; Indexicals; Demonstrative reference; Deictics; Situated vision

1. Background: what is missing in a purely conceptual representation

In this paper I argue that a theory of how visual information is analyzed and represented for the dual purposes of recognition and control of action will have to provide a system that does more than construct a conceptual representation from proximal stimulation. Such a theory, which we might call *a theory of situated vision*, will also have to provide a special kind of direct connection between elements of a visual representation and certain token elements in the visual field, a connection that is unmediated by an encoding of properties of the elements in question. In the first part of this paper I will give a number of empirical arguments for why such a function is needed. Then I will suggest that the *visual indexing* mechanism that we have been studying experimentally for some time (Pylyshyn, 1989) provides just this sort of function.

The most general view of what vision does is that it computes a representation of a scene that then becomes available to cognition so that we can draw inferences from it or decide what it is or what to do with it (and perhaps a somewhat different version of which may also become available for the immediate control of motor actions). When we represent something, whether in vision or in thought or even in a natural language, we typically represent a situation 'under a description', that is, we represent the elements of the situation as members of some category or as falling under a certain concept. So, for example, when we say or think 'the cat is on the mat', we refer to the elements under the categories 'cat' and 'mat'. This is, in fact, a fundamental characteristic of cognitive or intentional theories which distinguishes them from physical theories (see Pylyshyn, 1984). That is because what determines our behavior is not the physical properties of the stimuli around us, but how we interpret or classify them – what we *take them to be*. It is not the bright spot in the sky that determines which way we set out when we are lost, but the fact that we see it (or represent it) as the North Star. It is because we represent it *as* the North Star that our perception is brought into contact with our knowledge of such things as astronomy and navigation.[1] This is common ground for virtually all contemporary theories of cognition.

But this is not the whole story. Although it is not often recognized we do, under

---

[1] A useful heuristic in determining whether something is perceived or represented 'under a description' or 'conceptually' is to ask whether it could be *misperceived*. A preconceptual (purely causal) connection has no room for misperception. We can misperceive something only when we perceive it *as* something it is not. But when we react (mechanically, neurally or biochemically) to a physical stimulus the reaction does not depend on the category under which we perceive or conceptualize it. Consequently, we cannot react to it in this way in error (or 'mis-react' to it).

certain conditions, also represent some things without representing them in terms of concepts. We can refer to some things, as I will say, *preconceptually*. For example, in the presence of a visual stimulus, we can think thoughts such as '*that* is red' where the term '*that*' refers to something we have picked out in our field of view without reference to what category it falls under or what properties it may have. A term such as *this* or *that* is called a 'demonstrative'. Philosophers like Perry (1979) have argued that demonstratives are ineliminable in language and thought. The reasons for the ineliminability of demonstratives in language and thought also apply to visual representations. Not only can we represent visual scenes in which parts are not classified according to some category, but there are good reasons why at least some things *must* be referenced in this preconceptual way. If we could only refer to things in terms of their category membership, our concepts would always be related only to other concepts (the concepts for categories) and would never be grounded in experience. Sooner or later the regress of specifying concepts in terms of other concepts has to bottom out. Traditionally, the 'bottoming out' was assumed to occur at sensory properties, but this 'sense data' view of concepts has never been able to account for the grounding of anything more than simple sensory concepts and has been largely abandoned. The present proposal is that the grounding begins at the point where something is picked out directly by a mechanism that works like a demonstrative. We will later propose that visual indexes do the picking out and the things that they pick out in the case of vision are what many people have been calling *visual objects* or proto-objects.

A second closely related problem with the view that representations consist solely of concepts or descriptions arises when we need to pick out particular token individuals. If our visual representations encoded a scene solely in terms of concepts or categories, then we would have no way to pick out or to refer to particular individuals in a scene except through concepts or descriptions involving other concepts, and so on. In what follows I will suggest a number of ways in which such a recursion is inadequate, especially if our theory of vision is to be situated, in the sense of making bidirectional contact with the world – i.e. contact in which individual elements in a scene causally invoke certain elements in a representation, and in which the elements in the representation can in turn be used to refer to particular individuals in the world.

It is this second problem – that of establishing a correspondence between individual things in the world and their counterparts in the visual representation – that I will focus on in this paper, since this is where the notion of a visual index played its first theoretical role in our work. Before I describe how a visual index is relevant to this connection function, I offer a few illustrations of how this function is missing from the sorts of representations that visual theories typically provide. Theories of visual perception universally attempt to provide an effective (i.e. computable) mapping from dynamic 2D patterns of proximal stimulation to a representation of a 3D scene. Both the world and its visual representation contain certain individuals or elements. The world contains objects, or whatever your ontology takes to be the relevant *individuals*, while the representation contains symbols or symbol structures (or codes, nodes, geons, logogens, engrams, etc. as the theory specifies). The problem of keeping *tokens* of the representing elements in correspondence with *tokens* of individual things in the world turns out to be rather more difficult than one might have expected.

With the typical sort of conceptual representation, there is no way to pick out an individual in the world other than by finding the tokens in a scene that fall under a particular concept, or satisfy a particular description, or that have the properties encoded in the representation. What I will try to show is that this cannot be what goes on in general; it can't be the case that the visual system can only pick out things in the scene by finding instances that satisfy its conceptual representation. There are phenomena that suggest that the visual system must be able to pick out individuals in a more direct manner, without using encoded properties or categories. If this claim is correct then the visual system needs a mechanism for selecting and keeping track of individual visual objects that is more like a demonstrative reference (the sort of reference we make in language when we use demonstrative terms like *this* or *that*) than a description. And that, I suggest, is why we must have something like a visual indexing mechanism which *preconceptually* picks out a small number of individuals, keeps track of them, and provides a means by which the cognitive system can further examine them in order to encode their properties, to move focal attention to them or to carry out a motor command in relation to them (e.g. to point to them).

The idea that we need to have a means of direct reference is not new. In the study of robotic control, researchers like Lespérance and Levesque (1995) recognized that in order for a robot to function in a real environment, its system of representations must be able to deal with indexicals, or agent-centered ways of representing the world. In such representations, instead of referring expressions like 'a large red round object located at $<x,y>$' we might have 'the object in line with the direction I am heading and located between me and what I am looking at right now...'). Our notion of an index is a special case of such an indexical (other cases include locatives, such as 'here', or 'now' and personal deictic references such as 'I' or 'you'). Other artificial intelligence writers, such as Agre (1997) and Brooks (1999), have gone even further and suggested that focussing on indexical information changes the computational problems associated with planning and executing actions so radically that symbolic representations will play little or no role in these problems. While such issues are beyond the scope of this paper, I wish merely to point out that, one way or another, indexicals are playing a larger role in current theories of cognition, especially where cognition eventuates in action.

What I intend to do in this paper is first lay out some general empirical motivations for hypothesizing the existence of primitive indexing mechanisms (sometimes called FINSTs for purely historical reasons, going back to Pylyshyn, Elcock, Marmor, & Sander, 1978, where indexes were referred to as 'FINgers of INSTantiation') that *individuate* and *index*, or keep track of about four or five individual objects in the visual field. I will then present some experimental evidence showing that something like an index must be available inasmuch as people can select and keep track of four or five individual objects in controlled experiments. I will briefly review and defend the so-called FINST theory of visual indexing. Then I will discuss the relation of these ideas to other work, including work on *deictic strategies*, on *object files* and on infants' sensitivity to numerosity. Finally, I will very briefly relate these ideas to some classical problems in psychology, including the problem of transsaccadic integration and the problem of grounding concepts in experience.

2. The need for individuating and indexing: empirical motivations

There are two general problems raised by the description view of visual representations, i.e. the view that we pick out and refer to objects solely in terms of their categories or their encoded properties. One problem is that there are always an unlimited number of things in the world that can satisfy any particular category or description, so that if it is necessary to refer to a unique individual object among many similar ones in the visual field (especially when its location or properties are changing), a description will often be either too complex or inadequate. A second problem is deeper. The visual system needs to be able to pick out a particular individual *regardless* of what properties the individual happens to have at any instant of time. It is often necessary to pick out an element in the visual field *as a particular enduring individual*, rather than as whatever happens to have a certain set of properties. An individual remains the same individual when it moves about or when it changes any (or even all) of its visible properties. Yet *being the same individual* is something that the visual system often needs to compute, as we shall see in the examples below.

In arguing for the insufficiency of conceptual (or descriptive) representations as the sole form of visual representation, I will appeal to three empirical assumptions about early vision: the assumption that the detection of properties proceeds by the prior detection of objects that bear those properties, the assumption that the detection of objects is primitive and preconceptual (i.e. does not itself involve the appeal to any properties), and the assumption that visual representations are built up incrementally.

2.1. Detection of visual properties is the detection of properties of objects

The *first assumption* is that when a property is detected and encoded by the visual system it is typically detected not just as a property existing in the visual field, but as the property of an individual perceived object. I will assume that the visual system does not just detect the presence of redness or circularity or collinearity in the visual field: it detects that certain individual objects are red or circular or are arranged linearly. There are a number of sources of evidence supporting this assumption, most of which were collected in connection with asking somewhat different questions.

(a) There is a great deal of evidence showing that several properties are most easily extracted from a display when they occur within a single visual object, and therefore that focal attention (which is assumed to be required for encoding conjunctions of properties) is object-based (Baylis & Driver, 1993). Evidence supporting this conclusion comes from a variety of sources (many of which are reviewed in Scholl, 2001), including clinical cases of hemispatial visual neglect and Balint syndrome, which implicate an object-centered frame of reference. This sort of object-specificity of feature encoding is exactly what would be expected if properties are always detected as belonging to an object.

(b) Evidence often cited in support of the assumption that properties are detected in terms of their *location* is compatible with the view that it is the object with which the property is associated, rather than its location, that is primary. A good example of a study that was explicitly directed at the question of whether location was central was one carried out by Nissen (1985). She argued that in reporting the conjunction of two features, observers must first locate the *place* in the visual field that has both features. In Nissen's studies this conclusion comes from a comparison of the probability of reporting a stimulus property (e.g. shape or color or location) or a pair of such properties, given one of the other properties as cue. Nissen found that accuracy for reporting shape and color were statistically independent, but accuracy for reporting shape and location, or for reporting color and location, were *not* statistically independent. More importantly, the conditional probabilities conformed to what would be expected if the way observers judged both color and shape was by using the detected (or cued) color to determine a location for that color and then using that location to access the shape. For example, the probability of correctly reporting both the location and the shape of a target, given its color as cue, was equal (within statistical sampling error) to the product of the probability of reporting its location, given its color, and of reporting its shape, given its location. From this, Nissen concluded that detection of location underlies the detection of either the color or shape feature given the other as cue. Similarly, Pashler (1998, pp. 97–99) reviewed a number of relevant studies and argued that location is special and is the means by which other information is selected. Note, however, that since the objects in all these studies had fixed locations, these results are equally compatible with the conclusion that detection of properties is mediated by the prior detection of the individuals that bear these properties, rather than of their location. If the individuals had been moving in the course of a trial it might have been possible to disentangle these two alternatives and to ascertain whether detection of properties is associated with the instantaneous location of the properties or with the individuals that had those properties.

(c) A number of experimental paradigms have used moving objects to explore the question of whether the encoding of properties is associated with individual objects, as opposed to locations. These include the studies of Kahneman, Treisman, and Gibbs (1992) on 'object files' and our own studies using multiple object tracking (MOT) (see Section 3.2 below, as well as Pylyshyn, 1998; Pylyshyn et al., 1994). Kahneman et al. showed that the priming effect of letters presented briefly in a moving box remains attached to the box in which the letter had appeared, rather than to its location at the time it was presented. Similarly, related studies by Tipper, Driver, and Weaver (1991) showed that the phenomenon known as *inhibition of return* (whereby the latency for switching attention to an object increases if the object has been attended in the past 300 ms to about 1000 ms) was specific to particular objects rather than particular locations within the visual field (though later work by Tipper, Weaver, Jerreat, & Burak, 1994, suggests that location-specific IOR also occurs).

While there is evidence that unitary focal attention, sometimes referred to as the 'spotlight of attention', is often location-based, and appears to spread away from its central spatial locus, the sort of attention-like phenomena that were investigated in connection with object files and IOR (and other studies to be sketched in Section 3) appear to be far more attached to objects with little evidence of spreading to points in between the objects. Using the MOT paradigm, we found that in a shape discrimination task using MOT, changes are more readily discriminated when they are associated with objects that are being tracked, with little spread to inter-object locations (Sears & Pylyshyn, 2000; see also Intriligator & Cavanagh, 1992). In all these cases what appears most relevant to the detection of properties is not their instantaneous location, but the continuing individuality – or some writers say, the continuing numerical identity – of the objects that bear those properties.

2.2. Individuation of object tokens is primitive and precedes the detection of properties

The *second assumption* is that the process of individuating object tokens is distinct from the process of recognizing and encoding the objects' types or their properties. Clearly, the visual system can distinguish two or more distinct token individuals regardless of the type to which each belongs, or to put it slightly differently, we can tell visually that there are several distinct individuals independent of the particular properties that each has; we can distinguish distinct objects (and count them) even if their visible properties are identical. What is usually diagnostic of (though not essential to) there being several token individuals is that they have different spatiotemporal properties (or locations). Without a mechanism for individuating objects independent of encoding their properties it is hard to see how one could judge that the six elements in Fig. 1 are arranged linearly, especially if the elements in the figure were gradually changing their properties or if the figure as a whole was moving while maintaining the collinear arrangement of elements. In general, featural properties of elements tend to be factored out when computing global patterns, regardless of the size and complexity of the global pattern (Navon, 1977). Computing global patterns such as collinearity, or others discussed by Ullman (1984), requires that elements be registered as individuals while their local properties are ignored. This 'ignoring' might make use of whatever selectional mechanisms may be available, perhaps including, in the collinearity example, focusing attention on lower spatial frequencies or functionally replacing the objects with points. Whatever the particular algorithm used to detect collinearity among elements, it is clear that specifying *which* points form a collinear pattern is a necessary part of the computation.

Here is another way to think of the process of computing relational properties among a set of objects. In order to recognize a relational property, such as **Collinear**$(X_1,X_2,...X_n)$ or **Inside**(X_1,C_1) or **Part-of**(F_1,F_2), which apply over a number of particular individual objects, there must be some way to specify which objects are the ones referred to in the relationship. For example, we cannot recognize the **Collinear** relation without somehow picking out *which* objects are collinear. If

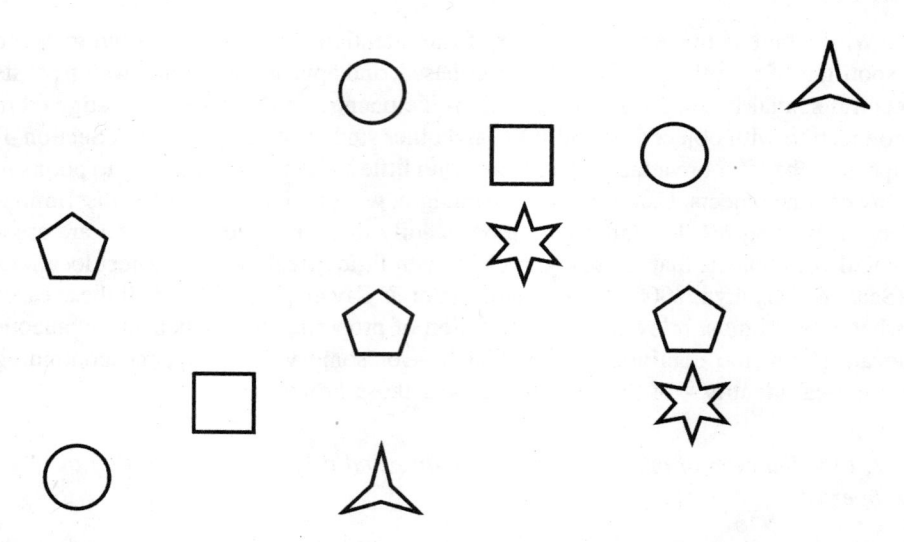

Fig. 1. Judging collinearity requires both selecting the relevant individual objects and ignoring all their local properties.

there are many objects in a scene only some of them may be collinear, so we must *bind* the objects in question to argument positions in the relational predicate. Ullman (1984) as well as a large number of other investigators (Ballard, Hayhoe, Pook, & Rao, 1997; Watson & Humphreys, 1997; Yantis, 1998; Yantis & Johnson, 1990; Yantis & Jones, 1991) refer to the objects in such examples as being 'marked' or 'tagged'. The notion of a tag is an intuitively appealing one since it suggests a way of labeling objects to allow us to subsequently refer to them. Yet the operation of tagging only makes sense if there is something on which a tag literally can be placed. It does no good to tag an internal representation since the relation we wish to encode holds in the world and may not yet be encoded in the representation. So we need a way of 'tagging' that enables us to get back to tagged objects in the world to update our representation of them. But how do we tag parts of the world? It appears that what we need is what labels give us in diagrams: a way to name or refer to individual parts of a scene *independent of their properties or their locations*. This label-like function that goes along with object individuation is an essential aspect of the indexing mechanism that will be described in greater detail below.

There are a number of other sources of evidence suggesting that individuation is distinct from discrimination and recognition. For example, individuation has its own psychophysical discriminability function. He et al. (1997) have shown that even at separations where objects can be visually resolved they may nonetheless fail to be *individuated* or attentionally resolved, preventing the individual objects from being picked out from among the others. Without such individuation one could not count the objects or carry out a sequence of commands that require moving attention from one to another. Given a 2D array of points lying closer than their threshold of attentional resolution, one could not successfully follow such instructions as:

'move up one, right one, right one, down one,...' and so on. Such instructions were used by Intriligator (1997) to measure attentional resolution. Fig. 2 illustrates another difference between individuating and recognizing. It shows that you may be able to recognize the shape of objects and distinguish between a group of objects and a single (larger) object, and yet not be able to focus attention on an individual object within the group (in order to, say, pick out the third object from the left). Studies reported in He et al. (1997) show that the process of individuating objects is separate and distinct from that of recognizing or encoding the properties of the objects.

Studies of rapid enumeration (called *subitizing*) described in Trick and Pylyshyn (1994) also show that individuating is distinct from (and prior to) computing the cardinality of a small set of objects. Trick and Pylyshyn showed that items arranged so they cannot be preattentively individuated (or items that require focal attention in order to individuate them – as in the case of items lying on a particular curve or specified in terms of conjunctions of features) cannot be subitized, even when there are only a few of them (i.e. there was no break in the function relating reaction time to number of items). For example, in Fig. 3, when the squares are arranged concentrically (as on the left) they cannot be subitized, whereas the same squares arranged side by side can easily be subitized. According to our explanation of the subitizing phenomenon, small sets are enumerated faster than large sets when items are preattentively individuated because in that case each item attracts an index, so observers only need to count the number of active indexes without having to first search for the items. Thus, we also predicted that precuing the location of preattentively individuated items would not affect the speed at which they were subitized, though it would affect counting larger numbers of items – a prediction borne out by our experiments (Trick & Pylyshyn, 1994).

2.3. Visual representations are constructed incrementally

The *third assumption* is that our visual representation of a scene is not arrived at in one step, but rather is built up incrementally. This assumption has strong support. Theoretical analyses (e.g. Tsotsos, 1988; Ullman, 1984) have provided good reasons for believing that some relational properties that hold between visual elements, such as the property of being inside or on the same contour, must be acquired serially by scanning a display. We also know from empirical studies that percepts are generally built up by scanning attention and/or one's gaze. Even when attention may not be scanned there is evidence that the achievement of simple percepts occurs in stages over a period of time (e.g. Calis, Sterenborg, & Maarse, 1984; Reynolds, 1981; Schulz, 1991; Sekuler & Palmer, 1992). If that is so then the following problem immediately arises. If the representation is built up incrementally, we need a mechanism for determining the correspondence between representations of individual elements across different stages of construction of the representation or across different periods of time. As we elaborate the representation by uncovering new properties of a dynamic scene, we need to know which individual objects in the current representation should be associated with the new information. In other

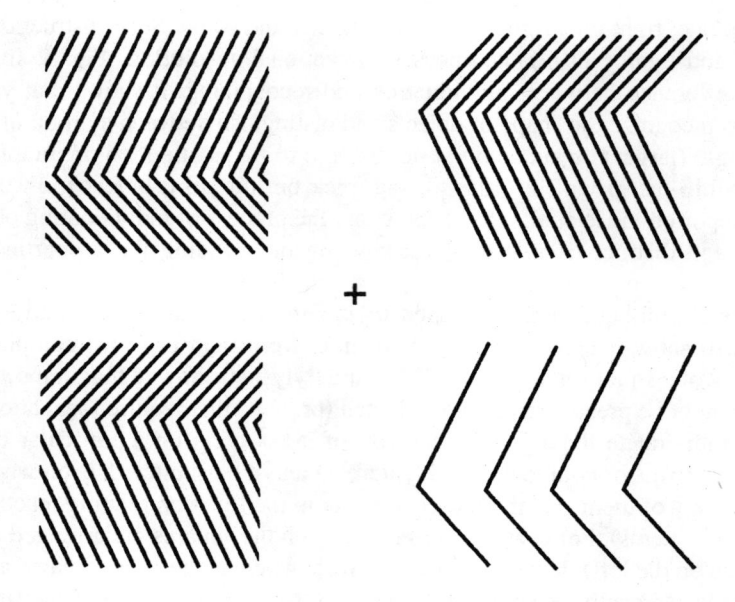

Fig. 2. At a certain distance if you fixate on the cross you can easily tell which groups consist of similar-shaped lines, although you can only *individuate* lines in the bottom right group. For example, you cannot count the lines or pick out the third line from the left, etc., in the other three groups (based on He, Cavanagh, & Intriligator, 1997).

words, we need to know when a certain token in the existing representation should be taken as corresponding to the same individual object as a particular token in the new representation. We need that so that we can attribute newly noticed properties to the representation of the appropriate individual objects. This problem remains even if the scene changes gradually so that updating can occur continuously – indeed the problem arises even if the scene remains fixed while the representation is incrementally computed (or when the percept is bistable, as in Fig. 4).

Suppose we have a representation of a scene such as the one shown on the right of Fig. 4 (a possible form of representation, which was used by Feldman & Ballard, 1982, is shown on the right). From the representation one might be able to infer that there are 12 lines in the figure. But we don't have a way to refer to the lines

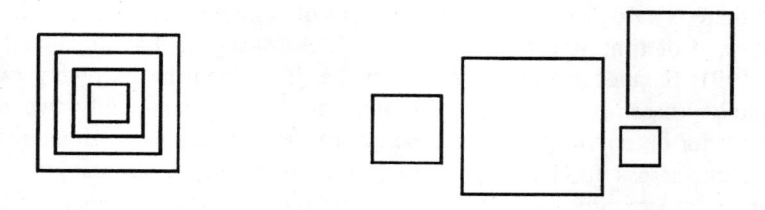

Fig. 3. Squares that are arranged so they cannot be preattentively individuated (on the left) cannot be subitized, whereas the ones on the right are easily subitized (based on Trick & Pylyshyn, 1994).

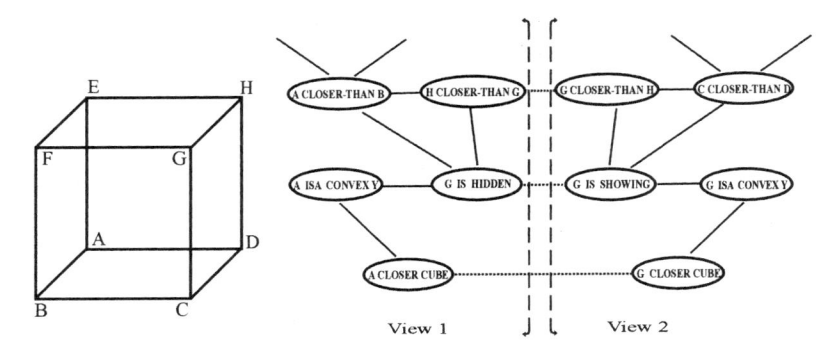

Fig. 4. One possible form of representation of a figure such as the reversing cube on the left. The figure on the right shows a connectionist network (as described by Feldman & Ballard, 1982), with solid lines corresponding to activating links and dotted lines corresponding to inhibitory links. This example assumes that vertices in the diagram are labeled. How could you represent the figure if they were not labeled?

individually. Yet without identifying particular lines we could not add further information to elaborate the representation. If, for example, on further examination, we discover that some lines are longer than others, some vertices form certain recognized angles, and so on, we would not be able to connect this new information to the representation of particular individual objects in the current representation. Because conjunctions of properties (e.g. red AND right-angled AND smaller-than, etc.) are defined with respect to particular objects, individual objects must be identified in order to determine whether there are property conjunctions.

A general requirement for adding information to a representation is that we be able to relate the newly discovered properties to *particular* elements in the existing representation of the figure. If you notice, say, that a certain angle is a right angle, you need to add this information to the representation of a particular vertex. How do you know which represented vertex it is so you can add the information to the appropriate item? In this example, as in using diagrams in general, we label lines or vertices. But of course the world does not come with every object conveniently labeled. What constraints does the need to pick out individual objects impose on the form and content of an adequate representation?

In principle it is possible to pick out an individual object by using an encoded description of its properties. All you need is a description that is unique to the individual in question, say 'the object α with property P' where P happens to uniquely pick out a particular object. But consider how this would have to work. If you want to add to a representation the newly noticed property Q (which, by assumption, is a property of a particular object, say object α), you must first locate the representation of object α in the current representation. Assuming that individuals are represented as expressions or individual nodes in some conceptual network, you might detect that the object that you just noticed as having property Q also had property P which uniquely identifies it. You might then assume that it had been previously stored as an object with property P. So you find an object in the current representation that is described as having P and conjoin the property Q to it (or use an identity statement to assert that the object with property P is identical to the object with property Q). There are many ways to accomplish this, depending on exactly what form the representation takes. But whatever the details of such an augmentation process, it must be able to locate the representation of a *particular individual* in order to update the representation properly. Yet this may well be too much to ask of a general procedure for updating representations. It requires working backward from a particular individual in the scene to its previous representation. There is no reason to think that locating a previous representation of an individual is even a well-defined function since representations are highly partial and schematic (and indeed, the representation of a particular object may not even exist in the current representation) and an individual object may change any of its properties over time while continuing to be the same object. In fact the rapidly-growing literature on change blindness would suggest that unless objects are attended they may change their properties without their representation being updated (Rensink, 2000a,b; Rensink, O'Regan, & Clark, 1997, 2000; Simons, 1996; Simons & Levin, 1997).

The basic problem can be stated as follows: in order to properly update a representation upon noticing a new property Q, what you need to find in the current representation is not a representation of an individual with certain properties, but rather the representation of the *very individual* on which the new property Q has been detected, and you have to do that independent of what properties of the display you have already encoded at that point in time. The alternative to the unwieldy method described in the past paragraph for locating a representation of a particular individual is to allow the descriptive apparatus to make use of some functional equivalent of *demonstrative* reference (such as the type of reference corresponding to the natural language words *this* or *that*). If we had such a mechanism, then adding newly noticed information would consist of adding the predicate $Q(\alpha)$ to the representation of a particular object α, where α is the object directly picked out by this demonstrative indexing mechanism. Since, by hypothesis, the visual system's Q detectors recognize instances of the property Q *as a property of a particular visual object* (in this case of α), being able to refer to α provides the most natural way to view the introduction of new visual properties by the sensorium.[2] In order to introduce new properties into a representation in that way, however, there would have to be a non-descriptive way of picking out the unique object in question. In the following section I examine experimental evidence suggesting that such a mechanism is needed for independent reasons – and in fact was proposed some time ago in order to account for certain empirical findings.

Note that although the above discussion has been concerned mainly with reidentifying individual objects within the foveal field of view, a very similar problem

---

[2] The reader will have noticed that this way of putting it makes the reference mechanism appear to be a *name* (in fact the name 'α'). What I have in mind is very like a proper name insofar as it allows reference to a particular individual. However, this reference relation is less general than a name since it ceases to exist when the referent (i.e. the visual object) is no longer in view. In that respect it functions exactly like a demonstrative, which is why I continue to call it that, even as I use examples involving names like α.

arises when the objects appear across different views, as when a display is examined by moving the eyes. Interestingly, the problem that led to the postulation of a visual index mechanism in the first instance arose in connection with the attempt to model the process of reasoning with the aid of a diagram (Pylyshyn et al., 1978). The problem there is rather similar to the updating problem discussed above. But since relevant objects might have moved off the fovea into the parafovea in the course of drawing the figure, a new dimension is added to the problem of updating the representation: we need to be able to pick out individual objects that have left the high-resolution field of view and then returned again as the eyes moved about. This problem will be raised again in discussing the relation of visual indexing theory to theories of saccadic integration in Section 4.2.

3. Experimental evidence for a visual index mechanism

3.1. Preconceptual selection

The following experiment by Burkell and Pylyshyn (1997) illustrates and provides evidence in favor of the assumption that the visual system has a mechanism for picking out and accessing individual objects prior to encoding their properties. Burkell and Pylyshyn showed that sudden-onset location cues (which we assumed caused the assignment of indexes) could be used to control search so that only the locations precued in this way are visited in the course of the search. This is what we would expect if the onset of such cues draws indexes and indexes can be used to determine where to direct focal attention.

In these studies (illustrated in Fig. 5) a number of placeholders (11 in this example), consisting of black Xs, appeared on the screen and remained there for 1 s. Then an additional three to five placeholders (which we refer to as the 'late-onset cues') were displayed. After 100 ms one of the segments of each X disappeared and the remaining segment changed color, producing a display of right-oblique and left-oblique lines in either green or red. The subject had to search the cued subset for a line segment with a particular color and orientation (say a left-oblique green line). Since the entire display had exemplars of all four combinations of color and orientation, search through the entire display was always what is known as a conjunction-search task (which is known to produce slow searches in which the time it takes to locate a target increases rapidly with increasing numbers of items in the display). As expected, the target was detected more rapidly when it was one of the subsets that had been precued by a late-onset cue, suggesting that subjects could directly access those items and ignore the rest. There were, however, two additional findings that are even more relevant to the present discussion. These depend on the fact that we manipulated the nature of the precued subset to be either a single-feature search task (i.e. in which the target differed from all other items in the search set by no more than one feature) or a conjunction-search task (in which only a combination of two features could identify the target because some of the non-targets in the search set differed from it in one feature and others differed from it in another feature).

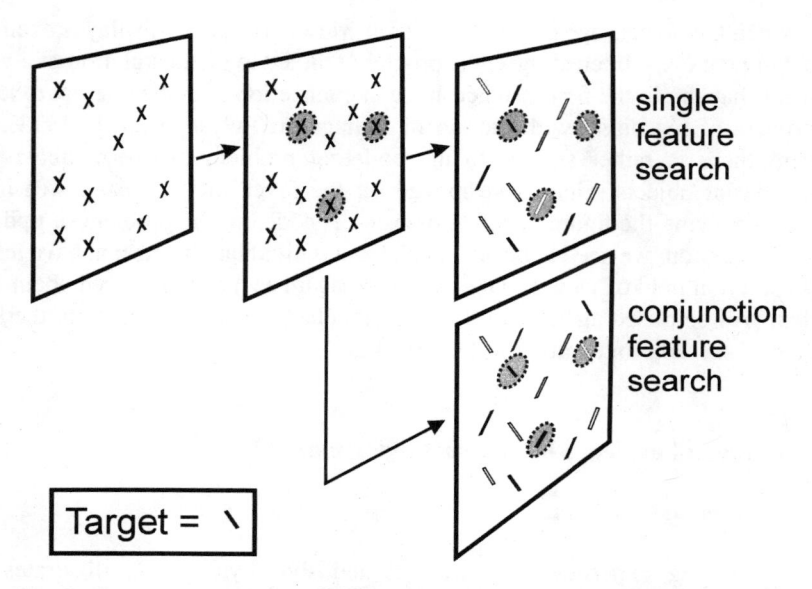

Fig. 5. Sequence of events in the Burkell and Pylyshyn (1997) study. In the first frame the observer sees a set of placeholder Xs for 1000 ms. In the second frame, 'late-onset' placeholders appear for 100 ms, signaling the items that will constitute the search subset. In the third frame, all placeholders change to search items and the subject must try to find the specified target in one of two conditions. In the top display the target differs from all the non-targets by one feature (color), whereas in the bottom display, a combination of two features is required to distinguish the target. In the experiment the bars were either red or green and the faint circles did not appear – they are only for expository purposes.

Although a search through the entire display would always constitute a conjunction-feature search, the subset that was precued by late-onset cues could be either a simple or a conjunction-feature subset. So the critical question is this: is it the property of the entire display or the property of only the subset that determines the observed search behavior? We found clear evidence that only the property of the *subset* (i.e. whether it constituted a simple-search or a conjunction-search task) determined the relation between the number of search items and the reaction time. This provides strong evidence that only the cued subset is being selected as the search set. Notice that the distinction between a single-feature and a conjunction-feature search is a distinction that depends on the entire search set, so it must be the case that the entire precued subset is being treated as the search set: the subset effect could not be the result of the items in the subset being visited or otherwise processed one by one.

Of particular relevance to the present thesis was the additional finding that when we systematically increased the distance between precued items there was *no* increase in search time per item, contrary to what one would expect if subset items were being spatially searched for. It seems that increasing the spatial dispersion of the items does not increase the time it takes to examine them, even when the examination appears to be serial (e.g. the time increases linearly as the number of non-targets in the subset increases). This is precisely what one would expect if, as we predict, the cued items are indexed and indexes can be used to access the items *directly* (although serially), without having to scan over the display for the subset items.

This type of study provides a clear picture of the property of indexes that we have been emphasizing: they provide a *direct access mechanism*, rather like the random access provided by addresses or pointers in a computer. Certain primitive visual objects can be indexed without appealing to their properties (the indexing being due to their sudden appearance on the scene) and once indexed, they can be individually examined either in series or in parallel. In other words, one can ask 'Is x red?' so long as x is bound to some visual object by an index.

It should be noted that Watson and Humphreys (1997) independently reported a set of very similar studies and found very similar results to those of Burkell and Pylyshyn (1997). They presented a set of search items in two successive displays and showed that as long as the temporal gap between early and late items was more than about 400 ms and as long as there was no luminance change in the early items at the time the late items appeared, the late-onset items behaved as though they were the only items displayed. However, these authors argued that the underlying priority-assignment process involved 'marking' the early items for inhibition in the subsequent selection task. While we are not persuaded that the Watson and Humphreys results imply that selectional priority of late-onset items is due to the inhibition of the old items, their explanation of the selectional effect is compatible with the visual indexing theory since visual indexes could in principle be implemented by activation or inhibition of object representations or by some combination of the two (in fact an earlier implementation, following the work of Koch & Ullman, 1985, does use both activation and inhibition; see Box 4 of Pylyshyn, 2000; Pylyshyn & Eagleson, 1994). The point we make is that once 'selected', the objects can be accessed directly without using an encoding of their properties and without further scanning of the display – i.e. we assume that the mechanism of selection provides an access path or binding between objects and the cognitive processes that need to refer to them (e.g. the comparison or test operation in the search process). This is why it is significant that we found that the spatial dispersion of the objects did not affect search time.

3.2. Multiple object tracking (MOT)

We have argued that the visual system needs a mechanism to *individuate and keep track of particular individuals in a scene* in a way that does not require appeal to their properties (including their locations). Thus, what we need is a way to realize the following two functions: (a) pick out or individuate *primitive visual objects*, and (b) provide a means for referring to these objects as though they had labels or, more accurately, as though the visual system had a system of pointers. Although these two functions are distinct, I have proposed that they are both realized by a primitive mechanism called a *visual index*, the details of which are sketched in Section 4. In this section I illustrate the claim that there is a primitive mechanism that picks out and maintains the identity of visual objects, by describing an experimental paradigm

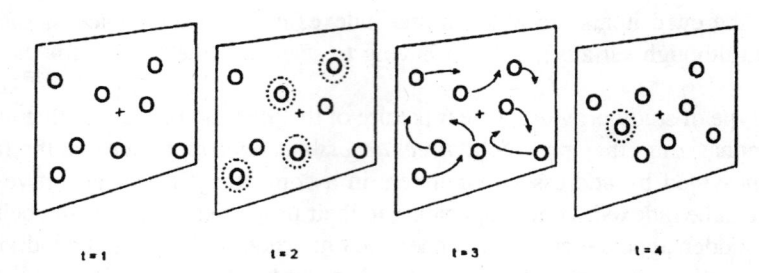

Fig. 6. Illustration of a typical MOT experiment. A number (here eight) of identical objects are shown (at $t = 1$), and a subset (the 'targets') is selected by, say, flashing them (at $t = 2$), after which the objects move in unpredictable ways (with or without self-occlusion) for about 10 s. At the end of the trial the observer has to either pick out all the targets using a pointing device or judge whether one that is selected by the experimenter (e.g. by flashing it, as shown at $t = 4$) is a target.

we have been using to explore the nature of such a mechanism. It is called the *Multiple Object Tracking (MOT) Task* and is illustrated in Fig. 6.

In a typical experiment, observers are shown anywhere from eight to 24 simple identical objects (points, plus signs, circles, figure-eight shapes). A subset of these objects is briefly rendered distinct (usually by flashing them on and off a few times). Then all the identical objects move about in the display in unpredictable ways. The subject's task is to keep track of this subset of objects (called 'targets'). At some later time in the experiment (say 10 s into the tracking trial) one of the objects is probed by flashing it on and off. The observer must then indicate whether the probed object was one of the targets. (In other studies the subject had to indicate *all* the targets using a mouse.) A large number of experiments, beginning with the studies described in Pylyshyn and Storm (1988), have shown that observers can indeed track up to five independently moving targets within a field of ten identical items. In the original Pylyshyn and Storm study we showed that the motion and dispersion parameters of that experiment were such that tracking could not have been accomplished using a serial strategy consisting of scanning focal attention to each figure in turn, encoding and storing its location, and then on the next iteration, returning to the figure closest to that location, updating that location, and so on. Based on some conservative assumptions about how fast focal attention might be scanned and using the actual trajectories of the objects of the experiments we simulated this strategy as it would apply to our experimental materials. From this we were able to conclude that such a serial tracking process would frequently end up switching to the wrong objects in the course of its tracking and would result in a performance that was very much worse than the performance we actually observed in our experiments (over 85% correct). This means that the moving objects could not have been tracked by a unitary beam of attention *using a unique stored description of each figure*, inasmuch as the only possible descriptor that was unique to each figure at any particular instant in time was its location. If we are correct in arguing from the nature of the tracking parameters that stored locations cannot be used as the basis for tracking then all that is left is the figure's identity over time, or its persisting *individuality*. This is exactly what I claim – viz., that we have a mechanism that allows preconceptual tracking of a primitive perceptual individuality.[3]

Recently, a large number of additional studies in our laboratory (Blaser, Pylyshyn, & Domini, 1999; Blaser, Pylyshyn, & Holcombe, 2000; McKeever, 1991; Pylyshyn, 1998; Scholl & Pylyshyn, 1999; Scholl, Pylyshyn, & Feldman, 2001; Scholl, Pylyshyn, & Franconeri, 2001; Sears & Pylyshyn, 2000) as well as in other laboratories (Culham et al., 1998; Intriligator & Cavanagh, 1992; Viswanathan & Mingolla, in press; Yantis, 1992, and others) have replicated these MOT results using a variety of different methods, confirming that observers can successfully track around four or five independently moving objects. The results also showed that merely widening one's breadth of attention (as assumed in the so-called zoom lens model of attention spreading, Eriksen & St. James, 1986) would not account for the data. Performance in detecting changes to elements located inside the convex hull outline of the set of targets was no better than performance on elements outside this region, contrary to what would be expected if the area of attention were simply widened or shaped to conform to an appropriate outline (Sears & Pylyshyn, 2000). Using a different tracking methodology, Intriligator and Cavanagh (1992) also failed to find any evidence of a 'spread of attention' to regions between targets (see also Awh & Pashler, 2000). It appears, then, that items can be tracked despite the lack of distinctive properties (and, indeed when their properties are changing) and despite constantly changing locations and unpredictable motions.[4] Taken together, these studies suggest that what Marr (1982) referred to as the *early vision system* (an essentially encapsulated system, discussed at length in Pylyshyn, 1999) is able to individuate and keep track of about five visual objects and does so without using an encoding of any of their visual properties.

The MOT task exemplifies what is meant by 'tracking' and by 'maintaining the

---

[3] As usual one can't exclude all logically possible alternative processes for achieving these results. For example, we cannot exclude the possibility that location encoding occurs in parallel at each tracked object and then serially allocated focal attention is used for tracking, or that four parallel 'beams of attention' independently track the four targets. Another alternative that has been proposed (e.g. Yantis, 1992) is that the objects are tracked by imagining that they are vertices of a deforming polygon and tracking the polygon as a whole. This 'polygon tracking' view may describe a useful strategy for chunking the tracking objects and thus improve one's memory for where they are (which is useful for recovering from errors, as noted in Sears & Pylyshyn, 2000), but it does not supplant the need to track the individual objects since the statistically independent movement of these objects continues to define the vertices of the imagined distorting polygon. One logically cannot track the polygon without *somehow* tracking the independently-moving individual targets. Moreover, observers can track the targets perfectly well whether or not they maintain a convex polygon and whether or not they use this strategy. The strongest case for the indexing mechanism comes from the convergence of a variety of different studies (described in Pylyshyn et al., 1994, and elsewhere), no one of which is definitive, but the pattern of which supports the view that there is a distinct mechanism for individuating and keeping track of token visual objects.

[4] In a set of yet-unpublished studies (Scholl, Pylyshyn, & Franconeri, 2001) we have even shown that observers do not notice and cannot report changes of color or shape of objects they are tracking when the change occurs while they are behind an occluder or during a short period of blank screen, thus lending credence to the view that properties are ignored during tracking.

identity' of objects. It also operationalizes the notion of 'primitive visual object' as whatever allows preconceptual selection and MOT.[5] Note that objecthood and object-identity are thus defined in terms of an empirically established mechanism in the human early vision system. A certain (possibly smooth) sequence of object locations will count as the movement of a single visual object if the early vision system groups it this way – i.e. if it is so perceived. Of course it is of interest to discover what sorts of events will in fact count as visual objects from this perspective. We are just beginning to investigate this question. We know from MOT studies that simple figures count as objects and also that certain well-defined clusters of features do not (Scholl, Pylyshyn, & Feldman, 2001). Indeed, as we saw in Section 2, some well-defined visually-resolvable features do not allow individuation (see Figs. 2 and 3). We also know that the visual system may count as a single persisting individual, certain cases where clusters of features disappear and reappear. For example, Scholl and Pylyshyn (1999) showed that if the objects being tracked in the MOT paradigm disappear and reappear in certain ways, they are tracked as though they had a continuous existence. If, for example, they disappear and reappear by deletion and accretion along a fixed contour, the way they would have if they were moving behind an occluding surface (even if the edges of the occluder are not invisible), they are successfully tracked. However, performance in the MOT task degrades significantly in the control conditions where objects suddenly go out of existence and reappear at the appropriate matching time and place, or if they slowly shrink away to a point and then reappear by slowly growing again at exactly the same relative time and place as they had accreted in the occlusion condition. The persistence of objecthood despite certain kinds of disappearances was also shown in a different context by Yantis (1998) who found that when an object disappears either for a very short time or under conditions where it is seen to have been occluded by an opaque surface, the visual system treats the two exposures of the object as a single persisting object. These findings are compatible with the thesis (Nakayama, He, & Shimojo, 1995) that occlusion plays an important role in early vision. Beyond that, what qualifies as a primitive (potentially indexable) object remains an open empirical question. In fact, recent evidence (Blaser et al., 2000) has even shown that objects can be tracked even though they are not specified by unique spatiotemporal coordinates (e.g. when they share a common spatial locus and move through 'feature space' rather than real space).

---

[5] The concept of a 'proto-object' is a general one that has been used by a number of writers (sometimes using the same term, Di Lollo, Enns, & Rensink, 2000; Rensink, 2000a, and sometimes using some other term, such as 'preattentive object', Wolfe & Bennett, 1997) in reference to clusters of proximal features that serve as precursors in the detection of real physical objects. What these uses have in common is that they refer to something more than a localized property or 'feature' and less than a recognized 3D distal object. Beyond that, the exact nature of a proto-object depends on the theory in question.

4. A theory of visual indexing and binding: the FINST mechanism

4.1. Background motivation and assumptions of the theory

The basic motivation for postulating indexes is that, as we saw at the beginning of this essay, there are a number of reasons for thinking that a certain number of individual objects in the field of view must first be *picked out* from the rest of the visual field and the identity of these objects *qua individuals* (sometimes called their *numerical identity*) must be maintained or tracked despite changes in the individuals' properties, including their location in the visual field. The visual index hypothesis claims that this is done *primitively* by the FINST mechanism of the early vision system, without identifying the object through a unique descriptor. In other words, it is done without cognitive or conceptual intervention. In assigning indexes, some cluster of visual features must first be segregated from the background or picked out as a unit (the Gestalt notion of making a figure-ground distinction is closely related to this sort of 'picking out', although it carries with it other implications that we do not need to assume in the present context – for example that bounding contours are designated as belonging to one of the possible resulting figures). Until some part of the visual field is segregated in this way, no visual operation can be applied to it since it does not exist as something distinct from the entire field.[6]

But segregating a region of visual space is not the only thing that is required. The second part of the individuation process is that of providing a way for the cognitive system to refer to that particular individual or visual object, as distinct from other individuals. It must be possible to bind one of a small number (perhaps four or five) of internal symbols or elements of a visual representation to individual clusters or visual proto-objects. Moreover, the binding must be such that the representation can continue to refer to a visual object, treating it as the *same* individual despite changes in its location or any other property (subject to certain constraints which need to be empirically determined). The existence of such a capacity would make it possible, under certain conditions, to pick out a small number if individual visual objects and also to keep track of them as individuals over time. We are beginning to map out some of the conditions under which such individuation and tracking can occur; for example, they include spatiotemporal continuity of motion, or discontinuity in the presence of local occlusion

---

[6] Only *visual* objects have been considered in this paper. However, objecthood need not be specific to a particular modality, and more general notions of objecthood might turn out to be theoretically useful. For example, if we define objecthood in terms of trackability (as I do when I half-seriously introduce the term 'FINGs' at the end of this paper, or as we do in Scholl, Pylyshyn, & Feldman, 2001), then objecthood may become a broader, and perhaps theoretically more interesting notion. For example, it appears that even when visual 'objects' are not distinguished by distinct spatiotemporal boundaries and trajectories, they still function as objects in many other respects. They may, for example, be tracked as individuals and they may exhibit such object-based attention phenomena as the single-object detection superiority (Blaser et al., 2000). The auditory domain offers additional possibilities: auditory objects can be tracked either when a moving auditory source is distinguished and followed or when patterns or 'streams' are followed over time (Bregman, 1990; Kubovy & Van Valkenburg, 2001). Whether these various distinct phenomena involve the same sort of indexing mechanism remains an open research question.

cues such as those mentioned above in discussing the Scholl and Pylyshyn (1999) and the Yantis (1998) results. They also include the requirement that the element being tracked be a perceptual whole as opposed to some arbitrary, but well-defined, set of features (see Scholl, Pylyshyn, & Feldman, 2001).

Visual index or FINST theory is described in several publications cited earlier and will not be described in detail here beyond the sketch given above. The essential assumptions may be summarized as follows: (1) early visual processes segment the visual field into feature-clusters which tend to be reliable proximal counterparts of distinct individual objects in a distal scene; (2) recently activated clusters compete for a pool of four to five visual indexes or FINSTs; (3) index assignment is primarily stimulus-driven, although some restricted cognitively mediated processes, such as scanning focal attention until an object is encountered that elicits an index, may also result in the assignment of an index; (4) indexes keep being bound to the same individual visual objects as the latter change their properties and locations, within certain as-yet-unknown constraints (which is what makes them perceptually the same objects); and (5) only indexed objects can enter into subsequent cognitive processes, such as recognizing their individual or relational properties, or moving focal attention or gaze or making other motor gestures to them.

The basic idea of the visual indexing and binding mechanism is illustrated schematically in Fig. 7. Certain proximal events (e.g. the appearance of a new visual object) cause an index to be *grabbed* (since there is only a small pool of such indexes this may sometimes result in an existing binding being lost). As new properties of this object are noticed and encoded they are associated with the index that points to that object. This, in effect, provides a mechanism for connecting elements of an evolving representation with elements (i.e. objects) in the world. By virtue of this causal connection, the cognitive system can *refer to* any of a small number of primitive visual objects. The sense of reference that is relevant here is one that appears in computer science when we speak of pointers or when variables are assigned values. In this sense, when we speak of having a reference we mean that

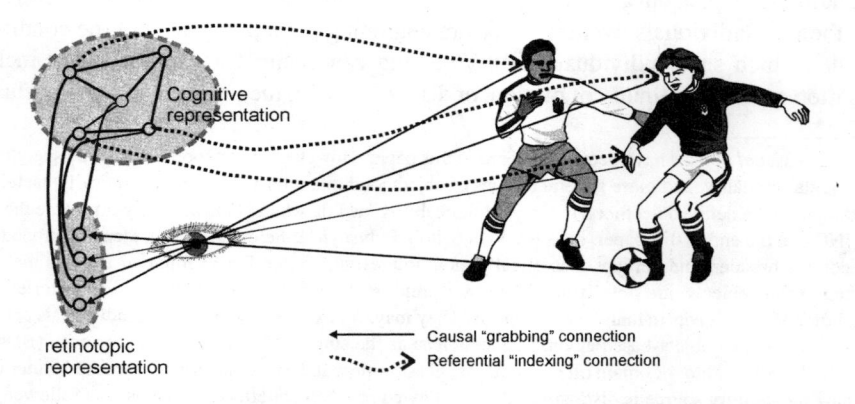

Fig. 7. Sketch of the types of connections established by visual indexes between the primitive visual objects or proto-objects and parts of conceptual structures, depicted here as a network.

we are able to access the things being referred to (the referents) in certain ways: to interrogate them in order to determine some of their properties, to evaluate multiple-argument (polyadic) predicates over them, to move focal attention to them, and in general to *bind* cognitive arguments to them. The important thing here is that the inward arrows are purely causal and are instantiated by the preconceptual apparatus which, following the terminology suggested by Marr (1982), we call *early vision* (Pylyshyn, 1999). The indexing system latches on to certain kinds of spatiotemporal objects because it is 'wired' to do so, or because it is in the nature of its functional architecture to do so, not because those entities satisfy a certain cognitive predicate – i.e. not because they fall under a certain concept. This sort of causal connection between a perceptual system and an object in a scene is quite different from a representational or intentional or conceptual connection. For one thing there can be no question of the object being *mis*represented since it is not represented *as* something (see also Footnote 1).

Although this sort of seizing of indexes by primitive visual objects is essentially a bottom-up process, it could in some cases be guided in an indirect way by intentional processes. For example, it is known (Posner, Snyder, & Davidson, 1980) that people can scan their focal attention along some path (by simply moving it continuously through space like a spotlight beam) and thereby locate certain sorts of objects. A possible consequence of such scanning is that an index may get assigned to some primitive objects encountered along the way. This is no different from the sort of indirect influence that cognition has over vision when one chooses to direct one's gaze or focal attention or the sort of indirect influence we have over other automatic functions (including such autonomic functions as heart rate) when we choose to carry out a voluntary action that leads to a change in the automatic function.

The indexing notion being hypothesized is extremely simple and only seems complicated because ordinary language fails to respect certain distinctions (such as the distinction between individuating and recognizing, or between indexing and knowing where something is, and so on). In fact a very simple network, such as the one described by Koch and Ullman (1985) can implement such a function[7] (the application of the Koch and Ullman network to visual index theory has been

---

[7] Although we do not address the question of how such a mechanism might be implemented in the nervous system or otherwise, alternatives are not difficult to imagine in the case of vision. Any early vision system will contain sensors and a way of clustering features (e.g. Marr, 1982). In order to maintain the identity of moving clusters (i.e. to implement a 'sticky' binding) all one needs is a mechanism that treats time-slices of clusters that move continuously over the retina as the same cluster. It could do so, for example, by following the rule that if the majority of the elements in a cluster (represented, for example, in a 'list of contributing points') continue to be present in a succeeding cluster then consider both clusters to be the same. Or alternatively, one could simply spread the activation arising from a cluster of elements to neighboring elements, thereby favoring the activation of nearby regions and so favoring continuously moving clusters. This is essentially the technique suggested by Koch and Ullman (1985) in their proposal for a neural implementation of attentional scanning. The point is that there is no in-principle puzzle about how one could implement the notion that indexes are assigned by a bottom-up causal mechanism so that once assigned the indexes are maintained as the clusters move about. Once we have such a clustering mechanism, assigning pointers to the most active of the ensuing clusters is a trivial matter and common ground to most theories of attention (e.g. the guided search theory of Wolfe et al., 1989).

explored in Acton, 1993; Pylyshyn & Eagleson, 1994). All that is required is a winner-take-all circuit whose convergence on a certain active region (or node) on a spatiotopic map enables a signal to be sent to that region, thus allowing it to be probed for the presence of specific properties (a simple sketch of such a system is given in Box 4 of Pylyshyn, 2000). The important point about such a network, which makes its pointing function essentially preconceptual, is that the process that sends the probe signal to a particular object *uses no encoding of properties of that object, not even its location*. Being able to probe a certain object depends only on its instantaneous location (say in some feature map) being the most active by some measure (such as the activation measures assumed in many theories of visual search, like those of Treisman & Gelade, 1980; Wolfe, Cave, & Franzel, 1989). What makes this system object-based, rather than location-based, is certain provisions in the network (i.e. enhancing of the immediate neighboring places) which result in the probe location moving in response to the movement of the primitive object (see Koch & Ullman, 1985).

4.1.1. A note on 'property-dependence' of indexing and on the attentive nature of tracking

There has been some misunderstanding about the role of object properties and of attention in tasks such as MOT. To claim that the indexing process is preconceptual is not to claim that the assignment and maintenance of indexes does not depend on properties of the objects. Clearly indexes get assigned and maintained because the objects in question possess certain properties rather than other properties. The issue is whether an *encoding* of these properties is used by the cognitive system to assign and track an index. It is also clear that objects are being tracked in the MOT paradigm because observers in these studies intend to solve a certain problem and in doing so they must pay attention to the task – indeed they often find the task very attention-demanding. What makes indexing preconceptual is not that it does not depend on properties of objects or that it is not connected with the cognitive system – it clearly is. Like other mechanisms of early (non-cognitive) vision, such as edge detectors, these mechanisms are both modular (i.e. operate on a manner that is independent of cognitive processes) and at the same time are deployed by cognitive processes in pursuit of some task. Red detectors are presumably preconceptual too, they work the way they do because of their physical–chemical properties, but they can nonetheless be deployed in a cognitive task, such as to search for a red car in a parking lot. None of these facts mean that *indexing* per se is conceptual or cognitive or even attentive.

Cognitive factors clearly enter into many aspects of performance in tasks such as MOT. Even if tracking is data-driven, as we have claimed, observers can also decide to move their attention from target to target (that they can do so is an explicit claim of indexing theory). And when they do so they can encode the relative location of targets, even if tracking does not make use of that information. In Sears and Pylyshyn (2000) we argue that one purpose for encoding this location information might be to help recover from errors. If indexes are occasionally lost due to visual distractions, a 'shadow model' of the display can be used to aid in their recovery. Sears and

Pylyshyn argued that such a strategy could account for several aspects of their data, and also might explain why constraining the targets to maintaining a more memorable configuration, such as the convex hull shape investigated by Yantis (1992), helps to improve tracking performance. In any case it is clear that more is going on in MOT experiments than just tracking based on data-driven index maintenance. There is always an overlay of cognitive activity: observers may choose to keep track of designated targets or to switch their attention to other indexed objects, or they may choose to scan their attention around until new objects capture indexes. As we suggested earlier, the cognitive system may be able to influence the indexing process in such indirect ways, and in so doing make it possible for different objects to be indexed (thus allowing objects other than flickered ones to be designated as targets). Observers are free agents, and they don't have to use the indexing mechanism provided by early vision to track targets – they may choose to attend to the sound in the next room or leave the experiment. The *total task* in these (and all other human subject) studies is clearly under cognitive control and typically requires considerable concentration.

In the past I have referred to indexing as 'preattentive' because the theory hypothesizes that indexes are not mediated by a conceptual description. But as just noted, even if the indexing and tracking mechanism is preattentive in this sense, the *task* of tracking multiple objects may require a great deal of effort and attention. In fact the theory predicts that indexes would be readily grabbed by any new object that appears in the field of view, so 'attention' may be involved in orienting the system to the relevant part of the visual field (i.e. attention may be required to control eye movements and to provide some selection of the inputs to the visual indexing system). The notion of an automatic data-driven mechanism is also compatible with the possibility that index binding decays over time and therefore requires periodic reactivation. Since many investigators take susceptibility to disruption and the need for effort as an indication that the process is 'attentive', I now avoid referring to indexing as preattentive. I continue to assume, however, that indexing and tracking are realized by an automatic and preconceptual mechanism, despite the fact that it may require that certain additional conditions be satisfied (e.g. objects must have certain properties in order to capture an index) in order for MOT to occur. This is in part because I believe the bulk of the evidence favors this view and in part because it is the alternative with the more far-reaching consequences and therefore the more interesting hypothesis to pursue, pending evidence to the contrary.

4.2. Relation to other theories

Visual index theory is closely related to a number of other theoretical frameworks. As mentioned earlier, it is very close in spirit to the object file theory of Kahneman et al. (1992) although the latter has been applied in the context of memory retrieval and has consequently emphasized the memory content of the information associated with the objects in memory. Kahneman et al. are correct when they suggest that, "We might think of [a visual index] as the initial spatiotemporal label that is entered in the object file and that is used to address it... [A] FINST might be the initial phase of a simple object file before any features have been attached to it" (p. 216). Because of this difference in focus, research on visual indexes has been more concerned with the nature of the mechanism that allows cognition to refer to and track objects, whereas object file theory has been concerned with the question of which features of the objects are (eventually) encoded and associated with the object in memory. Thus, other investigators who appeal to the object file idea have typically asked what object-related information is encoded (Wolfe & Bennett, 1997), whereas we have looked at conditions under which only the individuality of objects is relevant to the task.

There is also a close connection between the proposed visual index mechanism and the notion of a *deictic code* discussed by Ballard et al. (1997), although their term 'deictic *code*' misleadingly suggests that the pointer actually encodes some property of the scene, as opposed to providing access to the object's properties. In the Ballard et al. discussion, the authors also point out the importance of having some way to refer to objects in a scene, without using some unique encoded properties to pick out such objects. They introduce the need for such reference both on the grounds of computational complexity and on experimental grounds, because it makes it possible to use what they call a *deictic strategy* which, in effect, allows the perceiver to minimize storage by encoding visual information only when it is needed. In their experiments they found that when observers examine a scene for the purpose of such tasks as copying a pattern of blocks, they encode very little (only the color or location of one block) on each fixation, preferring instead to revisit the scene for each new piece of information. From this Ballard et al. conclude that the object being fixated serves as a deictic reference point in building a minimal description. This is very similar to the view taken here, except that according to the present theory, such deictic references need not involve eye fixations (though they may frequently do so) and they can be directed at more than one object at a time. Indeed, we know from the work of Ullman (1984), as well as from our own work discussed earlier, that they must involve several objects.

There is also a close connection, noted earlier, between updating a representation as new properties of a scene are noticed, and updating a representation in the course of moving one's eyes about, the problem of saccadic integration. If visual indexes were able to keep track of a small number of objects as the same persisting individuals over the course of saccadic eye movements we would have a mechanism that might help to solve one of the central problems of saccadic integration: the problem of determining correspondences between objects in successive views. It had been widely believed that we maintain a large panoramic display and superimpose successive views in registration with eye movements (the registration being accomplished by using a 'corollary discharge' signal). This view has now been thoroughly discredited (Irwin, 1996; O'Regan, 1992), leaving the saccadic integration problem as an open problem in vision research.

The correspondence problem has always been at the heart of the saccadic integration problem, as well as for theories of apparent motion (Dawson & Pylyshyn, 1988), stereo vision (Marr, 1982), visual-auditory integration of location information, visual-motor adaptation, and many other psychophysical phenomena that require a perceptual correspondence to be established between individuals. Various mechanisms have been proposed for dealing with this problem. The possible mechanisms for solving this problem rely on one or another of the two distinct ways of picking out and keeping track of individual objects that were discussed earlier: ones that appeal to a unique description of a individual object and ones that do not. The first type includes an interesting proposal called the saccade-target theory (Currie, McConkie, & Carlson-Radvansky, 2000; Irwin, McConkie, Carlson-Radvansky, & Currie, 1994; McConkie & Currie, 1996), which postulates that unique properties of *one* object (the one that serves as the target of the saccade) are encoded and searched for in the second fixation in order to establish a cross-fixation correspondence. Since Irwin (1996) has found that subjects can retain the locations of about four objects across a saccade, the other three objects would have to be located by recalling their (encoded) locations relative to the saccade target. The second option is exemplified by the visual index theory. In contrast to the saccade-target theory, visual index theory assumes that a small number of objects can be recovered from the second fixation as a side effect of their having been indexed and tracked across the saccade, without the benefit of an encoding of their properties. Of course this assumes that indexes survive the very rapid saccadic motion. Some informal indication that this may be the case comes from our own observations that MOT occurs equally well when saccades are freely permitted as when they are prevented (as in the original studies of Pylyshyn & Storm, 1988). Moreover, Henderson and Anes (1994) showed that object files were retained during saccades since object-specific priming occurred across eye fixations.

5. Discussion: objects and the mind–world connection

Visual indexing (FINST) theory hypothesizes a mechanism for picking out, tracking and providing *cognitive access* to *visual objects* or *proto-objects*. The notion of an *object* is ubiquitous in cognitive science, not only in vision but much more widely. Indeed, in a recent ambitious work inspired by ideas from computer science, Brian Cantwell Smith has made the generalized notion of object the centerpiece of a radical reformulation of metaphysics (Smith, 1996). The present work shares with Smith an interest in the question of how a connection can be established between a concept and an object (or in Smith's terms, how the world can be 'registered'), and it also shares the view that the phenomenon of tracking is central to understanding this notion. But our concern in this essay has not been to construct a notion of object free of metaphysical assumptions about the world (a sort of Cartesian skepticism), but with the notion of object beginning with some basic facts about the nature of our early vision system. We take for granted that the world consists of physical objects. The view being proposed takes its initial inspiration from the many studies that have shown that attention (and hence information access to the visual world) is allocated primarily, though not exclusively, to individual visual objects rather than to properties or to unfilled locations (Baylis & Driver, 1993). This general conclusion is also supported by evidence from clinical neuroscience, where it has been argued that deficits such as unilateral neglect (Driver & Halligan, 1991) or Balint syndrome (Robertson, Treisman, Friedman-Hill, & Grabowecky, 1997) apply over frames of reference that include ones that are object-based, where deficits appear to be specified with respect to individual objects. From this initial idea we have sought to analyze the process of attention into distinct stages. One of these involves the detection and tracking of primitive visual objects. This stage allows attention and other more cognitive processes to access and to operate on these primitive visual objects.

Although our focus has been on *visual* objects there are a number of findings in cognitive development that appear to be relevant to our notion of object and index. For example, the notion of object has played an important role in several works (Carey & Xu, 2001; Leslie, Xu, Tremoulet, & Scholl, 1998; Spelke, Gutheil, & Van de Walle, 1995; Xu & Carey, 1996). Leslie et al. have explicitly recognized the close relation between this notion of object and the one that is involved in our theory of visual indexes. Typical experiments show that in certain situations, 8-month-old infants are sensitive to the cardinality of a set of (one or two) objects even before they use the properties of the individual objects in predicting what will happen in certain situations where objects are placed behind a screen and then the screen is removed. For example, Leslie et al. (1998) describe a number of studies in which one or two objects are placed behind a screen and the screen is then removed to reveal two or one objects. Infants exhibit longer looking times (relative to a baseline) when the *number* of objects revealed is different from the number that the infant sees being placed behind the screen, but not when the objects have different visual properties. This has widely been taken to suggest that registering the individuality of objects ontologically precedes the encoding of their properties in tasks involving objects' disappearance and reappearance.

While it is tempting to identify these empirical phenomena with the same notion of 'object', it remains an open question whether all these uses of the term refer to the same thing. My present use of the term is inextricably connected with the theoretical mechanism of visual indexing, and therefore to the phenomena of individuation and tracking, and assumes that such objects are picked out in a preconceptual manner. If the sense of 'object' that is needed in other contexts entails that individuating and tracking must appeal to a conceptual category, defined in terms of how the observer represents it or what the observer takes it to be, then it will not help us to ground our concepts nor will it help with the problem of keeping track of individuals during incremental construction of a percept. In the case of the MOT examples, the notion of primitive visual object introduced here does fill these functions. But of course this leaves open the question of what the connection is between the primitive visual object so-defined and the more usual notion of physical object, and in particular with the notion of object often appealed to in the infant studies. In those studies, an object is sometimes defined as a "bounded, coherent, three-dimensional physical object that moves as a whole" (Spelke, 1990). Are such Spelke objects different from what we have been calling visual objects?

The speculative answer to the question of the relation between these two notions of object is that primitive visual objects are *typically* the proximal counterparts of real physical objects (which include Spelke objects). According to this view, the visual system is so structured that it detects visual patterns which *in our kind of world* tend to be reliably associated with entities that meet the Spelke criteria. If that is the case, then it suggests that, contrary to claims made by developmental psychologists like Spelke et al. (1995) and Xu (1997), quite possibly the *concept* of an object is not involved in picking out these objects, just as no concept at all of the individual objects (i.e. no description) plays a role in such phenomena as MOT. Despite this speculative suggestion, it is less clear whether a concept is involved in all the cases discussed in the developmental literature. From the sorts of considerations raised here, it seems likely that something more than just concepts may be involved in at least some cases of infants' picking out objects. It seems likely that a direct demonstrative reference or *indexing* is involved in at least some of the phenomena (see Leslie et al., 1998). However, there also appear to be cases in which clusters of features that one would expect would be perfectly good objects from the perspective of their visual properties may nonetheless fail to be tracked as objects by 8-month-old infants. Chiang and Wynn (2000) have argued that *if the infants are given evidence that the things that look like individual objects are actually collections of objects* then they do not keep track of them in the studies involving placing objects behind a screen, despite the fact that they do track the visually-identical collections when this evidence is not provided. For example, if infants see the putative objects being disassembled and reassembled, or if they see them come into existence by being *poured from a beaker* (Carey & Xu, 2001; Huntley-Fenner, Carey, & Salimando, 2001), they fail to track them as individual objects. This *could* mean that whether or not something is treated as an object depends on prior knowledge (which would make them conceptual in this case). On the other hand it may just mean that certain aspects of the recent visual history of the objects affects whether or not the visual system treats them as individual objects. What makes the latter at least a possibility is that something like this appears to be the case with other cases of the disappearance and reappearance of visual objects. As mentioned earlier, it has been shown that the precise *manner* in which objects disappear and reappear matters to whether or not they continue to be tracked (Scholl & Pylyshyn, 1999). In particular, if their disappearance is by a pattern of accretion such as occurs when the object goes behind an occluding surface and reappears in a complementary manner (by disocclusion), then it continues to be tracked in a MOT paradigm. But this sort of effect of recent visual history is quite plausibly subsumed under the operation of a preconceptual mechanism of the early vision system (for other examples of what appear on the surface as knowledge-based phenomena but which can be understood as the consequence of a non-cognitive mechanism, see Pylyshyn, 1999).

The central role that objects play in vision has another, perhaps deeper, consequence worth noting. The primacy of objects as the focus through which properties are encoded suggests a rather different way to view the role of objects in visual perception and cognition. Just as it is natural to think that we apprehend properties such as color and shape as properties of *objects*, so it has also been natural to think that we apprehend objects as a kind of property that particular *places* have. In other words, we usually think of the matrix of space-time as being primary and of objects as being occupants of places and times. Yet the present proposal suggests an alternative and rather intriguing possibility. It is the notion that *primitive visual object* is the primary and more primitive category of early (preconceptual) vision. It may be that we detect *objecthood* first and determine location the way we might determine color or shape – as a property associated with the detected objects. If this is true then it raises some interesting possibilities concerning the nature of the mechanisms of early vision. In particular, it adds further credence to the claim that we must have a way of referring directly to primitive visual objects without using a unique description under which that object falls. Perhaps this function can be served in part by the mechanism I referred to as a visual index or a visual demonstrative (or a FINST).

Notice that what I have been describing is not the notion of an individual physical object. The usual notion of a *physical* object, such as a particular table or chair or a particular individual person, *does* require concepts (in particular it requires what are called *sortal* concepts) in order to establish criteria of identity, as philosophers like Hirsch (1982) and others have argued. The individual items that are picked out by the visual system and tracked primitively are something less than full-blooded individual objects. Yet because they are what our visual system gives us through a brute causal mechanism (because that is its nature), and also because the proto-objects picked out in this way are typically associated with real objects in our kind of world, indexes may serve as the basis for real individuation of physical objects. While it is clear that you cannot individuate objects in the full-blooded sense without a conceptual apparatus, it is also clear that you cannot individuate them with *only* a conceptual apparatus. Sooner or later concepts must be grounded in a primitive causal connection between thoughts and things. The project of grounding concepts in sense data has not fared well and has been abandoned in cognitive science. However, the principle of grounding concepts in perception remains an essential requirement if we are to avoid an infinite regress. Visual indexes provide a putative grounding for basic objects – the individuals to which perceptual predicates apply, and hence about which cognitive judgments and plans of action are made (see the interesting discussion of the latter in Miller, Galanter, & Pribram, 1960). Without such a preconceptual grounding, our percepts and our thoughts would be disconnected from causal links to the real-world objects of those thoughts. With indexes we can think about things (I am sometimes tempted to call them *FINGs* since they are inter-defined with *FINSTs*) without having any concepts of them: one might say that we can have *demonstrative thoughts*. We can think thoughts about *this* without *any description* under which the object of that thought falls: you can pick out one speck among countless identical specks on a beach. What's even more important is that at some stage we *must* be able to make judgments about things for which we do not have a description. For if all we had was descriptions, we would not be able to tell whether a particular description D was satisfied by some particular thing in the world, since we would have no independent way to select or refer to the thing that satisfied D. Without preconceptual reference we would not be able to decide that a particular description D was satisfied by a particular individual (i.e. by *that* individual) and thus we could not make judgments about nor decide to act upon a particular individual. It is because you can pick out a particular individual that you can move your gaze to it or you can reach for it – your motor system cannot be commanded to reach for something that is red, only to reach for a particular individual object.

Needless to say there are some details to be worked out so this is a work-in-progress. But there are real problems to be solved in connecting visual representations to the world in the right way, and whatever the eventual solution turns out to be, it will have to respect a set of both logical and empirical considerations, some of which are sketched here. Moreover, any visual or attentional mechanism that might be hypothesized for this purpose will have far-reaching implications, not only for theories of situated vision, but also for grounding the content of visual representations and perhaps for grounding perceptual concepts in general.

Acknowledgements

I wish to thank Jerry Fodor for his considerable help with this paper, particularly with regard to the many conceptual and philosophical questions raised by this work, and Brian Scholl for his careful reading of several drafts of this manuscript and for our many useful discussions and arguments over the interpretation of our results. This research was supported in part by NIHM grant 1R01-MH60924.

References

Acton, B. (1993). *A network model of visual indexing and attention*. Unpublished master's thesis, University of Western Ontario, London, Canada.

Agre, P. E. (1997). *Computation and human experience*. Cambridge: Cambridge University Press.

Awh, E., & Pashler, H. (2000). Evidence for split attentional foci. *Journal of Experimental Psychology: Human Perception and Performance*, 26 (2), 834–846.

Ballard, D. H., Hayhoe, M. M., Pook, P. K., & Rao, R. P. N. (1997). Deictic codes for the embodiment of cognition. *Behavioral and Brain Sciences*, 20 (4), 723–767.

Baylis, G. C., & Driver, J. (1993). Visual attention and objects: evidence for hierarchical coding of location. *Journal of Experimental Psychology: Human Perception and Performance*, 19, 451–470.

Blaser, E., Pylyshyn, Z. W., & Domini, F. (1999). Measuring attention during 3D multielement tracking (abstract). *Investigative Ophthalmology and Visual Science*, 40 (4), 552.

Blaser, E., Pylyshyn, Z. W., & Holcombe, A. O. (2000). Tracking an object through feature-space. *Nature*, 408 (Nov 9), 196–199.

Bregman, A. (1990). *Auditory scene analysis: the perceptual organization of sound*. Cambridge, MA: MIT Press.

Brooks, R. A. (1999). *Cambrian intelligence*. Cambridge, MA: MIT Press (A Bradford Book).

Burkell, J., & Pylyshyn, Z. W. (1997). Searching through subsets: a test of the visual indexing hypothesis. *Spatial Vision*, 11 (2), 225–258.

Calis, G. J., Sterenborg, J., & Maarse, F. (1984). Initial microgenetic steps in single-glance face recognition. *Acta Psychologica*, 55 (3), 215–230.

Carey, S., & Xu, F. (2001). Infants' knowledge of objects: beyond object files and object tracking. *Cognition*, this issue, 80, 179–213.

Chiang, W. -C., & Wynn, K. (2000). Infants' representation and tracking of multiple objects. *Cognition*, 75, 1–27.

Culham, J. C., Brandt, S. A., Cavanagh, P., Kanwisher, N. G., Dale, A. M., & Tootell, R. B. H. (1998).

Cortical fMRI activation produced by attentive tracking of moving targets. *Journal of Neurophysiology*, 80 (5), 2657–2670.

Currie, C. B., McConkie, G. W., & Carlson-Radvansky, L. A. (2000). The role of the saccade target object in the perception of a visually stable world. *Perception & Psychophysics*, 62, 673–683.

Dawson, M., & Pylyshyn, Z. W. (1988). Natural constraints in apparent motion. In Z. W. Pylyshyn (Ed.), *Computational processes in human vision: an interdisciplinary perspective* (pp. 99–120). Stamford, CT: Ablex.

Di Lollo, V., Enns, J. T., & Rensink, R. A. (2000). Competition for consciousness among visual events: the psychophysics of reentrant visual processes. *Journal of Experimental Psychology: General*, 129 (4), 481–507.

Driver, J., & Halligan, P. (1991). Can visual neglect operate in object-centered coordinates? An affirmative single case study. *Cognitive Neuropsychology*, 8, 475–494.

Eriksen, C. W., & St. James, J. D. (1986). Visual attention within and around the field of focal attention: a zoom lens model. *Perception & Psychophysics*, 40, 225–240.

Feldman, J. A., & Ballard, D. H. (1982). Connectionist models and their properties. *Cognitive Science*, 6, 205–254.

He, S., Cavanagh, P., & Intriligator, J. (1997). Attentional resolution. *Trends in Cognitive Sciences*, 1 (3), 115–121.

Henderson, J. M., & Anes, M. D. (1994). Roles of object-file review and type priming in visual identification within and across eye fixations. *Journal of Experimental Psychology: Human Perception and Performance*, 20 (4), 826–839.

Hirsch, E. (1982). *The concept of identity*. Oxford: Oxford University Press.

Huntley-Fenner, G., Carey, S., & Salimando, A. (2001). Sand does not count: infant individuation of objects and non-solid substances. Manuscript submitted for publication.

Intriligator, J. M. (1997). *The spatial resolution of attention*. Unpublished Ph.D., Harvard University, Cambridge, MA.

Intriligator, J., & Cavanagh, P. (1992). Object-specific spatial attention facilitation that does not travel to adjacent spatial locations (abstract). *Investigative Ophthalmology and Visual Science*, 33, 2849.

Irwin, D. E. (1996). Integrating information across saccadic eye movements. *Current Directions in Psychological Science*, 5 (3), 94–100.

Irwin, D. E., McConkie, G. W., Carlson-Radvansky, L. A., & Currie, C. (1994). A localist evaluation solution for visual stability across saccades. *Behavioral and Brain Sciences*, 17, 265–266.

Kahneman, D., Treisman, A., & Gibbs, B. J. (1992). The reviewing of object files: object-specific integration of information. *Cognitive Psychology*, 24 (2), 175–219.

Koch, C., & Ullman, S. (1985). Shifts in selective visual attention: towards the underlying neural circuitry. *Human Neurobiology*, 4, 219–227.

Kubovy, M., & Van Valkenburg, D. (2001). Auditory and visual objects. *Cognition*, this issue, 80, 97–126.

Leslie, A. M., Xu, F., Tremoulet, P. D., & Scholl, B. J. (1998). Indexing and the object concept: developing 'what' and 'where' systems. *Trends in Cognitive Sciences*, 2 (1), 10–18.

Lespérance, Y., & Levesque, H. J. (1995). Indexical knowledge and robot action – a logical account. *Artificial Intelligence*, 73, 69–115.

Marr, D. (1982). *Vision: a computational investigation into the human representation and processing of visual information*. San Francisco, CA: W.H. Freeman.

McConkie, G. M., & Currie, C. B. (1996). Visual stability across saccades while viewing complex pictures. *Journal of Experimental Psychology: Human Perception and Performance*, 22 (3), 563–581.

McKeever, P. (1991). *Nontarget numerosity and identity maintenance with FINSTs: a two component account of multiple-target tracking*. Unpublished master's thesis, University of Western Ontario, London, Canada.

Miller, G. A., Galanter, E., & Pribram, K. H. (1960). *Plans and the structure of behavior*. New York: Holt, Rinehart & Winston.

Nakayama, K., He, Z. J., & Shimojo, S. (1995). Visual surface representation: a critical link between lower-level and higher-level vision. In S. M. Kosslyn, & D. N. Osherson (Eds.), *Visual cognition* (pp. 1–70). Cambridge, MA: MIT Press.

Navon, D. (1977). Forest before trees: the precedence of global features in visual perception. *Cognitive Psychology, 9*, 353–383.

Nissen, M. J. (1985). Accessing features and objects: is location special? In M. I. Posner, & O. S. Marin (Eds.), *Attention and performance* (Vol. XI, pp. 205–219). Hillsdale, NJ: Lawrence Erlbaum.

O'Regan, J. K. (1992). Solving the "real" mysteries of visual perception: the world as an outside memory. *Canadian Journal of Psychology, 46*, 461–488.

Pashler, H. E. (1998). *The psychology of attention.* Cambridge, MA: MIT Press (A Bradford Book).

Perry, J. (1979). The problem of the essential indexical. *Noûs, 13*, 3–21.

Posner, M. I., Snyder, C., & Davidson, B. (1980). Attention and the detection of signals. *Journal of Experimental Psychology: General, 109*, 160–174.

Pylyshyn, Z. W. (1984). *Computation and cognition: toward a foundation for cognitive science.* Cambridge, MA: MIT Press.

Pylyshyn, Z. W. (1989). The role of location indexes in spatial perception: a sketch of the FINST spatial-index model. *Cognition, 32*, 65–97.

Pylyshyn, Z. W. (1998). Visual indexes in spatial vision and imagery. In R. D. Wright (Ed.), *Visual attention* (pp. 215–231). New York: Oxford University Press.

Pylyshyn, Z. W. (1999). Is vision continuous with cognition? The case for cognitive impenetrability of visual perception. *Behavioral and Brain Sciences, 22* (3), 341–423.

Pylyshyn, Z. W. (2000). Situating vision in the world. *Trends in Cognitive Sciences, 4* (5), 197–207.

Pylyshyn, Z. W., Burkell, J., Fisher, B., Sears, C., Schmidt, W., & Trick, L. (1994). Multiple parallel access in visual attention. *Canadian Journal of Experimental Psychology, 48* (2), 260–283.

Pylyshyn, Z. W., & Eagleson, R. A. (1994). Developing a network model of multiple visual indexing (abstract). *Investigative Ophthalmology and Visual Science, 35* (4), 2007.

Pylyshyn, Z. W., Elcock, E. W., Marmor, M., & Sander, P. (1978). *Explorations in visual-motor spaces.* Paper presented at the Proceedings of the Second International Conference of the Canadian Society for Computational Studies of Intelligence, University of Toronto, Toronto, Canada.

Pylyshyn, Z. W., & Storm, R. W. (1988). Tracking multiple independent targets: evidence for a parallel tracking mechanism. *Spatial Vision, 3* (3), 1–19.

Rensink, R. A. (2000a). The dynamic representation of scenes. *Visual Cognition, 7*, 17–42.

Rensink, R. A. (2000b). Visual search for change: a probe into the nature of attentional processing. *Visual Cognition, 7*, 345–376.

Rensink, R. A., O'Regan, J. K., & Clark, J. J. (1997). To see or not to see: the need for attention to perceive changes in scenes. *Psychological Science, 8* (5), 368–373.

Rensink, R. A., O'Regan, J. K., & Clark, J. J. (2000). On the failure to detect changes in scenes across brief interruptions. *Visual Cognition, 7*, 127–145.

Reynolds, R. (1981). Perception of an illusory contour as a function of processing time. *Perception, 10*, 107–115.

Robertson, L., Treisman, A., Friedman-Hill, S., & Grabowecky, M. (1997). The interaction of spatial and object pathways: evidence from Balint's syndrome. *Journal of Cognitive Neuroscience, 9* (3), 295–317.

Scholl, B. J. (2001). Objects and attention: the state of the art. *Cognition*, this issue, *80*, 1–46.

Scholl, B. J., & Pylyshyn, Z. W. (1999). Tracking multiple items through occlusion: clues to visual objecthood. *Cognitive Psychology, 38* (2), 259–290.

Scholl, B. J., Pylyshyn, Z. W., & Feldman, J. (2001). What is a visual object: evidence from multiple-object tracking. *Cognition*, this issue, *80*, 159–177.

Scholl, B. J., Pylyshyn, Z. W., & Franconeri, S. L. (2001). The relationship between property-encoding and object-based attention: evidence from multiple-object tracking, submitted for publication.

Schulz, T. (1991). A microgenetic study of the Mueller-Lyer illusion. *Perception, 20* (4), 501–512.

Sears, C. R., & Pylyshyn, Z. W. (2000). Multiple object tracking and attentional processes. *Canadian Journal of Experimental Psychology, 54* (1), 1–14.

Sekuler, A. B., & Palmer, S. E. (1992). Visual completion of partly occluded objects: a microgenetic analysis. *Journal of Experimental Psychology: General, 121*, 95–111.

Simons, D. J. (1996). In sight, out of mind: when object representations fail. *Psychological Science, 7* (5), 301–305.

Simons, D. J., & Levin, D. T. (1997). Change blindness. *Trends in Cognitive Sciences, 1*, 261–267.
Smith, B. C. (1996). *On the origin of objects*. Cambridge, MA: MIT Press.
Spelke, E. S. (1990). Principles of object perception. *Cognitive Science, 14*, 29–56.
Spelke, E. S., Gutheil, G., & Van de Walle, G. (1995). The development of object perception. In S. M. Kosslyn, & D. N. Osherson (Eds.), *Visual cognition* (Vol. 2, pp. 297–330). Cambridge, MA: MIT Press.
Tipper, S., Driver, J., & Weaver, B. (1991). Object-centered inhibition of return of visual attention. *Quarterly Journal of Experimental Psychology, 43A*, 289–298.
Tipper, S. P., Weaver, B., Jerreat, L. M., & Burak, A. L. (1994). Object-based and environment-based inhibition of return of selective attention. *Journal of Experimental Psychology: Human Perception and Performance, 20*, 478–499.
Treisman, A., & Gelade, G. (1980). A feature integration theory of attention. *Cognitive Psychology, 12*, 97–136.
Trick, L. M., & Pylyshyn, Z. W. (1994). Why are small and large numbers enumerated differently? A limited capacity preattentive stage in vision. *Psychological Review, 10* (1), 1–23.
Tsotsos, J. K. (1988). How does human vision beat the computational complexity of visual perception. In Z. W. Pylyshyn (Ed.), *Computational processes in human vision: an interdisciplinary perspective* (pp. 286–340). Stamford, CT: Ablex.
Ullman, S. (1984). Visual routines. *Cognition, 18*, 97–159.
Viswanathan, L., & Mingolla, E. (in press). Dynamics of attention in depth: evidence from multi-element tracking. *Perception*.
Watson, D. G., & Humphreys, G. W. (1997). Visual marking: prioritizing selection for new objects by top-down attentional inhibition of old objects. *Psychological Review, 104* (1), 90–122.
Wolfe, J. M., & Bennett, S. C. (1997). Preattentive object files: shapeless bundles of basic features. *Vision Research, 37* (1), 25–43.
Wolfe, J. M., Cave, K. R., & Franzel, S. L. (1989). Guided search: an alternative to the feature integration model for visual search. *Journal of Experimental Psychology: Human Perception and Performance, 15* (3), 419–433.
Xu, F. (1997). From Lot's wife to a pillar of salt: evidence that *physical object* is a sortal concept. *Mind and Language, 12*, 365–392.
Xu, F., & Carey, S. (1996). Infants' metaphysics: the case of numerical identity. *Cognitive Psychology, 30*, 111–153.
Yantis, S. (1992). Multielement visual tracking: attention and perceptual organization. *Cognitive Psychology, 24*, 295–340.
Yantis, S. (1998). Objects, attention, and perceptual experience. In R. Wright (Ed.), *Visual attention* (pp. 187–214). Oxford: Oxford University Press.
Yantis, S., & Johnson, D. N. (1990). Mechanisms of attentional priority. *Journal of Experimental Psychology: Human Perception and Performance, 16* (4), 812–825.
Yantis, S., & Jones, E. (1991). Mechanisms of attentional selection: temporally modulated priority tags. *Perception & Psychophysics, 50* (2), 166–178.

6

What is a visual object? Evidence from target merging in multiple object tracking

Brian J. Scholl[a,*], Zenon W. Pylyshyn[b], Jacob Feldman[b]

[a]*Harvard University, Cambridge, MA, USA*
[b]*Rutgers University, New Brunswick, NJ, USA*

Abstract

The notion that visual attention can operate over visual objects in addition to spatial locations has recently received much empirical support, but there has been relatively little empirical consideration of what can count as an 'object' in the first place. We have investigated this question in the context of the multiple object tracking paradigm, in which subjects must track a number of independently and unpredictably moving identical items in a field of identical distractors. What types of feature clusters can be tracked in this manner? In other words, what counts as an 'object' in this task? We investigated this question with a technique we call *target merging*: we alter tracking displays so that distinct target and distractor locations appear perceptually to be parts of the same object by merging pairs of items (one target with one distractor) in various ways – for example, by connecting item locations with a simple line segment, by drawing the convex hull of the two items, and so forth. The data show that target merging makes the tracking task far more difficult to varying degrees depending on exactly how the items are merged. The effect is perceptually salient, involving in some conditions a total destruction of subjects' capacity to track multiple items. These studies provide strong evidence for the object-based nature of tracking, confirming that in some contexts attention must be allocated to objects rather than arbitrary collections of features. In addition, the results begin to reveal the types of spatially organized scene components that can be independently attended as a function of properties such as connectedness, part structure, and other types of perceptual grouping. © 2001 Elsevier Science B.V. All rights reserved.

Keywords: Visual object; Target merging; Multiple object tracking

---

* Corresponding author. Present address: Department of Psychology, Yale University, P.O. Box 208205, New Haven, CT 06520-8205, USA. Fax: +1-203-432-7172.
E-mail address: brian.scholl@yale.edu (B.J. Scholl).

1. Introduction

Attention imposes a limit on our capacity to process visual information, but there has been much debate recently concerning the correct *units* for characterizing this limitation. It was traditionally argued or assumed that attention restricts various types of visual processing to certain spatial areas of the visual field – for example, in 'spotlight' and 'zoom lens' models of visual attention (e.g. Eriksen & St. James, 1986; Posner, Snyder, & Davidson, 1980). It has recently been demonstrated, however, that there must also be an object-based component to visual attention, in which discrete objects are directly attended, and in which attentional limitations are characterized in terms of the number of objects which can be simultaneously selected. The excitement which this shift has generated is apparent in the recent proliferation of empirical demonstrations of object-based attention using many different paradigms in both normal and impaired observers (see Scholl, 2001, for a review).

The notion that visual attention can select visual objects has thus been well confirmed, and has engendered many new theories of visual attention. The surprising lacuna in all of this research, however, is that we do not know what sorts of stimuli can count as visual objects in the first place. (By 'object' here, we simply mean an independently attendable feature cluster; for discussion of the distinction between 'objects', 'groups', 'parts', etc., see Scholl (2001).) The research program of object-based attention has until now largely concentrated on evidence *that* attention can be allocated to discrete objects, rather than on what the objects of attention can be. (For recent exceptions, see Avraham (1999) and Watson and Kramer (1999).) The importance of this issue is clear: among the most crucial tasks in the study of any cognitive or perceptual process is to determine the nature of the fundamental units over which that process operates. It has become abundantly clear that visual attention can operate over objects, but we do not as yet know what qualifies as an object except in certain simple cases.[1]

---

[1] Of course, there is a wealth of evidence concerning the factors that mediate perceptual grouping, starting with the seminal demonstrations of the Gestalt psychologists. These investigations are distinct from our question, though, for two reasons. First, as will be clear below, several of the manipulations used in our experiments do not involve standard grouping principles (e.g. to take a simple case, a line is typically thought of as a single unit, and not as a 'group' of points). Second, it is not a foregone conclusion that the units of attention will obey standard principles of perceptual grouping. It may be, for example, that attention will automatically spread only within a subset of those perceptual groups that we can intentionally perceive. Another way to put this is that attention may automatically spread only within groups defined primarily by 'bottom-up' factors, but 'top-down' factors may additionally form groups which are perceived as such, but which don't readily constrain the automatic spread of attention. For a more complete discussion of the relation between perceptual grouping and objecthood, see Feldman (1999). For a different perspective on the relation between grouping and attention, see Driver, Davis, Russell, Turatto, and Freeman (2001).

The experiments reported here address this question in the context of the multiple object tracking (MOT) paradigm, in which subjects must track a number of independently and unpredictably moving identical items in a field of identical distractors. What types of spatially organized components can be independently tracked in this manner? In other words, what counts as an 'object' in this task?

1.1. Multiple object tracking (MOT)

Most studies of object-based visual attention have employed static stimuli, for example in the large literature spawned by seminal studies of spatial cueing (e.g. Egly, Driver, & Rafal, 1994) and divided attention (e.g. Duncan, 1984). Others have used dynamic displays, but observers have typically had to attend to only a single moving item (e.g. Kahneman, Treisman, & Gibbs, 1992; Tipper, Brehaut, & Driver, 1990; Tipper, Driver, & Weaver, 1991). We suspect, however, that an entirely different set of constraints on objecthood may come into play when observers must simultaneously attend to multiple feature clusters which are allowed to move about the visual field while attentional selection is being assessed. One such context is the MOT task used here.

Observers in the first MOT experiment (Pylyshyn & Storm, 1988) were initially presented with a display containing a number of small identical crosses. After a moment, a subset of these crosses were blinked several times to indicate their status as targets. As soon as this blinking ceased, all of the identical crosses began moving independently and unpredictably about the display. At various times during this motion a small probe appeared, and observers had to indicate whether the probe had occurred on a target cross, a distractor cross, or neither. Note that this task can only be done by tracking the individual target items throughout the motion phase, since they all have identical features. Subjects were able to perform this task with over 85% accuracy when tracking up to five targets (but not more) in a field containing five other identical distractors, and computer simulations revealed that this performance could not be explained in terms of a single attentional spotlight which cyclically visited all of the targets in sequence (see Pylyshyn & Storm, 1988, for details). Other studies have demonstrated in other ways that attention is truly 'split' between the items in a MOT task, rather than being 'spread' between them (Intriligator, 1997; though cf. Yantis, 1992). Both Intriligator (1997, Experiment 2) and Sears and Pylyshyn (2000), for instance, demonstrated that various benefits which accrue to tracked items and locations (such as speeding response times to detect luminance increments) held only for the targets themselves, and not for the space between them or for other items which happened to be located within the polygon bounded by the targets. This selection is dynamic, and can survive occlusion, but not other similar disruptions in spatiotemporal continuity (Scholl and Pylyshyn, 1999). Recent neuroimaging experiments, which controlled for passive viewing, eye movements, and discrete attentional shifts, have localized the processes involved in this sort of task to parts of both parietal and frontal cortex

(Culham et al., 1998; Culham, Cavanagh, & Kanwisher, 2001). In this paper, we will regard this MOT as a paradigmatically *attention-demanding* task.[2]

1.2. What is an object that a person may track it?

To investigate the nature of visual objects in the context of MOT, we ask what types of configural properties a scene component must have in order to be tracked. Observers attempt to track arbitrary collections of features, for example as when a target (to be tracked) and a distractor (to be disregarded) are drawn as opposite endpoints of a single line segment. Here, in order to perform the tracking task, subjects must separately select one endpoint of the line segment, keeping track of which is the target and which is the distractor. (As in any tracking task, targets and distractors move independently.) But if, as we hypothesize, such undifferentiated ends are not parsed as objects, then this manipulation should substantially impair tracking performance. Subjects will be unable to separately track each of the two endpoints, but rather will only be able to track whole lines, and will be forced to guess which end is actually a target. This manipulation, which we call *target merging*, is the basis of all the experiments reported below.

We start with a baseline tracking task in which subjects are asked to track four targets from a total of eight independently moving items, a task most subjects can perform at or above 85% accuracy. In each trial, the eight items (drawn as identical boxes) are initially shown in a static display. After 1 s, four of these items are highlighted by small blinking probes which appear and disappear from the items to indicate that they are targets. Then all eight begin moving independently and unpredictably about the display. After 10 s of such motion, the items stop moving, and the subject must use the mouse to indicate which four of the eight items were the targets.

In all of the target merging conditions reported below, we used the same set of item trajectories and target selections as in the above baseline condition: the only difference is in how the targets and distractors are drawn. Instead of drawing each target and each distractor as a separate object (e.g. a dot), we randomly paired each target with a distractor and then *merged* the pair in some way so that they would be perceived as parts of the same object – for example, by drawing a line between them, drawing a convex hull around them, etc. (see details and schematic drawings of the conditions below). Because all items move independently (as in the baseline tracking task) the new 'combined' objects which result from this target merging are not rigid, but rather shrink as the constituent target and distractor approach each other and elongate as they recede from each other. Because one end of each pair is a target,

---

[2] MOT is clearly attentionally demanding and effortful, leading most researchers to talk of MOT as an attentional process (Culham et al., 1998, 2001; He, Cavanagh, & Intriligator, 1997; Intriligator, 1997; Scholl, 2001; Treisman, 1993; Viswanathan & Mingolla, in press; Yantis, 1992). However, Pylyshyn (1989, 1994, 2001) has proposed that this task may involve several stages, and that the mechanism responsible for tracking the continuing identity of individual objects could itself be preattentive. Pylyshyn has hypothesized such a mechanism, called a visual index or 'FINST', that individuates objects and keeps track of their identity in a data-driven manner, despite changes in their properties or locations. We will not discuss this hypothesis here, though it is discussed at length in Pylyshyn (2001).

while the other end is a distractor, in order to perform the task subjects need to select and track just part of each pair. Again, the actual trajectories to be tracked are exactly the same as in the baseline condition. Hence, this paradigm tests the hypothesis that attention can only be allocated to distinct objects, and not simply arbitrary collections of features. Moreover, by varying the exact manner in which target and distractor locations are merged, we can test exactly what configural cues – connectedness, part structure, and other aspects of perceptual organization – make a part of the scene count as a 'distinct object' (see also Watson & Kramer, 1999).

Though the design of our experiment is completely between-subjects, the conditions we used were of two main types, which we now discuss in turn. Given the inherently dynamic nature of these displays, readers may wish to view animations of these conditions, several of which are available for viewing or downloading with a web browser at http://pantheon.yale.edu/~bs265/bjs-demos.html.

1.3. Group #1: undifferentiated parts of objects

1.3.1. Boxes

In our baseline condition, each item was simply drawn as a small individual outlined square, similar to the items used in previous MOT experiments (see Fig. 1a). Because the items in this experiment employed completely independent trajectories, these items were allowed to intersect during their motion, and when this happened one of the squares would occlude the other, with T-junctions at the occluding borders to indicate a depth relation. Viswanathan and Mingolla (in press) demonstrated that this method results in tracking performance which is comparable to earlier studies (a fact which we confirmed in pilot studies).

1.3.2. Lines

In this condition, we simply connected each pair of target/distractor locations with a single line, so that the entire display consisted of four lines (see Fig. 1b). One end of each line was then highlighted during the target designation phase, so that subjects had to track one end of each of the four lines throughout the motion period. We expected impaired performance in this condition: if attention must be allocated to objects as wholes, then it should be very difficult to confine attention to undifferentiated ends of objects, even if such loci move through the very same trajectories that can be tracked quite well when using individual points or boxes. (Note that when there *are* easily differentiated parts or surfaces of objects, it seems likely that attention could be selectively applied to those parts or surfaces. For discussion, see the 'dumbbells' condition below, and see also Hochberg and Peterson (1987) and Peterson and Gibson (1991) for cases where attention does seem to select well defined intra-object surfaces.)

1.3.3. 'Rubber bands' (with occlusion)

One concern with the 'lines' condition is that such stimuli involve much less of an overall enclosed area than do the 'boxes'. In order to control for the possible confounding effect of size, we replicated the effect of the 'lines' by essentially stretch-

Condition	Diagram	Note
(a) **Boxes**		Serves as baseline; Occlude each other when intersecting
(b) **Lines**		Subjects have to track one end of each line
(c) **Rubber Bands with Occlusion**		Subjects track one end of each RB; controls for size
(d) **Rubber Bands without Occlusion**		Like rubber bands, but without any occlusion
(e) **Necker Cubes**		Subjects track one of the two squares present in each 'cube'
(f) **Necker Control**		Controls for visual clutter in 'Necker cubes'

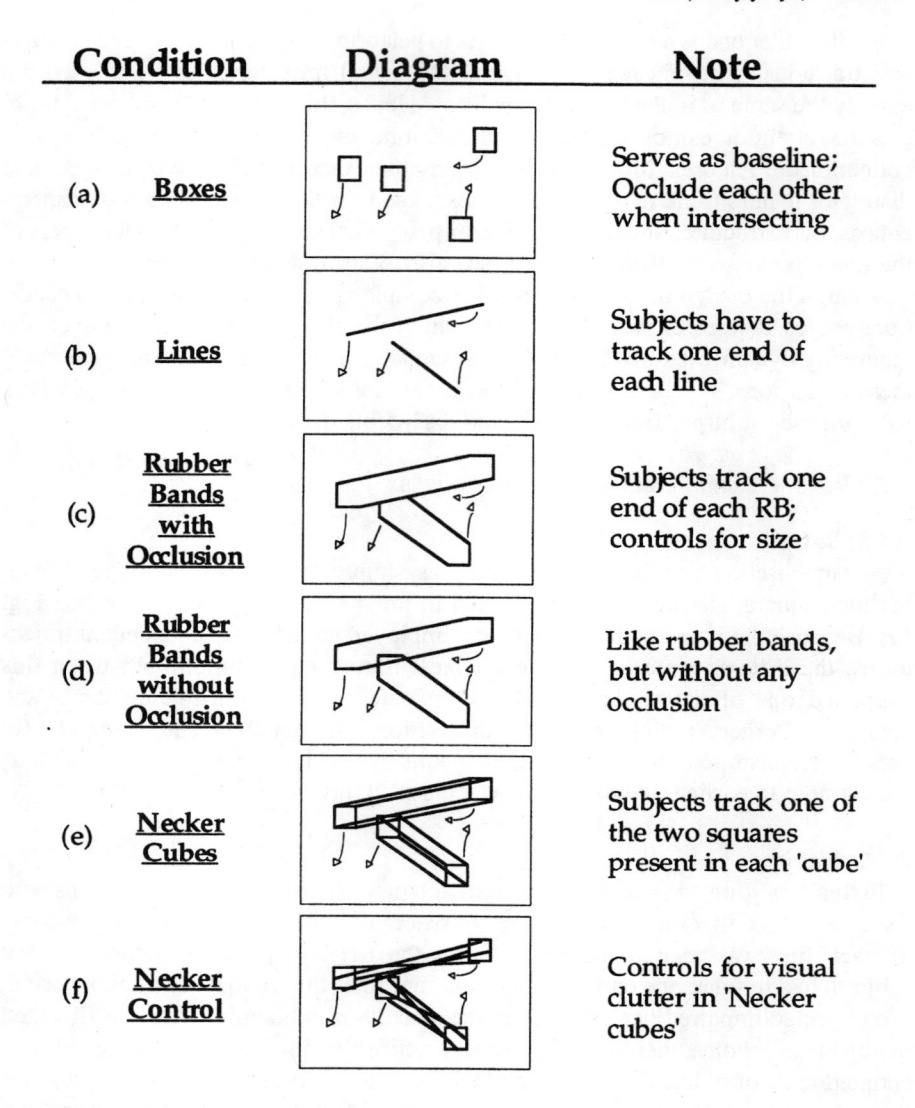

Fig. 1. A group of conditions designed to test whether undifferentiated parts or ends of objects can be independently selected by attention and tracked over time. See the text for discussion. The diagrams are not drawn to scale. Each diagram depicts only four items (two pairs), whereas the displays used in the experiments each involved eight items, four of which were targets and four of which were distractors. One 'end' of each item is a target; the other is a distractor. Dynamic animations of several of these conditions are available for viewing or downloading with a web browser at http://pantheon.yale.edu/~bs265/bjs-demos.html.

ing a single line 'rubber band' around each target/distractor pair of boxes, and then drawing only that rubber band (see Fig. 1c). This method again results in undifferentiated 'ends' of items which must be tracked, but such loci now occupy an equivalent amount of space to the individual boxes. Since the items each move independently, however, it is possible for one such rubber band to occlude another.

1.3.4. 'Rubber bands' (without occlusion)

To control for the possible deleterious effects of such occlusion, we also tested this condition when the region bounded by a rubber band was not a 'solid' outlined shape, but just a set of lines, so that the full contours of each rubber band were always visible (see Fig. 1d).

1.3.5. Necker cubes

Another reason why boxes might be trackable but ends of rubber bands might not be is that the boxes provide a closed contour for selection and tracking (i.e. the square), whereas only two or three of a box's four sides are ever drawn in the rubber bands. To examine this, one could just draw both entire boxes in a target/distractor pair and then simply connect them with a line to form a 'dumbbell' (see below). The problem with this is that such a scheme might not necessarily involve a single object, but could rather involve two objects connected by a line! How can we draw both boxes in each pair, but still have those boxes subsumed into a configuration that is likely to be parsed as a single object? Our solution was to connect *each* vertex of a box to the corresponding vertex of its pair-mate, resulting in long thin 'Necker cubes' (see Fig. 1e). In this condition, each locus to be tracked still involves the enclosed contour of an entire square, as in the baseline 'boxes' condition, but these squares are subsumed into more global units.

1.3.6. Necker controls

The 'Necker cubes' condition also adds a substantial amount of visual clutter: each pair now involves four lines connecting the two squares. Any impairment of tracking for Necker cubes might thus simply reflect an intolerance for visual clutter. To control for this, we also employed a condition in which each pair of squares was connected by the same number of lines, but in a way which did support the perceptual interpretation of a single 'Necker cube': we instead attached the lines at the middles of each side of each square, and furthermore did not always connect equivalent sides (see Fig. 1f). We hypothesized that this condition would result in better performance than the Necker cubes, since, although it suffered from an equivalent degree of visual clutter, it might not be parsed as a single object. (In motion, this stimulus looked rather like two individual squares moving about independently, which happened to have some sticky substance stuck between them.)

1.4. Group #2: 'dumbbells'

The target merging conditions above were designed to examine whether undifferentiated parts or ends of objects can be independently selected and tracked over time. In three other conditions, we also explored how such 'attentional objecthood' is mediated by connectedness, part structure, and other configural properties. Connectedness and other aspects of perceptual grouping have been found to play a role in object-based attention in earlier studies. Some of the relevant evidence concerning perceptual grouping involves the role of occlusion. Several studies have shown that mechanisms of object-based attention treat partially occluded objects as wholes, as they are perceptually grouped (e.g. Behrmann, Zemel, & Mozer, 1998; Moore, Yantis, & Vaughan, 1998), and that dynamic object representations can survive even moments of complete occlusion (e.g. Scholl & Pylyshyn, 1999; Tipper et al., 1990; Yantis, 1995). In addition, some neuropsychological studies suggest a more direct role of grouping (e.g. Boutsen & Humphreys, 2000; Driver, Baylis, Goodrich, & Rafal, 1994; Ward, Goodrich, & Driver, 1994). Driver et al. (1994), for example, had neglect patients report whether a small triangle had a gap in its contour, where this triangle was surrounded by other triangles such that it was perceptually grouped into a right-leaning or a left-leaning global figure. When the critical triangle was grouped into the left-leaning global figure, the gap was on the right side of this overall group; when it was perceptually grouped into the right-leaning figure, in contrast, the gap was on the left of the overall group. This manipulation greatly affected whether the patients perceived the gap, even though the critical triangle was always drawn identically. With regard to connectedness in particular, several recent studies have demonstrated that connected regions are often represented as single objects (e.g. Kramer & Watson, 1996; Van Lier & Wagemans, 1998; Watson & Kramer, 1999). The literature on perceptual grouping itself, however, has been largely silent on what configural properties make a scene component count as a distinct whole 'object' (as opposed to a contour, surface, 'unit', or other figural component at some lower level of the hierarchy; see Feldman, 1999, for discussion).

To explore the roles which such issues play in the ability to track multiple items, we employed three other types of 'dumbbell' conditions (see Fig. 2).

1.4.1. Dumbbells

In the simplest of these conditions, we just combined the 'boxes' and 'lines', so that a line was drawn between each pair of boxes (with the boxes occluding the lines, so that the lines began at the boxes' contours; see Fig. 2a). It is difficult to formulate a specific prediction for this condition. On the one hand, unlike lines and rubber bands, these stimuli now possess salient curvature minima indicating the ends to be tracked. There is a large body of research stemming from Hoffman and Richards (1984) which has demonstrated that such discontinuities are precisely where perceptual *parts* of objects are parsed, and indeed the parts in this context may be parsed as visual objects of their own (at a different hierarchical level), which might not predict impaired performance. On the other hand, each pair of items in a dumbbell is still physically connected, and we might expect this to lead to impaired performance, as we do with lines and rubber bands. Several neuropsychological studies have demonstrated that merely connecting two items with a thin line will greatly affect the percepts of both neglect patients (e.g. Behrmann & Tipper, 1994; Tipper and Behrmann, 1996) and of patients suffering from Balint syndrome, who will typically perceive only one of two unconnected discs, but yet will perceive an entire dumbbell (e.g. Humphreys & Riddoch, 1993; Luria, 1959).

	Condition	Diagram	Note
(a)	**Dumbbells**		Connected, but with obvious part-structure
(b)	**Dashed Dumbbells**		Same grouping as 'dumbbells', but not physically connected
(c)	**Unconnected Dumbbells**		Unconnected, and controls for lines

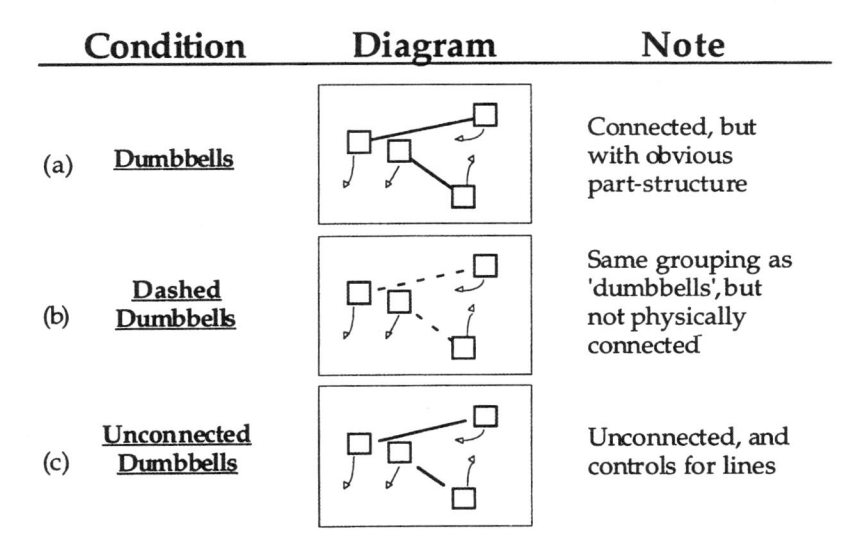

Fig. 2. A group of conditions (not to scale) designed to examine the roles of grouping, connectedness, and part structure. Each diagram depicts only four items (two pairs), whereas the displays used in the experiments each involved eight items, four of which were targets and four of which were distractors. One 'end' of each item is a target; the other is a distractor. Dynamic animations of several of these conditions are available for viewing or downloading with a web browser at http://pantheon.yale.edu/~bs265/bjs-demos.html.

1.4.2. Dashed dumbbells

In the basic dumbbells case, we might expect physical connectedness to impair tracking. In an effort to distinguish actual physical connectedness from more general perceptual grouping, we also tested a condition wherein the lines connecting the boxes were 'dashed' (see Fig. 2b), which disrupted the physical connectivity but not the grouping.

1.4.3. Unconnected dumbbells

In another condition, we used a solid connecting line which ended before it actually contacted a square, leaving a gap on either end the length of which was always 75% of the item size (see Fig. 2c). In addition to testing the role of connectedness, this condition also serves as another control for possible impairments arising simply from the existence of other lines in the display.

These conditions collectively embody an initial exploration of what types of feature clusters can be tracked in MOT. To ensure that any differences in performance are due to the stimulus manipulations and not to any other haphazard differences in trajectories, we used an entirely between-subjects design in which the same trajectories and target selections are used in all conditions – such that the *only* difference between the trials in each condition is the way in which the stimuli are drawn. In particular, each 'item' (or 'end' of an item pair) still moves on an independent trajectory, and on the *same* independent trajectory that it moves on in each of the other conditions.

2. Method

2.1. Participants

Eighty-one Rutgers University undergraduates, nine for each of the nine conditions, participated in one individual session either to fulfill an introductory psychology course requirement or to receive extra credit in another course. Each participant completed only one of the target merging conditions. Three subjects chose to terminate the experiment before completion, and were replaced. All subjects had normal or corrected-to-normal vision.

2.2. Apparatus

The tracking displays were presented on a monitor controlled by a Power Macintosh 6500 computer. Subjects were positioned with their heads in a chinrest 36.8 cm from the display monitor, the viewable extent of which subtended 45 × 33.75°. All displays were controlled by custom software written in the C programming language, using the VisionShell libraries of programming routines (Comtois, 1998).

2.3. Stimuli

Each trial employed four target items and four distractor items, drawn as described below. Initial item positions were generated randomly, with the constraint that each had to be at least 5.62° from the edges of the display monitor and at least 4.22° from each other. A 10 s animation sequence was generated for every trial to produce unpredictable trajectories for each item as follows. Items were each assigned initial random horizontal and vertical velocity vectors which could vary by single integer steps between −3 and 3 (with '0' indicating a stationary position with regard to that dimension), and which determined how fast an item moved in the specified direction. There was a 10% chance after each frame of motion that this value would be updated by a single step (i.e. ±1) in a randomly chosen direction (with −3 and 3 always serving as the most extreme values possible). Each item was updated independently, resulting in completely independent and unpredictable trajectories. The resulting set of trajectories for a trial, along with randomly selected target items, were stored off-line as 335 static frames to be presented for 30 ms each for a total of 10 s of motion. In the resulting motion, items could move a maximum of 0.21°/frame. Since frames were displayed for 30 ms each, the resulting item velocities were in the range from 0 to 7.02°/s, with an average velocity across all items and trials of 2.37°/s.

2.4. Drawing conditions

The individual lines comprising each item were all one pixel (0.07°) wide, except as noted below, and were clearly visible. In the *boxes* condition, each item was drawn independently as a square subtending 2.81°, centered on the item position. The squares were all randomly assigned to different depth planes, such that they would occlude each other when their trajectories intersected. In the *lines* condition, each target was randomly paired with a distractor to result in four target/distractor pairs, and each pair was drawn as a single line connecting the center of each item. In the *rubber bands with occlusion* condition, each target/distractor pair was drawn as the smallest convex polygon encompassing both of the areas drawn as squares in the 'boxes' condition. Each of the four resulting polygons was randomly assigned to a separate depth plane, such that they would occlude each other when they intersected. The *rubber bands without occlusion* condition was identical to the 'rubber bands with occlusion' condition, except that items never occluded each other: each polygon was always drawn simply as a collection of six line segments (or possibly four line segments, when the items were momentarily horizontally or vertically aligned). In the *Necker cube* condition, the squares were drawn as in the 'boxes' condition, and in addition each vertex of each square was connected to the same vertex of its pair-mate square with a single line. The resulting figures appeared to be extended three-dimensional boxes, with their depth relation appearing bistable. There was no occlusion involved. The *Necker control* condition was identical to the 'Necker cube' condition, except in the organization of the extra lines: instead of connecting the corresponding vertices, the four lines were drawn from the midpoints of the squares' sides, connecting the left side of one square to the top side of the other, and similarly top to bottom, bottom to left, and right to right (see Fig. 1e). The *dumbbell* condition was implemented simply by drawing both the lines and the boxes, with the boxes occluding the lines such that the lines connected at the borders of the squares (see Fig. 2a). The *dashed dumbbell* condition was identical to the 'dumbbell' condition, except that the line was dashed, with the lengths of both the line segments and gaps always 0.7° each, regardless of the total line length. Finally, the *unconnected dumbbell* condition was identical to the 'dumbbell' condition, except that the lines always terminated 2.11° from the squares' borders.

2.5. Procedure and design

At the beginning of each trial, the eight items were displayed, drawn as described above. After 1 s, the four target items were highlighted with small flashing probes (disappearing and reappearing for 165 ms each on each of five flashes). The 10 s of item motion then ensued. After 10 s, all of the items stopped moving, and the subject had to indicate the four target items using the mouse. The fourth mouse-click caused the display to disappear, and the subject initiated the next trial with a keypress. Eye movements were not monitored, and no special instructions were given concerning fixation, since different fixation conditions have been found not to affect performance on this task.[3]

Forty sets of trajectories (along with target selections) were generated and stored

---

[3] Pylyshyn and Storm (1988) monitored and ensured fixation by discarding trials on which subjects made eye movements, and obtained qualitatively identical results to other investigators who either employed no special constraints or instructions concerning fixation – for example, Intriligator (1997) and Yantis (1992) – or else instructed subjects to maintain fixation but did not monitor eye movements – for example, Scholl and Pylyshyn (1999).

off-line. Nine different subjects were run on these 40 trials in each of the nine different conditions (for total of 81 subjects in total). Subjects first completed ten practice trials for which data were not collected, and then completed the 40 experimental trials in a randomized order (different for each subject). The entire experimental session took about 20 min.

3. Results

Tracking accuracy was recorded on each trial. Because there were always four targets, percent correct P was always 0, 25, 50, 75, or 100%. Mean P and standard errors for each condition averaged across the nine subjects per condition are shown

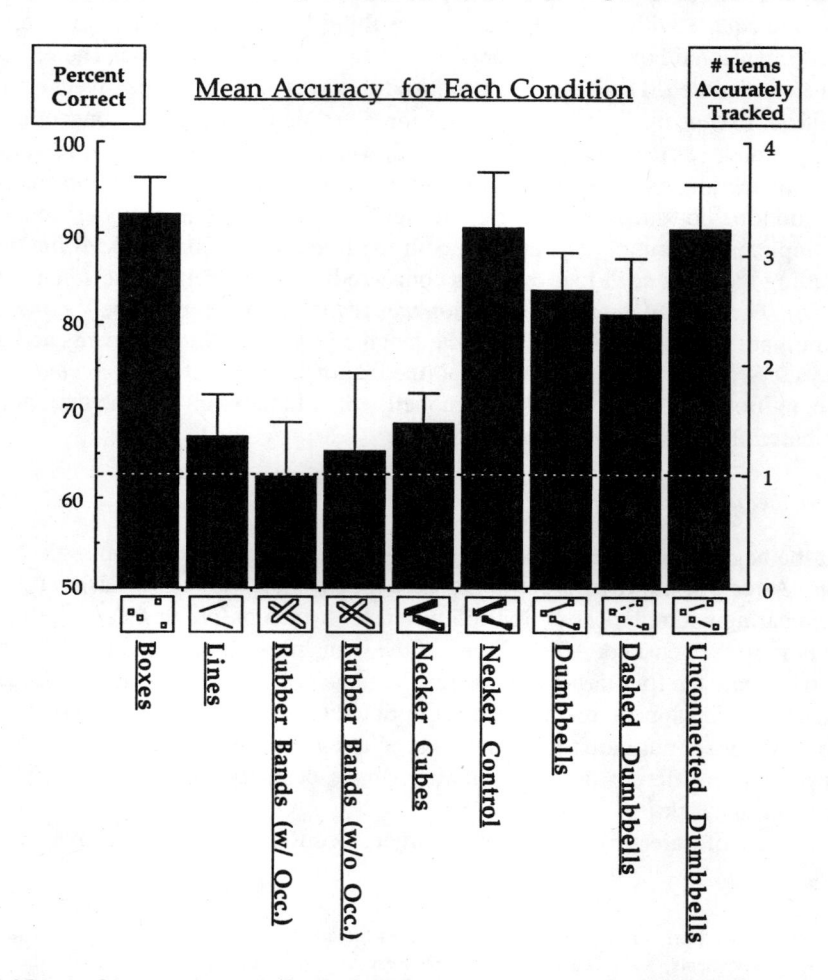

Fig. 3. Mean performance and standard errors in all conditions plotted in terms of both percent correct and the number of items successfully tracked (see Appendix A for details). Chance performance, as discussed in Section 3, is indicated by the dashed line.

in Fig. 3. It is also possible to translate P linearly into a measure m giving the *effective number of items tracked* by each subject in each condition – i.e. the number of items that had to be independently tracked in order to give rise to the observed percent correct P. (A derivation and justification of m is given in Appendix A.) One advantage of the alternate performance measure m is that it allows us to mark the performance level consistent with the subject's having only tracked one target throughout a trial. A value of $m = 1$ means that his or her capacity to divide attention among multiple objects has been effectively obliterated, which in the current case is equivalent to $P = 62.5\%$ (though note that with other numbers of targets $m = 1$ will correspond to different values of P). In Fig. 3, percent correct P is given on the left scale and m is given on the right scale, and both chance ($P = 50\%$) and single-item tracking performance ($m = 1$) levels are marked.

An analysis of variance on these accuracy data revealed a significant effect of the drawing condition ($F(8, 72) = 41.12$, $P < 0.05$). Additional planned comparisons indicated that:

(a) performance with 'boxes' was significantly better than performance with 'lines' ($t(16) = 12.11$, $P < 0.01$), 'Necker cubes' ($t(16) = 13.44$, $P < 0.01$), and 'rubber bands' both with occlusion ($t(16) = 12.04$, $P < 0.01$) and without occlusion ($t(16) = 8.29$, $P < 0.01$);

(b) performance on 'rubber bands' did not differ based on whether the rubber bands occluded each other or not ($t(16) = 0.82$, $P > 0.3$);

(c) performance in the 'Necker control' was significantly better than performance with 'Necker cubes' ($t(16) = 9.35$, $P < 0.01$), but did not differ from performance with 'boxes' ($t(16) = 0.59$, $P > 0.3$);

(d) performance with 'dumbbells' was significantly *worse* than with 'boxes' ($t(16) = 4.24$, $P < 0.01$), and also significantly *better* than with both 'lines' ($t(16) = 7.85$, $P < 0.01$), and with 'rubber bands with occlusion' ($t(16) = 8.46$, $P < 0.01$);

(e) performance with 'dumbbells' was significantly worse than performance with 'unconnected dumbbells' ($t(16) = 3.07$, $P < 0.01$), but did not differ from performance with 'dashed dumbbells' ($t(16) = 1.07$, $P > 0.2$); and finally

(f) performance with 'unconnected dumbbells' did not differ from performance with 'boxes' ($t(16) = 0.74$, $P > 0.3$).

4. Discussion

These results from target merging displays in MOT are, in the first instance, strong evidence for the object-based nature of tracking, since the different stimulus conditions engendered very different levels of performance, despite the fact that the particular targets that subjects were being asked to track were identical in every other way across the conditions, and in particular moved through exactly the same trajectories. (The 'multiple *object* tracking' task, in other words, does appear to be aptly named.) Performance was greatly impaired when subjects had to track ends of lines, rubber bands, or Necker cubes; apparently, such undifferentiated *ends* of such stimuli are not treated as objects, since observers were unable to independently individuate, select, and track them. In these target merging conditions, each pair in its entirety seems to constitute a single visual object, but this fact only impairs performance, since each pair consists of both a target and a distractor. This impaired performance is especially striking given that there are other reasons to expect that subjects should actually do better in such conditions. For instance, subjects know that each pair consists of a target and distractor, and therefore they know that any item about which they are confident can be used to fix the correct target status of another item: 'I know that this one way down here wasn't one of the targets, so that means that I can just follow the line up ... to this one, which must be a target.' This interpretation is supported by the fact that performance in the 'Necker control' condition (see Fig. 1f) did *not* differ from the baseline, even though it differed only minimally in its physical constitution from the 'Necker cube' condition. This result may be related to the fact that 'Necker control' pairs tended to look like two separate items with some gooey substance stuck between them. (This odd percept may also be related to the intriguing result that 'Necker control' performance was actually better than with 'dumbbells', despite the additional clutter.)[4]

Another advantage of target merging is methodological. Other studies of object-based attentional effects have relied on reliable but small differences in accuracy or in reaction times across conditions (see Duncan, 1984; Egly et al., 1994; and the many follow-up studies generated by each), with differences between conditions seldom perceptually apparent to observers. By contrast, our method results in large differences in accuracy and a phenomenologically salient effect (like other phenomenological demonstrations of perceptual grouping, but unlike many measures of object-based attention). These results confirm not only that attention *can* be object-based, but that in some cases it *must* be object-based (see Driver & Baylis, 1998; He & Nakayama, 1995). Attention involuntarily spreads to the entire rubber band, for instance, even though subjects are attempting to track only the end of the rubber band.

Note that this explanation in terms of objecthood is distinct from concerns about segmentability in general. One might argue that perhaps observers are worse on 'Necker cubes' than on 'Necker controls', for instance, not because of how such displays are parsed in terms of objects, but simply because the ends of the pairs that subjects must track are more easily segmented from the 'Necker control' display: in the 'Necker cube' display, in contrast, there are many other rectangles and parallel lines that might make the ends harder to segment.[5] If so, then the deleterious effects of the Necker cubes should occur regardless of their connection to the targets – i.e.

---

[4] This 'Necker cube' versus 'Necker control' comparison also calls into question an explanation in terms of perceived depth: since both of these conditions appear to some degree to involve rotation in depth, that fact cannot be responsible for the impaired performance found here in some conditions. In addition, other studies have shown that multiple objects can be tracked in depth quite easily, as would be expected if this type of attention were to be useful in the real world (Blaser, Pylyshyn, & Domini, 1999; Viswanathan & Mingolla, in press).

[5] Thanks to an anonymous reviewer for suggesting this interpretation, and the resulting control experiment.

the impairment should simply be a function of their presence in the display as a whole. To test this, we ran an additional control experiment wherein nine new observers (the same number as in the main experiment) tracked four boxes in a field of eight boxes. In the background of the displays, however, were four additional boxes, connected into either 'Necker cube' or 'Necker control' pairs. Observers viewed 30 trials of each type in separate blocks, the order of which was counterbalanced. Overall, performance was impaired in these conditions (85% combined compared to 92% for the 'boxes' alone in the main experiment; $t(16) = 2.82$, $P < 0.05$), which demonstrates that the added background items were salient enough to impair performance, probably due to increased crowding in the display as a whole. The extent of this impairment did not differ depending on whether 'Necker cubes' or 'Necker controls' were in the background, however: subjects were 86% accurate for displays with background 'Necker cubes', and 85% accurate for displays with background 'Necker controls' ($t(8) = 0.71, P > 0.4$). The fact that these two stimuli yielded very different levels of performance in the main experiment, but did not do so here (and were in fact in the wrong direction), suggests that our object-based results are distinct from general concerns about segmentation.[6]

In addition, this initial exploratory study has begun to examine some of the factors which mediate the degree to which various feature clusters can 'count' as objects for purposes of MOT. Connectedness, for example, appears to play a role, since performance was impaired with 'dumbbells' but not with 'unconnected dumbbells'. On the other hand, this result might reflect perceptual grouping rather than physical connectedness, since there was no difference between performance with 'dumbbells' and 'dashed dumbbells', nor between 'rubber bands' and 'occluded rubber bands'. Finally, however, the deleterious effects of perceptual grouping and connectedness appear to be attenuated by the presence of easily parsable object 'parts', since performance with 'dumbbells' was still significantly better than with 'rubber bands'. In other studies, we are now investigating more precisely the roles of the curvature minima which signal the existence of these object parts (see also Driver & Baylis, 1995; Hoffman & Singh, 1997; Watson & Kramer, 1999).

The conditions reported here are only an initial investigation of the types of properties which can mediate 'attentional objecthood', but this paradigm has proven

---

[6] Yantis (1992) suggested that MOT can be enhanced by imagining the targets as being grouped into a single virtual polygon (VP), and then tracking deformations of this polygon. He demonstrated that such grouping does indeed play a role in MOT by showing that performance was facilitated simply by informing subjects of this strategy, or by constraining the items' trajectories such that the polygon could never collapse upon itself. Perhaps, then, performance is impaired simply because such manipulations disrupt the formation of the VP. While we agree that performance in the basic MOT task can be improved by using this strategy (or indeed, by any grouping strategy, e.g. pairing items into virtual line segments), the improvement seems likely to be due to an improved error-recovery process when one item is lost: when items are being perceptually tracked as virtual groups, one can make an educated guess as to where a lost item 'should' be, given the overall contour of the virtual shape (see Sears & Pylyshyn, 2000). In addition, Scholl and Pylyshyn (1999) have shown that information which is local to each item (or 'vertex' in the VP strategy) does greatly impact tracking performance. In any case, the VP strategy cannot easily explain the particulars of our results: for example, the 'Necker cube' and 'Necker control' conditions should disrupt performance to an equal degree on the VP story, but they do not.

a useful way to explore these issues. First, MOT provides a way to check the generalizability of other object-based attention results, the majority of which have been collected using only a few experimental paradigms involving static displays (or dynamic displays in which there is still a single locus of attention). Second, there are also several intrinsic advantages to using MOT to study object-based attention: the results obtained in this paradigm consist of large perceptually salient differences in accuracy, unlike most earlier results, and it also seems likely that this paradigm will have more power to reveal subtle differences between different conditions, since the 'objects' in this paradigm must not only be parsed from the display, but must be maintained throughout the tracking period. The experiments reported here, and others using this paradigm, will help us to provide a missing link in the study of object-based attention, by revealing what types of spatially organized visual components can be independently attended.

Acknowledgements

For helpful conversation and/or comments on earlier drafts, we thank Erik Blaser, Susan Carey, Patrick Cavanagh, Jon Driver, Steve Franconeri, Peter Gerhardstein, Glyn Humphreys, James Intriligator, Allan Kugel, Alan Leslie, Ken Nakayama, Mary Peterson, Dan Simons, Joe Tanniru, Anne Treisman, and Steve Yantis. We also thank Steve Franconeri, Damien Henderson, and Joe Tanniru for assistance with data collection. Some of these results were presented at the 2000 meeting of the Association for Research in Vision and Ophthalmology. B.J.S. was supported by NIH F32-MH12483-01, Z.W.P. was supported by NIH 1R01-MH60924, and J.F. was supported by NSF SBR-9875175.

Appendix A. Derivation of m, the effective number of items tracked

For simplicity, assume a display with n targets and n distractors ($2n$ objects total). A variation of the following with a target proportion other than one-half can easily be derived.

Assume the following idealized strategy: track m objects, and guess randomly on the others. We assume that the observer knows that half the items are targets and thus for each unknown item guesses 'target' with a probability of 0.5.

Assuming this strategy, the observer will correctly track m of the n targets, and guess correctly on half of the remaining $n - m$ targets. This yields a proportion correct P of

$$P = \frac{m}{n} + \frac{1}{2}\left(1 - \frac{m}{n}\right) = \frac{1}{2}\left(\frac{m}{n} + 1\right)$$

Solving for m, we have

$$m = n(2P - 1)$$

We interpret the performance score m as the 'effective number of items tracked' (because it is the number of items which, when tracked correctly, gives rise to the given proportion performance P). This measure is advantageous because it allows percent correct scores from trials with different numbers of targets to be uniformly combined to estimate observers' tracking capacity.

Of course, m is based on an idealized conception of subjects' strategy, and must be interpreted with some caution. On a given trial a subject may track two items for a while, and perhaps lose track of one, thus in the end scoring $m = 1$ while having tracked more than one item for part of the trial. Note, however, that once lost a target cannot be 'picked up again' at better than a chance rate, so $m = 1$ performance does suggest that *at least* one object, but no more than one, was tracked from the beginning of the trial to the end. On the other hand, a capacity to track $m > n$ trials will still yield $P = 100\%$; hence, the estimate of tracking capacity derived from a given trial is necessarily capped at n.

References

Avrahami, J. (1999). Objects of attention, objects of perception. *Perception & Psychophysics, 61*, 1604–1612.

Behrmann, M., & Tipper, S. (1994). Object-based visual attention: evidence from unilateral neglect. In C. Umilta, & M. Moscovitch (Eds.), *Attention and performance. Conscious and nonconscious processing and cognitive functioning* (Vol. 15. pp. 351–375). Cambridge, MA: MIT Press.

Behrmann, M., Zemel, R., & Mozer, M. (1998). Object-based attention and occlusion: evidence from normal participants and a computational model. *Journal of Experimental Psychology: Human Perception and Performance, 24*, 1011–1036.

Blaser, E., Pylyshyn, Z., & Domini, F. (1999). Measuring attention during 3D multi-element tracking (abstract). *Investigative Ophthalmology & Visual Science, 40* (4), 552.

Boutsen, L., & Humphreys, G. (2000). Axis-based grouping reduces visual extinction. *Neuropsychologia, 38*, 896–905.

Comtois, R. (1998). *VisionShell [Software libraries]*. Cambridge, MA: author.

Culham, J. C., Brandt, S., Cavanagh, P., Kanwisher, N. G., Dale, A. M., & Tootell, R. B. H. (1998). Cortical fMRI activation produced by attentive tracking of moving targets. *Journal of Neurophysiology, 80*, 2657–2670.

Culham, J. C., Cavanagh, P., & Kanwisher, N. (2001). Attention response functions of the human brain measured with fMRI. Manuscript submitted for publication.

Driver, J., & Baylis, G. (1995). One-sided edge assignment in vision: II. Part decomposition, shape description, and attention to objects. *Current Directions in Psychological Science, 4*, 201–206.

Driver, J., & Baylis, G. (1998). Attention and visual object segmentation. In R. Parasuraman (Ed.), *The attentive brain* (pp. 299–325). Cambridge, MA: MIT Press.

Driver, J., Baylis, G., Goodrich, S., & Rafal, R. (1994). Axis-based neglect of visual shapes. *Neuropsychologia, 32*, 1353–1365.

Driver, J., Davis, G., Russell, C., Turatto, M., & Freeman, E. (2001). Segmentation, attention, and phenomenal visual objects. *Cognition*, this issue, *80*, 61–95.

Duncan, J. (1984). Selective attention and the organization of visual information. *Journal of Experimental Psychology: General, 113*, 501–517.

Egly, R., Driver, J., & Rafal, R. (1994). Shifting visual attention between objects and locations: evidence for normal and parietal lesion subjects. *Journal of Experimental Psychology: General, 123*, 161–177.

Eriksen, C. W., & St. James, J. D. (1986). Visual attention within and around the field of focal attention: a zoom lens model. *Perception & Psychophysics, 40*, 225–240.

Feldman, J. (1999). The role of objects in perceptual grouping. *Acta Psychologica, 102*, 137–163.

He, S., Cavanagh, P., & Intriligator, J. (1997). Attentional resolution. *Trends in Cognitive Sciences, 1,* 115–121.

He, Z. J., & Nakayama, K. (1995). Visual attention to surfaces in 3-D space. *Proceedings of the National Academy of Sciences USA, 92,* 11155–11159.

Hochberg, J., & Peterson, M. A. (1987). Piecemeal perception and cognitive components in object perception: perceptually coupled responses to moving objects. *Journal of Experimental Psychology: General, 116,* 370–380.

Hoffman, D., & Richards, W. (1984). Parts of recognition. *Cognition, 18,* 65–96.

Hoffman, D., & Singh, M. (1997). Salience of visual parts. *Cognition, 69,* 29–78.

Humphreys, G. W., & Riddoch, M. J. (1993). Interactions between object and space systems revealed through neuropsychology. In D. Meyer & S. Kornblum, *Attention and performance* (Vol. XIV, pp. 183–218). Cambridge, MA: MIT Press.

Intriligator, J. M. (1997). *The spatial resolution of visual attention.* Unpublished doctoral dissertation, Harvard University, Cambridge, MA.

Kahneman, D., Treisman, A., & Gibbs, B. J. (1992). The reviewing of object files: object-specific integration of information. *Cognitive Psychology, 24,* 174–219.

Kramer, A., & Watson, S. (1996). Object-based visual selection and the principle of uniform connectedness. In A. Kramer, M. Coles, & G. Logan (Eds.), *Converging operations in the study of visual selective attention* (pp. 395–414). Washington, DC: APA Press.

Luria, A. R. (1959). Disorders of 'simultaneous perception' in a case of bilateral occipito-parietal brain injury. *Brain, 83,* 437–449.

Moore, C., Yantis, S., & Vaughan, B. (1998). Object-based visual selection: evidence from perceptual completion. *Psychological Science, 9,* 104–110.

Peterson, M. A., & Gibson, B. S. (1991). Directing spatial attention within an object: altering the functional equivalence of shape descriptions. *Journal of Experimental Psychology: Human Perception and Performance, 17,* 170–182.

Posner, M. I., Snyder, C. R. R., & Davidson, B. J. (1980). Attention and the detection of signals. *Journal of Experimental Psychology: General, 109,* 160–174.

Pylyshyn, Z. W. (1989). The role of location indexes in spatial perception: a sketch of the FINST spatial index model. *Cognition, 32,* 65–97.

Pylyshyn, Z. W. (1994). Some primitive mechanisms of spatial attention. *Cognition, 50,* 363–384.

Pylyshyn, Z. W. (2001). Visual indexes, preconceptual objects, and situated vision. *Cognition,* this issue, 80, 127–158.

Pylyshyn, Z. W., & Storm, R. W. (1988). Tracking multiple independent targets: evidence for a parallel tracking mechanism. *Spatial Vision, 3,* 179–197.

Scholl, B. J. (2001). Objects and attention: the state of the art. *Cognition,* this issue, 80, 1–46.

Scholl, B. J., & Pylyshyn, Z. W. (1998). Tracking multiple items through occlusion: clues to visual objecthood. *Cognitive Psychology, 38,* 259–290.

Sears, C. R., & Pylyshyn, Z. W. (2000). Multiple object tracking and attentional processing. *Canadian Journal of Experimental Psychology, 54,* 1–14.

Tipper, S., & Behrmann, M. (1996). Object-centered not scene-based visual neglect. *Journal of Experimental Psychology: Human Perception and Performance, 22,* 1261–1278.

Tipper, S., Brehaut, J., & Driver, J. (1990). Selection of moving and static objects for the control of spatially directed action. *Journal of Experimental Psychology: Human Perception and Performance, 16,* 492–504.

Tipper, S. P., Driver, J., & Weaver, B. (1991). Object-centered inhibition of return of visual attention. *Quarterly Journal of Experimental Psychology, 43A,* 289–298.

Treisman, A. (1993). The perception of features and objects. In A. Baddeley, & L. Weiskrantz (Eds.), *Attention: selection, awareness, and control* (pp. 5–35). Oxford: Clarendon Press.

Van Lier, R., & Wagemans, J. (1998). Effects of physical connectivity on the representational unity of multi-part configurations. *Cognition, 69,* B1–B9.

Viswanathan, L., & Mingolla, E. (in press). Attention in depth: disparity and occlusion cues facilitate multi-element visual tracking. *Perception.*

Ward, R., Goodrich, S., & Driver, J. (1994). Grouping reduces visual extinction: neuropsychological evidence for weight-linkage in visual selection. *Visual Cognition, 1*, 101–129.

Watson, S., & Kramer, A. (1999). Object-based visual selective attention and perceptual organization. *Perception & Psychophysics, 61*, 31–49.

Yantis, S. (1992). Multielement visual tracking: attention and perceptual organization. *Cognitive Psychology, 24*, 295–340.

Yantis, S. (1995). Perceived continuity of occluded visual objects. *Psychological Science, 6*, 182–186.

7

Infants' knowledge of objects: beyond object files and object tracking

Susan Carey[a,]*, Fei Xu[b]

[a]*Department of Psychology, New York University, 6 Washington Place, Rm 550, New York, NY 10003, USA*
[b]*125 NI, Department of Psychology, Northeastern University, Boston, MA 02115, USA*

Abstract

Two independent research communities have produced large bodies of data concerning object representations: the community concerned with the infant's object concept and the community concerned with adult object-based attention. We marshal evidence in support of the hypothesis that both communities have been studying the same natural kind. The discovery that the object representations of young infants are the same as the object files of mid-level visual cognition has implications for both fields. © 2001 Elsevier Science B.V. All rights reserved.

Keywords: Infants' knowledge of objects; Object files; Object tracking

1. Object individuation and numerical identity

Sensory input is continuous. The array of light on the retina, even processed up to the level of Marr's 2 1/2 D sketch (Marr, 1982), is not segregated into individual objects. Yet distinct individuals are provided by visual cognition as input to many other perceptual and cognitive processes. It is individuals we categorize into kinds; it is individuals we reach for; it is individuals we enumerate; it is individuals among which we represent spatial relations such as "behind" and "inside"; and it is individuals that enter into causal interactions and events. Because of the psychological importance of object individuation, the twin problems of how the visual system

---

* Corresponding author. Fax: +1-212-9954018.
E-mail addresses: scarey@psych.nyu.edu (S. Carey), fxu@neu.edu (F. Xu).

establishes representations of individuals from the continuous input it receives and the development of these processes in infancy have engaged psychologists for almost a century.

Human language, and cognition more generally, makes a principled distinction between *individuals* and their *properties*. One of the quantificational functions of noun phrases is to denote individuals and sets of individuals, whereas predicates denote properties of those individuals. Accordingly, the literatures of metaphysics and philosophy of language distinguish between *sortals* (concepts that provide criteria for individuation and numerical identity) and *non-sortals* (Gupta, 1980; Hirsch, 1982; Macnamara, 1986; Wiggins, 1980). Similarly, the object-based attention literature (see papers in this volume) argues for a principled distinction between processes that index individuals and track them through time and processes that bind representations of features to representations of those individuals.

The study of object representations in infancy has an intellectual history independent of the object-based attention literature. Piaget's pioneering studies of object permanence were motivated by Kantian considerations of the origins of ontological commitments (*space, time, object, causality*). Piaget (1954), like Quine (1960), wondered how infants, assumed to be endowed initially only with sensorimotor representations, could construct representations of individual objects which exist independent of them. Notice that the issue of Piagetian object permanence is at the heart of the problem of numerical identity of objects with which one has lost perceptual contact. When we credit infants with an appreciation of object permanence, we assume that they know it is the *same object* that they saw disappear under the cloth that they are now retrieving. As is well known, Piaget believed that infants did not acquire true object permanence until 18–24 months, the end of what he called the period of sensorimotor intelligence. Even successful retrieval of objects hidden under and behind barriers at around 9 months is consistent with mere empirical rules that lead the child to predict that if an object is seen disappearing behind the barrier, an object will be found there (with no commitment as to whether it is the same object or a different one). However, there is now ample evidence, some of which we will review here, that infants as young as 2.5 months establish representations of individuated objects and track them through time, even when occluded.

Thus, both literatures, that on mid-level object-based attention and that on object representations in infancy, involve parallel problems, in particular those of the bases of object individuation and numerical identity. Recently, many have suggested that both communities have actually been studying the same psychological mechanisms; that is, that the object representations of young infants are identical to those that are served up by mid-level object-based attention (Leslie, Xu, Tremoulet, & Scholl, 1998; Scholl & Leslie, 1999; Simon, 1997; Uller, Carey, Huntley-Fenner, & Klatt, 1999). We endorse this proposal, with an important emphasis on *young*. Our paper has three main goals. First, we wish to introduce the literature on infant object representations to researchers studying object-based attention. Next, we summarize the considerations in favor of the hypothesis that the representations of the mid-level object tracking system are those that subserve object representations of young infants. Finally, we consider what practitioners of each discipline have to learn from those of the other if we accept this hypothesis. Although many of the arguments in this paper are highly speculative, we believe that this exercise will inform both communities and open new venues of empirical research.

2. Two distinct representational systems in the service of object individuation

In adults, there is *prima facie* evidence that *at least* two distinct representational systems underlie object individuation. The first is the mid-level vision system (mid-level because it falls between low level sensory processing and high level placement into kind categories) that establishes object file representations, and that indexes attended objects and tracks them through time (see the papers in this volume). This first system (called in this paper the mid-level object file system) privileges spatiotemporal information in the service of individuation and numerical identity. Individual objects are coherent, spatially separate and separately movable, spatiotemporally continuous entities.[1] Features such as color, shape, and texture may be bound in the representations of already individuated objects; they play a secondary role in decisions about numerical identity, when spatiotemporal evidence is neutral. Furthermore, a small number of attended objects may be indexed in parallel, the indexed individuals tracked through time and occlusion, the spatial relations among indexed individuals represented. Pylyshyn (2001) dubs these indexes FINSTs (FINgers of INSTantiation), for they serve a deictic function, like a finger point at an individual object. Here we adopt the assumption made by Kahneman, Treisman, and Gibbs (1992), and endorsed by Pylyshyn, about the relation between the indexing processes (Pylyshyn's FINSTs) and object files. Object files are symbols for individuals and FINSTs are the initial spatiotemporal addresses of those individuals. FINSTs might be thought of as the initial phase of an object file, before any features have been bound to it.

The second system (called in this paper the kind-based object individuation system) is fully conceptual, drawing on kind information for decisions about individuation and numerical identity. For adults, individuation is based on kind information when no relevant spatiotemporal evidence is available, as when we decide that the cup on the windowsill is the same one we left there yesterday, but the cat on the windowsill is not the same individual as the cup we left there yesterday. Sometimes kind information overrides spatiotemporal continuity, as when we decide that a person ceases to exist when she dies, in spite of the spatiotemporal continuity of her body. Property/featural changes are relevant to individuation at the conceptual level, but not on their own. Our inferences concerning the relevance of property changes to individuation are kind-relative. For example, a puppy may be the same individual as a large dog a month later, but a small cup will not be the same

---

[1] The exact characterization of the individuals that are indexed by FINSTs and are represented by object files is a matter awaiting empirical investigation. See Scholl, Pylyshyn, and Feldman (2001) for a first investigation into what individuals can be tracked in multiple object tracking (MOT) studies. It seems likely that groups of spatially separate entities undergoing common motion are construed as individuals in these studies. As we argue in Section 6, the infant literature bears on this issue.

Panel 1

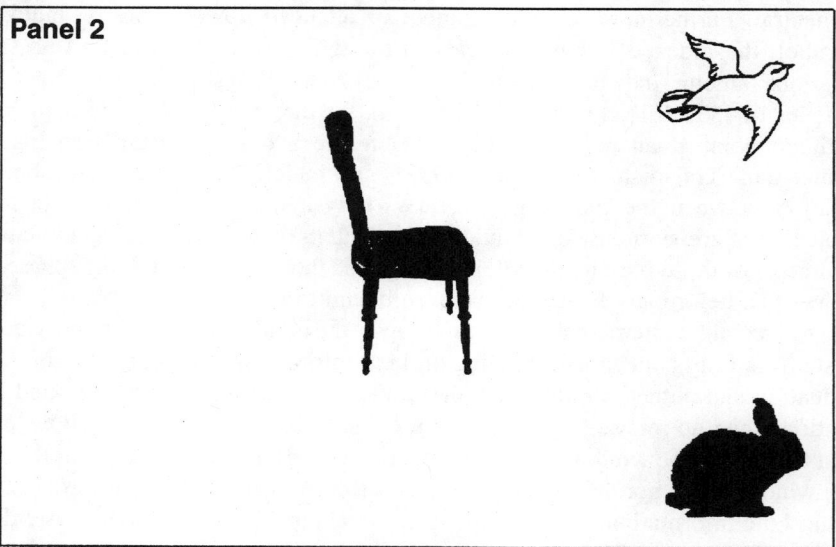

Panel 2

Fig. 1. *Prima facie* evidence for two mechanisms of object individuation.

individual as a large cup a month later. Similarly, color differences do not signal distinct individual chameleons, but they do signal distinct individual frogs.

Fig. 1 illustrates the operation of the two systems in establishing numerical identity. First examine Panel 1. Imagine that you lose perceptual contact with the scene, and return 5 min later to view Panel 2. How would you describe what has happened? You would probably say that the rabbit has moved from above and to the left of the chair to below and to the right of it, while the bird has moved from the bottom left to the top right. In this account, numerical identity (sameness in the sense of *same one*) is being carried by kind membership; it is the rabbit and the bird each of whom you assume has moved through time. The conceptual, kind-based, system of individuation is responsible for establishing the object tokens in this case. Now imagine that a fixation point replaces the chair, and Panels 1 and 2 are projected one after the other onto a screen, while you maintain fixation on the common fixation point. If the timing of the stimuli supports apparent motion, what would your perception be? Rather than seeing a bird and a rabbit each moving diagonally, you see two individuals each changing back and forth between a white bird-shaped object and a black rabbit-shaped object as they move side to side. The visual system that computes the numerical identity of the objects that undergo apparent motion in arrays such as Fig. 1 minimizes the total amount of movement; this system takes into account property or kind information only when spatiotemporal considerations are equated (see Nakayama, He, & Shimojo, 1995, for a review). The mid-level object file system is responsible for establishing the object tokens in this case, and it settles on a different solution than does the kind-based object individuation system.

We shall argue that studies on object individuation in infancy lend support for the suggestion that kind-based object individuation is architecturally distinct from the mid-level object file system. But we must begin by providing some evidence that, contra Piaget, young infants establish representations of individual objects and track them through time. Before we consider the nature of the processes that subserve object representations in early infancy, we must be convinced that there *are* object representations in early infancy.

3. Object individuation and numerical identity in the first year of life

Studies using the violation of expectancy looking time methodology have pushed back the age of the representation of object permanence to 2.5 months (Baillargeon & DeVos, 1991; Hespos & Baillargeon, in press; Spelke, Breinlinger, Macomber, & Jacobson, 1992). In these experiments, infants watch events unfold before them. After being familiarized or habituated to the events, typically they are shown, in alternation, an expected outcome (an outcome that is consistent with adults' understanding of the physical world) and an unexpected outcome (an outcome that is inconsistent with adults' understanding of the physical world, a magic trick). If infants have the same understanding of the events as do adults, they should look longer at the unexpected outcome relative to the expected outcome. Often, but not always, these studies involve events unfolding behind screens, the outcome of the magic trick being revealed upon removal of the screen. These studies require no training; one simply monitors looking times as the infant watches what is happening. Thus, this method taps spontaneous representation of objects and events.

This method yields interpretable findings in newborns (e.g. Slater, Johnson, Brown, & Badenoch, 1996), and is widely used in studies of infants of 2 months

1.   ▮   ▮   Screen introduced

2.   ▮   ▮ → 🦆   Object 1 brought out

3.   ▮   ▮ ←   Object 1 returned

4. 🦆 ← ▮   ▮   Object 2 brought out

5.   → ▮   ▮   Object 2 returned

Steps 2-5 repeated

6.   Screen removed revealing:
       🦆   🦆   Expected outcome
                  or
           🦆   Unexpected outcome

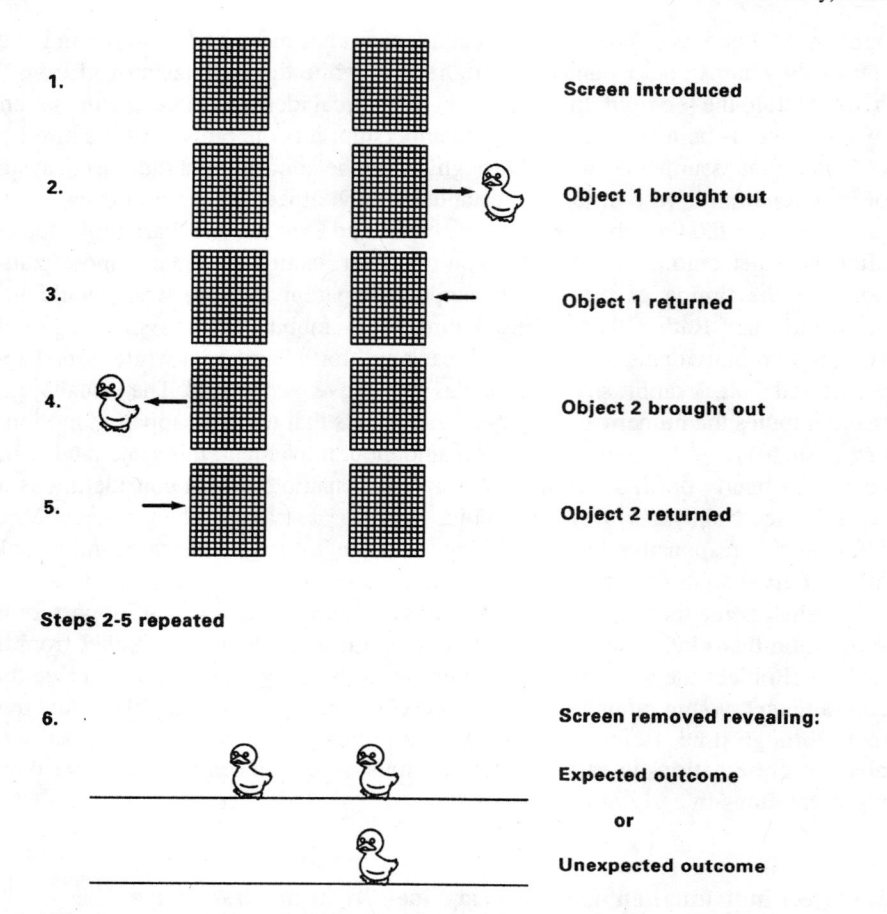

Fig. 2. Schematic representation of experimental paradigm in Spelke, Kestenbaum, Simons, and Wein (1995).

and older. Here we briefly describe two studies using this methodology that illuminate the relation between object permanence and infants' use of spatiotemporal information in the service of object individuation. By spatiotemporal information we mean location or motion information – spatial separation in the frontal plane or in depth, and continuity or discontinuity in an object's trajectory.

Spelke, Kestenbaum, Simons, and Wein (1995) showed that infants do not merely expect objects to continue to exist when out of view, but also that they interpret spatiotemporal discontinuity as evidence for two numerically distinct objects. They showed 4.5-month-old infants two screens with a gap in between, from which objects emerged as in Fig. 2. One object emerged from the left edge of the left screen and then returned behind that screen, and after a suitable delay, a second, physically identical object emerged from the right edge of the right screen and then returned behind it. No object ever appeared in the space between the two screens.

Since an object cannot get from point A to point B without traversing a spatiotemporally continuous path, adults conclude that there must be two numerically distinct objects involved in this event. What about these young infants? After habituation, the screens were removed, revealing only one object (the unexpected outcome) or two objects (the expected outcome). The infants looked reliably longer at the one-object outcome, suggesting they, too, established representations of two distinct objects in this event. A control condition established that infants indeed analyzed the path of motion, and did not expect two objects just because there were two screens. If the object did appear in the space between the two screens, a different pattern of looking was obtained.[2]

Using a different procedure, Wynn (1992) provided further evidence that infants are able to use spatiotemporal discontinuity in object individuation. Five-month-old infants watched a Mickey Mouse doll being placed on a puppet stage. The experimenter then occluded the doll from the infant's view by raising a screen, and placed a second doll behind the screen. The screen was then lowered, revealing either the expected outcome of 2 dolls, or the unexpected outcome of 1 doll or 3 dolls. Infants looked longer at the unexpected outcomes of 1 or 3 objects than at the expected outcome of 2 objects. Wynn interpreted these studies as showing that infants can add 1 + 1 to yield precisely 2.[3] Whatever these studies tell us about infants' capacity for addition, success depends on the infant's ability to use spatiotemporal discontinuity to infer that the second Mickey Mouse doll was numerically distinct from the first one.

These results suggest that (1) infants represent objects as continuing to exist when they are invisible behind barriers, (2) infants distinguish one object from two numerically distinct but featurally identical objects, distinguishing *one object* from *one object and another object*, and (3) the information infants draw upon for object individuation and for establishing numerical identity is spatiotemporal. If spatiotemporal discontinuity is detected, young infants establish representations of two numerically distinct objects.

Contrary to Piaget's position that processes for establishing representations that trace individual objects through time and occlusion develop slowly over the first 2 years of human life, these studies indicate that they are in place by 4 months of age.

---

[2] In Spelke, Kestenbaum, Simons, and Wein (1995), 5-month-old infants were agnostic as to how many objects were involved in the continuous event; in a replication with 10-month-olds, infants established a representation of a single object in the continuous motion event, reversing the pattern of preference from the outcomes of the discontinuous motion condition (Xu & Carey, 1996). What is important is that in both experiments the pattern of looking differed between the two conditions (continuous motion vs. discontinuous motion). Thus, when they detected spatiotemporal discontinuity, infants created representations of two numerically distinct, though featurally identical, objects.

[3] Wynn (1992) and her many replicators (Feigenson, Carey, & Spelke, in press; Koechlin, Dehaene, & Mehler, 1998; Simon, Hespos, & Rochat, 1995) also included a subtraction condition: 2 − 1 = 2 or 1. Infants looked longer at the outcomes of two objects, the unexpected outcome in this condition. Irrespective of what these studies show about infant representation of number (see Simon, 1997; Uller et al., 1999), here we emphasize their implications for infant representations of objects.

Other studies push this age as low as 2 months (e.g. Hespos & Baillargeon, in press), and some have argued that these abilities may be given innately (e.g. Spelke, 1996).

4. Does the mid-level object file system underlie infant object representations?

As argued by Leslie et al. (1998) and Scholl and Leslie (1999), the identification of object representations in young infants with the object files of object-based attention rests on several considerations. First, and most importantly, both systems privilege spatiotemporal information in decisions about individuation and numerical identity. Second, both systems are subject to the same set size limitation of parallel individuation; that is, only three (or four) objects can be indexed and tracked simultaneously. Third, the object representations of both systems survive occlusion, and object tracking is sensitive to the distinction between loss of visual contact that signals cessation of existence and loss of visual contact that does not.

4.1. Primacy of spatiotemporal information

In the mid-level object file system, the questions of individuation and numerical identity concern the bases on which an indexed object retains its index, as opposed to a new object file being established or a new index being assigned. Pylyshyn (2001) and Scholl (2001) both touch on evidence suggesting that spatiotemporal continuity is the primary determinant of numerical identity in this system. Features of an indexed object can change and may be represented as such (see also Kahneman et al., 1992). This is seen clearly in apparent motion studies; the visual system has no problem seeing totally distinct features as states of a single moving object. In order to see apparent motion in cases such as that illustrated in Fig. 1, the visual system must decide which object to pair with which object. To a first approximation, spatiotemporal considerations decide the matter. In such simple displays, the system will minimize the total amount of movement, and will happily override featural information in favor of a motion of two objects each changing color, size and shape as well as kind. However, featural information can play a secondary role: when spatiotemporal information does not unambiguously favor one solution over the other, featural changes are taken into account (see Nakayama et al., 1995, for a review).

The phenomenon of the "tunnel effect" (Burke, 1952) further underscores that new object files are not opened on the basis of featural differences. The tunnel effect is the perception of object unity when objects disappear behind a barrier, reappearing later out the other side. Michotte and Burke (1951) dubbed this phenomenon "amodal completion" because observers do not *see* the object behind the screen (unlike in apparent motion or subjective contours). Rather, observers encode the event as involving a single object despite the discontinuity of perceptual input, and they can even describe its hidden trajectory. Spatiotemporal considerations determine amodal completion (the speed of the object, the time behind the occluder, the relative sizes of the objects to that of the occluder). What do *not* matter are the features of the objects; a green circle entering behind the screen may emerge as a red

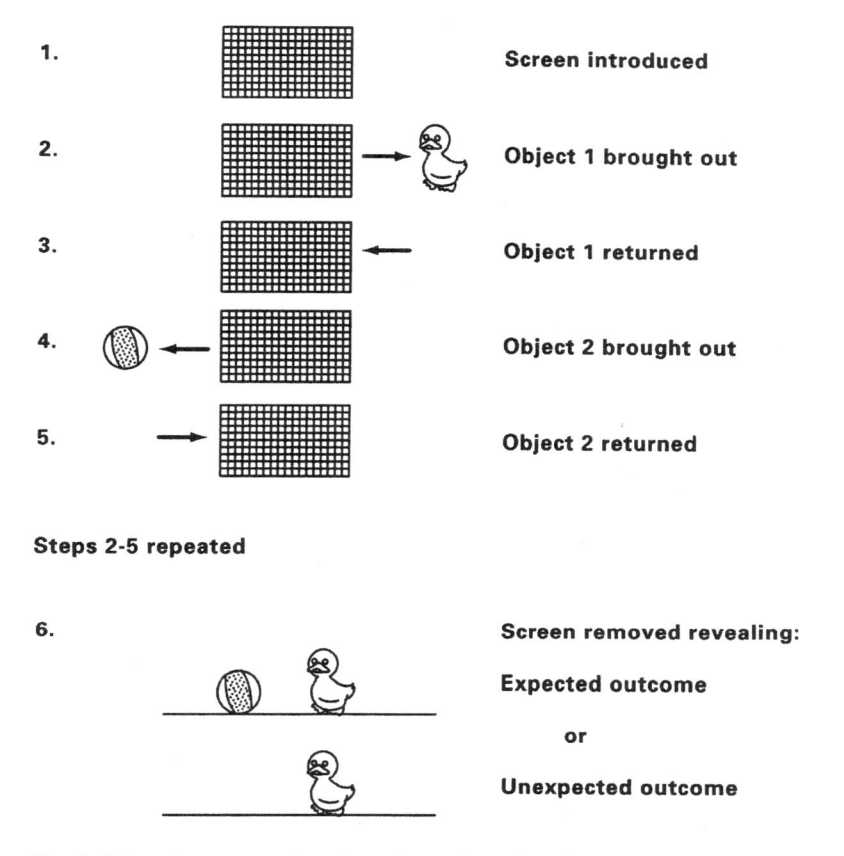

1.	[screen]		Screen introduced
2.	[screen] → 🦆		Object 1 brought out
3.	[screen] ←		Object 1 returned
4.	🏐 ← [screen]		Object 2 brought out
5.	→ [screen]		Object 2 returned

Steps 2-5 repeated

6.	🏐 🦆	Screen removed revealing:
		Expected outcome
		or
	🦆	Unexpected outcome

Fig. 3. Schematic representation of experimental paradigm from Xu and Carey (1996).

square and yet be seen as the same object just as strongly as if it emerges a green circle, so long as the spatiotemporal parameters supporting amodal completion are met (Burke, 1952).

Consistent with the claim that featural changes do not signal the opening of new object files, object tracking in the MOT studies is not disrupted by indexed objects changing color, size, shape or kind during tracking (Pylyshyn, 2001). Finally, a recent study by Scholl, Pylyshyn, and Franconeri (2001) underscores the primacy of spatiotemporal information in the establishing and tracking of object files. In the MOT paradigm, if tracking is stopped and one of the objects disappears, the subjects can indicate its location and direction of motion. But if objects are changing properties during tracking, subjects are not aware of the momentary color or shape of a tracked object.

In sum, the computations that maintain indexes to attended objects rely heavily on spatiotemporal information; objects are tracked on the basis of spatiotemporal continuity. Once an object file is opened, features may be bound to it, and updated as the object moves through space. (The study just described shows that features are not automatically bound to open object files, perhaps because of the high attentional demands of tracking four independently moving objects at once.) These generalizations hold for the young infant's object representations as well, the point to which we now turn.

The Spelke, Kestenbaum, Simons, and Wein (1995) and Wynn (1992) studies described above suggest that infants as young as 4 months of age draw on spatiotemporal information in object individuation and tracking, but they do not show that spatiotemporal information is privileged, for they did not explore whether infants could also use property or kind differences as a basis for object individuation. Recent studies suggest that young infants do not use property or kind differences as a basis for opening new object files (Xu & Carey, 1996), especially when spatiotemporal evidence is strong (e.g. continuous trajectory specifying one object, a single location specifying one object). Imagine the following scenario. One screen is put on a puppet stage. A duck emerges from behind the screen and returns behind it, and then a ball emerges from behind the same screen and then returns (Fig. 3). How many objects are behind the screen? For adults, the answer is clear: At least two, a duck and a ball. But since there is only a single screen occluding the objects, there is no clear spatiotemporal evidence that there are two objects. We must rely on our knowledge about object properties or object kinds to succeed at this task. In our studies, infants were shown the above event. The contrast was either at the superordinate (as well as basic) level (e.g. a duck and a ball, an elephant and a truck; or an animal and a vehicle) or just at the basic level (e.g. a cup and a ball); some objects were toy models (e.g. truck, duck) where others were from highly familiar everyday kinds (e.g. cup, bottle, book, ball). On the test trials, the screen was removed to reveal either the expected outcome of two objects or the unexpected outcome of only one of them. If infants have the same expectations as adults, they should look longer at the unexpected outcome. The results, however, were surprising: 10-month-old infants failed to draw the inference that there should be two objects behind the screen, whereas 12-month-old infants succeeded in doing so.

Control conditions established that the method was sensitive. Ten-month-old infants succeeded at the task if they were given spatiotemporal evidence that there were two numerically distinct objects, e.g. if they were shown the two objects *simultaneously* for 2 or 3 s at the beginning of the experiment. Furthermore, Xu and Carey (1996) showed that infants are sensitive to object properties under the circumstances of their experimental paradigm: it takes infants longer to habituate to a duck and a car alternately appearing from behind the screen than to a car repeatedly appearing from behind the screen. In this task, infants failed to draw on object kind information for object individuation (e.g. animal, vehicle, duck, truck, ball, cup, etc.); they also failed to draw on property contrasts (e.g. the contrast between being yellow, curvilinear, and rubber vs. being red, rectilinear, and metal). The property differences which infants under 10 months of age are sensitive to may be irrelevant to object individuation. Other laboratories have replicated these findings (Wilcox & Baillargeon, 1998a, Experiments 1 and 2; see Xu & Carey, 2000, and Section 5.2 below, for a discussion of some apparently conflicting data from Wilcox, 1999; Wilcox & Baillargeon, 1998a,b).

Van de Walle, Carey, and Prevor (in press) sought convergent evidence for the claim that infants below 12 months of age do not use kind membership as a basis for opening new object files. In these studies, a manual search measure was used instead of the violation of expectancy looking time procedure. Ten- and 12-month-old infants were trained to reach through a spandex slit into a box into which they could not see in order to retrieve objects. Three types of trials were contrasted: one-object trials, two-object trials in which individuation must be based on property/kind contrasts, and two-object trials in which spatiotemporal evidence specified numerically distinct objects. On a one-object trial, the experimenter pulled out the same object (e.g. the toy telephone) twice, replacing it into the box each time. On two-object trials in which individuation is based on property/kind information, infants watched the experimenter pull out an object (e.g. a toy telephone), return it to the box, then pull out a second object (e.g. a toy duck), and return it to the box. On two-object trials in which spatiotemporal evidence supported individuation, the experimenter pulled out the first object (e.g. the telephone), left it on top of the box, pulled out the second object (e.g. the duck) so that they were simultaneously visible, and then returned both to the box.

The boxes were then pushed into the child's reach, and patterns of search revealed how many objects the child had represented as being in the box. Both 10- and 12-month-olds differentiated the one- and two-object trials when given spatiotemporal evidence for two objects. That is, they searched for a second object after having retrieved the first one on two-object trials but not on one-object trials, and having retrieved the second object on two-object trials, they did not search further. Twelve-month-olds also succeeded when given property/kind information alone. In contrast, the 10-month-olds failed in this condition; their pattern of search on the two-object trials was the same as on the one-object trials. Ten-month-olds failed to use kind differences such as telephone, duck or car, book or property differences such as black, yellow, telephone-shaped, duck-shaped, rubber, or plastic to establish representations of two numerically distinct objects in the box. These results are consistent with those of the looking time studies of Xu and Carey (1996).

We draw two conclusions from these studies. First, they support the identification of the young infants' object representations with those of the mid-level object file system, for they show that infants under 10 months of age rely almost exclusively on spatiotemporal information in decisions about numerical identity of objects seen at different times. Second, they are consistent with the possibility that a second system of object individuation, a kind-based system, emerges at around 12 months of age (see Section 6.1 for further discussion).

4.2. Set size limitations

Pylyshyn's MOT paradigm provides direct evidence regarding the number of objects that may be simultaneously indexed and tracked through time. Although various task variables affect the set size at which performance is virtually errorless, a good approximation is that about four objects are the limit (see Pylyshyn, 2001; Trick & Pylyshyn, 1994, for a discussion of the relations between the limits on parallel individuation and indexing of objects and the limits on subitization, the rapid apprehension of precise numerosity of small sets of objects, in the absence of counting).

Results from several experimental paradigms suggest that young infants' limit on parallel individuation of objects is in the same range. In the interest of space, we mention just two lines of relevant work. The studies by Spelke, Kestenbaum, Simons, and Wein (1995) and Wynn (1992), described above, show that infants represent events in terms of precisely one object or precisely two objects. Success with sets of three objects, however, is mixed: Wynn (1992) showed that 4-month-old infants expected $1 + 1$ to be precisely 2 (they looked longer at impossible outcomes of 3 than at possible outcomes of 2, as well as at impossible outcomes of 1). Wynn also found that young infants succeeded at a $3 - 1 = 2$ compared to a $2 + 1 = 2$ comparison. Baillargeon, Miller, and Constantino (1993) found that 10-month-olds succeeded in a $2 + 1 = 3$ or 2 comparison, but they failed at a $1 + 1 + 1 = 3$ or 2 comparison. Finally, Uller and Leslie (1999) found that 10-month-olds succeeded in a $2 - 0 = 1$ vs. $2 - 1 = 1$ comparison, but failed in a $3 - 0 = 2$ vs. $3 - 1 = 2$ comparison. Thus, there appears to be robust successes with sets of 1 and 2, and some fragile successes with sets of 3.

Similarly, in simple habituation paradigms, in which, over time, infants look less at successive presentations of arrays of a single set size (e.g. 3) and recover interest when shown an array of a different set size (e.g. 2), performance often falls apart at 3 vs. 4 (Starkey & Cooper, 1980). That parallel individuation of small sets of objects underlies success in these studies, rather than a symbolic representation of number such as that computed by analog magnitude systems (Dehaene, 1997), shows that success is not predicted by Weber fraction considerations; infants succeed at 2 vs. 3 but fail at 4 vs. 6 (e.g. Starkey & Cooper, 1980).[4] Thus, that the limits on set sizes of object tokens that may be simultaneously attended and tracked are in the same range supports the identification of the system that supports object individuation in infancy with that underlying object-based attention in adults.

4.3. Occlusion vs. existence cessation

Another parallel between the two systems is that indexed objects, just like the objects represented by infants, survive occlusion, as revealed in studies of the tunnel effect (Burke, 1952). Further, Scholl and Pylyshyn (1999) showed that object tracking in the MOT paradigm was not disrupted by the objects going behind real or virtual occluders. Almost all of the infant studies cited above involve occlusion.

In Scholl and Pylyshyn (1999) it mattered that the objects disappeared behind an occluder by regular deletion along its contour, reemerging from the other side by regular accretion along its opposite contour. If the objects disappeared at the same rate by shrinking to nothing, reappearing farther along the trajectory at the same rate

---

[4] Although experiments with small sets of objects reveal the set size signature of object file representations (Feigenson et al., 2001), under some circumstances infants also create numerical representations of large sets that show the Weber fraction signature of analog magnitude representations (Xu, 2000; Xu & Spelke, 2000).

by expanding from a point, tracking was totally disrupted. Thus, the system distinguished the object's going behind an occluder from its going out of existence, to be later replaced by another object coming into existence. Bower (1974) provided evidence that young infants draw the same distinction. Bower compared infants' visual search for objects that disappeared by shrinking down to nothing with their visual search for objects that disappeared by progressive deletion along a boundary. Infants searched for the missing object in the latter case but not the former. This early experiment bears replication, perhaps with a manual search paradigm along the lines of Van de Walle et al. (in press).

4.4. Conclusions

Section 4 has outlined the considerations in favor of identifying infants' object representations and object files, as well as identifying the computations that underlie young infants' tracking of moving with the adult mid-level system of object indexing. For the rest of this review, we will adopt this identification as a working hypothesis, and consider its implications for each of the two research communities.

What is to be gained from the discovery that students of adult mid-level object-based attention and students of infant object representations are exploring the same natural kind? Some have argued that this discovery *explains* some of the properties of infant object representations, such as the primacy of spatiotemporal information in individuation or the set size limitations. Of course, this is not so; at best, the identification reduces two sets of mysteries to one. Still, both communities stand to benefit from this discovery. Understanding hard won in one community may be applied to the other, and phenomena explored in one literature become a source of hypothesis for the other.

5. Lessons to be learned regarding infants' object representations

5.1. Object representations in infancy: perceptual or conceptual?

As Scholl and Leslie (1999) discussed at length, that infant object representations are object files has important implications for the controversies in the infant literature concerning whether infants' object representations are *conceptual* or *perceptual*. In the attention literature, object file representations are considered *mid-level* between low-level sensory representations and fully conceptual representations. Object file representations do not depend upon categorizing individuals into antecedently represented object kinds. To a large extent, the mechanisms that index and track objects through time work the same way whether the objects are instances of familiar kinds or not (see Nakayama et al., 1995, for a review), and are thus *mid-level* in not requiring placement into conceptual categories.

Scholl and Leslie (1999) had a different sense of *mid-level* in mind. They were concerned with the status of the spatiotemporal and featural information that enters into the processes of object indexing and object file creation. It is consistent with their position that the object files themselves are symbolic representations (see

Sections 6.4–6.7 below). Nonetheless, spatiotemporal and featural information that is drawn upon in the creation and maintenance of object files is most likely represented in an encapsulated perceptual system (see Pylyshyn, 2001). If so, it is misleading to say that the infant "believes" that objects trace spatiotemporally continuous paths, or "knows" that objects are permanent, for the infant represents no such propositions in any accessible form. We are in agreement with Scholl and Leslie, and with Pylyshyn, on this point.

5.2. Object featural information and the tunnel effect

The identification of the two literatures is a source of insight into the different status of spatiotemporal information and object feature information in the young infant's object representations. However, it is controversial that spatiotemporal information takes precedence over featural information in infants' individuation of objects (Needham & Baillargeon, 1997; Wilcox, 1999; Wilcox & Baillargeon, 1998a,b). This controversy potentially undermines the identification of the two literatures. However, when we look more closely at these apparent conflicts, uniting the two literatures helps us resolve them, and thereby strengthens the integration.

A central piece of evidence for the identification of the two literatures is the failure of infants to draw on featural differences in establishing representations of two objects in the studies of Van de Walle et al. (in press) and Xu and Carey (1996) described above. Recent studies by Wilcox and her colleagues (Wilcox & Baillargeon, 1998a,b) have challenged our interpretation of these results. In Wilcox and Baillargeon's narrow/wide-screen studies, infants watched a blue ball and a red box emerge, one at a time, from opposite sides of a screen. In each cycle, both objects were out of view, behind the screen, for a short period of time. Two conditions were contrasted. In the wide-screen condition, the occluding screen was 30 cm wide, wide enough for both objects to simultaneously fit behind, since the sum of the widths of the ball and the box was 22 cm. In the narrow-screen condition, however, the screen was too narrow (21 cm or even narrower) for both objects to fit behind. Infants as young as 4.5 months of age looked longer at the narrow-screen event than at the wide-screen event. Wilcox and Baillargeon interpreted the infants' behavior as follows: in the narrow-screen event, the infants must have used the featural (or kind) differences between the box and the ball to infer that two distinct objects were involved in this event and must have realized that the two objects could not fit behind the screen simultaneously.

These are extremely creative and interesting studies. However, there is another possible interpretation of the results. The narrow/wide-screen events are very similar to those in studies of the tunnel effect described above (e.g. Burke, 1952). In amodal completion, the visual system takes into account various spatiotemporal parameters and yields a representation of a single object persisting through occlusion. Perhaps the conditions of the narrow-screen event are those that support amodal completion, such that the infant represents it as a single object persisting through occlusion, and finds the change of properties anomalous. Although babies, by hypothesis deploying the mid-level object tracking system, can update representations of single objects when properties change, they nonetheless expect an object's properties to stay constant.[5] On this alternative account, infants are not using the property differences as a basis for opening a second object file in the narrow-screen events; rather the property change of a single object is anomalous, and thus attention grabbing. On this account, the wide-screen events do not yield amodal completion so there is no single object-token whose properties changed during occlusion.

To explore the amodal completion hypothesis, Carey and Bassin (1998) assessed adults' spontaneous perception of the events upon seeing them (without any verbal prompting, a situation identical to what the infant experienced). Virtually all of the participants shown a very narrow-screen (15 cm) event spontaneously noted that something was anomalous, as did 40% of those shown a 21 cm narrow-screen event. Most importantly, *all but one* of the participants, when they noticed the anomaly, whether in the 15 cm or the 21 cm version, described it as follows: "It went in a ball and it came out a box." That is, they described the event as a single object magically changing properties (as described in the tunnel effect literature), rather than two objects that could not fit behind the screen.

Notice that the tunnel effect alternative interpretation assumes that infants, like adults, used the relative size of the objects and the occluder to establish a representation of a single object persisting behind the screen, and that infants, like adults, expect that properties of objects remain constant while occluded, and thus find the property changes interesting or anomalous. On this interpretation, the developmental changes reported in Wilcox (1999) concern *which* property changes of a single object infants find anomalous or interesting (first size and shape, then surface pattern, then color). On this interpretation, the narrow-screen findings do *not* reflect the child's ability to use featural information as a basis for decisions of numerical identity of object files.

It is, of course, an open question whether our interpretation of the narrow-screen/wide-screen studies is correct. We offer it here as an example of how the identification of the two literatures might guide the interpretation of apparently conflicting results. Furthermore, our hypothesis suggests experiments on the tunnel effect in adults. To our knowledge, there has been no systematic study of the effects of the relative size of the objects and the occluders in producing an illusion of a single object behind the barrier. The screens in the adult studies of the tunnel effect are much wider, relative to the objects, than those in these infant studies. The Carey and Bassin (1998) findings should be systematically followed up; the conditions of the narrow-screen events should produce very strong amodal completion, irrespective of object speed.

---

[5] There is ample evidence that infants expect properties bound to a represented object to remain constant during occlusion. For example, in Baillargeon's rotating screen studies, infants predict when the screen's motion should be arrested from the height of the occluded object (Baillargeon, 1991), and in Aguilar and Baillargeon's studies of when objects should be visible after going behind screens with a window, infants again take into account the height of the occluded object (e.g. Aguilar & Baillargeon, 1999).

5.3. A second challenge to the Xu and Carey (1996) findings

Experiments 7 and 8 of Wilcox and Baillargeon (1998a) show that young infants use featural information for object individuation, and are not subject to the tunnel effect interpretation. In their study, 9.5-month-old infants were shown a box moving from one side of the stage and disappearing behind a screen, followed by a ball emerging from the other side of the screen. The screen was then lowered and the infant saw *only* the ball on the stage. Infants looked longer at this outcome relative to a condition where the same ball disappeared behind the screen and reappeared from the other side. However, this positive result goes away completely if the first object, the box, appeared from behind the screen, moved to the side of the stage, then reversed its trajectory and disappeared behind the same screen, the ball then emerging from behind the same screen. The test outcome was identical to the experiment described above.

Wilcox and Baillargeon (1998a) argued that the infants' success in the first condition is due to their using the differences between the box and the ball to create representations of two objects, their attention being drawn by the anomalous ball only outcome in the ball–box condition. We agree with their argument. One possible interpretation for the success in the single trajectory condition, in the face of failure in the double trajectory condition (as well as in Van de Walle et al., in press; Xu & Carey, 1996), is that the single trajectory condition provided very little spatiotemporal information that there was a single object. Analogous to the case of apparent motion, when spatiotemporal evidence does not favor one solution over another, infants can use featural differences for object individuation. However, slightly stronger spatio-temporal evidence for the presence of a single object (as in the second experiment with a reversal of trajectory and both objects appearing from behind the same location, namely the screen) overrides any sensitivity to features and the object file system computes a representation of a single one object. In the Xu and Carey (1996) studies, spatiotemporal evidence for one object was even greater; the objects emerged from behind the same screen several times, and reversed trajectory several times.

5.4. Object segregation vs. object files

Xu, Carey, and Welch (1999) explored when infants could use feature or kind information to individuate objects in static arrays, and found age shifts that converged with those found in the individuation within object tracking experiments cited above. Consider Fig. 4. How many objects are there in this array? Adults respond that there are two objects, a duck and a car, and if the duck is lifted from above, adults predict that the duck will come alone and are surprised if the duck/car moves as a single object. Xu et al. (1999) habituated 10- and 12-month-old infants to the stationary duck/car stimulus (and to an analogous cup/shoe stimulus), after which the top object was grasped and lifted, and two outcomes shown in alternation. In one outcome, just the top object came up (move-apart outcome) and in the other, both objects came up (move-together outcome). At 10 months, the infants did not look longer at the unexpected, move-together, outcome. They failed to use the

HABITUATION

APART (EXPECTED)

TOGETHER (UNEXPECTED)

Fig. 4. Schematic representation of experimental paradigm from Xu et al. (1999).

contrast between the duck and the car, or the cup and the shoe, to infer that there were two individual objects in the array. That is, 10-month-olds failed to draw on kind contrasts (duck/car, cup/shoe) or property contrasts (yellow-rubber-duck shaped/red-metal-car shaped) to resolve the ambiguous object into two. At 12 months, however, the infants succeed at the task, looking longer at the unexpected outcome in which the cup/shoe or duck/car moved as a single object. Furthermore, as in Van de Walle et al. (in press) and Xu and Carey (1996), when 10-month-olds were given spatiotemporal evidence that there were two objects (e.g. if the objects were briefly moved, laterally, relative to each at the beginning of each habituation trial), they now succeeded, looking longer at the unexpected move-together outcome. These results converge with the data of Van de Walle et al. (in press) and Xu and Carey (1996). However, these results are in apparent conflict with other experiments by Needham and her colleagues.

Needham and her colleagues (Needham, 1998; Needham & Baillargeon, 1997,

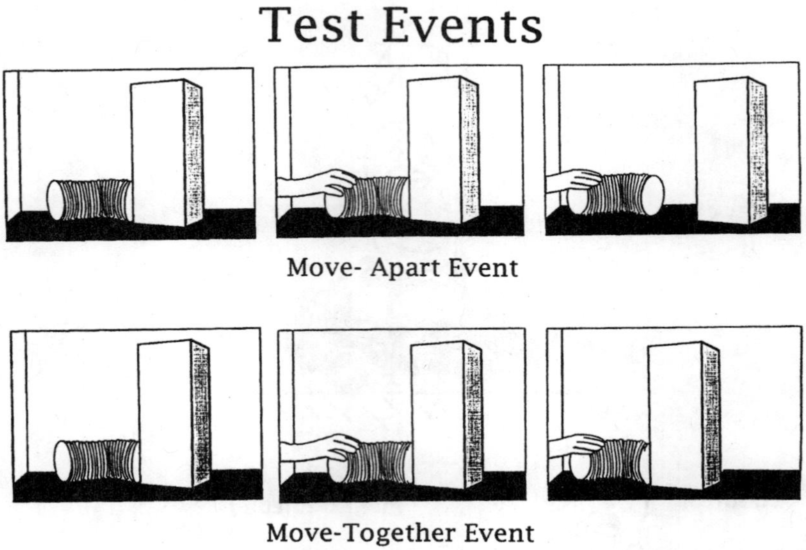

Test Events

Move-Apart Event

Move-Together Event

Fig. 5. Schematic representation of ambiguous stimulus from Needham box/hose object segregation studies.

1998) demonstrated that even infants as young as 5 months of age succeed in using featural information to segment objects that share boundaries. Consider Fig. 5. The rectangular box is blue and made of wood, and the cylinder is bright yellow and made of plastic. Young infants use the contrast between blue, rectangular, wood and yellow, cylindrical, plastic, or some subset of these contrasts, to resolve the ambiguity derived from a shared boundary and to parse this figure into two distinct objects. This is demonstrated in experiments in which infants view this ambiguous display for a few seconds, after which one of the objects is grasped and pulled. Infants look longer if the box/hose object moves as a single whole than if it comes apart.

Thus, featural information plays a role in object segregation problems in early infancy, but this does not undermine the arguments of Section 4.1 above, for the processes of object indexing, creating object files, and tracking objects through time engage two quite distinct individuation problems. First, there is the segregation of objects that share boundaries, which, like figure/ground segregation, concerns the problem of assigning edges and surfaces to individuals. In these problems, such as those posed by the displays in Figs. 4 and 5, ambiguity arises from shared boundaries. Second, there is the *different* individuation problem than that which arises in object tracking experiments. Object tracking experiments concern, among other things, whether already perceptually segregated individuals are numerically distinct. Ambiguity in the latter case arises because perceptual contact specifying spatiotemporal continuity has been lost (as in occlusion, or due to attentional shifts). As we have indicated at length, it is in the latter problem that featural information plays a decidedly secondary role. But in the former cases (figure/ground and object segregation in static arrays), featural information *must* play a primary role, for edges are specified by color and brightness contrasts. Other featural cues, such as gestalt cues (good form, symmetry, feature similarity) also enter into the earliest stages of figure/ground segregation, as does spatiotemporal information such as spatial segregation in depth. It is very likely that all of these cues would influence infants' object segregation as well, an empirical matter worth exploring.

In sum, the adult literature distinguishes the processes through which edges are assigned to figures, or surfaces to objects, on the one hand, from those through which already segmented figures or objects are tracked through time, their features updated as they change. In the former processes, featural information plays a pivotal role, in part with and in interaction with spatiotemporal information, while in the latter spatiotemporal information is sharply privileged. Thus, that young infants (at least as young as 4 months of age) make robust use of featural information for object segregation does not undermine the claim that they almost always fail to do so in the service of tracing numerical identity of already segmented objects.

Why then did infants in Xu et al. (1999) fail to use the distinctions between the duck and the car, or the cup and shoe to segment the arrays as in Fig. 4 into two objects? We recruit two further distinctions in our speculative answer to this question.

5.5. On distinguishing featural/property information from kind information

The merging of the two literatures supports another distinction that might help resolve some of the apparent empirical conflicts in the infant literature. Recall that very young infants succeed at segmenting the ambiguous box/hose arrays (Fig. 5) on the basis of featural differences between the two objects, but it was not until 12 months that infants segmented the ambiguous duck/car display (Fig. 4) into two objects. Needham and colleagues have found that success at any given object segmentation task is sensitive to object complexity. For instance, making the hose curved and rotating the array so that the boundary between the box and hose isn't fully visible pushes the age of success a few months older (Needham, Baillargeon, & Kauffman, 1997).

The duck/car and cup/shoe stimuli of Xu et al. (1999) were more complex than any that have been used in the Needham et al. studies. They are multicolored and multi-parted, with each object having a complex, irregular shape. Their properties alone do not support an unambiguous parse; property contrasts support segmenting the head from the body, the beak from the rest of the head, the body from the feet, the windowed part of the car from the rest of the car, the wheels from the rest of the car, as well as the duck from the car.[6]

---

[6] Needham and Baillargeon (2000) and Xu and Carey (2000) discuss many other respects in which the Xu et al. (1999) paradigm poses a more difficult problem for infants than does the paradigm used by Needham and her collaborators. For example, babies in our studies are habituated to the stationary display, perhaps supporting an interpretation of the array as a single object. Also, Needham and Baillargeon (2000) review unpublished work that shows that infants succeed in segmenting side by side objects at a younger age than they do objects one on top of the other. We suggest that each of these factors makes it more likely that infants need to draw on kind representations to solve the problem, and that it is kind representations that are becoming available between 10 and 12 months of age.

It is important to distinguish the encapsulated processes that draw on property information in object segregation from processes that draw on conceptually mediated kind representations, as in recognizing the top part of Fig. 5 as a duck (see Pylyshyn, 2001, for an extended discussion of this distinction). Xu and Carey (2000) suggest that various features of our task, including the fact that the property differences do not support an unambiguous parse, make a property-based parse less likely, and require that the child draw on kind representations to succeed. Thus, the 10–12 month shift in these studies may reflect the emergence of kind representations, or the ability to draw upon them in object individuation, just as do the 10–12 month shifts in Van de Walle et al. (in press) and Xu and Carey (1996).

5.6. On distinguishing between kind representations and experience-based shape representations

There is one more apparent conflict in findings between the box/hose experiments of Needham and the duck/shoe experiments of Xu et al. Needham found that at an age at which infants do not succeed at parsing an ambiguous stationary display, a few seconds exposure to one of the objects (e.g. the box alone or the hose alone) before presentation of the ambiguous display leads infants as young as 5 months of age to succeed (see Needham et al., 1997, for a review). That is, early in infancy, experience-based representations may be recruited in the service of object segregation. To check if such prior exposure would help in the duck/car case, Xu et al. (1999) included a condition in which 10-month-olds were given 30 s exposure to the duck alone and 30 s exposure to the car alone, before being habituated to the stationary duck/car display (Fig. 4). Ten-month-old infants still failed. Why would experience help in the box/hose case but not the duck/car case?

The work of Peterson (1994) suggests another distinction we must make in thinking about the representations that play a role in object individuation: representations of kinds and representation of experientially derived shapes. Her work has shown that these two types of representations play distinct roles in the process of figure/ground segregation, suggesting that they might also play distinct roles in the process of object segregation.[7]

In a series of studies, Peterson and her colleagues have studied figure/ground displays in which one of the surfaces is bounded by a meaningful shape (e.g. a face profile or a sea horse) and in which its complement is not. She often manipulates other cues to figure/ground segregation as well (e.g. symmetry, binocular depth cues). What she finds is that meaningfulness of shape (which can only have been derived from experience) enters in parallel with and in interaction with encapsulated perceptual processes at the very earliest stages of figure determination. That is, the meaningful shape is more often seen as figure than its complement, and this

---

[7] We are not claiming here that the problem of object segmentation and the problem of figure/ground segmentation are one and the same problem, just that they are analogous and should be differentiated from the problem of object identity in tracking experiments.

factor sometimes overrides other cues to figure such as symmetry or depth cues (e.g. Peterson & Gibson, 1993; see Peterson, 1994, for a review).

This state of affairs is perhaps paradoxical. Logically, it would seem that object recognition (place an individual token with respect to an antecedently represented kind) would require prior figure/ground segregation, for one needs the individual to match against stored representations. Peterson resolves the paradox by pointing out that familiarity of shape may enter into the process without requiring that actual recognition (accessing a familiar kind) has taken place. In support of this observation, Peterson, de Gelder, Rapcsak, Gerhardstein, and Bachoud-Levis (in press) presented neuropsychological evidence that the experientially derived shape representations that enter into figure/ground segregation are *not* the kind representations that mediate object recognition. They presented a double dissociation between a visual agnosic patient with bilateral temporal-occipital lobe lesions and a patient with bilateral occipital lesions who was impaired on a variety of sensory and perceptual capacities. Agnosic patients cannot recognize familiar objects; they cannot name them, say what they are for, describe them, or show any other evidence of having placed them with respect to a familiar kind. The agnosic patient nonetheless showed the effects of experientially derived shape on figure determination to an equal extent as normal participants in these studies. That is, she was more likely to see a sea horse as figure than an upside-down sea horse (inversion controls for all other cues to figure/ground segregation), even though she could not recognize the sea horse. The occipital patient showed no effect of experientially derived shape representations in figure/ground decisions, but when he saw the meaningful shape as figure, he could recognize it as well as did normal participants in this experiment.

The Peterson work is relevant to the present discussion because it shows that representations of shape may enter into individuation processes in at least two different ways, only one of which involves recognition with respect to antecedently represented kinds. Although the Peterson work concerns figure/ground segregation, the same may be true for object segregation. As Peterson shows, the representations of shape that enter into the encapsulated early processes are fragmentary and simpler than those that support full-blown object recognition. It is possible that the experientially-based shape representations of the geometrically simple box or hose are influencing these early perceptual processes, and that the child cannot form such representations of the more complex duck or car with so little contact with these stimuli. Continuing along this line of speculation, it may be that only when infants have formed kind representations of ducks and cars does recognition of the objects as members of those categories play a role in the object segregation task posed by the stimulus array of Fig. 4, as well as the numerical identity tasks of Van de Walle et al. (in press) and Xu and Carey (1996).

Thus, in all these cases the adult vision literature on object representations contributes to a *possible* resolution of several apparent conflicts in the infant literature. We suggest that the resolution will depend upon distinguishing between mid-level object file representations, property representations, experience-based shape representations and kind representations, and the respective roles these play in distinct individuation problems (figure/ground segregation, object segregation, object files, and kind-based object individuation).

6. Lessons from the infant literature concerning adult object representations

Section 5 considered lessons gained from the adult literature on mid-level object tracking for our understanding of young infants' object representations. Here we ask how the infant literature can return the favor. What lessons about object individuation in adults might be gleaned from the infant literature?

6.1. Distinguishing object file individuation from kind-based individuation

Until now, we have merely asserted that the adult literature distinguishes kind-based individuation from mid-level object file-based individuation. Actually, the literature is not unequivocal on this matter. On some treatments there is no such thing as kind-based individuation. For example, in the standard treatment of logical form in the literature on formal semantics, "The dog is black" is formalized as "$((x)(dog(x) \& black(x)))$". That is, being a dog is a property of an existentially quantified individual picked out in some other way, just as being black is. Similarly, Kahneman et al. (1992) suggest that object files represent individual tokens of objects and that "is a truck" or "is a dog" are features of objects rather than themselves sortals that directly provide criteria of individuation and numerical identity. In support of this way of looking at things, they offer the observation that we can felicitously say, "Its a bird, its a plane, its Superman", referring all along to the same individual.

For reasons beyond the scope of this paper, we do not consider this position tenable (see Carey & Xu, 1999; Macnamara, 1986; Xu, 1997, for discussions of the relevant philosophical literature as it relates to the psychological questions). In adult conceptual life, criteria for individuation and numerical identity are sortal-specific. As mentioned earlier, kind-relevant considerations often override spatio-temporal continuity in judgments of numerical identity. A person, just dead, is not identical to her corpse, in spite of the spatiotemporal continuity of her body. Some philosophers (e.g. Hirsch, 1982) would push this point even further, arguing that not only is spatiotemporal continuity not sufficient for our judgment of identity, but that it is not even necessary. A paradigm example is the following. Suppose you have a watch whose interior needs to be cleaned. You dismantle the watch, scattering the various parts on the desk, then you reassemble the watch after cleaning. During this process, spatiotemporal continuity was lost when the parts were scattered on the desk yet our intuition is clear that when the watch has been reassembled, it is the same watch as the one you started with.

In addition, kinds provide criteria of individuation and numerical identity directly, whereas properties do not. One can count the dogs or the shoes or the fingers in this room, but not the red in this room. Thus, at least as articulated in adult language, kind representations are sharply differentiated from property representations. They are not merely features to be bound to individuals picked out by FINSTs or to individual object files.

The infant literature could bear on this controversy. If it turns out that infant cognitive architecture distinguishes between kinds and properties, and between kinds and object files, the position that these must be distinguished in adult cognitive architecture would receive support. We touched on this suggestion in our attempts to resolve the apparent discrepancies between the box/hose studies (Fig. 5) and the duck/car studies (Fig. 4), but we have not yet really marshaled the evidence for this position. Twelve-month-olds robustly succeed in experiments where individuation is signaled by kind distinctions (Van de Walle et al., in press; Xu & Carey, 1996; Xu et al., 1999). However, it does not follow that *is a duck* has a different status in the 12-month-old's conceptual system than does *is yellow*. The fact that 12-month-olds in these studies formed representations of two objects on the basis of the distinction, for example, between a telephone and a book does not mean that they were using kind representations to do so. After all, adults would assume that a black plastic object was numerically distinct from a red cardboard and paper object, even in the absence of having identified these objects as a telephone and a book.

We have recently completed a series of experiments with 12-month-olds (Xu, Carey, Quint, & Bassin, 2001) to establish whether 12-month-olds' success in our studies was based on property contrasts or kind contrasts. Using the paradigm of Xu and Carey (1996), infants were shown an event in which an object (e.g. a red ball) emerged from behind a screen and returned, followed by an object (e.g. a green ball) emerging from behind the screen from the other side and returning. On the test trials, infants were shown two objects (e.g. a red ball *and* a green ball) or just a single object (e.g. a red ball *or* a green ball) when the screen was removed. We found that even though 12-month-old infants were sensitive to the perceptual differences between the objects, these property changes (i.e. color change alone, size change alone, or the combination of the two) did not lead to successful object individuation. That is, upon seeing a red ball alternating with a green ball (or a big ball and a small ball, or a big red ball and a small green ball), the infant did not conclude that there were two distinct objects behind the screen. In the last experiment of this series, infants were shown two types of shape changes (holding color and size of objects constant) – a within-kind shape change (e.g. a sippy cup with two handles vs. a regular cup with one handle) or a cross-kind shape change (e.g. a cup and a bottle). During habituation trials, we found that the infants were equally sensitive to both types of shape change. On the test trials, however, only the infants who saw the cross-kind shape change showed evidence of successful object individuation by looking longer at the one-object, unexpected outcome than the two-object, expected outcome. These results provide preliminary evidence that kind representations (and not just property representations) underlie the success at 12 months.

Furthermore, the capacity to individuate in the absence of spatiotemporal information that emerges between 10 and 12 months of age is closely tied to linguistic competence in ways that implicate kind concepts. Xu and Carey (1996) found that 10-month-olds who knew the labels for the objects succeeded at individuating familiar objects on the basis of kind distinctions (the objects were a ball, a bottle, a book, and a cup). A new set of studies showed that labeling facilitates individuation in this paradigm. Xu (1998) tested 9-month-old infants using the Xu and Carey (1996) paradigm and gave the infants verbal labels for the objects. When the toy duck emerged from behind the screen, the experimenter said, in infant directed speech, "Look, [baby's name], a duck". When the duck returned behind the screen and the ball emerged from the other side, the experimenter said, "Look, [baby's name], a ball". On the test trials, infants were shown an expected outcome of two objects, a duck and a ball, or an unexpected outcome of just one object, a duck or a ball. Infants looked longer at the unexpected outcome of a single object. In a control condition, infants heard "a toy" for both the duck and the ball, and their looking time pattern on the test trials was not different from their baseline preference. In a second study, two tones were used instead of two labels and infants again failed to look longer at the one-object outcome. Our interpretation of this finding is that contrasting labels provide signals to the infant that two kinds of objects are present, and that there must therefore be two numerically distinct objects behind the screen. The negative finding with tones suggests that perhaps language in the form of labeling plays a specific role in signaling object kinds for the infants. It is unclear whether labels are necessary for the formation of kind representations (cf. the experiments of Mandler and her colleagues cited below; we are agnostic as to the format of representation of symbols for kinds). We take these results as part of a general pattern of findings that infants expect labels to refer to kinds, and that kind membership has consequences for both individuation and categorization (e.g. Balaban & Waxman, 1997; Waxman, 1999).

Kind concepts differ from property concepts in ways other than that kinds provide criteria for individuation and numerical identity. Other infant studies confirm that kind representations are differentiated from property representations by the end of the first year of life (see Mandler, 2000; Xu & Carey, 2000, for reviews), and that labeling facilitates kind representations (Balaban & Waxman, 1997; Waxman & Markow, 1995). Furthermore, Waxman (1999) showed that by 13 months, infants distinguish linguistically between kind representations and property representations. Upon hearing a series of objects described by a count noun ("Look, its a blicket") they extract kind similarity (at both the basic and superordinate levels) but not property similarity (texture and color), whereas upon hearing an adjective ("Look, its a blickish one") they extract property similarity as well.

In sum, these studies support the claims that kind representations are architecturally distinct from property representations, as they play distinct roles in individuation, categorization, and language. These studies also lend support to the architectural distinction between object file-based individuation and kind-based individuation, for this latter system emerges markedly later in development.

6.2. Lessons concerning the mid-level object file/object tracking system itself

Suppose it is true that kind-based individuation is architecturally distinct from the mid-level object tracking system, that the mid-level system underlies object individuation and tracking early in early infancy and that the kind-based system is not developed until the end of the first year of life. If so, studies of young infants provide us with a wonderful methodological tool – a chance to study the object tracking system pure, so to speak, uncontaminated by kind representations. Before the emergence of the kind-based system, the processes that create representations of individual objects create only object files. Properties of objects are represented as features bound to object files. After this developmental change, the processes that create representations of individual objects also create symbols for kind sortals, such as *duck*, and properties of these individuals may be bound directly to them, as in *yellow duck*. Once this second system of kind-based object individuation has become available, it creates the representations that articulate thought. That is, it preempts object file representations in our experiences of the world. This is why, in the absence of direct spatiotemporal evidence to the contrary, we infer that the duck and the cat moved in Fig. 1, and why we consider that a person ceases to exist when he or she dies, in spite of the spatiotemporal continuity of bodies. Thus, for adults, we need to set up situations that prevent the operation of the second system (high attentional load, as in MOT or search studies, or very brief exposures, as in apparent-motion studies or feature conjunction studies) or situations that separate perception from judgment in order to study the operation of the mid-level object file and object tracking systems.

If we accept the arguments of the paper so far, then the study of object representations in very young infants can provide invaluable evidence concerning the nature of the mid-level systems, for very young infants do not yet have available the kind-based systems which preempt the output of the mid-level vision in adult conceptual representations. In the remaining sections of this paper, we sketch what might be learned about the object file and object tracking system from studies of the object representations of very young infants.

6.3. Short-term memory and object file representations

In MOT experiments and in studies of object-based attention in which the objects undergo real or apparent motion (Kahneman et al., 1992), subjects are in nearly continuous visual contact with the objects. Occlusion, if present at all, is momentary. FINSTs are indices that depend upon spatiotemporal information in order to remain assigned to individuals. It is unclear from these studies, then, whether object files are stable object representations that may be placed into longer lasting short-term memory stores, perhaps even losing their current spatiotemporal indices. The object permanence and number studies of young infants suggest that they can.

Many of the infant studies cited above involve occlusion, sometimes for as long as 10 s or more. In Wynn's 1 + 1 (or 2 − 1) studies, for instance, the first object (or pair) remains hidden for several seconds, and a memory representation of that object (or pair) must be updated, in memory, as the result of the addition (or subtraction). Then when the outcome array is revealed object file representations are again computed, and the resultant models (the short-term memory object file representation, and the current outcome object file representation) are compared.[8] Koechlin et al. (1998) showed that 5-month-old infants succeed in 1 + 1 = 2 or 1 and 2 − 1 = 2 or 1 addition/subtraction studies even when the objects behind the screen are placed on a rotating plate. Under these conditions, the infant cannot maintain an index on a hidden object; that is, when the outcome is revealed, the infant has no way of knowing which object on the plate is the same object as the first one placed behind the screen and which one is the same object as the second one. This finding supports the assumption by Simon (1997) and Uller et al. (1999) that *two* object file models, one of the set-up event and one of the outcome array, are being compared.

Feigenson, Carey, and Hauser (2001) have new findings that lend support to the hypothesis that the infant can create and store more than one memory model of sets of objects, and compare them numerically in memory. Furthermore, these studies show that the total number of objects represented in two separate short-term memory stores can exceed the limits of object indexing, showing that short-term memory stores may include object files that are not currently indexed. Ten-month-old infants were shown a given number of graham crackers placed into one box, and a different number placed into another box. The infants could not see the crackers in the box. The infants watched the crackers being placed into the two boxes, and then they were allowed to crawl to one or the other. At issue was whether they would go to the box with the larger number of crackers. This is what they did, when the choice was 1 vs. 2 or 2 vs. 3. Performance fell apart at 3 vs. 4 and at 3 vs. 6. This latter finding is important, for it rules out that analog magnitude number representations (see Dehaene, 1997; Gallistel, 1990, for characterizations of and evidence for analog magnitude number representations of number) could be underlying performance on this task. Success when analog magnitude number representations are activated is a function of the ratio between the set sizes; 3 vs. 6 is the same Weber fraction as 1 vs. 2 and is more discriminable than 2 vs. 3. Success within the range of parallel individuation and failure outside it, controlling for ratio, is the set size signature of object file representations of these individuals. This is the earliest demonstration of an ordinal quantitative judgment in infants, but it is the success at 2 vs. 3 that is of theoretical importance in the present context. Sets of 2 or 3 objects are each within the infants' limits of object indexing, but sets of 5 are not. Thus, infants cannot be indexing a single set of objects in this experiment. Rather, they must be establishing two short-term memory models, one consisting of 2 object files and one consisting of 3 object

---

[8] In the Simon (1997) and Uller et al. (1999) accounts of these experiments it was assumed that the comparisons were based on 1 − 1 correspondence among object files in the two models. Subsequent experiments (Clearfield & Mix, 1999; Feigenson et al., 2001, in press) make it clear that object file models are often compared on the basis of total surface area or volume, or on the basis of properties of the individual objects, and that these properties of object file representations are more salient than is the number of object files in a model. These facts do not undermine the conclusion that object file representations are underlying the infants' behavior in these studies, but they do undermine the conclusion that these experiments reflect numerical computations over object file representations.

files, and then comparing them in memory.[9] Thus, object file representations do not merely underlie momentary tracking of objects. Rather, object files are symbols that articulate relatively long lasting short-term memory models, which, in turn, support other computations; in this case, comparisons with respect to more or less.

6.4. Mid-level object representations: preconceptual? Or, what kinds of things are FINGs?

Pylyshyn (2001) suggests that the individuals that are indexed in the mid-level object tracking experiments are non-conceptual. Of course, the individuals that are indexed are in the world (hence neither preconceptual or conceptual). At issue is whether the symbols for these individuals, the object files themselves, are preconceptual or conceptual symbols. Recall that Pylyshyn (2001) agrees that the assignment of a FINST is the initial phase of creating an object file, and thus that FINGs (the individuals FINSTs point to) are the same individuals as those represented by object files.

We have discussed at length one sense in which object files are preconceptual symbols; they do not represent object kinds such as *dog* or *cup*. In addition, Pylyshyn (2001) is mainly concerned with the issue of whether the processes that use features or spatiotemporal information to assign indexes are themselves conceptual processes. He argues that individuals are picked out by perceptual processes, perhaps in a bottom-up manner; individuals are *not* determined by a process that examines explicitly represented definitional or probabilistic features, even spatiotemporal ones.

Although we believe that Pylyshyn is right about this, the question still remains concerning object files as symbols themselves. Notice that the fact that perceptual processes (figure/ground segregation, surface representation, object tracking on the basis of spatiotemporal information) establish object files does not make them perceptual symbols. Perceptual processes may deliver symbols that are conceptual, as seen by their conceptual role.

An analogy may clarify our argument here. Michotte (1963) specified the spatiotemporal parameters of the relation between two moving bodies sufficient for the perception of causal interaction, e.g. for the perception that contact with one moving body caused a second one to move. That there are perceptual processes that yield representations of causality does not mean that that these representations themselves are perceptual. Causal attribution transcends the spatiotemporal parameters, being contributed by the mind, and guides further inferences and actions, being in that sense informationally promiscuous. In these senses, then, representations of caus-

---

[9] See previous footnote. In the infant choice experiment, infants were maximizing the total amount of graham cracker. Given a choice between one large cracker in one container and two small crackers, summing to half the volume of the large one, infants chose the single large cracker. Still, the set size signature of object file representations obtained success at 2 vs. 3, but not at 3 vs. 6, indicating that the comparison was mediated by object file representations and not representations that could keep a running total of volume apart from the individual objects.

ality are conceptual, even though there are dedicated perceptual processors that compute them.

To explore the issue of whether object files are conceptual symbols, we must begin by considering their *content*. What do object files represent? Two types of empirical evidence bear on this question: (1) studies of the extensions of object files (What entities in the world cause object files to be established? What are FINGs (an empirical question)?) and (2) studies of the conceptual role of object files (What computations do object file symbols participate in?). We shall argue that the content object files is *physical objects*, by which we mean what is sometimes called "Spelke-objects", namely, bounded, coherent, 3D, separable and moveable wholes. And we will argue that object file representations are conceptual in the sense that they articulate physical reasoning, enter into number-relevant computations, and support intentional action. Sections 6.5–6.7 review the evidence in support of these claims.

6.5. The extension of object files

The claim that object files represent real 3D objects may seem hardly surprising, but in fact, there are reasons to doubt it. The arrays are *actually* 2D objects in virtually all of the adult studies on mid-level vision, as well as in some of the infant studies (e.g. those of Johnson, 2000, and his colleagues on amodal completion behind barriers and those of Johnson and Gilmore, 1998, on object-based attention). But because we can present many of the cues for depth in 2D arrays, surfaces arrayed in 3D are routinely perceived in such displays. That the system can be fooled (similarly for Michotte causality) does not mean that it is not representing the stimuli as Spelke-objects. What reasons do we have for thinking that this may be the case?

We have already presented one line of evidence that object files represent Spelke-objects. The processes that establish and maintain object file representations are sensitive to the distinction between the spatiotemporal information that specifies occlusion, on the one hand, and that that specifies the cessation of existence, on the other. Occlusion and existence cessation are properties of real physical objects. Furthermore, studies of infants shown pictures suggest that infants sometimes misperceive 2D representations as if they were real 3D objects. Many studies have shown that infants attempt to grasp pictured objects well into the second year of life (see DeLoache, Pierroutsakos, Uttal, Rosengren, & Gottlieb, 1998).

Two series of studies with 8-month-old infants underline the point that the individuals being tracked in the infant studies are physical objects, and not just any perceptual objects specified by figure/ground processes. A hallmark of physical objects is that they maintain their boundaries through time. Neither a pile of sand nor a pile of blocks is a Spelke-object, in spite of the fact that when stationary it may be perceptually indistinguishable from one. One may make a pile-shaped cone and coat it with sand, or one may put together a set of small objects, yielding a single pile-shaped entity. It is only upon viewing such entities in motion (do they fall apart, or do they maintain their boundaries?) that unequivocal evidence for their ontological status is obtained. Infants track Spelke-objects that are perceptually identical to piles of sand (Huntley-Fenner, Carey, & Salimando, 2001) or piles of little blocks (Chiang & Wynn, in press) under conditions where they will not track the perceptually identical non-objects.

Take Huntley-Fenner et al. (2001) for example. They carried out $1 + 1 = 2$ or 1 studies involving sand poured behind or sand objects being lowered behind the barriers. When the sand was resting on the stage, it formed a pile, and the sand objects, when resting on the stage, were perceptually indistinguishable, being pile-shaped objects coated in sand. It was only upon seeing the entity being poured (sand) or lowered (object) onto the stage that infants could identify the resulting pile-shaped entity as sand or as an object. Stimulus type was a between-participant variable, and infants were familiarized with the stimuli before the study by handling the sand or the sand object. One study involved a single screen; another involved two screens. Eight-month-old infants succeeded in the sand object conditions, but failed in the sand conditions. The failure in the two-screen study is especially striking, for it shows that infants do not have "sand permanence". In this study, the infant watched as a pile of sand was poured onto the stage floor, and then hidden behind a screen. A second, spatially separate, screen was introduced and a second pile of sand was poured behind it. The screens were then removed, revealing either two piles of sand (one behind each screen) or only one (the original pile seen on the stage floor initially). Eight-month-olds did not differentiate the two outcomes, although they succeeded if the stimuli were sand-pile-shaped Spelke-objects lowered as a whole onto the stage floor. As mentioned above, object permanence requires an individual whose identity is being tracked; it is the *same individual* we represent behind the screen. Apparently, 8-month-old infants cannot establish representations of individual portions of sand and trace them through time.

These infant studies suggest that the object tracking system is just that: an *object* tracking system, where *object* means 3D, bounded, coherent physical object. It fails to track perceptually specified figures that have a history of non-cohesion. That the system can be fooled, can *misrepresent* 2D stimuli as objects, does not militate against this conclusion.

One final line of work on infant object representations bolsters this conclusion. Identical spatiotemporal principles (e.g. independent motion) specify tactile and visual objects, and infants map representations across the two modalities. Streri and Spelke (1988) allowed young infants to handle rings (one in each hand) that they could not see. When the rings moved independently of each other, infants preferred to look at a display containing two spatially separate objects. In contrast, when handling rings connected by a rigid rod (again, one in each hand), such that they did not move independently of each other, they preferred to look at a display containing a single object. (In cross-modal experiments of this sort, infants typically prefer to look at the visual stimulus that matches the tactually represented stimulus, presumably because they seek a consistent representation of their world.)

In sum, infant object representations appear to have 3D, bounded, coherent, separately moving objects in their extensions. On the assumption that infant object representations are object files, we conclude that "object files" are well named: they represent real physical objects.

6.6. Conceptual role: object file representations are the input into volitional action

Section 6.5 concerns what real world individuals are represented by object files. This is one part of the project of specifying the content of a symbol; the other part is specifying its conceptual role. Files representing currently visible attended objects, as well as those stored in short-term memory, guide actions directed towards the physical world. By 8 months, infants solve Stage 4 object permanence tasks (retrieving objects hidden under cloths, behind barriers). Similarly, at 10 months, before kind representations support individuation, object file representations support manual search in the Van de Walle et al. (in press) object retrieval tasks and in the Feigenson et al. (2001) number comparison experiments cited above. Insofar as being available to guide volitional action (informational promiscuity) is evidence that a representation is conceptual, these studies suggest that object files are.

6.7. Conceptual role: object representations articulate physical knowledge

The actions in the Feigenson et al. studies were based on the output of computations that established which container contained more crackers. That object file representations enter into comparative quantity computations suggests that they have conceptual roles that far transcend merely representing objects that the infant may reach for. Indeed, it is in the exploration of the conceptual role of object representations that the infant studies most dramatically transcend the literature on mid-level vision, for these studies have not been concerned with the inferences that are drawn about objects. If the identification of the infant's object representations with object files is correct, then these studies show that object file representations articulate considerable physical knowledge. Some of this physical knowledge may be innate, instantiated in the computations that establish representations of object files in the first place. But other aspects are learned – object files are representations of objects about which infants can learn, and in this learning they learn about objects as a class, not just about individual object tokens.

6.7.1. Innate physical knowledge about objects

By 2 months of age, infant object file representations are quite adult-like. For example, Johnson, 2000 reviews the literature on surface perception in infancy. By 2 months of age, infants are sensitive to almost all the same information adults are in building representations of the amodally complete surfaces behind barriers, although young infants need more redundant cues than do older children or adults. Astoundingly, 2-month-olds are also able to represent physical relations such as inside and behind, and their representations are constrained by knowledge of solidity, a property of Spelke-objects but not of 2D visual objects. Spelke et al. (1992) habituated 2-month-olds to a ball rolling behind a screen, the screen then being removed and the ball shown resting against the back wall. They then inserted a barrier behind the screen, perpendicular to it with its top visible, and rolled the ball behind again. Upon removal of the screen, infants looked longer if the ball ended up against the back wall, having apparently passed through the solid barrier, than if the ball was revealed resting against the barrier. Convergent evidence is provided by Hespos and Baillargeon (in press), who showed that 2-month-olds expect objects inside other objects to move with them, in contrast to objects behind other objects, and also that they expect objects can be inserted into open containers but not into closed containers (the latter being a violation of solidity).

Besides expecting objects to be solid, and thus not to pass through other ones, by 6 months infants also expect objects to be subject to the laws of contact causality (Leslie & Keeble, 1986). Young infants look longer if an object goes into motion without having been contacted by another moving object than if it has (Spelke, Philips, & Woodward, 1995) and they look longer if a small object hitting another makes it move farther than if a larger object going the same speed does (Baillargeon, 1995).

Thus, the conceptual role of the infant's object representations is that of 3D Spelke-objects; objects are represented as solid entities in spatial relations with each other that cannot pass through other objects, and which move only upon contact. If we accept the identification of the infant's object concept with object files, then we must accept that object file representations also have the same conceptual role.

6.7.2. Learning generalizations about objects

Still under debate is what aspects of the conceptual role of object representations described above are innate and what are learned. There is no doubt, however, that infants learn many generalizations about objects during their early months. Thus, the processes that yield object representations yield representations about which the infant learns. To take just one example – infants do not innately know that unsupported objects fall (Baillargeon, 1995). That is, if they watch an object slowly pushed off a platform until it is completely unconnected to it, apparently suspended in mid-air, 3-month-olds show no differential interest relative to whether it is adequately supported from below. Just a few weeks later, though, this event draws long looking, relative to events in which the object is supported. In a series of beautiful experiments, Baillargeon has shown that infants' learning about support unfolds in a regular way. First they are not surprised that the object does not fall so long as there is any contact with the support, then the contact must be from below, then more than half of the base of the object must be supported from below, and finally they take into account the geometry of the object. Furthermore, the initial stages of this learning occur, in the ordinary course of events, from infants' own attempts to place objects on surfaces, but it can also be driven from observational evidence alone.

One important conclusion from these studies is that they reveal generalizations that infants make about *objects*; experience placing stuffed animals on tables enables infants to predict whether any unsupported Spelke-object will fall. Systematic study of generalization from observational evidence would be of great interest in constraining our models of the learning process. At the very least, infants have not had previous experience with the specific objects in the Baillargeon support studies. That is, physical reasoning about Spelke-objects embodies knowledge formulated over the category *object*, whatever the format of this knowledge.

6.8. Interim conclusions: what are object files symbols of?

Two lines of evidence support the conclusion that infants' object representations have Spelke-objects as their content. First, the extensions of the symbols seem to be real 3D, bounded, coherent objects. Infants do not track individuals that cannot be construed as Spelke-objects, like piles of sand or piles of blocks, or entities that shrink to nothing or explode. Infants sometimes attempt to pick up pictured objects, providing evidence that they sometimes misconstrue 2D representations of objects as Spelke-objects. And infants have cross-modal representations of individuated 3D objects; not only do the same principles specify object number, but infants map the object representations built on tactile spatiotemporal evidence to visual representations of objects. Second, studies of the conceptual role of object representations show that they support action, quantitative comparisons, and articulate physical reasoning. If we accept the identification of infants' object representations with object files, then we must correspondingly enrich our conception of the latter.

7. A summary overview

This paper is speculative. We do not know for sure that young infants' object representations are identical to those computed by the mid-level object-based attention system. As one reviewer pointed out, it may be that the two are quite distinct representational systems, and their similarities reflect the fact that both are designed to solve similar problems – picking out individuals and tracking them through time. Of course this is possible, but we doubt it, for the similarities we draw upon in making the identification are non-veridical. Objects do not change color and texture over the short time course in which both systems allow object representations to be updated, and there is no particular reason for the limitations on the set size of objects that may be individuated in parallel to be so similar if the systems are distinct. But these are early days in exploring the relations between the two literatures, and no doubt in many details our speculations will turn out to be wrong.

We have argued here that the discovery, if true, that young infants' object representations are the same natural kind as the object files of mid-level vision has important consequences for both literatures. Merging the two literatures brings new data to bear on very general theoretical disputes within each literature, such as the content of object representations, the relative roles of spatiotemporal, featural and kind information in object individuation and tracking, and the senses in which object representations are preconceptual and the senses in which they are conceptual.

Acknowledgements

The research reported here was supported by NSF grants (SBR-9712103 and SBR-951465) to S.C., and NIH B/START grant (R03MH59040-01) and NSF grant (SBR-9910729) to F.X. We thank Zenon Pylyshyn, Brian Scholl, Cristina

Sorrentino, Joshua Tenenbaum, Gretchen Van de Walle, and two anonymous reviewers for helpful discussion and very helpful comments on an earlier draft.

References

Aguilar, A., & Baillargeon, R. (1999). 2.5-month-old infants' reasoning about when objects should and should not be occluded. *Cognitive Psychology, 39*, 116–157.

Baillargeon, R. (1991). Reasoning about the height and location of a hidden object in 4.5- and 6.5-month-old infants. *Cognition, 38*, 13–42.

Baillargeon, R. (1995). A model of physical reasoning in infancy. In C. Rovee-Collier & L. Lipsitt (Eds.), *Advances in infancy research* (Vol. 9, pp. 305–371). Norwood, NJ: Ablex.

Baillargeon, R., & DeVos, J. (1991). Object permanence in young infants: further evidence. *Child Development, 62*, 1227–1246.

Baillargeon, R., Miller, K., & Constantino, J. (1993). *Ten-month-old infants' intuitions about addition*. Unpublished manuscript, University of Illinois at Urbana, Champaign, IL.

Balaban, M. T., & Waxman, S. R. (1997). Do words facilitate object categorization in 9-month-old infants? *Journal of Experimental Child Psychology, 64*, 3–26.

Bower, T. G. R. (1974). *Development of infancy*. San Francisco, CA: W.H. Freeman.

Burke, L. (1952). On the tunnel effect. *Quarterly Journal of Experimental Psychology, 4*, 121–138.

Carey, S., & Bassin, S. (1998). *When adults fail to see the trick. Adult judgments of events in an infant violation of expectancy looking time study*. Poster presented at the 11th biennial meeting of the International Society for Infant Studies, Atlanta, GA.

Carey, S., & Xu, F. (1999). Sortals and kinds: an appreciation of John Macnamara. In R. Jackendoff, P. Bloom, & K. Wynn (Eds.), *Language, logic, and concepts: essays in honor of John Macnamara*. Cambridge, MA: MIT Press.

Chiang, W. C., & Wynn, K. (in press). Infants representations and teaching of objects: implications from collections. *Cognition*.

Clearfield, M. W., & Mix, K. S. (1999). Number versus contour length in infants' discrimination of small visual sets. *Psychological Science, 10* (5), 408–411.

Dehaene, S. (1997). *The number sense: how the mind creates mathematics*. Oxford: Oxford University Press.

DeLoache, J. S., Pierroutsakos, S. L., Uttal, D. H., Rosengren, K. S., & Gottlieb, A. (1998). Grasping the nature of pictures. *Psychological Science, 9* (3), 205–210.

Feigenson, L., Carey, S., & Hauser, M. (2001). Infants' spontaneous ordinal choices, submitted for publication.

Feigenson, L., Carey, S., & Spelke, E. S. (in press). Infants' discrimination of number vs. continuous extent. *Cognitive Psychology*.

Gallistel, C. R. (1990). *The organization of learning*. Cambridge, MA: MIT Press.

Gupta, A. (1980). *The logic of common nouns*. New Haven, CT: Yale University Press.

Hespos, S., & Baillargeon, R. (in press). Knowledge about containment events in very young infants. *Cognition*.

Hirsch, E. (1982). *The concept of identity*. New York: Oxford University Press.

Huntley-Fenner, G., Carey, S., & Salimando, A. (2001). Objects are individuals but stuff doesn't count: perceived rigidity and cohesiveness influence infants' representation of small numbers of discrete entities, submitted for publication.

Johnson, M. H., & Gilmore, R. O. (1998). Object-centered attention in 8-month-old infants. *Developmental Science, 1* (2), 221–225.

Johnson, S. (2000). The development of visual surface perception: insights into the ontogeny of knowledge. In C. Rovee-Collier, L. Lipsitt, & H. Hayne (Eds.), *Progress in infancy research* (Vol. 1, pp. 113–154). Mahwah, NJ: Erlbaum.

Kahneman, D., Treisman, A., & Gibbs, B. (1992). The reviewing of object files: object specific integration of information. *Cognitive Psychology, 24*, 175–219.

Koechlin, E., Dehaene, S., & Mehler, J. (1998). Numerical transformations in five-month-old infants. *Mathematical Cognition, 3*, 89–104.

Leslie, A. M., & Keeble, S. (1986). Do six-month-old infants perceive causality? *Cognition, 25*, 265–288.

Leslie, A., Xu, F., Tremoulet, P., & Scholl, B. (1998). Indexing and the object concept: developing "what" and "where" systems. *Trends in Cognitive Sciences, 2* (1), 10–18.

Macnamara, J. (1986). *A border dispute: the place of logic in psychology.* Cambridge, MA: MIT Press.

Mandler, J. M. (2000). Perceptual and conceptual processes in infancy. *Journal of Cognition and Development, 1*, 3–36.

Marr, D. (1982). *Vision.* New York: Freedman.

Michotte, A. (1963). *The perception of causality.* New York: Basic Books.

Michotte, A., & Burke, L. (1951). *Une novelle enigme de la psychologie de la perception: le "donee amodal" dans l'experience sensorielle.* Aces du 13 eme Congrages Internationale de Psychologie, Stockholm, pp. 179–180.

Nakayama, K., He, Z. J., & Shimojo, S. (1995). Visual surface representation: a critical link between lower-level and higher-level vision. In S. M. Kosslyn, & D. N. Osherson (Eds.), *Visual cognition* (2nd ed., pp. 1–70). Cambridge, MA: MIT Press.

Needham, A. (1998). Infants' use of featural information in the segregation of stationary objects. *Infant Behavior and Development, 21* (1), 47–76.

Needham, A., & Baillargeon, R. (1997). Object segregation in 8-month-old infants. *Cognition, 62*, 121–149.

Needham, A., & Baillargeon, R. (1998). Effects of prior experience on 4.5-month-old infants' object segregation. *Infant Behavior and Development, 21* (1), 1–24.

Needham, A., & Baillargeon, R. (2000). Infants' use of featural and experiential information in segregating and individuating objects: a reply to Xu, Carey, & Welch (1999). *Cognition, 74*, 255–284.

Needham, A., Baillargeon, R., & Kauffman, L. (1997). Object segregation in infancy. In C. Rovee-Collier, & L. Lipsitt (Eds.), *Advances in infancy research* (Vol. 11, pp. 1–39). Greenwich, CT: Ablex.

Peterson, M. A. (1994). Object recognition processes can and do operate before figure-ground organization. *Current Directions in Psychological Science, 3* (4), 105–111.

Peterson, M. A., de Gelder, B., Rapcsak, S. Z., Gerhardstein, P., & Bachoud-Levis, A. (in press). A double dissociation between conscious and unconscious object recognition processes revealed by figure-ground segregation. *Vision Research.*

Peterson, M. A., & Gibson, B. (1993). Shape recognition inputs to figure-ground organization in three-dimensional displays. *Cognitive Psychology, 25*, 383–429.

Piaget, J. (1954). *The construction of reality in the child.* New York: Basic Books.

Pylyshyn, Z. W. (2001). Visual indexes, preconceptual objects and situated vision. *Cognition*, this issue, *80*, 127–158.

Quine, W. V. O. (1960). *Word and object.* Cambridge, MA: MIT Press.

Scholl, B. J. (2001). Objects and attention: the state of the art. *Cognition*, this issue, *80*, 1–46.

Scholl, B. J., & Leslie, A. M. (1999). Explaining the infant's object concept: beyond the perception/cognition dichotomy. In E. Lepore, & Z. Pylyshyn (Eds.), *What is cognitive science?* (pp. 26–73). Oxford: Blackwell.

Scholl, B. J., & Pylyshyn, Z. W. (1999). Tracking multiple items through occlusion: clues to visual objecthood. *Cognitive Psychology, 38*, 259–290.

Scholl, B. J., Pylyshyn, Z. W., & Feldman, J. (2001). What is a visual object? Evidence from target merging in multi-element tracking. *Cognition*, this issue, *80*, 159–177.

Scholl, B. J., Pylyshyn, Z. W., & Franconeri, S. L. (2001). The relationship between property-encoding and object-based attention: evidence from multiple-object tracking, submitted for publication.

Simon, T. J. (1997). Reconceptualizing the origins of number knowledge: a "non-numerical" account. *Cognitive Development, 12*, 349–372.

Simon, T., Hespos, S., & Rochat, P. (1995). Do infants understand simple arithmetic? A replication of Wynn (1992). *Cognitive Development, 10*, 253–269.

Slater, A., Johnson, S. P., Brown, E., & Badenoch, M. (1996). Newborn infants' perception of partly occluded objects. *Infant Behavior and Development, 19*, 145–148.

Spelke, E. S. (1996). Initial knowledge: six suggestions. *Cognition, 50*, 431–445.

Spelke, E. S., Brelinger, K., Macomber, J., & Jacobson, K. (1992). Origins of knowledge. *Psychological Review*, *99*, 605–632.

Spelke, E. S., Kestenbaum, R., Simons, D. J., & Wein, D. (1995). Spatio-temporal continuity, smoothness of motion and object identity in infancy. *British Journal of Developmental Psychology*, *13*, 113–142.

Spelke, E. S., Phillips, A., & Woodward, A. L. (1995). Infants' knowledge of object motion and human action. In D. Sperber, D. Premack, & A. J. Premack (Eds.), *Causal cognition: a multidisciplinary debate*. Oxford: Clarendon Press.

Starkey, P., & Cooper, R. (1980). Perception of numbers by human infants. *Science*, *210* (28), 1033–1034.

Streri, A., & Spelke, E. S. (1988). Haptic perception of objects in infancy. *Cognitive Psychology*, *20*, 1–23.

Trick, L., & Pylyshyn, Z. (1994). Why are small and large numbers enumerated differently? A limited capacity preattentive stage in vision. *Psychological Review*, *101*, 80–102.

Uller, C., Huntley-Fenner, G., Carey, S., & Klatt, L. (1999). What representations might underlie infant numerical knowledge? *Cognitive Development*, *14*, 1–36.

Uller, C., & Leslie, A. (1999, April). *Assessing the infant counting limit*. Poster presented at the biennial meeting of the Society for Research on Child Development, Albuquerque, NM.

Van de Walle, G., Carey, S., & Prevor, M. (in press). The use of kind distinctions for object individuation: evidence from reaching. *Journal of Cognition and Development*.

Waxman, S. R. (1999). Specifying the scope of 13-month-olds' expectations for novel words. *Cognition*, *70*, B35–B50.

Waxman, S. R., & Markow, D. R. (1995). Words as invitations to form categories: evidence from 12- to 13-month-old infants. *Cognitive Psychology*, *29*, 257–302.

Wiggins, D. (1980). *Sameness and substance*. Oxford: Basil Blackwell.

Wilcox, T. (1999). Object individuation: infants' use of shape, size, pattern, and color. *Cognition*, *72*, 125–166.

Wilcox, T., & Baillargeon, R. (1998a). Object individuation in infancy: the use of featural information in reasoning about occlusion events. *Cognitive Psychology*, *37*, 97–155.

Wilcox, T., & Baillargeon, R. (1998b). Object individuation in young infants: further evidence with an event-monitoring paradigm. *Developmental Science*, *1*, 127–142.

Wynn, K. (1992). Addition and subtraction by human infants. *Nature*, *358*, 749–750.

Xu, F. (1997). From Lot's wife to a pillar of salt: evidence that physical object is a sortal concept. *Mind and Language*, *12*, 365–392.

Xu, F. (1998). Distinct labels provide pointers to distinct sortals in 9-month-old infants. In E. Hughes, M. Hughes, & A. Greenhill (Eds.), *Proceedings of the 22nd Annual Boston University Conference on Language Development* (pp. 791–796). Somerville, MA: Cascadilla Press.

Xu, F. (1999). Object individuation and object identity in infancy: the role of spatiotemporal information, object property information, and language. *Acta Psychologica*, *102*, 113–136.

Xu, F. (2000). *Numerical competence in infancy: two systems of representations*. Paper presented at the 12th International Conference on Infant Studies, Brighton.

Xu, F., & Carey, S. (1996). Infants' metaphysics: the case of numerical identity. *Cognitive Psychology*, *30*, 111–153.

Xu, F., & Carey, S. (2000). The emergence of kind concepts: a rejoinder to Needham & Baillargeon. *Cognition*, *74*, 285–301.

Xu, F., Carey, S., Quint, N., & Bassin, S. (2001). Kind-based object individuation in infancy. Manuscript in preparation.

Xu, F., Carey, S., & Welch, J. (1999). Infants' ability to use object kind information for object individuation. *Cognition*, *70*, 137–166.

Xu, F., & Spelke, E. S. (2000). Large number discrimination in 6-month-old infants. *Cognition*, *74*, B1–B11.

Index

Agnosia, 12-13
Alexia, 13
Amnesia, 67
Amodal completion, 73-85, 92
Attention. See also Objects
  auditory, 33-36 (see also Audition)
  defined, 3-5
  demonstrative thoughts and, 154-155
  event perception and, 29-30
  explananda of, 4
  FINST mechanism and, 27-28, 145-151, 154 (see also FINST mechanism)
  infants and, 36-39, 179-213
  MOT and, 9-10, 28, 141-144 (see also Multiple object tracking (MOT))
  proto-objects and, 20-21, 62, 127, 129, 144n5, 145-151, 154
  same-object advantages and, 6-9, 18-19, 30-32
  segmentation and, 20-21, 61-95
  sprites and, 29-30, 47-60
  stages of, 63-64
  surfaces and, 19-20
Attentional blink, 118-120
Audition, 2, 33-36, 123-126
  ATIA and, 115-116
  attentional blink and, 118-120
  dichotic tones and, 112
  directional discrimination and, 100-120
  distortion and, 98-99
  dual subsystems of, 112-113
  edges and, 103-111
  emergent properties and, 106-109
  fundamental frequency and, 110-111
  grouping and, 106-109
  indispensable attributes and, 106-111, 115-120
  IOR and, 116-118
  objects vs. events, 97-99
  pitch, 108-109
  plensensory functions and, 103-106
  spatiotemporal mapping and, 113-115
  streams of, 33-36
  visual location and, 100-102, 113-122

Balint syndrome, 12-13, 131
Baylis, Gordon, 92
Beck, Diane, 92
Blaser, Erik, 174
Bolia, R. S., 122
Bregman, A., 122

Capacity limitation, 4
Carey, Susan, 3, 36-39, 174, 179-213
Cartesian skepticism, 151
Causality, 29, 180
Cavanagh, Patrick, 3, 29-30, 47-60, 174
Change blindness, 5, 70-72
Cognition. See Attention
Color, 24
  auditory streams and, 34
  change blindness and, 72
  coincidence and, 109
  grouping and, 75
  infants and, 200-201
  Metelli rule and, 80
  object file systems and, 38
  preconceptual selection and, 139-141
  property detection and, 132
  segregation and, 194-197
  transparent, 80-83
  tunnel effect and, 186-187, 192-193
Contour integration, 86
Contrast thresholds, 88
Critique of Pure Reason (Kant), 114

Davis, Greg, 61-95
Deictic strategies, 130-131, 150
Demonstrative thoughts, 154-155
Dichotic tones, 112
Distortion, 98-99
Dorsal cochlear nucleus, 101
Dorsal stream, 112-113
Driver, Jon, 3, 21, 39, 61-95, 174
Drones, 103n3
Dumbbells, 11-12
  MOT experimentation and, 165-167, 169
Dynamic events. See Motion

Ears. *See* Audition
Edges
 audition and, 103-106, 110-111
 indispensable attributes and, 110-111
Ellis, A. J., 114
Emergent properties, 106-109

Features, 21
 encoding and, 22-23
 infants and, 192-193
 kind information and, 197-198
 MOT and, 23-24
 priority and, 23-24
 segregation and, 194-197
 tunnel effect and, 192-193
Feldman, Jacob, 39, 159-177
FINST (FINgers of INSTantiation)
mechanism, 27-29, 127, 154
 individuation and, 130-131, 181
 infants and, 200, 203, 205-206
 multiple object tracking and, 27-29, 145-151
 property dependence and, 148-149
 visual indexing and, 27-29, 130, 145-151
Flankers, 85-89
Flicker paradigm, 71
Fodor, Jerry, 39, 155
Franconeri, Steve, 174
Freeman, Elliot, 61-95
Frontal cortex, 161-162
Fundamental frequency, 110-111
Fusiform face area (FFA), 22-23
Fusion, 82

Gabor patches, 85, 92
 lateral interactions paradigm and, 86-89
Gerhardstein, Peter, 174
Gestalt psychology, 16, 160
 audition and, 102
 change blindness and, 72
 FINST mechanism and, 145
 inattentional blindness and, 66-70
 modal/amodal completion and, 85
 phenomenology and, 75
 segmentation and, 62-70
Grouped-array theory, 15
Grouping, 16-17, 160
 audition and, 102-120
 change blindness and, 70-72
 color and, 75
 connectedness and, 166-167, 173
 dumbbells and, 165-167
 edges and, 103-106, 110-111
 emergent properties and, 106-109
 Gestalt approach and, 16-17, 62-70, 160
 inattentional blindness and, 66-70
 indispensable attributes and, 106-111, 115-120
 introspection and, 66
 phenomenology and, 75, 160
 plensensory functions and, 103-106
 preattentive stage and, 65
 reference frames and, 15-16
 segmentation and, 61-62

Handel, S., 122
Helmholtz, Hermann, 114
Hemispheric lesions, 112-113
Henderson, Damien, 174
Heteromodal cortex, 101
Howlett, Henry, 92
Humphreys, Glyn, 174

Inattentional blindness
 change blindness and, 70-72
 Gestalt psychology and, 66-70
Infants
 audition and, 100
 conceptual role and, 208
 kind information and, 36-39, 198-202
 mid-level object file system and, 186-191, 202-203, 205-206
 multiple-object tracking (MOT) and, 36-39, 187, 189-190
 occlusion and, 36-39, 190-191, 193n5
 perceptual/conceptual representation and, 36-39, 191-192
 shape representations and, 198-200
 short-term memory and, 203-205
 size limitations and, 189-190
 tunnel effect and, 186-187, 192-193
Inhibition of return (IOR), 13, 116-118
Inter-aural time disparity (ITD), 112, 116
Inter-click interval (ICI), 112
Intriligator, James, 174

James, William, 17

Kanizsa subjective figures, 73-74
Kant, Immanuel, 114
Kind information
 experience and, 198-200
 features and, 197-198
 individuation and, 200-202

object files and, 37-38, 200-210
Krumhansl, C. L., 122
Kubovy, Michael, 97-126

Labianca, Angela T., 47-60
Language, 39, 127, 180
Leslie, Alan, 39, 174
Location, 14
    audition and, 100-120
    indispensable attributes and, 106-111, 115-120
    individuation and, 133-135
    multiple object tracking and, 143n3
    orthogonal orientation and, 86
    pitch and, 108-109
    property detection and, 132-133
    reference frames and, 15-16, 27-29, 131-135
    token studies and, 133-135
    visual indexing and, 153-154
Luminance, 79-83. See also Color

Marr, David, 30-31
Mehler, J., 122
Metelli rule, 79-83, 85, 89
Misperception, 128n1
Modal completion, 92
    attentional effects of, 83-85
    Metelli rule and, 79-83, 85, 89
    phenomenology and, 73, 75-76
    specific segmentation and, 73
    visual studies of, 76-79
Motion
    dumbbell technique and, 11-12, 165-167, 169
    features and, 22-23
    FINST mechanism and, 145-151
    indexing and, 27-29 (see also Visual indexing)
    infants and, 191-200, 197n6, 207
    object-file theory and, 25-27
    occlusion and, 24-25
    orbital, 49-54
    property detection and, 132-133
    representation maintenance and, 24-29
    sprites and, 29-30, 47-60
    trajectory and, 59, 163, 169-170, 194
    tumbling, 49-54, 58
    walking, 55-58
Multiple object tracking (MOT), 9-10, 10n4, 10n5, 159-161
    auditory streams and, 34-35

dumbbells and, 165-167
effort and, 28n11, 162n2
features and, 23-24
FINST mechanism and, 27-29, 145-151
indexing and, 27-29
infants and, 36-38, 187, 189-190, 202-205
Necker cubes and, 164-165, 169, 172-173
object definition and, 162-163
occlusion and, 25, 35, 163-165
property detection and, 23-24, 132-133
rubber bands and, 163-165
short-term memory and, 203-205
target merging and, 31-32, 168-174
visual indexing and, 27-29, 127, 141-144, 151-153
Music, 103n3, 108

Nakayama, Ken, 39, 174
Natural language, 127, 180
Necker cubes, 32
    MOT experiments and, 164-165, 169, 172-173
Neglect, 10-13, 15-17, 90, 131
Neisser, Ulric, 6
Neuhoff, J. G., 122
Newton, Isaac, 114

Object files, 25-27, 37-38, 130-131, 186-197, 200-210
Objects
    auditory, 33-36, 97-126
    Balint syndrome and, 12-13
    collections and, 153
    complex, 18-19
    context and, 13-21
    defined, 30-32, 98
    divided attention and, 6-8
    features and, 21-24
    infants and, 2, 36-39, 179-213
    location and, 14 (see also Location)
    modal/amodal completion and, 73, 76-85
    multiple-object tracking (MOT) and, 9-10, 31-32, 159-177 (see also Multiple object tracking (MOT))
    neglect and, 10-17, 90, 131
    numerical identity and, 145, 179-181
    perceptual groups and, 16-17 (see also Grouping)
    physical knowledge and, 208-209
    reference frames and, 15-16, 27-29, 131-135

reviewing paradigm and, 27
same-object advantages and, 6-9
segmentation and, 20-21, 61-95 (see also Segmentation)
segregation and, 194-197
selective looking and, 5-6
spatial selection and, 5 (see also Spatial selection)
subitizing and, 127, 135
surfaces and, 9, 19-20, 80-83, 103-111
time/motion and, 24-29
visual indexing and, 27-29, 127-158
Occlusion, 25-26, 30, 35-36, 56
FINST mechanism and, 145-151
infants and, 190-191, 193n5
Metelli rule and, 79-83, 85, 89
modal/amodal completion studies and, 76-85
parallel vision and, 78
rubber bands and, 163-165, 169
Orbital motion, 29-30, 49-54
Overlapping strategy, 6-9

Parahippocampal place area (PPA), 23
Parallel search, 76
Peterson, Mary, 174
Phenomenology
Gestalt approach and, 62-70, 75
grouping and, 75
introspection and, 76
modal/amodal completion and, 73, 75-85
over-reliance upon, 75
parallel vision and, 78
segmentation constraints and, 89-90
selective attention and, 62-64
Philosophy of mind, 2
Physical knowledge, 208-209
Pitch
separation, 108, 110-111
TIA and, 116-120
Plensensory functions, 103-106
Point-light walkers, 54-58
Primary visual cortex, 85-89, 92
Prosopagnosia, 13
Proto-objects, 20-21, 62, 91, 127, 129, 144n5, 145-151, 154
Pylyshyn, Zenon W., 39, 127-158, 159-177, 210

Raymond, Jane, 60
Reaction time (RT), 68, 70
attentional blink and, 119
audition and, 112
directional discrimination and, 100-101
indispensable attributes and, 117
modal/amodal completion and, 84
Reference frames, 15-16
indexing and, 27-29
property detection and, 131-135
Repp, B., 122
Rock, Irvin, 66, 75-76, 92
Rubber bands, 163-165, 169
Russell, Charlotte, 61-95

Saccadic integration, 150-151
Sagi, Dov, 88
Same-object advantages, 6-9
multiple parts and, 18-19
object definition and, 30-32
Scholl, Brian J., 1-46, 92, 122, 155, 159-177, 210
Search-subset selection, 127
Segmentation, 20-21, 61-63, 93-95
change blindness and, 70-73
early, 85-89
experience and, 198-200
Gestalt approach and, 62-70
inattentional blindness and, 66-70
Metelli rule and, 79-83
modal/amodal completion and, 73, 76-85
modulation of, 85-89
object files and, 194-197
other relationships of, 90-92
phenomenological limits and, 73-76
specific forms of, 73
traditional view and, 65
varying effects of, 83-85
Sensations of Tone (Helmholtz), 114
Sense data, 129
Short-term memory, 203-205
Simons, Dan, 39, 174
Simultanagnosia, 12-13
Sinha, Pawan, 60
Situated vision, 127
FINST mechanism and, 145-151
individuating and, 131-139
mind-world connection and, 151-155
multiple object tracking and, 127, 141-144, 151-153
preconceptual selection and, 139-141
property detection and, 131-135
pure conceptual representation and, 128-131
representation construction and, 135-139

Smith, Brian Cantwell, 151
Sorrentino, Cristina, 210-211
Sortals, 180
Sound. See Audition
Spatial selection, 5, 180
   audition and, 33-36, 100-120
   emergent properties and, 108
   file extension and, 206-207
   FINST mechanism and, 145-151
   Gabor patches and, 85-89, 92
   indispensable attributes and, 106-111, 115-120
   infants and, 183-186 (see also Infants)
   IOR and, 116-118, 132-133
   lateral interactions and, 86-89
   lesions and, 112-113
   location and, 14 (see also Location)
   mapping and, 113-115, 117
   object-file theory and, 25-27
   occlusion and, 25-26 (see also Occlusion)
   packaging and, 2-3, 14
   perceptual groups and, 15-17 (see also Grouping)
   preconception and, 205-206
   reference frames and, 15-16, 27-29, 131-135
   same-object advantages and, 6-9, 18-19, 30-32
   selective looking and, 5-6
   tunnel effect and, 186-187, 192-193
Spelke-objects, 206-207, 209-210
Spence, C., 122
Spotlights, 1, 5
   indexing and, 27-29
   multiple-object tracking (MOT) and, 9-10, 160
Sprites, 29-30, 47
   effort and, 48
   familiarity and, 59-60
   orbital motion and, 49-54
   point-light walkers and, 55-58
   procedural aspects of, 48-49
Subitizing, 127, 135
Surfaces, 19-20
   edges and, 103-111
   illusory contours and, 9
   indispensable attributes and, 106-111
   transparent, 80-83

Tenenbaum, Joshua, 211
Theory of indispensable attributes (TIA)
   attentional (ATIA), 115-116
   benefits of, 118-120
   cost of ignoring, 116-118
   edges and, 110-111
   emergent properties and, 106-109
   grouping and, 106-109
   IOR and, 116-118
   mapping and, 115-118
   misinterpretations of, 108-109
Thornton, Ian M., 47-60
T-junctions, 163
Tracking. See Multiple-object tracking (MOT)
Treisman, Anne, 39, 174
Tumbling motion, 49-54, 58
Tunnel effect, 186-187, 192-193
Turatto, Massimo, 61-95
Turgéon, M., 122

Unilateral neglect. See Neglect

V1 neurons, 85-89
Van de Walle, Gretchen, 211
Van Valkenburg, David, 97-126
Ventral stream, 112-113
Viewer-based reference frames, 15
Virtual polygon (VP), 10n5, 173n6
Visual indexing, 27-29, 156-158
   conceptual representation and, 128-131
   experimental evidence for, 139-144
   FINST mechanism and, 145-151, 154
   grabbing and, 146
   incrementation and, 135-139
   individuation tokens and, 133-135
   mind-world connection and, 151-155
   misperception and, 128n1
   multiple object tracking and, 127, 141-144, 151-153
   need for, 131-139
   object property detection and, 131-135
   preconception and, 128-131, 139-141
   representation construction and, 135-139
   serial access and, 140-141
Visual working memory (VWM), 20-24
Volitional action, 208

Watkins, A. J., 122
Watt algorithm, 7
What/Where subsystem, 97-98, 121
   audition vs. vision, 100-111, 113-120
   edges and, 102-106, 110-111
   evidence for, 112-113
   grouping and, 106-109

indispensable attributes and, 106-111, 115-120
spatiotemporal mapping and, 113-115

Xu, Fei, 179-213

Yantis, Steve, 174

Zoom lens, 1, 5, 160